P9-DNF-787

THE DEVIL PROBLEM

AND OTHER TRUE STORIES

THE
DEVIL PROBLEM

AND OTHER TRUE STORIES

DAVID REMNICK

RANDOM HOUSE

NEW YORK

All rights reserved under International and
Pan-American Copyright Conventions. Published in
the United States by Random House, Inc., New York,
and simultaneously in Canada by Random House
of Canada Limited, Toronto.

The essays in this work have been previously published in *Esquire*,
The New Yorker, and *The Washington Post*.

Grateful acknowledgment is made to the following for permission to reprint previously pub-
lished material:
Farrar, Straus & Giroux, Inc.: Excerpt from "Lullaby on Cape Cod" from *A Part of Speech* by
Joseph Brodsky. Translation copyright © 1980 by Farrar, Straus & Giroux, Inc. Excerpt from
"Uncommon Visage: The Nobel Lecture" from *On Grief and Reason* by Joseph Brodsky. Copy-
right © 1995 by Joseph Brodsky. Reprinted by permission of Farrar, Straus & Giroux, Inc.
Murray Kempton: Excerpts from *America Comes of Middle Age* by Murray Kempton. Reprinted
by permission of the author.
Random House, Inc.: Eight lines from "In Memory of William Butler Yeats" from *Collected Poems*
by W. H. Auden. Copyright © 1940 and renewed 1968 by W. H. Auden. Excerpt from *Shadow
and Act* by Ralph Ellison. Copyright © 1964 by Ralph Ellison. Reprinted by permission of
Random House, Inc.
Zephyr Press: Four lines from "I don't weep for myself now . . . ," from *The Complete Poems of
Anna Akhmatova*, Vol. II, translated by Judith Hemschemeyer (1990). Copyright © 1990 by
Judith Hemschemeyer. Reprinted by permission of Zephyr Press, Somerville, Massachusetts.

Cataloguing-in-Publication data is available.
ISBN 0-679-45255-9

Random House website address: http://www.randomhouse.com/

Printed in the United States of America on acid-free paper
24689753
First Edition

For Alex and Noah and, always, Esther

PREFACE

We order and excite our mental lives with stories. Mostly, they are the same stories over and over again. The tabloids (in print and, now, on television) have their set of stories: the wealthy brought low, betrayal in marriage and commerce, the murder of the innocent, the humbling of the celebrity, the ordinary man's triumph. They differ from the novels of, say, Dreiser, or the plays of Shakespeare, in the richness of detail, the complexity of thought and incident, the wealth of language, but in the story of O. J. Simpson (the tabloid story of the millennium) there were surely elements of *An American Tragedy* and *Othello*. There are other textures of mental life—the analytical, the pure emotions of lust or rage—but stories, the telling and listening, are much of what we are.

Reporters are interested in amassing information, in sorting through the latest trends, but above all we are interested in stories. They often contain useful information, but they are also patterns, morality plays, entertainments. To me, at least, Gary Hart's exile from public life after scandal drove him out of the 1988 presidential race is a story out of Dreiser, too. (It is surely a story that influ-

enced the way Bill Clinton told *his* story a few years later.) Ralph
Ellison's excruciating attempt, over many decades, to write a second novel after the great success of his first, *Invisible Man,* is a story.
There is something Greek about Ellison's tragedy, the way a
manuscript (with no copy) burned in a house fire, the way he died,
a couple of weeks after talking with me, having left his novel, frag-
mented, incomplete, in the hands of others. How a great religious
historian, Elaine Pagels, comes to write about evil and the devil
after the death of her husband and son is a story about the way
thought and creation begin.

The real subjects of these stories—the politicians, the scholars,
the artists, the athletes—do not necessarily recognize themselves in
the way they are depicted here. They don't see in the published
result the fullness of themselves and their experience. I don't blame
them. Journalism is not allowed the liberties of the novel or the evidence of the psychiatric dossier. "Stories" can only be a part, a
glimpse, of that fuller thing, the life.

Even though I am sure a number of the subjects of these pieces
were not at all pleased with the result—I don't expect another dinner invitation from Gary Hart, and Gerry Adams never sent a thank-
you note—I am grateful to all of them. Janet Malcolm is dead right
when she describes how the subjects of journalism so often feel
taken in when they discover that the story that comes out in the end
is not necessarily the story as they had pictured it in their heads. The
writer, and not the subject, chooses the details that will go into the
pieces and what ought to be ignored as irrelevant or dull.

In defense of these stories, the reader should know they are true.
Or, better to say, factual. These pieces range over many fields of
life—politics, scholarship, literature, sports—and touch on the
problems of race, sex, jealousy, aging, exile, and terror. But mostly,
they are about the gap between private life and public ambition, the
strange decisions someone like Gary Hart and Mario Cuomo will
make when faced with the possibility of becoming a president or a

justice of the Supreme Court; how Alger Hiss lives out his life when part of the world regards him as a pariah, another as a martyr; how an athlete faces the death of retirement; how two obscure scholars react when their relationship collapses into acrimony over a theory that both are convinced will revolutionize Shakespeare studies. The facts in all of them are straight, or at least the best I could do. In any case, I had the benefit of a ten-year-long apprenticeship at *The Washington Post,* the indulgence of the editors of *The New Yorker,* and, not least, the help of the magazine's rightly celebrated fact-checking department. That leaves me with no excuses.

CONTENTS

ONE

FORMS OF EXILE

I

———❧———

Winter on the Mountain

(April 1993)

It was freezing in the mountains, about ten degrees below zero.
All across Colorado, drifts of snow swept halfway up the sides of
the barns and the cabins. Without waking his wife, Gary Hart got up
before dawn and walked downstairs to his living room, a cavernous
place with a vaulted ceiling, high windows, and walls of lodgepole
pine. It is a mountain house out of a plutocrat's fondest four-color
dream. Hart could sit by the fire and see deer, elk, mountain lions,
and red fox move through the woods as the sun came up over the
foothills of Kittredge. Lately, a Corsican ram had been climbing
around the rocks near the house, and the dogs barked up at him.
Hart built the house a couple of years ago for his wife, Lee, he
would tell me, "because Lee had never had anything like this and
Lee deserved it."

Hart was making real money now, as a lawyer and an international businessman. Born to Nazarene evangelicals in Kansas, he
confessed to sometimes feeling "a little funny" about all the opu-
lence: the poolroom, the sauna, the walk-in closets, the state-of-
the-art appliances. It seemed sinful somehow. But the unease of

living here was more severe than a passing case of guilt; it was end-less and deep.

This was not the house that Gary Hart had thought he would be living in. At the start of the 1988 presidential campaign, he had been headed, as if on a greased chute of destiny, for the White House. But out of vanity, it seemed, and stubborn refusal to curb his extramarital liaisons for the purposes of high politics, he threw it all away long before the first primary. He could rage at the press for its blithe savagery, its puritan hypocrisy. But he should have known. In fact, he did know: he knew the risks and he ignored them. In May of 1987, he even invited the press to "follow me around" during the campaign. "I don't care. I'm serious," he told *The New York Times*. "If anybody wants to put a tail on me, go ahead. They'd be very bored." In the end, Hart paid for the sins of the flesh as no one else had done in two hundred years of American political history.

Hart's exile was immediate and absolute. To venture from the mountains of Colorado was to open himself to further humiliation. When he went to the 1988 Democratic Convention, in Atlanta, the only way he could enter the arena was with a Colorado delegate's pass. When he reached the convention floor, the Democratic chair-man, Paul Kirk, put a few security men between him and the tele-vision cameras. Hart's sense of martyrdom and piety was acute. "All our heroes are dead," he told Maureen Dowd, of the *Times*. "John is dead. Bobby is dead. And I'm dead—walking dead."

Now, five years on, Hart dispensed with self-pity and stuck to a handful of pitiful jokes. "Sometimes I'll be walking down the street in Washington and someone'll come up to me and say, 'Aren't you Gary Hart?' And I give 'em this little joke. I say, 'Yeah, I used to be.' And they laugh—'Ha! Ha! Ha!' "

After the convention was over, Hart had wanted to get on with his life. He was constantly on the road, especially in Russia, trying to set up business projects—seaports, airports, banks, phone systems—that would enrich his clients and connect him, in some marginal way, to public life. But the 1988 bruises still hurt. Hart was convinced that he would never have lost to George Bush, that his fall was "an accident, a car crash in history." When his friend and adviser Paul Tully died, last September, Hart ran into Richard Gephardt, the House majority leader, at the funeral. The election was only weeks away, and Gephardt, ever the Eagle Scout, could barely keep a cap on his fizzy enthusiasm.

"I think Bill's gonna do it!" Gephardt said.

"Yeah," Hart said darkly. "But Bush never should have won in the first place."

When Bill Clinton finally did win, Hart tried not to betray his mixed feelings. "He was glad Clinton won," his daughter, Andrea, said. "But he does have that feeling—'It could have been me, I could have done as good a job as this man.' " In 1972, when Hart was in charge of George McGovern's campaign for president, he had hired Clinton, a law student on summer break, to help lead the Texas organization. "My impression was of a guy with a lot of enthusiasm and a lot of hair," he said. Now that kid was president, the savior of his party. But didn't anyone see that Hart, and not Clinton, had reinvented the Democrats? He had been preaching military reform, national service, and economic investment as a senator from Colorado when Clinton was still getting to know the precincts of Arkansas. But no one much cared. Hart had lately sent memos to the White House but had got no answers.

Hart's frustration in exile was not just a matter of failed ambition—nothing as vain and petty as that. Take the winter of 1990–91. The Harts were moving into the new house, on Troublesome Gulch Road—just up the path from their old log cabin—but Gary felt no great happiness. Like everyone else in the country, he was spending hours in front of the television watching the bombing raids over Baghdad. In the press, many of the armchair analysts were predicting that when the land war finally began, thousands of American soldiers would die. Hart reflected that if he had been in the White House he would have gone the "sanctions route" a good deal longer. "I was terrified we'd lose a lot of people," he said later. "If thousands of American lives had been lost, I would have felt personally responsible."

Personal responsibility for thousands of dead—all for a weekend trip to Bimini on the good ship *Monkey Business*. This was what it was, at times, to be Gary Hart. "When you talk about Gary Hart now, people don't focus on anything except that here was this guy who got out of the race and the Donna Rice episode," Billy Shore, one of Hart's closest aides from the early days, said in February. "If he'd been hit by a bus the week before all that happened, the *Times* would have written an obituary paying tribute to 'a legislator's legislator.' " Now he was a living punch line.

"I don't like 'feel' questions," Hart said as we drove in his Jeep from Denver west to Kittredge. Over and over, in Kittredge, in Denver, and in Washington, Hart would dip lightly into the waters of the personal and then suddenly yank himself out. "It's all part of my death struggle with ego," he said.

Rarely has an American ego been more thoroughly probed, indulged, and, ultimately, destroyed. After his weekend became public knowledge, Hart quickly toppled from the pinnacle of public life, to join that shadowy population of Americans who are ready fodder for "Where Are They Now?" columns. They are figures first of irony and then of trivia; after a while, the game is guessing whether they are alive or dead. But Gary Hart's story will prove grander than that. His rise to prominence and fall from grace ring of Hawthorne and Dreiser, and played a critical role in the election of Bill Clinton.

Hart, whose parents forbid dancing, movies, alcohol, and the indulgences of the flesh, marries Lee Ludwig, a Nazarene girl from a good family, and they head east to New Haven. It is the age of John

Kennedy; and Hart, at Yale Law School, is swept up in Kennedy's charisma and call to public service. In 1972, he runs McGovern's children's campaign against the demonic Richard Nixon. The loss is overwhelming, but is eventually redeemed somewhat by Watergate. In 1974, Hart is elected to the Senate, where he gains a reputation as an innovative advocate of reform, the best of a new generation of "neoliberals." In 1984, he runs for president and stuns the experts by placing second in the Iowa caucus and winning the New Hampshire primary. One estimate has him suddenly gaining three million supporters a day. "Not since the Beatles had stormed onto the stage of *The Ed Sullivan Show* twenty years before had any new face so quickly captured the popular culture," Paul Taylor, of *The Washington Post,* writes. Hart is told by Warren Beatty, "Watch out. You've become famous too fast." If it hadn't been for the Democratic party machinery and a botched campaign in Illinois, Hart could well have won the nomination in 1984. He finishes the race with a string of victories, but loses narrowly to Walter Mondale. In 1987, Hart is the odds-on favorite to win the party's blessing and challenge George Bush in November. But then, in May of 1987, he vanishes under the wave of scandal as *The Miami Herald* stakes out his house and *The Washington Post* snags a detective report commissioned by a jealous husband. Hart quits the race. In December, he reenters it, but he can never regain his footing. In Iowa, he gets less than 1 percent of the vote and finishes last. Five weeks later, he goes home to stay.

Hart still has the rangy, handsome look that his handlers always hoped would be seen as a Colorado version of "Kennedyesque." In deepest winter, he still wears cowboy boots with his business suit, and no overcoat. Aware that his tag has come to be "aloof," or "imperious," Hart makes an effort to charm. As we drove through the foothills of the Rockies, past one old mining town after another, he told some familiar Nixon stories in a dead-on Nixon voice. His set piece is about the day he found himself seated next to Nixon at the funeral of Jacob Javits.

"All of a sudden I feel him tapping me on the knee. . . . Whap! Whap! Whap! . . . And he says, 'That music. Is that Bach or Brahms?' . . . Bach or Brahms? . . . I said I didn't know. And he says, 'Bach is much better than Brahms. Because Bach is *tougher* than Brahms.' "

Hart is fascinated by Nixon—by his cynicism and his uncanny ability to remain in the political limelight. Though Hart would be appalled by the idea, he and Nixon are historical partners. Both men were always remarkable analysts of everyone but themselves. Their downfalls were successive chapters in the history of the media and American politics. Watergate represented the apogee of investigative reporting on the presidential level; the Hart scandal took the public's right to know beyond any previous limit. It was Nixon who acknowledged this strange kinship when he wrote to Hart in 1987:

> Dear Gary,
> This is just a line to tell you that I thought you handled a very dif-ficult situation uncommonly well. . . . What you said about the media needed to be said. They demand the right to ruthlessly question the ethics of everyone else. But when anyone else dares to question their ethics, they hide behind the shield of freedom of speech. They refuse to make the distinction that philosophers throughout the centuries have made between freedom and license.

Hart drove slowly along the road that cuts through his property, of 170 acres. He pointed to a spot where he had seen a fox the week before and to the gate where, in 1987, hundreds of reporters had hunkered down, waiting for another glimpse of scandal. The Harts haven't had many reporters at their house since those days. They had invited me for dinner and to stay the night, and, in a clumsy attempt to thank them, I'd bought flowers in Denver and brought them as a gift.

Getting out of the Jeep, Hart smiled thinly at the bouquet. "It's gonna take a lot of flowers to make Lee feel any better about reporters," he said. "Lee was pretty brutalized, you know. I think she's all right now."

As we walked through the snow toward the house, we were greeted by the barking of dogs and then by Lee Hart, standing in the doorframe. She looked eager and nervous at the same time. Since "the events of 1987," as her husband often calls them, Lee Hart has kept out of the public eye. Even some of the Harts' closest friends are bewildered by the endurance of their marriage.

"Babe, why don't you give him the tour, and get that over with?" Hart said.

"That's what I was going to do, Gary."

Perhaps the thing that struck me most about the house, besides its sheer splendor, was how few signs there were that one of its owners had been so close to becoming the most powerful person on earth. Politicians usually keep several dozen grip-and-grin photos around—self-gilding memorabilia from the old campaigns or the trips abroad. At the Harts', just a few black-and-white pictures had been tacked up—familiar images from the campaign trail, with both Gary and Lee all smiles and looking a bit younger.

We sat by the fire and talked about *The Good Fight: The Education of an American Reformer,* a book that Hart was getting ready for publication. "I really wanted to title the book *The Diary of a Failed Reformer,* but they wouldn't let me," he said. "My editor had a fit. They give no credit to people for a sense of irony. The truth is, I don't think I was a failure. I just wasn't a success."

Hart's is a willfully soulless book. Throughout, he uses "the reformer" in place of the first person—a device that was intended to make the book seem less self-conscious and succeeds only in making it seem more so. Instead of paying tribute to Henry Adams with this device, as Hart had intended, he evokes Norman Mailer's old alter ego, Aquarius. That might not be so grating if Hart had written openly, bravely, even angrily, about his own experience. He has not. His reticence is at constant war with his sense of injury, and the conflict produces a tinny, self-righteous effect.

Hart wrote with far more passion in a number of letters to his editor at Random House, Jonathan Karp. One reads:

> You must condition yourself and your colleagues to the fact that nothing short of suicide will satisfy the skeptics and the cynics or even the asinine acquaintances. The reason simply is this: a newly aggressive and intrusive press establishment, never comfortable with my refusal to be categorized, exploited (and possibly created) an incident very near the bone. . . . I will never escape from this event, as you say, simply because the press cannot afford to let me escape it and because social and political exile is demanded to sustain the hypocrisy. *Nothing,* I repeat, *nothing,* I say in the foreword would solve these two problems. It would require an act of utmost contrition, which I am incapable of making.

In *The Good Fight,* Hart writes a skeletal history of various reformers in America and the ways they have been stifled, thwarted, or killed. Although he propounds no grand conspiracy theory, he is fascinated by the conspiratorial elements in the murders of Martin Luther King, Jr., and the Kennedys, and in the defeats of McGovern and the reformer. A prominent Washington journalist once told me that Hart, after a couple of drinks on an airplane five years ago, described his own fall in 1987 as a conspiracy of power elites: the military establishment, the energy industry—in short, all the institutions he planned to reform as president.

I told Hart I thought there was an acute sense of conspiracy running through the new book linking his own trials with those of the Kennedys and King.

He seemed genuinely surprised. "If you think that a paranoid sense of conspiracy runs through the book, then you're misreading it, or maybe I should rewrite it," he said. "And I may put myself in line with reformers, but it doesn't mean my loss was in any way equal to their losses. You can be a good Christian or a follower of Christ or Paul and not think you are Christ or Paul. My own impression of my experience in politics is that it was very minor. Virtually none of the things I wanted to get done got done."

Lee Hart called us in to dinner. She had prepared an elaborate salad of greens, bacon, cheese, and fruit, and then chicken breasts with wild rice and, for dessert, the richest chocolate cake this side of Lyons.

"This wine's a little tart, though, isn't it, babe?" Hart said. "Musta been a lemon vintage."

Lee Hart looked mortified. "Maybe another bottle . . ."

Hart smiled. "Don't bother, babe. This'll do."

I asked Lee Hart how the two of them had managed to pull themselves together after the disaster of 1987.

There was a pause. Then Lee said, "We were redoing the kitchen in the old house, where Andrea's living now. And Gary cut a lot of logs. Some were *The Miami Herald,* others were *The Washington Post*—"

Gary Hart's face turned the color of claret. "Now, babe," he said, in a voice freighted with anger and meaning.

"I just meant—"

"Babe, speak for yourself. Sure, it was hard. And if it was a career it was the tragic end of a career. But if you take it as public service, the way I did, then it's just the end of that part of your life."

"That's true, Gary. You always said that."

"The key thing is your attitude going into it. When I was elected to the Senate, I was eager to be there. But I never thought that this would be it, senator for life, or climb the ladder to the presidency. I just decided in the eighties that the Democratic party had to be the party of change. And 'up or out' became my attitude. I just could not stand to look at the lack of courage in the Senate. And then after I lost in '84—well, you really can't go back to the Senate after running for president, and rejoin those silly, inane discussions. I'm against the two-term limit, but people should leave voluntarily. They have to avoid being co-opted by the permanent Washington crowd—the journalists, the friendship. They get co-opted after a couple of terms. I want to go back to an earlier time, when politicians didn't hobnob with the press, and they saw themselves as public servants for a time. I was made fun of, even ridiculed, because I always said 'Mr. Koppel' or 'Mr. Brinkley' when I was on TV. My staff and family gave me hell about it . . ."

"I didn't," Lee said.

"Now, babe. C'mon. But for me it was an important thing. I thought I should be businesslike. Chumminess on television, the 'David' and 'Ted' stuff, was symbolic of the problem."

I tried to get back to the question of how the Harts went on with their lives in 1987.

"I left the presidential race at noon Friday and I was back in my law office at eight o'clock Monday morning," Hart said. "To prove something to everyone—that life goes on. Being president isn't everything in the world. If you are a mature adult and you have your values straight, you just go ahead and do the next thing. The hardest thing to deal with was the continual drumbeat of the press. I was out of politics, but it kept coming. I mean, how many times can you kill someone? How many times can you be dead?"

"Gary, don't make it seem as if—"

"Speak for yourself, babe," Hart said.

"Well, okay," she said. "A lot of people have the idea that you just didn't want to be president."

"Well, that's just . . . Look. We are at the stage where we think that you've got to be all-consumed by the idea of becoming president. But it's nonsense. Thomas Jefferson gave his inaugural speech and then walked home through the mud to his boardinghouse. Now they think that your life is ruined if you fail. The danger of running for the presidency is that if you don't make it—and that's the case for almost everyone who tries—then you are considered a failure."

After dinner, we had coffee in the living room, and I asked the Harts about the '92 race.

"When Clinton began to pick people for his team, there was a moment of elation for me when I saw Eli Segal, John Emerson, and those people—people who had been with me once—getting serious jobs in the administration," Hart said.

I asked him whom he had supported initially in the race. He seemed embarrassed, and Lee broke in, saying, "I supported Tsongas in the primaries. Clinton's idea of a middle-class tax cut was just pandering to voters. I also didn't like the Japanese-bashing. Gary, you said the same thing."

Hart reddened once more.

"Just let me recollect, babe," he said, and then, "Tsongas's famous little book looked like a lot of my stuff. When he called me and said, 'I'm going to run for president,' I started laughing. And he did, too. It was like an unspoken thing on how crazy it is to run for president."

"I remember you said, 'Paul, I knew you weren't feeling well, but I didn't think you were sick in the head.' "

"Maybe, babe. Maybe. But we went on laughing for three minutes or so, and then, a few days later, he announced." Hart said he was tired and ready for bed, but before he left I asked him what he did now on a typical day when he was not traveling abroad.

"It's very boring," he said. "I sit behind a desk. I make telephone calls, draft proposals. I give speeches. I negotiate proposals for airports and seaports. I'm an advocate. In '88, I tried to figure out a way to maintain a link to the private sector, to do something in the private sector related to what my goals had been in the public. I went to Taiwan, to Argentina, but it didn't lead to anything."

"You got to play a lot of tennis," Lee Hart said.

"Yeah, babe. And to Czechoslovakia, Japan. When I traveled, I discovered there was a lot of bewilderment out in the world about why I hadn't succeeded. They still thought I had something to say, even if no one at home did. That was very vivid."

Lee Hart and I stayed up and talked awhile in the kitchen. I was grateful to her for the trouble she had gone to. No matter how much the Harts steered away from the "events" that Hart had ruled out of bounds, the presence of yet another reporter could only have been painful to both of them.

"You know, it's different for Gary from what it is for me," she said. "He was the one running for office, and, contrary to what some people might have thought, I really never fantasized about being in the White House. That was putting the cart before the horse. I did think Gary should have been president. I didn't fear the White House. There were all sorts of things I would have worked on. But I had no long-standing ambitions. Maybe that was a mechanism of self-protection. You protect yourself against disappointment. I'm delighted with Hillary. Early on, she made a few faux pas, which happens, but she's a good speaker and doesn't have a lot of mannerisms that drive you crazy."

I said it seemed strange that the Clinton administration had asked Mondale, Hart's 1984 opponent, to be the ambassador in Moscow—an appointment that Mondale eventually turned down, and that went to Thomas Pickering. Friends and family had told me that Hart, who wrote a book on perestroika and travels to Moscow several times a year, was particularly galled by the Mondale appointment.

Lee Hart's face tightened into an expression infinitely sad.

"I'd have been stunned if he had been asked," she said. "But it tells you something. Gary has never, ever, abused the public trust. And when we know the garbage that's come out of that city . . . The truth is, Gary is trashed anytime there's anything negative brought up about anyone else. Clinton would never have been president had it not been for what happened to Gary. The Clinton people know that they got off easier than Gary did. Clinton also had the support of the Democratic party people, who hung in there with him, which Gary never had. I was just very happy that they survived. The press seemed to have learned—or I hope so, for the sake of the country. Otherwise, who would ever run for office?" Lee Hart's eyes widened and filled. "In many respects," she said slowly, "our situation was just so simple, but it was not what they thought it was or said it was. It never was."

While Gary Hart was still running for president in 1988, he mapped out in his mind the first months of his term. The first thing he would do was invite Gorbachev to the inauguration, and then he'd get a quick arms-control treaty on strategic arms and nuclear testing. "I may flatter myself, but I think Gorbachev sensed in me a dramatic figure who was like him, at least in some small way," he said. Then he would get started on the Middle East, break some of the old molds on defense policy, the economy, energy policy.

Some of Hart's former aides found themselves wandering through the inaugural events in Washington this year and thinking, This should have been us—four years ago.

Hart had hoped that Clinton, as president, would make a bold gesture to the Russians, as he said he himself would have done. He told some of Clinton's aides that they ought to invite Boris Yeltsin to the inauguration, as an indication of support for democratic reform. "I got back mumbo-jumbo about who was where last, the protocol of it," he said, rolling his eyes. "They missed the whole point."

But even if Clinton didn't ape Hart's inaugural strategy, the political debt of the new president to the exile is undeniable. For one thing, the White House is stocked with former Hart people: John Emerson, the deputy director of personnel; Eli Segal, the head of the fledgling national service program; David Dreyer, the director of planning; Jeremy Rosner, the counselor and director of legislative affairs at the National Security Council. And Larry Smith, who was Hart's key aide on defense policy, became the counselor to Secretary Les Aspin, at the Pentagon.

The influence goes beyond mere personnel. In Denver, Hart and I watched the State of the Union speech together. He spent some of the time laughing at the standing ovations and the primping of his old colleagues, and the rest of it, and he nodded paternal assent to the policy initiatives coming from the podium: a streamlined defense, an economy based on investment rather than on consumption, a program of national service. In Hart's time, all this was known as neoliberalism, the sharp break with the ideological orthodoxy of the Hubert Humphreys and Walter Mondales of the Democratic party. "In 1984, Hart fired the first shot at the fortress of the Democratic party and lived to tell the story, which inspired a bunch of others who might have been scared off," Bruce Reed, a domestic policy adviser to Clinton, told me. "To the extent that he made the world safe for new ideas, Gary Hart made his mark."

Where Hart and Clinton differed profoundly was in their style of personal politics. Hart's was cool, intellectual, while Clinton's is more that of a populist, a hugger, a figure of almost preternatural resilience. The joke about Hart among his aides during the 1984 and 1987 campaigns was that the candidate would go to a reception for five hundred people, and after it was over his aides would ask, "Well, did he meet any of them?" The joke about Clinton last year was that the duty of the Secret Service was to protect the people from the candidate.

But Clinton's edge didn't consist only of his natural warmth toward people and crowds; he had history, and Gary Hart, to learn from. In 1987, when the press first started asking Hart questions about his marriage and his sex life, he knew there was static in the Washington air. At the same time, he had faith—an unwise and luckless faith—in precedent and the secrets that the press had always kept. Hart's staff members were far from ignorant about "the Issue." They had prepared explanations in 1984, too. But they continued to suspend disbelief. They wished away disaster. Then, in April of 1987, just two weeks before the scandal broke, Larry Smith went to Colorado for a "blue skies" meeting with the campaign leadership. He asked the group what they intended to do about rumors of Hart's womanizing. "One of the campaign's leaders laughed, and said, 'We never talk about it,' " Smith recalled. "I said, 'Well, you'd better think about it.' "

Reporters might whisper, but what would the papers actually print? Just look at what had gone on before, they said. Andrew Jackson was married to a bigamist. Grover Cleveland supported an illegitimate child. Wendell Willkie had an affair with an editor of the *New York Herald Tribune* at the very time the paper was promoting his candidacy. Franklin D. Roosevelt and Dwight Eisenhower had affairs, and the Homeric catalog of John Kennedy's afternoons of leisure surely needs no recounting.

But, as Hart well knew, the atmosphere had changed immeasurably after the Watergate scandal. The press had become adversarial, wary of being duped or of being seen as "in the tank" for a public official. And the truth was that reporters never really warmed to Gary Hart. They found him imperious, aloof, reckless, a little strange. Somehow, that made it easier to bring him down.

"It's like with George Romney in 1967," I was told by Richard Cohen, the *Washington Post* columnist who traveled with the Hart campaign in 1984. "The press knew that Romney was an idiot, but the question was: How do you write it? So along come his comments about being brainwashed, and—*wham!*—they take him out. He's history. Same with Hart. There was always this sense among the press that he just wasn't—well, right. That he was weird. But how do you write it? And then along comes Donna Rice."

After *The Miami Herald* rushed into print with the results of its stakeout of Hart's townhouse, on Capitol Hill, "Hell Week" began for the campaign. Nothing like this had ever happened in American politics. The rules had suddenly changed, and the Hart cadres, young, and scattered across the country, were utterly confused. The newspapers and the television stations were in a mad dash to win the race to nail Hart. "I thought the whole system had gone awry," says Kathy Bushkin, who was once a close aide of Hart's and is now an executive at *U.S. News & World Report*. "For whatever reason, Gary Hart showed bad judgment, and for whatever reason, the press seemed determined to get something on him. Inside the campaign, people were stunned, frightened, frustrated. These were people who had come to politics out of great idealism. They weren't prepared for things like spin control and damage control."

John Holum, who worked with Hart in both presidential campaigns, told me, "When the story broke, Gary called me. No one else was talking to the press. We needed to do something. I said, 'What's going on?' He said, 'John, I'm not crazy.' So I said, 'So it's not true.' He said, 'Right, it's not true.' So I went on television and got hung out to dry saying that I had known Gary Hart for seventeen years and I believed him. Now I think he did lie. I was very angry. What really made me angry is that he could let all those people pin their hopes on him and then not have the personal discipline to make his candidacy viable."

While Hart struggled to keep his candidacy alive—while he faced unprecedented questions from the press on the order of "Have you ever committed adultery?"—editors and reporters at *The Washington Post* looked into a detective's report they had been given which provided evidence that Hart had been carrying on an affair with a Washington lobbyist. When the *Post* called Hart and said that it was preparing to run a story on the subject, Hart quit the race and went home to Kittredge.

"No one looks back on that with great memories, but the rules evolve," says Dan Balz, a political writer at the *Post*. "We're in a period like that now, with baby-sitters and nannies sinking cabinet appointees. What Hart did was wrong, because he misrepresented his own marriage and life in a way that became fatal. For a lot of people in this country, the simple fact of infidelity is disqualifying. Also, his actions were contemporaneous with the race. He stretched the limits."

David Dreyer, who was a key Hart aide in the Senate and is now a member of Clinton's staff, naturally sees it otherwise. "I think he was treated shabbily by the press," he says. "His privacy was invaded. The trials he went through after the campaign were disproportionate to what he had done. He was treated as a nonperson, almost as a political prisoner in a totalitarian system. He's off the political radar screen."

While Hart always denied to his staff that there was a problem, Bill Clinton acknowledged from the start that there would be questions, and he intended to act before the press did. In September of 1991, John Holum and other Democratic activists went to a meeting of an exploratory committee of the Clinton campaign at the Quality Inn on New Jersey Avenue in Washington. "Clinton himself brought up the question of the marriage," Holum told me. "Clinton said, 'I know you are all concerned about this. Here's the situation:

There were problems in our marriage and we've worked them out.'
I was so gratified. No, I was *thrilled* that he was doing this."

To compare Hart's shock and his steely defensiveness at his
press conferences during Hell Week with Bill and Hillary Clinton's command of the same subject in the early stages of their
campaign is to see consummate politicians learning from the
foibles of a deeply flawed teacher. Hart made himself into a martyr. He went before his supporters and the cameras and said that
his campaign was a "crusade," and that "if I'm right about that, it
really doesn't matter if the leader is struck down in battle or with
a knife in the back, because the cause goes on and the crusade continues."

Clinton and his aides watched Gennifer Flowers unleash her
unholy confession in the *Star* and went immediately on the coun-
teroffensive, charging her with profiteering and saying that taped
conversations with the candidate had been doctored. On January 26,
1992, just after the Super Bowl, Clinton and his wife went on *60 Minutes* and seemed to speak past the host, Steve Kroft, and straight to the
voters, in a way never seen before in presidential politics. When Kroft
asked for the specifics of the problems in the marriage, Clinton
replied with a combination of frankness, indirection, and a knowing
vocabulary which was designed to admit imperfection and, at the
same time, shield him from further assault. "I think the American
people—at least, people that have been married for a long time—
know what it means and know the whole range of things it can
mean," he said. "You go back and listen to what I've said. You know, I
have acknowledged wrongdoing. I have acknowledged causing pain in
my marriage. I have said things to you tonight and to the American
people from the beginning that no American politician ever has. I
think most Americans who are watching this tonight, they'll know
what we're saying; they'll get it, and they'll feel that we have been
more than candid."

And then, perhaps even more important, Hillary Clinton echoed her husband, and did so without apology or embarrassment: "You know, I'm not sitting here—some little woman standing by my man, like Tammy Wynette. I'm sitting here because I love him, and I respect him, and I honor what he's been through and what we've been through together. And, you know, if that's not enough for people, then, heck, don't vote for him."

The Clinton campaign had it easier. If there had been extramarital affairs, they were presumably not going on during the campaign. Hart had not given voters reason to believe the same of him. And Clinton was not taken by surprise. His young campaign handlers, some of whom run the White House communications office today, were no longer fooled by even the friendliest of reporters.

"The Clinton cadre had no illusions about what the press was capable of doing, while the Hart people were stunned by it," a party activist who worked in both candidates' campaigns said. "With the Hart episode, people on the Democratic side began to understand about reporters. 'Okay,' they said about the reporters, 'they may be our age, they may look like us, and even vote like us, but they are not us. They are another political force, an adversary.' The Clinton people hated the press even more than the Hart people."

On a clear, cold evening this winter, I went out to the Pentagon and was led to Larry Smith's office. Smith's rooms were newly painted and bare. "We're just finding out where the coffeepot is," Smith said by way of greeting. Smith worked as Hart's top aide in the Senate from 1978 to 1982, leaving the office just as the other aides were discussing strategy for the first presidential race.

"Let me begin by saying this," he said. "Gary is a truly tragic figure. Though I love him, I left him in the late spring, early summer of 1982 because I lost confidence in him. I believed he felt himself in a way to be divine."

A mixture of anger, dismay, and real, lasting affection was characteristic of every former Hart aide I had met, but Smith was the one who was most willing, or able, to display his feelings.

"There is a theology that says that if you sin you are cast into the outer darkness called hell," Smith said. "If you are mortal, like most of us, you have to deal with the fact of sin, so when you do sin you are in your own mind condemned to hell. That is, if you are human and do not deny that fact. The only other way is to insist that you are above the usual rules. I came to believe that Gary Hart felt that the fate of Gary Hart was that he was destined to be president of the United States and he was not bound by the disciplines that impinge on the rest of us. In the end, the guy broke everybody's heart.

"Look at what Clinton did. He signaled that he had come short of the glory of God. But he looked into the camera and acknowledged it and said he still felt worthy of support. In other words, he is like us. He is human. That was a powerful political act."

I interrupted Smith to say that Hart had told me he could not have stayed in the race, because "other lives" would have been dragged through the press and ruined.

"Maybe so, maybe so," Smith said. Then he said, "I want you to hear something."

Smith crossed the room and found a hardbound copy of the collected poems of Yeats, a gift from Gary Hart. He leafed to one of the later poems—"Come Gather Round Me, Parnellites," an ode to the Irish hero and statesman whose political career faltered when he became a corespondent in the divorce case of his mistress, Kitty O'Shea.

"I can't read this without thinking of Gary," Smith said. And he read:

> The Bishops and the Party
> That tragic story made,

A husband that had sold his wife
And after that betrayed;
But stories that live longest
Are sung above the glass,
And Parnell loved his country,
And Parnell loved his lass.

Larry Smith's eyes filled with tears as he closed the book. "That's the tragedy," he said. "But with Gary it's worse. He didn't even love the lass. Now he is walking around like a ghost. What I want for my friend is to have a fine peace on this earth."

Gary Hart is in Washington looking for work at a new law firm. He sits by the window of a trendy Washington restaurant, i Ricchi, drinking cappuccino.

"Clinton was a watershed," he says. "There was the scandal, and it was dealt with for a couple of weeks, and then it went away. It wasn't just how he handled it. I hate that word 'handle.' They say Clinton handled his situation better than I did. Poppycock. It wasn't the decision to go on *60 Minutes*. It was the editorial decision not to pursue it any further. I didn't see editors this time sending reporters halfway around the world to peek in a politician's window. And that was good for the country. The wife of a very prominent Washington journalist told me the other day that everyone in Washington thinks Bill Clinton never would have been elected president without Gary Hart. Maybe. The idea is that I somehow carried away the burden of scandal. Maybe she also means that I plowed new ground on the party and the issues. If that's the case, I'm a happy man. You don't always have to win to win. You don't always have to achieve the highest office to succeed.

"The hardest adjustment was having a platform for twelve years and then having it disappear overnight. See, you don't have to be president to have a platform, but when you lose you've lost your platform. Even if you are speaking in an empty Senate, when it's a sea of mahogany, you can feel you are contributing. That urge doesn't end overnight. Imagine a writer told he could not write. It was a way of expressing myself, my convictions. One day, you're speaking ten times a day, and then, suddenly, you're not. I was in London, and one of the papers sent around a reporter to interview me. They also sent over a photographer to take my picture. I'd met her before, and we started talking to kill time while she set up. I kind of interviewed her. She said she was married, but the marriage wasn't too happy, and someone had suggested she get involved in photography. And now, she said, her camera had become her whole life. 'If someone ever took away my camera,' she said, 'I'd be lost.' Then she started asking about my life and my situation. And I said, 'Well, you know how you would feel if someone took away your camera? You'd be completely lost. Well, that is how I feel. I've lost my platform, my chance to influence things and contribute.' And when she turned around there were tears streaming down her face.

"So now I have no public role. I don't have a platform. You are limited at the *Times* op-ed page to one appearance every six months or so. I tell them that doesn't seem to apply to Henry Kissinger, but that doesn't matter. Every time I call there with something to say, I get a new young thing on the line. Very nice, smart, but they just don't want to hear from me. This is not an American ethos, it's an American journalistic ethos. There are a handful of people who decide who is going to have a platform and who will not. The golden Rolodex. My category—my place in the Rolodex—is the Privacy Issue for Public Officials. Which is the only thing I won't talk about. My friend Billy Shore gets on me to write about Yugoslavia, and I say, 'For whom? Who cares what I think about Yugoslavia?' The young thing at the other end of the phone says, 'When were you last in Yugoslavia?' I'll bet they never ask Nixon that."

———◆◆◆———

In 1995, Hart considered running for the Senate in Colorado, but decided to stay out of the race.

2

The Situationist

(September 1994)

One morning not long ago, Marion Barry saw on the front page of his newspaper the signpost to redemption. The signpost came in the form of poll numbers that gave him reason to believe that to be filmed by the Federal Bureau of Investigation in the act of smoking crack cocaine is not necessarily a disqualification for a fourth term as mayor of the District of Columbia. In fact, there are those in the capital who would say that at this point in the peculiar career of Marion Barry, arrest and incarceration are assets, stigmata.

Barry had a long day ahead of him—the funeral of a close friend, then a complicated flight to a civil rights reunion in Jackson, Mississippi—but for the moment he was absorbed in the numbers published in *The Washington Post*. The *Post*'s story, played above the fold and across two columns, declared that in the race for the Democratic primary, on September 13, Barry was running twelve points ahead of a city councilman and hardy perennial named John Ray and, more remarkably, twenty-two points ahead of the incumbent mayor, Sharon Pratt Kelly. Even with such a commanding lead,

Barry was more skeptical than elated. He had seen other polls, with less encouraging numbers, and, besides, he did not trust the *Post,* especially its owners and the editorial board. They had endorsed him three times for mayor—the first endorsement, in an editorial in 1978, elevated Barry from the bottom of the polls to city hall— but they would not do it again. He was sure of that. The *Post* wanted no part of his redemption story. Indeed, Barry wondered if the *Post* might not be trumpeting this late-June poll precisely to arouse the "ABBs"—the Anybody But Barry vote.

The *Post* poll was not merely a horse-race accounting; it also showed that Barry's negatives were dangerously high. More than a third of the respondents said that under no circumstances would they vote for him. The reasons were obvious, and have become part of the folklore of local politics in Washington. Barry's arrest on a drug charge, in January of 1990, near the end of his third term as mayor, and then his trial and his imprisonment for six months on a misdemeanor narcotics charge had all been international news. Around the world, people had seen on television how a police-and-FBI sting operation brought low the mayor of the United States capital: they had seen the government's videotape of Barry in room 727 of the Vista International Hotel trying to coax a former model named Rasheeda Moore into bed and then, at her urging, taking long stiff drags on a pipe stuffed with crack; they had seen him surrounded by agents, crying out, "Got me set up! Ain't that a bitch?" The agents searched the mayor's pockets, finding, among other items, business cards, breath mints, and, ultimate proof of his municipal powers, a photograph of potholes.

Barry's downfall had not been sudden, or even a surprise. He began as an effective executive, creating programs for the old and the jobless, and leading a downtown-development program that had all the benefits and the gaucheries of business in the roaring eighties. But Barry apparently began snorting and smoking drugs at least four years before the arrest, and he had been drinking heavily—cognac, usually—for far longer. A married man, Barry chased other women with such ferocity that he would one day go on *Sally Jessy Raphael* to describe his sex "addiction." Barry's second wife, Mary Treadwell, once said of her husband's infidelities, "I'm just going to blow his dick off. It will save us all a lot of trouble." For many months during Barry's decline, readers of the *Post* were treated to a series of reports of mayoral escapades: Barry falling asleep at dinner parties; Barry, wearing a tracksuit and a baseball cap emblazoned "Mayor," trying to talk his way into a young mother's house; Barry on boondoggles in the tropics cavorting with drug dealers and other unsavories. After a while, the *Post* assigned reporters to "cover the body," and they would follow him until three, four, five in the morning, squinting into the distance, wondering what the mayor was doing with a raffish crowd on some yacht on the Potomac or with a woman known as Miss T in the Bahamas. A lot did not get into the paper, but enough did.

Barry's fall was not merely a matter of personal habits. His administration was already tainted in more traditional ways. After the high hopes of his first election, city hall sank slowly into the muck of corruption: kickbacks, expense-account shenanigans, and other varieties of municipal rip-off. Ivanhoe Donaldson, an old friend of Barry's from their days together in the civil rights movement, and perhaps his closest confidant, pleaded guilty in 1985 to stealing $190,000 in city funds and went to prison. With time, too, Barry depended more and more on his considerable abilities as a demagogue to cover up his, and the city's, decline; he played the race card when it suited him. And, all the while, everything got worse. The schools deteriorated. Deficits grew. The murder rate soared. The middle class fled. The tax base shrank. But Barry endured, the strongest survivor in a meager political pool.

Until the arrest at the Vista, Barry was defiant, declaring himself "invincible." The puckish local weekly the *City Paper* called him

Mayor for Life. Just weeks before the bust, Barry brought a reporter from the *Los Angeles Times* to one of his hangouts and, between drinks and a lengthy trip to the bathroom, bragged, "I'm gonna be like that lion the Romans had. They can just keep throwin' stuff at me, you know? But I'll be kickin' their asses, every time! In the end, I be sittin' there, lickin' my paws!"

The Barry affair, when it reached the stages of arrest and trial, undermined the spirit of the city. Most of all, perhaps, it was a terrible blow to the African-American majority in a town that had once seen him as its answer to the successful black mayors in Atlanta and Los Angeles. After Barry was arrested, the *Post*'s editorial cartoonist Herblock published a drawing of a black child in a decrepit apartment watching the videotape of the mayor smoking crack. The boy's face was pure sadness, his body slack. The mayor, who had led rallies for schoolchildren urging them to stay off drugs, who had campaigned hard for the support of the clergy, turned out to be a liar and an addict.

Even after Barry's conviction, the city dwelled uneasily in his shadow. He did not allow what is known in the current therapeutic language of newspapers as "the healing process" to proceed. Two months into his six-month jail term, an inmate told a reporter that in a crowded visiting room he had seen the former mayor abuse his visiting privileges with a woman. The inmate, a drug dealer named Floyd Robertson, said he had been sitting only eight feet from the mayor, and the woman, in plain view of other people in the room, "leaned her head over [Barry's] lap, and then I saw her head go up and down." Robertson told another reporter, "There's no way I wouldn't have seen it. My wife's eyes were as big as saucers." Although prison officials quickly moved Barry to another prison, Barry, for his part, denied the charge, telling a local television station, "My character is such I wouldn't do it. My principles are [so] strong I wouldn't do it."

Now, in 1994, Barry is basing his comeback campaign for mayor on precisely his character and his principles—on his own declarations of sobriety and redemption. On street corners and on radio shows, he talks dutifully of the city's financial crisis, its struggle to lose the title Murder Capital of America. He offers a few proposals. He lightly attacks his opponents as inexperienced (Ray) or incompetent (Kelly). He recites a charitable version of his own twelve years in office. But the center of Barry's campaign is his character, his story of exile and return. In 1992, he won a seat on the D.C. City Council representing Ward 8, the poorest section of the city. Now he intends to take back the office that he was forced to abandon.

If the numbers continue to go his way, Barry will prove to be more resilient than Richard Nixon; he will pull off the most bizarre victory since James Michael Curley managed to return as mayor of Boston half a century ago after serving time in prison for mail fraud. But, unlike Nixon or Curley, Barry does not ask voters to look past his flaws. He would prefer, in a sense, that they focus on them. In Barry's telling, his downfall was the result of personal weakness and, more profoundly, relentless persecution by racist "power structures": the FBI, Congress, the district attorney's office, *The Washington Post*. Using a campaign vocabulary that combines aspects of the Baptist Church, Afrocentrism, and twelve-step recovery programs, Barry means to run as a representative man, one who "has been there and back, just like so many folks." He has made his campaign an in-your-face Bible story in which the Deity is both Savior and precinct captain. To deny Barry would somehow be unforgiving, un-Christian, an apostasy against truths holier than any solution to the District's budget crisis. As for those who choose not to vote for him, he says, "That's between you and your God."

One morning this summer, while Barry was shaking hands at the Benning Road metro station, his sound truck boomed out the chapter headings of his story: "*The shock of the world! The biggest shock since*

Muhammad Ali beat Sonny Liston! Everyone will see! We will put the prodi-gal son back in office!"

Barry dressed for the funeral in a suit accented at the pockets and the lapels with the flaming colors of African kente cloth. Since he left prison, he has mostly given up the dark business suits he used to wear as mayor, and has filled his wardrobe with clothes made by a Ghanaian woman who runs a boutique on Society Hill, in Philadelphia. It's like the leaders in Africa, Barry tells friends: if you wear the suits of the European, you give up your own culture, your own self. The same is true of his choice of churches. Barry left a more traditional Baptist church for an Afrocentric one, the Union Temple Baptist Church, where the pastor, Willie Wilson, preaches in front of a gigantic mural of a black Christ and twelve black apostles, among them Nelson Mandela, Rosa Parks, Elijah Muhammad, Malcolm X, and Martin Luther King. In January, when Barry married for the fourth time, he and his bride, Cora Masters (a former chairman of the D.C. Boxing and Wrestling Commission), jumped over a broom at the end of an African-inflected ceremony. Barry has also taken an Arabic name—Anwar Amal, or Brightest Hope. In his City Council newsletter, a map of Ward 8 is superimposed on the southern tip of a map of Africa. As the campaign has progressed, however, Barry has toned down his African symbols. For an interview with editors and reporters at the *Post,* he wore a gray business suit and left his kufi hat at home.

The funeral was for Tom Skinner, a minister who had grown close to the Barry family. When Barry was considering the run for a fourth term as mayor, it was Skinner who told him to run as the standard-bearer of the poor: "God speaks through the people and the poor." The pews, upstairs and down, were filled when Barry arrived. He looked heavier than I remembered him, broader across the chest and the belly, but he had not changed much. As he paced slowly up the aisle, he clicked off a series of sharp nods of recognition to various friends. His warmest greeting was for Louis Farrakhan, who had stood by him during his trial.

The service was long and powerful—a mixture of tribute and gospel. Afterward, Marion and Cora stood on the church steps, talking quietly. The sun was white and hard, and the air was thick, promising rain. As Barry watched someone slam shut the door on the hearse, he winced and flicked sweat off his brow with his index finger. Soon the Barrys were surrounded, and were shaking hands in the shattering heat. It seemed that everyone who approached them came first to Cora. She has become her husband's lion at the gate, his press filter, his exhorter. Barry's previous wife, Effi, had been remote, a slender woman who always appeared uncomfortable as the political spouse and then aggrieved as the martyr wife. She, too, was at the funeral, but kept her distance. Cora is a far more formidable presence. "She'll keep Marion in line," friends say. "He doesn't dare cross her." To this day, Barry apologizes to Cora for the time, in 1987, when he had to force her to resign her post as boxing-and-wrestling chairman for double-billing more than $2,600 in expenses. Cora says the incident was "nothing," a mixup: "I'm just the worst mathematician in the world."

Early the next morning, I caught up with the Barrys in the dining room of a Holiday Inn in Jackson, Mississippi. There were more than two hundred people there, veterans of the 1964 Freedom Summer, when the Student Nonviolent Coordinating Committee dispatched demonstrators all over the state to overcome segregation. It was a summer marked by both triumph and the murder by Klansmen, in the town of Philadelphia, Mississippi, of three young activists—Michael Schwerner, James Chaney, and Andrew Goodman. Here and there was a well-known face from the movement: John Lewis, who is now a leading member of the House of Representatives from Georgia, and Julian Bond. People talked about their lives since 1964, their kids, their divorces. They patted their stomachs, made jokes about their bald spots. But the nostalgia was, most of all, political. The room was almost evenly divided, blacks and whites who had struggled together toward a common goal. It was a deflating reminder of how rare a thing that is in the racial politics of our times.

Barry worked the room with a pol's silken skill, gliding from one cluster of people to the next. He recognized faces, knew names, recalled the right anecdote, the common acquaintance. Cora and Christopher, Barry's teenage son from his marriage to Effi, trailed him around the room. Both seemed well accustomed to waiting, and were particularly indulgent at this homecoming. Barry was born in the Delta town of Itta Bena. His father, a sharecropper in the cotton fields, was forty-six and his mother eighteen at the time. Barry, who is fifty-eight, hardly remembers his father —"just a couple of images of him in the cotton field, riding the mules, maybe." When Barry was small, his mother struck out on her own, taking her children first to Arkansas, for the cotton-chopping season, then to Memphis, where she stayed on to work as a maid. For many years, Barry thought that his father had died, and that that was why the family had moved, but in fact his father died many years later. It turned out that his mother had left because her husband drank and sometimes beat her. "I guess she just got tired of it," Barry told me. Barry went to LeMoyne College, in Memphis, and supported a bus desegregation protest there. In 1960, at SNCC's founding meeting, in Raleigh, North Carolina, he became the group's first chairman. Most of Barry's work as an activist was in Tennessee and, beginning in 1965, as the civil rights movement worked its way north, in Washington, but from 1962 until 1964 he was one of a small army that tried to break through the resistant wall of segregation in Mississippi; namely, in McComb, an hour and a half south of Jackson.

After breakfast, the SNCC demonstrators boarded buses bound for the places where they had worked thirty years ago. The Barrys got on the bus headed for McComb. The day was impossibly bright, and even more humid than it had been in Washington. We all sat back in our seats, stunned by the air-conditioning. When we arrived at the McComb city hall, a crowd of local politicians and residents had gathered to greet the SNCC survivors. Barry was nearly the last to climb off the bus, and Christopher filmed the scene. This time, there were no nooses in the windows to scare the demonstrators, no fear of beatings in the holding cells. Local politicians, black and white, crowded around the SNCC people as homecoming heroes. "Man, I admire these people," Cora said. "I didn't before, but I do now. When it was going on, I was more radical in my ideas. The whole idea of getting hit and not hitting back—I just couldn't do that, I couldn't understand that."

After a meeting at the McComb city hall, the mayor of McComb suggested a visit to the Dinner Bell Restaurant, down the road, for a blowout lunch. A dozen to a table, we wheeled around an enormous lazy Susan that held platters heaped with fried chicken, fried green tomatoes, macaroni and cheese, greens, biscuits, ribs, sweet-potato pie, and red beans and rice. I sat next to Barry, and as he ate he seemed eager to explain himself. Everywhere he goes now, he tries to get the subject of his addictions and his current good health out into the air, not to put anyone at ease so much as to frame his story his way. Barry is only the latest American politician of many to attempt a comeback after humiliation; what makes him remarkable is not merely the elements of addiction and prison but the sheer speed of his return—the gall of it.

"Some people say it's too soon, from a recovery point of view, to take on the mayor's office," he began. "But what they don't know is that we recover by doing the things that make us happy. What dragged me down was not being mayor—it was insecurity, the need to be accepted by everyone, the pleasure syndrome. That's what brought me down. Alcohol and drugs—they make you feel good. They give you a sense of power you don't really have. So you have to do something that's satisfying. I love serving people. I love helping people empower themselves. Even some friends think it's too soon. Some genuinely think I'll go back. But it's been four years. To them, it seems like yesterday."

Barry told me about his "sponsor in recovery"—Darryl Colbert, a man who describes himself as "an ex-bum." When Barry was still mayor, he used to see Colbert hanging around East Capitol Street, drinking, strung out on drugs. Colbert told me that he had been drinking from the time he was seven until he was thirty-five. "I used everything known to man," he said. "I lost jobs, lost my marriage. I had three sons and I just wasn't there. I was down to a hundred and twenty-one pounds and one step from cirrhosis of the liver. I prayed to God to let me die. I cut my wrists open and the blood just dried. I healed." Colbert began treatment in 1987. Three years later, Barry, after he was arrested and went to a treatment center, attended an Alcoholics Anonymous meeting at a church in Southeast Washington. He saw Colbert there and could not believe that his old acquaintance had survived, much less made it into a recovery program. The two men started talking and going to AA meetings together.

As we ate, Barry said that, despite some "nasty" whispering in Washington, he had not had a relapse. I asked how often he went to AA meetings.

"I try to go once a week," he said. Colbert goes at least six times a week. "You can become addicted to AA meetings, too," Barry said, adding that he also calls "a therapist friend" when he feels the need. The most important thing, Cora said, was "the God force within."

After lunch, loaded down with the South's best sweet lard, we fairly waddled back to the bus and then slept all the way to Jackson.

Back at the lounge of the Holiday Inn, Cora and I talked awhile over drinks. It became clear that she and her husband feel betrayed, not only by the FBI and the policemen who laid the trap but by the press, old supporters, old friends.

"Everyone's friendship with Marion was tested," Cora said. "People who had benefited from him and people who had been involved in activities he was accused of deserted him. When you are somebody's friend, you may not approve of what they do, but you don't judge them. You minister to them, you pray with them, you stay with them. People are judgmental and hypocritical, and that puzzled and annoyed me. All of us have a life full of mistakes that no one knows anything about. We may not have been entrapped on video, but we've done some pretty not-so-hot things. Forgiveness is the hardest thing to do. But it's the most liberating thing in the world."

Barry had been making phone calls—a lingering addiction—and now he finally came to our table. But before he could join in the conversation a woman at the next table—drunk, it seemed—leaned over and touched Barry's arm, gently, not to interrupt, more to catch his eye.

"It's so terrible," she said, weepy now.

Barry held her hand and said, "Take care of yourself. Change will come."

"It's so awful. I thought we'd settled it," she said.

"We will," Barry said. "We will. And you take care."

Barry turned back to our table and took a sip of his drink.

"This orange juice is too orangey," he said.

The waitress was summoned, the drink was fixed, and Barry resumed just about where he had left off at lunch. "In prison, I had a chance to reflect," he said. "I read religious things, worked five, six hours a day. I worked the night shift at the power plant, reading meters, water temperatures. I also worked in the kitchen. In prison, working in the kitchen is considered the worst job by the inmates. But it's actually the best job. It's serving other people. So I saw it as an opportunity. Plus, I liked the hours—every other day, ten hours a shift. It gives you the chance to go to the gym, read, listen to tapes, go to the weight room. And I spent about ninety minutes every morning on the phone."

How did he get into drugs? When did it start?

"It's just drift," Barry said. "Control is an important factor. You begin to think you can do everything. It started with drinking. Alcohol was my drug of first choice. When you're into it, you lose your sense of perspective. You think you can control yourself. Very few people told me to stop. Cora told me. People that now say they did are not talking the truth. Most people are enablers. They make excuses for you. I'd call in to the staff and tell them I'm not coming in that morning, and they'd just adjust. We live in the kind of world where no one listens."

I remarked that Cora had said that prison was a blessing.

"Going to prison was one of the best things that ever happened to me," Barry said. "The government found a personal weakness. They'd tried everything else. I was under surveillance for years." Barry claims that government agents "went through my trash, they did tax audits, looking for everything they could find. So they found this weakness and they exploited it."

That night, after taking a drive in Barry's rented Lincoln along Route 49 in a failed mission to find a decent catfish place and a successful mission to buy fireworks, the Barrys went to a concert of the Freedom Singers, a group from the civil rights days. As was usual with Barry, he was running a couple of hours late, and we got to the concert just in time for Barry to grab a seat on the aisle, sing along through the encores, and get up to join in the big ovation.

Then something strange happened. As we were getting ready to go—or, at least, getting ready to watch Barry work the room—dozens of college-age kids, nearly all of them black, took the stage and stared out at the audience. Their leader, a striking young woman in an electric-red dress, announced that the doors had been locked. We would stay in our seats until we heard out a list of "non-negotiable demands," she said.

"We're here to take the torch!" she shouted, thrilled by her own nerve. "The youth of today feel helpless. They are being taught lies. They are not being taught their history, their culture."

She was never completely clear about what the students wanted. One of their demands was that the state keep its hands off black colleges. She called for the establishment of sixties-style freedom schools. What was even less apparent was why she came on so angry to this, of all groups. Just the same, Cora and Marion Barry were roused by the spirit of it.

"C'mon, Marion. Get up there. Help them out," Cora said. "These are kids! They need us!"

Barry jumped into the aisle and rushed the stage. He hugged the woman, who looked startled, and took the microphone. "The least we can do is pass the hat right now," Barry said. "We ought to start out right now, and I'll start with a hundred dollars." Barry dropped in his bill, and around went the hats and the baskets. Where all the money would go—that, too, was a mystery.

"So what if they go and splurge it all?" Barry said as we drove off. "They've got to learn. Take the initiative. Organize!"

Later, I called Taylor Branch, a veteran of the civil rights move-ment and the author of *Parting the Waters: America in the King Years 1954–1963*. When I asked him about Barry, Branch laughed and said he had been at the concert. "Marion's a political guy. He's not like the early Christian-martyr figures in the movement, like Diane Nash and John Lewis. He's no mystic, like Bob Moses was. Marion's a politician through and through. When he went up on that stage after the concert, he drew chuckles from the old movement people. Like 'Oh, there goes Marion. There he goes.' "

After returning to Washington, I called Chuck McDew, an old friend of Barry's from SNCC, and asked what it had been like to see Barry in Mississippi. "Well, he looked all right, which is good," McDew said. "Back in '90, when I saw what he was into, it made me so sad. Marion is a friend, a friend who screwed up. When a friend screws up, you don't try to stone the bastard. A lot of our people from SNCC became what I used to call the walking wounded. They took some heavy blows and—well, whatever gets you through the night.

"But I'm very hopeful. You know, I was with Ray Charles in Albany, Georgia. In the mid-sixties, SNCC had a project down there. Talking to Ray, I asked him, 'How can you justify having a habit and at the same time doing this?' Ray said, 'When you live in a world of darkness, sometimes you try to create your own light.' And that happens with a lot of people. Darkness is not just physical. Many black people—most black people in the struggle—lead lonely, solitary lives. Sometimes you try to create your own light, and that messes you up. That's something that most black people understand. They might use drugs or alcohol to create their own light, if only briefly. When they come to the realization that it doesn't work, most people in the black community won't totally condemn you for it. I think the white community doesn't understand that darkness quite as well, that there are people in despair trying to create a little light. If you're in New Rochelle, as opposed to central Harlem, or on Mulholland Drive, as opposed to South-Central L.A., you just don't understand it. But if you've been there, in the circles of despair, you can understand it. So when Marion got caught up in his difficulties I thought, Well, another man trying to create his own light just got burned in the process."

McDew spoke as a friend. His sympathy was a friend's sympathy. But Barry's narrative, his bid for redemption in the form of election to the city's highest office, is a public matter, and it threatens to split the city of Washington along its most obvious and treacherous divides: race, class, and even, as a kind of subtext of both, skin tone. Unlike New York, with its intricacies of ethnicity and geography, Washington is almost freakishly stark in its divides. The city is two-thirds black. Nearly a third of the city is on some form of public assistance. There are virtually no poor whites. The neighborhoods south of the Anacostia River are almost completely black and lower-income or, less frequently, middle-income. The region is all but ignored by "white Washington"; cabdrivers often refuse to make the trip there from downtown. The rate of violent crime has dropped, but not enough to stop the fear, the publicity, and the middle-class flight.

While Sharon Pratt Kelly is a lighter-skinned black and she and John Ray both live in more privileged sections of town, Barry is dark, the son of a sharecropper. His new house is a modest one, just off Martin Luther King Avenue, in Congress Heights. Ray and Kelly appeal to whites and middle- and upper-income blacks; Barry appeals to the poor, the lower middle class, the left-out. Ray and Kelly are mocked (east of the river) as "bougies"; for some upper-class blacks (west of the river), Barry is a " 'Bama," an unpolished southerner come to the big city. The polarities, naturally, fall apart even on the most cursory examination—Ray is from rural Georgia; Barry did graduate work in chemistry, and his son Christopher used to attend the posh St. Albans School, with the sons of senators, lobbyists, and developers—but to doubt that these categories, this language and folklore, exist is to live a wish. There are black Washingtonians who remember the days when upper-crust black folks used to do the "brown-paper-bag test" to determine who could come to a particular party; if the person in question was darker than an ordinary paper bag, there would be no invitation. "There's no question it's a factor that people whisper about," Cora Barry said. "It's a tragedy, but it's there."

No one has a more acute feeling for the divides of the city and their political possibilities than Marion Barry. When he ran for the school board, in 1971, he stopped using "motherfucker" as punctuation and "pigs" as a reference to the police; he put his dashikis aside and began wearing suits. When a reporter from the *Post* asked about the transformation, Barry explained, "I'm a situationist. I do what is necessary for the situation."

It has always been so. In 1978, Barry won his first term as mayor largely on the strength of the *Post* endorsement and votes from Ward 3, the main white ward. The permanent white population of Washington is nearly all Democratic and at least vaguely liberal, and Barry's background as a poor boy who became a civil rights leader touched the white-liberal imagination in Washington. But almost immediately Barry did his sums and saw Ward 3 as a political base with no future. Even as he conducted business with white developers, befriended them, and vacationed with them on Nantucket, he cultivated the city's powerful black ministers and created thousands of city jobs that were filled by African-Americans. By 1982, he had shifted his base, and that year and in 1986 he won with overwhelming black support.

In the interval between his conviction and sentencing, Barry ran for an at-large council seat. He lost, and, sifting through the results precinct by precinct, he learned just how clearly his story reflected the city's polarities. In 1992, he narrowed his focus and won the Ward 8 council seat. It is in poor neighborhoods like Ward 8, where so many people depend on city jobs or public assistance, and where the sense of victimhood is acute, that Barry is now strong. People there identify with his trials and his mistakes; they are grateful for the way he ran city hall, spending on summer programs and municipal jobs with secondary regard for the city purse. Julius Hobson, Jr., a lobbyist and former member of the school board, told me, "Downtown development shifted tax money to the neediest part of the city. Marion hired everyone. Marion's a great believer in 'I'd rather have you inside pissing out than outside pissing in.' "

Mary E. Cox, a lawyer, who stood by Barry during his trial, said that she thought that Barry's support was rooted, most of all, in a sense of injury and identification. "Of course it's racial," she said. "They treated Jeffrey Dahmer better than they treated Marion Barry. The black male is depicted as an animal. Whether it's Mike Tyson or Michael Jackson or O. J. Simpson, every year we see a black male sacrificed. Marion Barry represents the ordinary black man, not the black middle-class man. The way he walks, the way he talks, his skin color—the average black man in the street relates to him. There is a natural connection between Mr. Barry and men who have had troubles. He is not like Andrew Young or Julian Bond in this. By birthright, he connects to the ordinary man. So when the system holds up his weaknesses they react. It's a class thing."

Jamin Raskin, a professor at American University's Washington College of Law, who volunteered for Barry's first mayoral campaign, said, "No theme in this country has a greater resonance than fall and resurrection. Politics in the black community is especially rooted in religion. When other avenues were blocked, the church became the vehicle for political activism. Barry has a resonant theme. Even Clinton would show up in black churches and talk about condemning the sin and not the sinner."

Raskin went on to say, "There's another factor. The District of Columbia has the highest rate of criminal incarceration on earth, the most per hundred thousand. D.C. is higher than any state—and most cities—in the nation, and the U.S. is the highest in the world. The National Center on Institutions and Alternatives found in 1992 that on any given day in the District of Columbia forty-two percent of the black men aged eighteen to thirty-five were either in jail or prison or on probation or out on parole or awaiting trial or being sought on an arrest warrant. So the fact that Marion Barry has been in jail is not necessarily disqualifying for this community. Many people have had relatives or friends in jail."

Barry, the situationist, also seems to see "people in recovery" as a constituency. According to the D.C. Alcohol and Drug Abuse Services Administration, some eighty thousand District residents currently abuse drugs or alcohol. Barry has been showing up at Alcoholics Anonymous sessions, according to the *City Paper,* not only for his own recovery maintenance but sometimes in search of votes.

West of the Anacostia River—especially west of Rock Creek Park, in "white Washington"—Barry is anathema, a scoundrel. The *Post* poll gave Barry only 1 percent of the white vote. In the White House and on Capitol Hill, Democrats fear that Barry will win and hand comics and conservatives a lance with which to slay the party. *The Tonight Show*'s Jay Leno has already ventured that Barry might be running "not for mayor of the District of Columbia but for mayor of a district in Colombia." What jokes would victory bring? Subtly, congressional Democrats are doing what they can to support Kelly —or, at least, not embarrass her—not out of any love for Kelly but out of fear that her weakness will be to Barry's advantage.

Two white businessmen—Robert Linowes, a real estate lawyer, and John Hechinger, a hardware magnate—told me that while they could always do business with Barry and have had a more trying relationship with Kelly, they could not support him now, especially not when Washington is still run as a semicolony, under the tight control of congressional committees. "The memory of what happened may cause problems with Congress and hurt the image of the city," Linowes said. "We get more than six hundred million dollars a year now from Congress, and there is no guarantee they'll be willing to continue that without major supervision. The trains are not running on time, it's true, but there was an enormous train wreck. In Barry's last term, there were real problems with city finances. And there was just general disarray, a distrust of the government. Kelly has not been doing well, but she is getting all the blame. A lot of the financial trouble, the debts, dropped into her lap."

Hechinger agreed. "There is a saying around here: When Adam and Eve left the Garden of Eden, the Lord gave them redemption, but he didn't let them back into the Garden," he said. "Marion has had his three terms. He's got himself on the City Council, and he ought to stay there."

On the Fourth of July, Barry decided to take his campaign to the white neighborhoods of northwest Washington. "Open your minds, open your hearts, give me a chance," Barry kept telling the voters. Their reactions ranged from restrained applause to disgust. There was booing. Barry, with a smile, booed back. Rock Newman, the manager of the heavyweight champion Riddick Bowe and a close friend of the Barrys, went along with the campaign that day on a parade through the Palisades section of Washington and was shocked at the reaction to the green Barry button that he wore. "One middle-aged, respectable, pillar-of-the-community-looking lady looked at me and said, 'Are you supporting him?' " Newman told me. "I said, 'Yes, one hundred percent.' Well, she just looked at me, with all her humanity, and said, 'You poor son of a bitch.' "

Jim Nathanson represents Ward 3, the main "white ward," and he may have the best explanation of why his constituents refuse to read Barry's story the way it is read across the river. "An overwhelming majority of blacks feel the history of segregation and unequal treatment by the government in this city," Nathanson said. "This history carries with it a large burden, and most of my constituents have no immediate knowledge of that. My people are good-government,

Common Cause supporters. They see Marion Barry and see a guy who broke the law and devastated the city. They feel that he has no business running for mayor, and are even disgusted by his being on the Council. This ward will overwhelmingly come out to vote to make sure he doesn't win."

The most popular local Washington institution is the Redskins. The most influential is the *Post.* More than the Board of Trade, more than any other local institution, the *Post,* to many black Washingtonians, is the most powerful of white institutions. Anita Bonds, who helped manage Barry's campaigns, then worked for Mayor Kelly, told me, "The *Post* is in charge. It is *the* vehicle in this town that generates public opinion."

Everyone in Washington is aware of how the *Post*'s endorsements launched Barry into city hall in 1978 and Kelly in 1990. The Graham family, which controls the paper, and the editorial page editor, Meg Greenfield, are likely to stick with Kelly this time—or perhaps opt for Ray, after passing him over so many times before. Barry is out of the question. Those in the *Post* hierarchy regret their last endorsement of Barry, in 1986; today, they look back and wonder what might have happened if they had endorsed, if only symbolically, Carol Schwartz, the white Republican whom Barry trounced so thoroughly.

"There's no getting around it—you cannot have an election for mayor of D.C. in which the editorial page of the *Post* is not a factor," Milton Coleman, the assistant managing editor for metropolitan news, said. "Also, it's a part of the political landscape in this town that one of the ways to play racial politics is to go after this one big white institution—*The Washington Post,* the embodiment of 'them.' "

The paper's very top editors (with the exception of Coleman) are white, and, not unlike Ward 3 itself, they sometimes make odd decisions that reflect an insecurity about race in a town that is race-conscious in the extreme. In 1990, Farrakhan came to the *Post* to meet with editors and reporters over breakfast. Although he spent much of the on-the-record breakfast pushing aside charges that he was an anti-Semite, Farrakhan went on to say that powerful Jews in the media decided policy in the privacy of a Park Avenue apartment. He also described a vision he'd had, an encounter with Elijah Muhammad (dead since 1975) on a spacecraft that looked like a wheel; on the "wheel," Muhammad warned him of the various evil machinations of the federal government. Some of the *Post* people at the meeting left the room convinced that the man was a hater and a nut. Even so, the next morning's headline read, FARRAKHAN SEEKS LARGER ROLE IN U.S. POLITICS.

In my time with Barry, he continually showed his displeasure with the *Post*. And yet his complaints seem a form of demagoguery: he knows they will play well in the areas where he is looking hardest for votes. Barry has had, for many years, a sophisticated sense of the paper and a comprehensive knowledge of its reporters. (Nearly everyone on the city beat, at one time or another, has covered him.) He has toyed with the paper's liberal guilt, alternately campaigning for its good graces and berating it for its sins, real or imagined. Now he more often uses the *Post* as a foil. At a meeting with editors and reporters not long ago, Barry charged straight into his redemption-and-forgiveness speech and then, when the questions turned to the city's fiscal crisis and his role in it, he lectured, bullied, and stunned the journalists into exhaustion.

Milton Coleman knows all too well that the coverage of Barry by the city's "white" paper can influence the outcome and the emotions of all sides. "You get a guy like that, and if a whole people seems to dismiss him as nothing more than a cokehead, a womanizer, and the leader of a bloated bureaucracy—well, black folks get insulted by that," Coleman said. "They say, 'Why do you see Marion Barry only as that? Can't you see anything else? Then Marion Barry must be a metaphor for the way you see me.' "

A few days after the Mississippi trip, Barry scheduled a morning campaign appearance at a bus stop outside Marbury Plaza, a middle-class apartment complex in southeast Washington. As Barry pulled up in his midnight-blue Chrysler New Yorker, the sound truck was blaring, *"Marion S. Barry: a political genius! Marion S. Barry: he's never lost touch with the people! People like you and people like me!"*

Barry wore a green African suit buttoned to the neck. Before he had even crossed the street, people were yelling his name: "Hey, Barry!" and "Yo, Marion, you got mine!"

Barry looked as though he had spent a lifetime of mornings being applauded, but he was no less delighted. He waved and shook hands and asked the little questions that lock in a voter: "How you doin', dear? You registered to vote?" And "How many units you got up there?" And "How are your grades in school, dear? All B's? How 'bout some A's? You got to visualize it. Can you envision A's?" He seemed to know, by face, at least one out of every half-dozen people, and that was usually from a meeting at one of the city's black churches. With one woman he talked awhile about his "brand-new plan" to push prayer in the public schools.

"I know the power of persistent prayer from a personal point of view," he said. "To pray out loud, it doesn't just affect the person praying. It affects all those around who hear it. Let the courts decide the constitutional question. A large number of young people and ministers have asked me to do this, to introduce a bill permitting voluntary, student-led prayer in school."

"Marion S. Barry! Forgiven by God! Marion S. Barry! Raised by God to be the mayor of our nation's capital!"

"You know, mayors ought to be ministers, and ministers ought to be mayors," Barry told me in between handshakes. "Ministers save souls. So do mayors."

Barry's own minister, Willie Wilson, of the Union Temple Baptist Church, had told me that in his view (and Barry's) the interplay of politics and religion was an ethnic matter. "For the African, life is religion, and religion is life," Wilson said. "There is no division of church and state."

Every so often, Barry sprinted after a voter who seemed to have snubbed him. He bounded onto a bus and passed out pamphlets and registration forms. He is hoping to register thousands of voters. The driver did not complain. As Barry climbed down from the bus, a young woman pulled at his sleeve.

"Have you confessed to God our Savior?" she asked.

"Well, yes, I have," Barry said.

"That's good. That's good."

"Prayer, that's the thing."

"Well, God let me cross your path," the woman said.

"Pray on it," Barry said, a little ironic now. "Hallelujah!"

But he had misread her. She only became more earnest, nagging him. "Can you confess: 'I pray with my heart to Lord Jesus.'"

"Uh . . ."

When she finally left, Barry turned to me, smiling. He seemed relieved. "Sometimes you get these Bible-carrying evangelists and they don't want to hear what you say about anything other than Jesus Christ."

Later, I asked Barry if he had any models for himself as a man and as a politician. There was no hesitation. "Adam Clayton Powell, Jr., is the politician I admire most," he said. Powell was Harlem's shining light in Congress for over two decades. When Powell was under investigation for misconduct and, in 1967, was denied his seat in

Congress, he charged the House with racism. "If they can do this to me after twenty-four years of excellence . . . then you know what they can do to you," he told his black supporters. Running for reelection in Harlem in 1970, Powell lost to Charles Rangel in the Democratic primary by fewer than two hundred votes. Powell's political talents were vastly more extravagant than Barry's. What was important about Powell to Barry was the older man's story, his refusal to be judged by whites, his quest to return.

"Adam did a remarkable thing," Barry said. "He got a few steps from completing his journey. But they broke him at the end, when he went to Bimini. He didn't make it. When Adam was in Congress, I'd see him. I went up with Chuck Stone, one of his assistants. I used to know him. I was on the Hill the day the House voted to deny Adam his seat. Afterward, we went to his office. Adam was standing tall on the Capitol steps, but when I got to his office you could tell he was distraught. Adam said, 'I played the game the way the white folks played it, I even outplayed them.' In his heart, he didn't understand. It was a 'Why me?' thing. Then he felt, 'I know the difference. I'm black.'

"I know better about being black and playing the game the same way. They don't count the score the same way. Every black person knows that. It's just history. You have to know it. Even a nice guy like Tom Bradley, or Dick Arrington, nothing but nice guys, and look at them. But you can't stop. You keep going."

Barry's quest for redemption at the level of public endorsement is no less puzzling to many whites than "Free O.J." and "Mike Tyson: 'I'll Be Back'" T-shirts. Riding with Barry in his car one day, I said it seemed that the T-shirts were a reflection of the great divide in Washington and other American cities. I told him how, when he was working the Benning Road Metro station one morning, I'd met a carpenter named James Price. I'd asked Price about Barry and Tyson, whether there was some link between the two in his mind. Price said he thought there was. "What Barry went through was a learning experience," he said. "Even though he was convicted, look where he is now. I like his story. As for Tyson, we didn't see Mike Tyson rape that girl. But everyone makes mistakes. God forgives us for our sins. How can God forgive us for sins he's seen and we can't forgive for a sin we haven't seen?" I told Barry that the conversation was baffling to me and, what was more, was typical of dozens of others I'd had in Washington. Barry nodded his head, agreeing.

"It's a cultural difference, and religious, too," he said. "The African-American community, even guys on the streets, grew up in the church or around churches that represent something spiritual. I get the impression that the white community doesn't have the same intensity—the Presbyterians and the Episcopalians, it's not the same. The Baptist Church has more ritual. Redemptiveness is preached every Sunday. So it's cultural. They think, too, that the criminal justice system is corrupt, that there is no fairness in it. Or they've even had a bad experience in it themselves. The numbers would suggest that there is some validity in saying that the system is not fair to African-Americans, Hispanics, the poor. Nearly fifty percent of the prison population in America is African-American. Something's wrong. So when you see that every day you say, 'Well, we don't know if Mike Tyson is guilty or not, but something is wrong.' The cultural and historical differences don't mean the black community is less moral or lower in its standards. We're just as high, probably more so. There is a perception among some people that some African-Americans have a lower concept of ethics and standards. It's not true. Black people were just as outraged and disappointed and angry with me as whites. But they've had more personal experiences of grief in their lives, too."

In my conversations, a lot of people said more or less what Barry said. Among blacks, the chorus was near unanimous: Why can Ted Kennedy do what he has done and go on, while Marion Barry cannot? Why was Adam Clayton Powell brought down when the House of Representatives was filled with cads and cheats?

"There's no politician around who you can't get if you go after his weaknesses. Chuck Robb, JFK, Eisenhower. Maybe only Nixon could have got past that," Courtland Cox, one of Barry's oldest friends in Washington, said. "One has to understand that there was a vendetta to get Marion. People looked at that Vista tape and ignored it. People in the black community said, 'You sons of bitches were out to get him and used various practices to do it.' People felt that the government was out of control. And that's not just in Ward Eight. The people said, 'You are the same group of people who are always fucking with us.' So to me it's not a comeback but a never-left."

There are very few black politicians in Washington who challenge the Barry narrative—his opponents included. In 1990, Sharon Pratt Kelly won the *Post*'s endorsement, and then the election, largely because she was willing to run a "clean house" campaign directly attacking Barry. Since then, as Kelly has lost popularity and as Barry's narrative has taken its redemptive turn, she has steered well clear of direct criticism of her old rival. When I went to see Kelly in her new offices, at One Judiciary Square—an absurdly luxurious redoubt, whose final cost to the taxpayers will run close to three hundred million dollars—she swerved away from the Barry questions. She has next to no support east of the river, and if she is to get some it will not be from attacking Barry.

Kelly is not alone in her reluctance. Charlene Drew Jarvis, a councilwoman who represents Ward 4, an area with many middle-income and some upper-income blacks, was willing to say that this election is seen by many poorer blacks as Barry's quest to score a victory over white power structures. But when I asked her whether she would vote for Barry she laughed and said, "No comment, please!" Her constituents, she said, are divided. She didn't want to "alienate anyone."

Perhaps Barry's most influential black critic in Washington is Cathy Hughes, the woman known locally as the African-American Katharine Graham. Hughes owns a string of radio stations with

black-oriented programming, including WOL, in Washington. In
the past, she has supported Barry, but no longer. "Marion is a master pol," she told me. "Even when he can't help, he'll create smoke
and mirrors to make it seem like he is. It was a constant pep rally
when he was mayor until he was cracked out. There's something
about him that people connect to. He's a Farrakhan-type figure.
He's able to say 'Fuck you!' to the white power structure. Black
people mistakenly feel there is some value in saying 'In your face!'
He is our local 'in your face' leader, and he's exploiting the most
vulnerable people. But you can't dismiss him, any more than you
can dismiss Farrakhan. It's not what they've done for the people—
it's their ability to channel the frustration.

"I am anti-redemption-theme. This destroys our community. The
people who have not messed up should be the examples, not those
who mess up and come back. This man did not fix his problems. The
feds did it for him. But, for the community, that's a plus. They like
his boldness. Look at the whole drug culture. Drug kingpins are
idols because they are so bold. They go to jail and throw it in the
Man's face. This is the most painful thing in the world."

Ever since his trial, Barry and his supporters have claimed that the
government spent as much as fifty million dollars to investigate and
arrest him. (The government says that the real figure is many times
less.) Barry himself is convinced that the United States Information
Agency also spent "big money" and "a lot of energy" to distribute
the videotape of his arrest at the Vista hotel to foreign broadcasters
"for maximum airtime." His sense of conspiracy is not an aberra-
tion. Theories of conspiracy have always been a form of political
rage, a means of explaining clearly the sources of one's own misery.
More than ever, conspiracy theories are an integral part of the conversation in poorer black neighborhoods. There is the conspiracy to
entrap black elected officials. The conspiracy to eavesdrop on black

officials with spy satellites (once a favorite of Dick Gregory's). The conspiracy to target and destroy the black community with narcotics. The conspiracy of white (usually Jewish) doctors to create the AIDS virus at Fort Detrick, a research facility in Maryland, and infect blacks. The conspiracy among the white media elite to undermine, or even assassinate, Louis Farrakhan. The conspiracy, known as the Plan, in which white businesspeople and media elites have been plotting for the past twenty years to "take back" power from the blacks who have dominated local Washington government since the advent of home rule.

It is not hard to imagine the ground from which such fantastical thinking grows. How many black leaders have to be killed, how profound does the history of injustice have to be, before it throws the thinking of a community off balance? What Barry grasps intuitively—and what comes as a shock to most whites—is the political potential of conspiracy thinking. At various times in his career, Barry has made references to the Plan to rouse black audiences; these days, he refers to his personal downfall in conspiratorial terms.

One night, I rode around Ward 8 with Lieutenant Lowell Duckett, the head of the Delta Unit, an antigang force. His job is perhaps the roughest in the city: going after the drug gangs—the Barry Farms Crew, the Lynch Mob, the Black Mafia, the Galveston Street Crew—that are the source of so much narcotics trade and general mayhem in Washington. Duckett grew up in the city and played football at a junior college in Kansas. His build roughly approximates an elevator compartment. When he talks, he barks. Duckett has been on the police force for twenty-six years, and remembers well a time when it was nearly all white. He has gone on the radio to criticize his superiors and, while he was at it, the president of the United States. I was with him and Barry one afternoon when they appeared together on a call-in radio show. Duckett treated the three-time mayor to the verbal equivalent of a clothesline tackle.

We drove by Barry Farms, a public housing project, and Duckett said, "That's been a prime location for trouble in the past. That place used to be a plantation and became a place where freed slaves could live."

There are some middle-class houses in Duckett's district, but the middle class, in large part, has for years been fleeing the city for some of the most successful black suburban counties in the country: Prince Georges County and parts of Montgomery County, in Maryland. The poor are stuck. When Barry developed the downtown area of the city, the businesses that moved in created permanent jobs for yuppies, not for unskilled blacks. The underclass in Washington and cities like it is made up mainly of refugees from the industrial revolution, according to such experts in local demographics as Bart Landry, an associate professor of sociology at the University of Maryland at College Park, and Joel Garreau, an editor at the *Post*. Blacks came from the South to northern downtowns for unskilled jobs—loading, manual labor of all kinds—and now machines do the work. "There is a black middle-class miracle," Garreau told me. "But for the people left behind, the kids who have no place to study, who go to bed at night and wake up in the morning hearing gunfire, for the kids with no father in sight, no role model—for them, it's a nightmare."

Duckett knows those kids. They are the kids he has arrested and observed and lived among, and he understands their attraction to a leader like Marion Barry. "A lot of mothers in this town see Marion Barry as their son—he messed up, and then they kiss you and nurture you and send you back out," Duckett said as we drove by a series of abandoned lots. "Then, you take the black middle class. They're leaving anyway. And, man, what they're looking for they'll never find—white validation. They'll never get it.

"You got a class war going on in town," Duckett went on. "The mayor—she's up with the bougies. Her daddy was a judge. Mayor Kelly brought the bougies to the town, so there is a lot of resentment about that. Everything that was helping brothers—rec centers, summer jobs—is going out the window. The taxpayers ought to be willing to spend the way they did for white people on 4-H Clubs, Boys' Clubs. The government came up with things for them. If it don't happen, the race war is going to go down. The sleeping giant is just waking up.

"Barry's trial gains him credibility. It makes him a human being. I know what I'm talking about. Like most cops, I was addicted to alcohol. I almost lost my wife and kids, I was drinking on duty. I messed up, almost got indicted. Believe me, God will save your soul and AA will save your butt! My wife came back. I'm here. It's a success story. That's why I can look in Barry's eyes and know he's been redeemed. There's a redemptive quality in Marion Barry that's good for the city. If God is going to cure Marion Barry, then we might as well get on the bandwagon. He's seen it from the ground up and is making his way up."

Duckett pulled his cruiser up to a park at Atlantic Street and Livingston Road, where a go-go group, the Northeast Groovers, was playing. Duckett pointed out one gang member after another heading toward the band shell. He knew their affiliations by the bandannas they wore on their wrists, the style of their shorts, their T-shirts. They were children, most of them. Duckett said the concert would go just past dusk. "And then watch out," he said. "The guns are in the trunks of people's cars."

Duckett is a talkative man and has a way of careering into subjects without interruption. Occasionally, he would give an order to his men in the Delta Unit by walkie-talkie and then pick up the thread, saying, "And another thing . . ." The last couple of things he said shook me.

"And another thing. AIDS didn't come from no damn monkeys in Africa. It was developed at Fort Detrick, Maryland, to deal with different types and classes of people. You understand what I'm saying?"

Then, "And another thing. Integration? Integration is a social experiment that failed. We're more separate now than we were in 1968. I'm a realist, and I know America is not ready for no integration."

It is not always easy to pinpoint the sources of a conspiracy theory. But what Duckett had to say about the failure of integration, while not part of polite political discourse, was nothing less than the evident truth. Thanks to the civil rights movement, segregation has been outlawed in countless legal realms: education, public access, housing. But Duckett is right: Washington is not merely typical—it is a mirror of American separatism.

As Harry S. Jaffe and Tom Sherwood point out in *Dream City: Race, Power, and the Decline of Washington, D.C.,* their astute book on modern Washington, the city's plantation history is grotesque. For decades, the white elites in Congress and in local business kept tight control of money and politics. The tales of domination—all well known mainly among blacks—are legion. In the forties, Senator Theodore Bilbo, of Mississippi, a proud member of the Ku Klux Klan, was the chairman of the committee that ran the city. Bilbo, who had previously proposed an amendment to a work relief bill calling for the deportation of twelve million blacks to Liberia, used his position as chairman to suggest that thousands of black Washingtonians be driven onto farms or shipped to Africa or, at the very least, sequestered in a stadium. The city's one unifying institution, the Redskins, had also been a symbol of white reticence. The Redskins were the last team in the National Football League to integrate. It was only when Stewart Udall, the secretary of the interior under President Kennedy, spoke up, in 1961, that the team owner, George Preston Marshall, hired a black running back, the magnificent Bobby Mitchell. The *Post*'s sportswriter Shirley Povich cracked that the team colors should have been burgundy, gold, and Caucasian.

When Congress granted home rule to Washington, twenty years ago, there were dreams in the black community that the city would become Chocolate City, a showcase of black culture and political power. "But those days are so long ago, it just seems so sad what's happened since," Juan Williams, a black reporter at the *Post,* said.

Willie Wilson, Barry's spiritual leader, told me, "In Washington and everywhere else, the integrationist dream never occurred. Even the historical documents show that. America is as separate as it was thirty years ago. Many in the African-American community have concluded that the illusion of integration was the most detrimental force in the last thirty years. Thirty years ago, we had a sense of elders, of values that sustained us. The notion of integration was a total cultural-historical surrender. For example, prior to the fifties there were dozens of African-American hospitals; now there are seven. There were businesses, schools. We have walked away from that. Much of it was lost because, under the notion of integration, we walked away from what was ours. It was thought inherently inferior. Without integration, it's quite possible we would have been better off."

One afternoon, I was driving around the city with Barry, from one campaign stop to another, and I asked him about the question of integration. He had begun his political career when integration was among the country's highest goals, and now, it seemed, that had been lost.

"You see, whenever you try to integrate something, its culture, its history, very rarely do you achieve the purpose intended," Barry said. "Prior to 1954, we had many more African-American businesses than we have now. It's culture, too. When I was growing up, we understood who we were. We sang the Negro national anthem. We emphasized black history. We had the best teachers, because under segregation the system prevented the best and the brightest from doing other things. Now teaching is a lowly profession, unfortunately. Now we've lost our best and brightest who would have been teachers—lost them to IBM and General Motors. Our school systems have become havens for nonsuccess. Education in any culture is the way to transfer values and skills. That's why, even though some Jewish families send their kids to public schools, something else goes on that maintains the culture, your identity, as distinct and strong. That didn't happen in our community. Whenever you try to establish black schools, the larger society says you're being racist. In integration, you have two or three strong cultures together. Again, the Jewish people. Their model works well. That's why the Jewish people have disproportionate power, people would say, because of that strength. You got the Torah, the language, and the Ark.

"The African-American community was enslaved from 1619 or before, and every important thing an individual can have was taken from us: our history, our culture, our religion, even our names. Strip a person of all that, you strip him of everything. The African-American maintained some culture—the drums, dance—but, really, he was stripped. After 1863, four million people were freed without any education, because education had been illegal. We all supported the *Brown* v. *Board of Education* decision in 1954, but the infrastructure wasn't there. And it was our fault, quite frankly. So there was not the strength to integrate."

A little while later, Barry had some time to kill before one of his evening neighborhood campaign crawls, and he stopped at a beauty salon on Georgia Avenue.

"How long will a manicure take?" he asked.

"About twenty minutes."

"Can we do it in ten?"

Barry sat down and dipped his fingertips in moisturizer. A woman attended to his cuticles. As we talked, a young girl walked in the door. She was barefoot and dressed in a long white T-shirt, and was possessed of an almost comically voluptuous body. The girl walked back and forth across the salon and then stopped.

"You Barry?"

"Yes."

"No, you're not. You're not him." She was closer now, and it appeared that she was on drugs. Her speech was dreamy, her eyes vacant as echoing hallways.

"Yes, yes, I am," Barry said.

"No, c'mon. You're not the mayor. You're not Barry."

"How old are you?"

"Fifteen."

"You going to school?"

"Nah."

"Where are your parents?"

"My mother's in jail. My father's in jail. I live with my grandma. Sometimes."

"Sometimes?" Barry said. His mood had changed from delight to evident sadness. "Where do you get money?"

"People give it to me sometimes," the girl said, looking away.

"From guys, right? That's terrible. You gotta be careful."

The girl's voice took on a defensive, angry edge. "We're not gonna make you the mayor again," she said.

Barry asked the owner of the salon to keep checking on the girl, but he had no false hopes.

"Man, I see it all the time," he said. "I saw it growing up, too. What a tragedy. The odds of someone like that making it—well, it's zero."

Barry pulled the big Chrysler into a space along a commercial strip on Rhode Island Avenue Northeast. The plan was to shake some hands near the liquor store and the carryout places, and then move on to the houses and housing projects nearby. Before climbing out of the car, Barry peeled off his suit jacket. "Watch this," he said. "Superman! Presto!" He pulled on a T-shirt he'd bought earlier. "Support

African-American Business" was the logo, under a fist with dollars packed into it. The situationist was ready for the situation.

Barry climbed out of the car. At first, seven or eight guys sitting on plastic milk cartons across the street didn't notice, but as Barry walked closer, smiling all the way, they began to shout, "Hey, Barry!" and "Mistuh Mayor Man!" The few teenagers around were wearing huge hip-hop shorts and T-shirts advertising the innocence of O. J. Simpson. A big guy who identified himself as Big Hype grabbed Barry by the elbow and told him he ought to come around to the Kilimanjaro Club—his rap group was playing that night.

"Yo, Barry! Gimme two dollars!"

"Yo, Barry! You gonna win!"

Then the sound truck kicked in: *"Marion S. Barry, despised by a few, beloved by most! Marion S. Barry, a man of humble birth! His parents were sharecroppers making two hundred and fifty dollars a year in the Mississippi Delta! With God, all things are possible!"*

Barry started his tour of the neighborhoods nearby, hopping into a volunteer's Toyota and visiting every front-porch lounger he could find. Everywhere he went, people told him how disgusted they were with Kelly, how grateful they were for the civil service explosion under Barry. A man in his twenties wearing a "Don't Ask Me 4 Shit" T-shirt said he had got a summer job under Barry. Even at Edgewood Terrace, a public housing project, people spoke up for Barry.

"You think Sharon Pratt Kelly or John Ray would ever show up at a place like this?" one young woman said to me. "No way. They're terrified to come down here. Barry's ours."

One night, I went to the Greater New Hope Baptist Church, near Chinatown, for a Barry rally for potential volunteers. I arrived early, and met a young woman there named Dorothy Brooks. She lives across the river, and her belief that Marion Barry would make a better life for her and the city is near-absolute. Just as sure is her conviction that Barry was brought down by a government turned spy and temptress. "He was not himself," she said about his arrest. "It was the pressures of office, home. He was stressed out. It was his way of trying to unwind, by taking a chill pill."

As we sat waiting for Barry to arrive, Dorothy Brooks catalogued her burdens, and they were both extreme and typical. She works as a day-care provider in a city program and earns sixty dollars a week. She is taking this mayoral race very seriously. There are the three major Democratic contenders: Barry, Ray, and Kelly. In the fall, Carol Schwartz will run on the Republican line, and William Lightfoot, a wealthy black lawyer, will run as an independent if his friend John Ray does not get the Democratic party slot. Of them all, Dorothy Brooks said, only one candidate thinks what she thinks, cares about what she cares about.

"Marion Barry is not an Uncle Tom," she said. "He's not a yessir man. The people on the Hill cannot run him. . . . He's a God-fearing man who goes to church and wants to do for people, help people."

A few minutes later, Barry entered the room, and a chant went up: "Bar-ry! Bar-ry!" The candidate shook his fist, but shyly. "I want to thank God for this day, I want to thank him for allowing us to see this wonderful evening," he began. And then he talked about a thirteen-year-old who had been killed in a shootout in his neighborhood. He talked of the plague of violence, the need to build drug treatment centers: "We know it's a medical problem, don't we? So we treat it medically." And then he brought up the *Washington Post* poll. He gave it a conspiratorial edge: "We don't know what that poll was all about. What that poll did was mobilize those who don't like Marion Barry.

"But with the God force in us," he said, "there is not a problem we cannot solve." And then Marion Barry hoisted a box over his head and chanted, "Money! Money! Money! Who's got money?"

Dorothy Brooks was overcome. She was ready to pin all her hopes on Marion Barry, ready to volunteer if she could find the time.

"Everyone likes to see an underdog come back and be top dog," she said. "That's what he should be. Maybe because blacks have been attacked and knocked down since the beginning of time. Marion was toppled from his pedestal. It wasn't fair. He's due another chance. God says forgive. He is forgiven."

—◦—

Barry won his fourth term and, he declared, his redemption. Under Barry, however, the city deteriorated so rapidly that nearly every aspect of government was given over to a financial control board under congressional auspices. Barry, for his part, deteriorated just as quickly. Ill with prostate cancer and folding under the pressures of his municipal failures, he fell prey to the old addictions. By 1996 it was clear that nothing had been redeemed—not Barry and certainly not Washington, D.C.

3

Negative Capability

(November 1995)

On a miserable November morning, with his sinuses clogged and his throat raw and his ears filled with the bleat of the vox populi, Mario Cuomo sits in the modern politician's hell: a glassed-in radio studio, waiting for callers. Cuomo is host of *The Mario Cuomo Show,* broadcast from nine to noon Saturdays on more than thirty stations nationwide. Things might have been otherwise. A series of spectacular political refusals and then a loss at the polls a year ago landed Cuomo in this well-cooled inferno. The former governor tries never to admit to a moment of regret, but the fact is that the man who said no—no to a presidential run in 1991, and no in 1993 to a seat on the Supreme Court—is taking a call from "J.C. from San Diego." J.C. is a libertarian, and he would like to get rid of all laws.

"Now, *Marion,*" says J.C., "do you know why we have laws? Laws are to protect criminals, and . . ."

Cuomo peers sadly over his half glasses at the control booth. He knows that his producer is screening out most of the callers: the sleepless, the strange. J.C. is the cream. Cuomo sighs, but even now, when he is being paid for his patience toward the furious and the dim, he cannot suffer them for long. Finally, he interrupts, asking J.C. what he does for a living.

"I do some market research and collect tin cans."

"Well, good luck with your tin cans, J.C.," Cuomo says. "It really has been a pleasure."

The promise that Cuomo showed at the 1984 Democratic National Convention, his ability to frame an inclusive, liberal vision in a rhetoric suffused with the rhythms of Queens County and Lincoln, has come to this modest end. Ever since he lost the governorship to an obscure state legislator named George Pataki, he has been putting together a new life. In the weeks after the defeat, friends say, he struggled to understand what had happened when every trend—the polls, the endorsement by Rudolph Giuliani—had seemed to hint at victory. For several weeks, some of his friends thought he was depressed, disoriented. Cuomo and his wife, Matilda, moved from Albany to Sutton Place. He turned down the chance to do a daily radio show but took on the Saturday-morning gig. The rest of the week he makes speeches, writes books, and practices law at the firm of Willkie Farr & Gallagher. He says he's handling an interesting case for an Italian firm that makes a state-of-the-art composter and he's also involved in a matrimonial case for "one of the best-known people in the country." But Cuomo makes no secret of it: this is not how he envisioned his future. "It's tragic what's happened to Mario," one of his oldest friends says. "He gave up a seat on the Supreme Court, God knows why, to lose to a nobody like Pataki. Seeing Mario now is a little like seeing Muhammad Ali. It's terribly sad." Tim Russert, the host of NBC's *Meet the Press* and a former Cuomo staffer, says his old boss is "dying not being in the arena."

In his broadcast booth, Cuomo waits out the commercials for antibaldness salve, for an investment guide, for Preparation H. Then another caller, Adrian from San Diego, is on the line, crowing in triumph. He is a Gingrichite who was willing to wait half an hour on hold to announce it. "We've been playing it your way for forty years," he says. "And now . . ."

After a while, Cuomo tries to engage Adrian in much the same way Gunther Gebel-Williams engages his cats.

"Adrian, will you listen, please?"

Adrian will not be engaged.

"Adrian," Cuomo says finally, cracking the whip, "I think your factual command needs a little improvement. Then you'd have a little less aggravation."

As a talk-radio host, Cuomo went on the air last June advertising himself less as an ideological alternative to Rush Limbaugh and G. Gordon Liddy than as a man who would listen. He doesn't listen much. Cuomo's show lacks both the snap of drive-time entertainment and the velvety usefulness of National Public Radio. Limbaugh is a strange and effective mixture of propagandist and comedian, of V. I. Lenin and Jack E. Leonard. Liddy is a shock artist, the Karen Finley of radio. Cuomo, by contrast, often begins his show with an earnest sermon on the issues of the week and then seems to lose patience as the calls accumulate. He would like to believe that this is a good forum for rational debate, but it so rarely happens. You quickly get the sense that Cuomo would rather be somewhere else. "Somebody asked me about the difference between last year and this year," he says over a cup of coffee after the show. "Last year, I had my shoulder to the stone and was pushing it, and every once in a while the damn thing moved. You'd come home and be all scarred and sweaty and exhausted, your legs would pain you, but I made it move. As governor, I was changing the world just a little bit. Being there at the World Trade Center after the explosion and talking to the people of the world and saying exactly the right thing—or exactly the wrong thing. Or when they took the seventeen hostages at Ossining, getting them all out without a loss, fifty-odd hours without any sleep, constantly on the phone. Or making the budget, finally, without savaging all the programs for poor people. Doing what you had to do. I could make a hundred speeches a year, do radio every day, and be more visible than Rush Limbaugh, but it's not the same as having your shoulder to the stone. So I miss public service, because that is an immediate way to get it done. Now I only do it in a remote way, through surrogates. It's not what I want to be doing."

In the days that followed Colin Powell's announcement of noncandidacy, Cuomo studied the reruns with professional interest and a measure of satisfaction, for he was among the few commentators who had said all along that Powell would not run for president. No one could know better the motivation for and the pain of saying no. Now, as he relaxes in the lounge after his show, the mention of Powell's withdrawal vaults him into a kind of Joycean monologue, in which he is at once analyst and subject, outside and inside the mind of the refuser.

"I'd give him an A for his performance," Cuomo says. "It was highly competent. It was very military. It was unadorned, well strategized, well executed. On content, he did not satisfy me from my lawyer's point of view. If what you're saying, in effect, is that you don't feel it—which is what you said—then you knew that before the book tour. What were you looking for? Someone to light a fire in your belly? I mean, the logic escapes me a little bit. And the notion that I tried very hard to get the vocation. I mean—what?— you went up on a mountain? You prayed? You chanted? What were you talking to Ron Lauder for if you were looking for the vocation?

"The reason I thought he wouldn't run is that he is a general. He is accustomed to studying the weather, the terrain, all conditions and circumstances, plotting out every move, making sure you have overwhelming strength that blows them all away. But he was not about to blow away Pat Robertson, Jerry Falwell, Pat Buchanan, Phil Gramm, all these others. They would not go away. He's a general, unaccustomed to subordinates' challenging him. He never had to fight in the gutter. He was in the military, and now all of a sudden he was going to be out in the streets and people were going to be challenging you from your own party. But say you can deal with that. You say, okay, I can take it. I've been in wars. But it is a little messy. Now, let me think about my positions and how that works out. I'm for affirmative action; they're not. I'm for choice; they're not. What does that mean? What about all those cardinals we're counting on showing up for pictures the way they always did for Reagan and Bush?"

As Cuomo warms to the subject, he seems to light up. J.C. and his tin cans are a million miles away.

"There are bills being passed every day by the Republicans—what does General Powell say about them?" Cuomo goes on. "Is he for those Medicare cuts? As soon as I announce, I have to deal with the Gingrich-Dole package that is already there. What do I say? If I say I agree with them, can I go back on everything I've said about my positions? If I say I don't agree, I'm going to war with Gingrich and Dole at the beginning of a primary.

"Then, what happens if you win? Now you're the president. Does Gingrich come in, genuflect, make an act of humility, and say, 'From now on, I'm more moderate, just like you, Colin'? Or do you genuflect and say, 'I'm your president and I'm more conservative, just like you'? How do you reconcile that?"

Cuomo's advice to the Clinton administration is to seize the political opportunity, to invite Powell to take a top-level cabinet post. Co-opt him if you can—steal him, in effect, from the other side. Never mind that they tried once already. Never mind that Powell has declared himself a Republican. A top adviser to Clinton says that such an offer "hasn't been ruled out" by Clinton, but "we haven't spent a lot of time thinking about it, either."

"It's no-lose for Clinton," Cuomo says. "I'm Bill Clinton: Why should I invite him in? Because I want to show I agree with America, I think he's a terrific guy. I also want to show something to the African-Americans. . . . I'm prepared to add a Republican to my government. It's all good. What does Powell say? 'No, I wouldn't think of it, I would never serve in a Democratic administration'? You can't say that. Incidentally, your opinions on the issues are exactly the same as mine, right down the line. You won't serve your country. I'm very disappointed, Colin. That makes Powell less effective as, say, a vice presidential candidate. That takes a little chunk out of him."

Cuomo may question the wisdom of some of Powell's political choices, he may tease the general for his contradictions, and yet Powell's choices, just days after the fact, seem far more comprehensible than Mario Cuomo's. Even now, years after Cuomo refused to enter the presidential race or accept a seat on the Supreme Court, his reasoning defies understanding. Even those who have known him for decades cannot fathom his decisions.

"I think I can understand not running for president," Jack Newfield, a columnist for the *New York Post* who has been a friend of Cuomo's for twenty-five years, says. "It wasn't a matter of a skeleton in the closet. I think he's lived a life of extreme probity and integrity. But not everyone can stand what it takes to run. But for such a legal mind, for someone with those interpersonal skills, to have turned down a seat on the Supreme Court is beyond me. Mario Cuomo could have forged a center-left coalition on the court with Anthony Kennedy and David Souter. He could have held his own with Antonin Scalia. But no. He had to go for a fourth term as governor. And now he's doing talk radio. I don't get it."

Cuomo's most effective defender is his son Andrew, who works now in the Clinton Department of Housing and Urban Development. "They were rational choices," he says. "Might I have made different conclusions? Yes. But so what? He had the choices, not us."

Cuomo's explanations have not changed much over the years, and they are no less tortured than they ever were. He wants history to believe that he never really thought about the presidency until one of his friends brought it up on the eve of the 1992 race itself.

"There was a point in the fall of 1991, and I had a meeting with some contributors at a hotel," Cuomo says. "These were people who mostly went way back to the beginning of my political career—friends from St. John's and the neighborhood, who encouraged me. Some of them had done very well. One of them, Vincent Albanese, from Queens, who is a very successful lawyer and a close friend, said, 'Mario, what about the presidency?' I said, 'What do you mean?' He says, 'You don't have any right not to be interested. Let me tell you directly. We've been with you from the beginning. We don't agree with everything you do. But don't you think you owe it to us?' Well, that stopped me right in my tracks. I felt, suddenly, that I had been guilty of an injustice. These people had been supporting me, and it never occurred to me that maybe I should have gone to them, just out of respect, to say, 'How do you feel about it?' I was acting as if it were all my decision, which is what I'd always done. I'd never even talked about it with Matilda. . . .

"On the spot, I said, 'Vincent, I'll tell you what I'd like to do. If it's all right with Matilda, I think I'd like to get together some people and start immediately to look at this in an objective way—as fast as we can, because we're running out of time. I'll tell you in a matter of weeks whether we can do this.' Well, committees came from out of the blue. They reported to me in no time at all, and they all said, 'We'll get money. There's no question, we have a shot at this.' "

What stood in his way was Ralph Marino, the leader of the Republicans in the state senate, Cuomo claims. "I told him, 'How do you lose? We make the budget. I run. I win, I'm the president, and that's very good for you, good for New York. I lose, that's good for you, because you think you can beat Stan Lundine, the lieutenant governor. And you've gotten rid of me. I'm a pain in the neck to deal with, you all say that, so you're rid of me either way.' He said, 'We can't make the budget.' "

Cuomo will not say it directly, but it is clear he suspects that Marino and the Republican party, state and national, deliberately held up a budget agreement to keep him out of the race.

"What he did was consistent with the Republicans' political needs," Cuomo says. What does not figure into Cuomo's telling is the postscript: When he finally left office, the state had a projected deficit for 1995 of more than four billion dollars.

Some of Cuomo's closest advisers had recommended that he bolt the state before the budget issue ever arose. His son Andrew had counseled against his seeking a third term in 1990. Don't run, Andrew said, and the field will be clear for a run at the White House. "It was my fault for running for a third term," Cuomo says now. "The truth is I never thought about myself as a president. People hear that and they say, 'See, the guy has no self-confidence.' That's not it. I just didn't think I was the best you could find. I don't know if you can understand this, because you haven't been in the position, but, if you have any kind of intelligence, to run you have to conclude that you're better than all the other people. Either that or you have to have the fire in the belly, which is just stupid. Fire in the belly! I'm dying to be president? Why would anyone die for that? Are they crazy?"

If, in Cuomo's telling, Marino is the antagonist in the presidential epic, Stan Lundine, his lieutenant governor, plays a similar role in the Supreme Court story. "When the president asked me to go to the Supreme Court, I said, 'Mr. President, if I had someone who could win the Democratic nomination and then beat the Republican I'd do it.' . . . But I went to Stan Lundine, and I offered it to Stan, but Stan didn't want it. He said, 'I can't do it, Mario. Maybe together we can do it. Can you think of anyone else?' "

Cuomo shrugs. But even that explanation is incomplete. At the time, Cuomo told his friends that if he were an associate justice his "free-speech rights" would be hamstrung, that he couldn't make a dent in the economic and cultural issues that really mattered to him. He would be just one judge on a panel of nine, sworn to a kind of monastic existence. "I don't feel that by not being on the Supreme Court I lost out," he says. "The Supreme Court is very important and very prestigious and very easy. It's a very easy way to live out your life. But for a guy like me that's not where the problems are."

Cuomo remained a deeply provincial figure, a politician who rarely ventured for long out of his state. On his few trips overseas, he would keep his itinerary short and head back to Albany as soon as possible. To the end, he heeded his own counsel—and his counsel never permitted the highest level of ambition. His achievement was ever potential, vague, theoretical.

Cuomo is sixty-three. There might be another presidential shot for Colin Powell, but that is not likely for Mario Cuomo. He doesn't rule out running for office, but he says it's more likely that his son will run for something now. Political operatives in the state are already talking about Andrew as a candidate to run against Al D'Amato for the Senate in 1998. Mario Cuomo, for his part, will do this and that: make some money, do the radio show. He's got a book out called *Reason to Believe*—a lonely reply to the Contract with America. Last week, he appeared at Barnes & Noble and then at the 92nd Street Y.

"So, do I feel bad?" he says. "No. Do I feel cheated by fate? No. Do I kick myself around the corner for making a bad judgment? No. Do I think I missed anything? It's difficult for me to feel regret in that regard. When I sum up my whole life, I feel so lucky."

4

Belfast Confetti

(April 1994)

The blood-weary souls in Belfast whose fate it is to cover "the Troubles" have grown accustomed to the ritual of Gerry Adams's expressing his "sincere regret" after the latest act of terror. It is a *danse macabre*—the media and the revolutionary—and yet is surprisingly bland, workaday. A few of Adams's adjutants will call a press conference at the abandoned Conway Mill, off Falls Road, and string up a backdrop banner for the television cameras: "Towards a Lasting Peace." With everyone assembled, Adams appears before the microphones to trot out his homiletic explanations for one adventure or another of the Irish Republican Army: the blowing up of, say, a fish store and all the customers within; the point-blank assassination of an off-duty detective at the dog track; a mortar attack; a grenade through a picture window. The loss of life is "regrettable," of course, but not condemned, exactly. ("I do not engage in the politics of denunciation," he says.) It is, after all, the British who are ultimately at fault. This is just an "event" in a "broader conflict."

Then Adams may hint at more to come, a honeyed threat of new "spectaculars." A man of tweed, denim, and corduroy, he wants very much to appear professorial, distanced, clean. But if a reporter should press him too hard he will drop his collected tone. "I can understand an old hack's cynicism. Reporters are a very cynical breed of people," Adams said recently as he put an IRA bomb attack in its "proper context." Finally, the reporters will leave the mill, pleased to have their quote, their sound bite, but no less disgusted for having sat through the same performance dozens of times before.

The ritual does not quite end there, for now comes the complicated matter of packaging. In the United Kingdom, Gerry Adams is, by law, the Voice That Cannot Be Heard. British intelligence (and just about everyone else) is convinced that he is not merely the president of the small Sinn Fein political party but, far more important, the most influential figure in the republican movement, the IRA included. A terrorist, in other words. Sinn Fein, it is also assumed, is not the independent party that it pretends to be but, rather, the political wing of the IRA. For these associations, London has tried to inflict upon Adams a kind of media stigmata, a video bruise. When Adams appears on British television—and that means Northern Irish television, too—an actor dubs in his voice. Same face, same words, different voice. This is a practice rendered somewhat absurd when one considers that Adams first began negotiating directly with representatives of Her Majesty's Government when he was in his early twenties. He is now forty-five. Thanks to the Clinton administration, Adams was awarded a two-day visa to the United States earlier this year, despite fierce British objections. In New York, he was free to go on the morning shows and on *Donahue, Charlie Rose,* and *Larry King Live,* and he was free to speak in his own voice. With his more indulgent hosts, and with an audience that does not focus much anymore on the Irish question, Adams proved a master. Any untoward questions about his links to the IRA could be brushed aside with a coy denial. America also provided a ready constituency. Many Irish-Americans are more strident in their demand for immediate British withdrawal than even the Catholics of Northern Ireland. (In politics, distance creates uncomplicated vision. Witness the way many American Jews can be more Israel-right-or-wrong than the average Israeli.)

Without much friction from his hosts, Adams made a case for himself as an embattled historical figure who could drag his more absolutist brethren toward the olive branch if only London, Dublin, and the Protestant majority in Ulster would yield. More than once, it was suggested that his role in Northern Ireland was like that of Mandela in South Africa, or Arafat in the Middle East, and Adams, for his part, accepted the mantle: the reasonable man, the man of peace. He has no right to the comparison. Mandela and Arafat lead majority movements and have finally renounced terrorism. Adams does neither.

The leaders of Sinn Fein, unlike their opposite numbers among the Protestant unionists, are publicity-keen, and from the start they knew precisely how Adams should exploit his time in New York: which programs to visit, what charms to use. The current press spokesman, Richard McAuley, has a friendly manner and an earnest style that puts one in mind of a yuppie Democratic party operative. He is professionally likable, a pal. In the United Kingdom, people tend to be a bit skeptical about the Sinn Fein publicity apparatus. They are aware, for example, that one of McAuley's predecessors, Danny Morrison, is serving an eight-year jail sentence for "imprisoning" a police informer.

Back at home, opponents of the classic IRA posture (one hand at the ballot box, the other gripping an Armalite assault rifle) grew apoplectic as they saw Gerry Adams coasting from one talk show to the next as if he were on the brink of the Nobel Peace Prize. Even his supporters could not believe how smoothly it all went, what rapt attention their man received. They especially could not believe the convivial mood on *Larry King Live*.

"If we were to come over to Belfast," King said eagerly, "would you sit down with all the parties and show the world what's going on?"

"Of course I would," Adams said. "Absolutely."

"I'd like to do that."

"You'd be very welcome. I'll also buy you a pint of Guinness."

"I won't be shot, though?"

"No, no," Adams said. "You'll have your pint of Guinness."

Thus assured, King moved on: "Bedford, New Hampshire. Last call for Gerry Adams. Hello?"

On February 3, Adams returned to Ireland, and was greeted at Dublin Airport by a crowd somewhat less enchanted with his performance than Larry King had been. The leaders of a small Belfast-based group called Families Against Intimidation and Terror, or FAIT, had organized an angry welcoming party. The group assembled a few dozen people, mostly victims of terrorist acts inflicted either by the IRA or by the Protestant paramilitary groups—the Ulster Volunteer Force (UVF) and the larger Ulster Defence Association (UDA). FAIT's leaders issued a press release saying they wanted "to bring Gerry Adams back to reality" after he had "lived the lie of the 'Peacemaker' " on his trip to America.

Maurice Healy, a fifty-eight-year-old man from Cork, who says he was kidnapped and beaten by the IRA, lunged at Adams, shouting, "You fascist, psychotic bastard!" Later, Healy said of Adams, "He's got his Donegal-tweed coat. He's got his humanitarian dimension up front. It's easy to sell it to the Americans. He's projected himself as a peacemaker. What happened in America was totally unbalanced, in that people like me were not represented." Alan McBride, whose wife and father-in-law were killed last year in an IRA bombing on Shankill Road, in Belfast, was furious that in

America Adams had been treated "like some kind of pop star."
McBride told a reporter, "Adams is a murderer, because he supports
the killing of innocent men, women, and children. He is up to his
neck in blood."

Another demonstrator at Dublin Airport was a woman whose
losses to the Troubles have been so great, so numerous, that they are
almost freakish. Of the more than three thousand people who have
been killed in sectarian violence since the Troubles began and
British troops were sent into Northern Ireland, in 1969, ten of
them have been relatives of Sally McCartan. At the airport, she was
enraged—"revolted," she said—at being in the same room with
Adams. But her fury was no match for that of Maurice Healy or
Alan McBride. The press reports hardly mentioned her. A few
weeks later, out of camera range, at FAIT's small office, on High
Street in Belfast, she was more eager to talk.

The FAIT headquarters is a mess—stacked with clippings and
other papers. Among the posters on the walls are one of Mahatma
Gandhi and one of Gerry Adams, drenched to the elbows in blood.
Sally McCartan is fifty-five, and at times she looks years older;
when she talks about her losses to terrorism, her face clenches, the
lines deepen, her eyes lose their shine and focus, like broken windows. Though she and her husband, Sean, are Catholic, they used to
live peacefully near Protestant neighbors on Ormeau Road. When
the Troubles began, their tragedies started to accumulate, absurdly,
randomly, as if they were meant to stand for the city's terror.

"The first time anything happened was with my brother-in-law,
Jimmy McCartan," she said. "It was 1972, when things had really
got bad. Jimmy was twenty-one. He had an invitation to a wedding,
and he dressed himself up nice. There was a disco out at the Park
Avenue Hotel, near Hollywood, east of Belfast, on the water, and
they all decided to go. He was at the bar with a mate, and he over-
heard these UDA guys saying, 'He's a McCartan from the Markets
area.' By that time, the Protestants thought all Catholics were in the

IRA. Jimmy approached them and said, look, he didn't live in the Markets, he lived in Hollywood.

"But it was going wrong. Jimmy was really afraid. He asked the barman if there was a way to be protected. Could he slip out somehow? The barman opened a back door and let him out. But there were UDA all over, and Jimmy was out there in the dark with his mate. His mate ran one way and he ran the other. His mate was climbing a wall to get away, and, as he did, he heard voices shouting, 'We got him! We got McCartan.' And so this other lad ran home to tell my husband, Sean, and me there was trouble.

"This was about eleven forty-five at night. They found the body the next morning at six. They'd dumped Jimmy by a football pitch and a wee creek in East Belfast. He was mutilated, he was. They'd stripped him of his Chelsea boots and his new coat. The jeans were off him. He was stripped of his watch, his rings. They'd hung him first from the ceiling on a hook at some club and beat him dead. His fingers were all broken, his knuckles all busted. They cut his ears off. They cut him, uh, down below. A terrible death. They beat him with the starting handle of a car. He had two hundred and fifty cigarette burns on his hands and his face. They beat him so bad around the face that his face was swelled up like a gorilla's. When he was in the coffin, after the wake, when the people were gone, my sister-in-law and I decided to have a look. The undertaker said he'd never seen a corpse like it. He was right. Jimmy's legs and feet were black and blue, all swelled. He got a terrible death. The fear was in the family. Later, there were seven arrests, and they were all released except one, who took the rap. When they were released, the Protestant paramilitaries lit bonfires and held a celebration. They called them the Magnificent Seven."

On New Year's Day of 1974, a cousin of Sally McCartan's was shot and killed by an IRA man who had been aiming at a British soldier. A few months later, Sean's brother Noel and his sister Lily were walking home from a bar; a gunman jumped out, shot Noel

dead, and was seen escaping in the direction of a Protestant neighborhood. A week later, a few gunmen broke into Lily's house, probably looking for her, and fatally shot her husband, John. "Lily's never
recovered," Sally McCartan said. "She lives with relatives in an attic
room. She doesn't know day from night. Her food has to be brought
up to her, and she never leaves that room. She'd been a lovely girl
with a lovely figure and dark hair, and now she's all white and gray.
Her son went to drink. And then he was found in his house, bat-
tered, five or six years ago. It still puzzles us. They beat him to
death. We didn't have the heart to tell Lily her son was killed. Every
year, we send her an extra card at Christmas from her son. So she
won't know. That's a sad thing for you."

The shootings, the deaths, never seemed to stop. The latest came
in March of 1993. "My son Damien was driving a taxi part-time,
one of those hole-in-the-wall taxi places in the Markets district,"
Sally said. "One night, this young man came in and he seemed very
nervous. He asked Damien for a taxi to pick up his girlfriend. When
they were halfway there, the man said, 'I'm sorry to tell you this,
I'm IRA and we'll have to take your car.' Damien refused. But there
were three other IRA men waiting there, and there was some
wrestling about. Damien threw a couple of them out and then ran
to a social club. He called his older brother Sean and told him where
to try to cut off the car. And Sean did—he cut off the car. Damien
came with his friends, and the IRA guys gave the keys back.

"That was on a Saturday night at around midnight. The trouble
was, they'd embarrassed the IRA. On the Monday night, I got a call
from someone looking for young Sean. They said, 'Get someone
here quick. Damien's been shot, and they're looking for Sean now.'
I thought it was the loyalists, the Prods, who'd done it. They'd hit
the taxi depot before. I saw black and was crying something fierce.
Was Damien dead, or what? So I ran with my daughter, and we saw
smoke all around. They'd burned Damien's car. It was his own people, the IRA. Damien had been shot in the legs, eight shots. But it

was like that wasn't the most important thing to Damien. He was furious when they told him about his car. He went mad! Crazy! He was more worried about his car than his legs. He'd worked so hard to get it."

Sally knew that the IRA would likely come looking for young Sean, and it was then that she went public, appearing on television and in the local papers. When she did, Nancy Gracey, a woman who had started FAIT, in 1990, to protect her son, came calling. Like the rest of the people who had come to FAIT or eventually worked there, Sally McCartan saw publicity as the only way to prevent more bloodshed. (The IRA, for its part, dismisses FAIT as a front for British intelligence, or, alternatively, as a front for the tiny socialist Workers' party. A Protestant paramilitary told me he thought FAIT was "just a bunch of well-meaning sods, aren't they?")

So far, Sally's strategy has worked. Sean has gone unharmed. Sally now works at FAIT a few days a week, counseling other people who live in fear of the paramilitaries. While Sally McCartan has found a mission in her volunteer work, her husband, Sean, has drifted. He can no longer work. He doesn't talk much about what he has seen or about the relatives he has lost. He rarely goes out. Not long ago, Sally found him in a parked car, in an abandoned lot, his head leaning against the wheel, his eyes wide and staring.

Except in Ireland and Britain, the Troubles have become a minor story on the foreign-news pages. An explosion rates a two-paragraph notice in "Around the World," somewhere between an Indian bus crash and a Danish election. And not without reason. Compared with the carnage and the chaos lately in Bosnia, Burundi, Rwanda, Israel, South Africa, Georgia, Haiti, Tajikistan, Mexico, India, and a dozen other scenes of sectarian struggle and outright war, Northern Ireland is tranquillity itself. Every year, there are enough explosions and killings to generate a new packet of the familiar images—the bomb-shattered corpse, the child bicycling past the burned-out car—but the death toll has eased considerably. In 1972, 467 people were killed in sectarian violence; in the past decade, an average of about ninety have been killed every year. Paramilitaries on both sides still act brutally in their own communities, taking on the role of judge and jury and meting out punishment: kneecappings, beatings, exiles. But, with gangs at work on the Lower East Side and in South-Central Los Angeles, why should that rate many paragraphs in the American press?

To the newly arrived visitor, it is jarring to walk down a street in Belfast and see an armored car driving by, in which British soldiers are not merely holding their machine guns but aiming them, moving them slowly along the range of pedestrians. It is jarring to walk along Falls Road, a Catholic neighborhood, or along Shankill Road, a Protestant one, and see guard towers, police stations with twenty-foot walls, and barbed wire—the Peace Lines that seal off one neighborhood from another. The city bristles. It watches. Everywhere, there are teams of soldiers who guard the cop on the beat. Everywhere, there are infrared goggles; Starlight II LIEI "Twiggy" Night Observation Devices; self-loading rifles with image-intensification night sights; surveillance cameras; walkie-talkies; peepholes; helicopters hovering above Murder Mile, in North Belfast—going nowhere, whipping the air, waiting for new Troubles.

But there is a stasis at work. Over twenty-five years, a generation of people has grown accustomed to this life of nervousness. Belfast has achieved an acceptable level of tragedy. For anyone under thirty-five or so, political violence has been as much a feature of life as the rain showers and the rainbows that sweep across the city every few days. "It's the news every night, but unless it touches your close friends or family you don't pay it much mind," one young barman told me. And if you do not live in working-class Belfast, or near certain rural trouble spots along the border with the Republic, life is positively serene. Northern Ireland is, by modern standards, quiet, conservative, scrubbed, under control. One's chances of being murdered there are only a fifteenth of what they are in Washington, D.C. Drugs and street crime are also a fraction of what they are in London or Dublin. Catholics no longer suffer the level of discrimination they once knew as a fact of life. Ever since the rise of the civil rights movement, in the late sixties, the Protestant dominance of local politics, education, and culture has declined. Districts are no longer gerrymandered to the Protestants' advantage; discrimination in the workplace and the universities has diminished. As the linen mills and the docks have closed over the years, unemployment has soared (in some lower-income Catholic areas, the rate of male unemployment is as high as 80 percent), but welfare rates are generous—compared with those in the Republic of Ireland, at least. There are signs of upward mobility. Where once the middle-class and upper-middle-class neighborhoods around Malone Road in South Belfast were completely Protestant, more and more Catholics have moved into the area. And the middle classes have had some success in experimenting with integrated Catholic-and-Protestant schools.

There are figures of political hope in Northern Ireland: One is John Hume, a member of Parliament from Londonderry (Derry to the nationalists) and the leader of the main party among Catholics—the Social Democratic and Labour party, or SDLP. Hume's career began in the civil rights movement; he was one of its foremost thinkers and a key supporter of nonviolence during mass demonstrations in Londonderry in 1968. He has become the one politician universally accepted by Dublin, London, Washington, and Sinn Fein. A mesmeric speaker and an arm-bender of a traditional kind, he, and not Adams, is the most influential voice on Irish affairs on Capitol Hill. In the 1980s, the Irish foreign minister, Brian Lenihan, would try to press the Speaker of the House, Tip O'Neill, into one position or another. O'Neill would hear none of it. "I go by what John Hume says," he would growl. What Hume says is consistent with his position over the past three decades. He is committed to the establishment of a united Ireland, but renounces violent struggle and acknowledges the complexities of dealing with the Protestant majority in the North. He is convinced that the time will come when even the most obstinate unionists will come to the negotiating table. In this he has the support of the vast majority of the Catholics in Northern Ireland. Sinn Fein is a relatively small party: it wins about 11 percent of the vote in the North and less than 2 percent in the Republic.

In the past, Hume was uncompromising in his criticism of the militant republicans, going so far as to call Sinn Fein and the IRA fascist. But that rift has healed. In 1993, Hume and Adams together worked out a framework for at least the start of negotiations with London and Dublin; London and Dublin answered with a joint declaration that also promises, in effect, a devolution of British influence in Ulster. Although many political observers cannot see profound or irreconcilable differences between the two documents, Sinn Fein has demanded "clarifications" and has alternated armed attacks and brief cease-fires, while London, in turn, has said, in essence, "Put down your arms for good and then we'll talk." And so the beast keeps chasing its own tail.

Not to insult the suffering of those who have to live through sectarian conflicts all over the world, it must be said that for the visitor these conflicts often have about them a depressing sameness, a futility in which history and language are twisted beyond all recognition. Arrive in Armenia, say, and within half an hour you will hear of how the Azeris across the border started the horrific 1988 earthquake with a series of underground nuclear explosions; you will hear about a "secret alliance" of Azeris and Turks; you will hear about who was where first, who is the true owner of this church or that mountain pass. Cross the border into Azerbaijan, and you will hear the same tone of conspiracy, the same warring versions of history.

All this is true in Ireland, too, and has been for centuries. To the Protestant unionists, the signal moment in history is the seventeenth-century siege of Londonderry, a battle between the rival English kings William III (a Protestant) and James II (a Catholic). James nearly succeeded in pushing the Protestant settlers north and off the island, but failed; the Protestant victory at the Boyne River, in 1690, is celebrated every July. Even now, the graffito "Remember the Boyne" is to be seen on walls in Protestant neighborhoods. The license plate on the family Jaguar that belonged to the militant unionist Ian Paisley read "MOI 1690," a commemoration of the Battle of the Boyne. The attitude of endangerment, of siege, persists to this day.

To Catholic nationalists, the rise of the Celts is where history begins, and the 1916 Easter Rising is the signal event of the Cause, the great moment of promise and martyrdom. When I met with Gerry Adams at the Sinn Fein press center later in my stay in Belfast, the one decoration in the tiny, dingy room where we talked was a mounted reproduction of the 1916 "Proclamation of the Irish Republic," which was read outside the Dublin General Post Office on the day the uprising began. It was the republican answer to the Ulster Covenant of 1912—the Protestant document that called for eternal ties to England. Throughout our talks, Adams would glance up at the poster, as if for guidance.

Of all the twists and ironies of Irish history, perhaps the most profound is the reason for the presence in Ulster of thousands of British army troops. There is no disputing the Protestants' unchecked reign of discrimination well into the late sixties. When Catholic students and activists began civil rights protests in Belfast and Londonderry, in 1968, the police were clearly on the side of the Protestant government and did little to stop assaults on the republican protesters. When British troops arrived in Ulster with the expressed purpose of protecting the demonstrators, the Catholic population celebrated their arrival. The troops were to be their barrier. But soon the elaborate set of arrangements disintegrated. From 1971 to 1975, the British used their soldiers to round up suspected republican activists (and a few unionist ones as well) and jail them without trial. After setting out as protectors, the British army now behaved, in republican eyes, as an occupying force. The enmity reached its height in 1972, when British forces shot and killed thirteen Catholic protesters in Londonderry—an event memorialized among republicans as Bloody Sunday.

Of all the poets of Northern Ireland—and there have been a remarkable number of them for a country of a million and a half—Ciaran Carson is the one who captures best the futility of the Troubles, the geography of suspicion in Belfast, and, especially, this quality of historical argument: the way the two sides talk right past each other, speaking the same language but remaining incomprehensible to each other. In a few lines, Carson grasps just how the selective use of history creates the dividing wall of politics:

The flash-point of the current Trouble, though there's any God's amount
Of Nines and Sixes: 1916, 1690, The Nine Hundred Years' War, whatever.
Or maybe we can go back to the Year Dot. . . .

In any sectarian conflict, a political resolution never comes from resolving who was where and who was right in the Year Dot. To be visionary means to throw off the weight of history and take advantage of what few openings exist. The Israeli-PLO agreement in 1993 grew out of PLO weakness, Israeli weariness, and a leap of faith on both sides. But, as in Hebron or Johannesburg, there is no guarantee that even the most courageous leap will be rewarded with stability and civil peace.

In Ireland, a number of circumstances have been cause for hope. The British, for one, have admitted that they no longer have any strategic or economic interest in staying in Northern Ireland. "The British psychological process of detachment is beginning," the London *Independent*'s resident correspondent David McKittrick told me one day at a West Belfast pub. "They don't expect to be here forever. If it weren't for the unionists, they would leave right away. The old imperialism is gone. There is no security argument anymore. There are no Spanish galleons coming, no Russians storming the beaches." Not only have most Britons grown tired of sending thousands of troops off to Ulster, and not only do they see no point in just waiting for the next IRA attack, but there is also no money in what they're doing. Britain, the colonizer, puts more than three billion pounds into Northern Ireland every year, a billion of that in security. For years, in fact, the key questions for the British have been not if they should get out but, rather, when and how. The story goes that when the British foreign secretary, Douglas Hurd, was named secretary of state for Northern Ireland, in the fall of 1984, and was being driven around Belfast, he saw "Brits Out" written on walls in Catholic neighborhoods and is said to have remarked, " 'Brits Out'! But how? For God's sake, how?"

Perhaps the two most immediate obstacles to Britain's extricating itself from the Irish quagmire in the near future are John Major's tentative majority in Parliament and an unwillingness simply to abandon the Protestant majority of Ulster. At times, Major's hold on power seems to rely very strongly on the nine Ulster Unionist party MPs. All sides, including Sinn Fein, also acknowledge that if the British were simply to go home tomorrow—if they were to dismantle their military bases, their surveillance apparatus, and the barriers separating Falls Road from Shankill Road—the result could be violence far worse than anything seen in the last decade. There could even be a civil war. "If they were to leave tomorrow, what of these interfaces between neighborhoods?" Brian Feeney, a former Belfast city council member who is a spokesman for Hume's SDLP, told me. "This place could turn out to be a Sarajevo. The Brits will not allow a Bosnia on the western edge of Europe."

On an early-spring day, I spent an afternoon with a well-known poet named Michael Longley—a Protestant, who lives in South Belfast. Like Ciaran Carson, he is disgusted with the persistence of fundamentalism on both sides of the Irish question: with the IRA's unwillingness to forswear arms, with the unionists' Afrikaner-like sense of siege and superiority. "These sides are divided from each other in their souls," Longley said. We were walking along the soft turf of the Giant's Ring outside Belfast—a burial ground thought to date from the Bronze Age. "They adhere to ridiculous visions of themselves and their histories. I call it 'the green wank' and 'the orange wank.' The green wank, the republican delusion, is of some romantic, maudlin Ireland, poetry, the sod—all that shit. Sinn Fein is immersed in that, and yet Sinn Fein itself is so lacking in nimbleness and political imagination. It is so out of date. The only real border left in Europe is the Irish border, which Sinn Fein is intent on cementing. And then there's the orange wank, King William crossing the Boyne on a white horse. Sometimes these loyalists—it's as if all they'd got were their guns and their Bibles, and that's it.

"I am Protestant, went to Protestant schools, and, as I was growing up, there was nothing in the curriculum to suggest I lived in the North of Ireland. I was educated as a Brit. Sometimes I feel British, sometimes I feel Irish. That split is what I am. I listen to the BBC and Irish radio, I read the *Guardian* and the *Irish Times*. Yes, I would like to see a united Ireland, but that's a generation in the future—thanks to the IRA. So people from my background— Well, I understand how they feel. But that's changed. So much has changed. Despite what Gerry Adams says, there is little for the republicans to complain about. What the Brits do here is peanuts compared with what the Spanish do to the Basque separatists. The difference between the Hume-Adams agreement and the joint declaration doesn't warrant the loss of a finger, much less of a human life. We have the ability here to produce a Hebron or a Bosnia. Haven't we learned from history how an entire society can go off the rails without warning?"

Even though most of Ireland has grown sick of Gerry Adams's posturing, even though he lost his Westminister seat in his own home district in 1992, he is indispensable to the promise of peace in Northern Ireland. And here the comparison with Arafat is justifiable. The "hard men" of the IRA, no matter what the particulars of their relationship with Adams, will not put down their rifles and plastic explosives easily. Because of its willingness to carry out brutal acts, the IRA cannot be ignored. This is a hateful thing, but it is a fact, just as it was a fact for Israel that the armed division of the PLO could not be wished away. When one considers some of the other personalities at the head of Sinn Fein—Martin MacGuinness, of Londonderry, for one—Adams seems far more flexible, far more capable of making the leap of faith and the compromises necessary to bring about a peace. "If you are trying to make a deal, you try to preserve the person you need to deal with," Brian Feeney, of the SDLP, said. "If, by some chance, Adams ends up dead in a ditch, who is it you're going to deal with?"

Adams is the avatar of what is known as the class of '69, the nationalist leaders who were young men and women and were on the streets when the first riots broke out in Belfast and Londonderry. They were the ones who hurled Molotov cocktails and "Belfast confetti"—street rubble—first at the local police, and then at British soldiers and British armored cars. The movie *In the Name of the Father* has glamorized the Troubles for American audiences, but when people in Belfast talk admiringly about the film, a portrait of the Guildford Four and their unjust imprisonment for IRA bombings, they are often referring specifically to the opening scene, in which the entire West Belfast community acts as an organic whole, protecting one another and raining havoc on the British soldiers.

In Belfast, I sat in on the appeals hearing of one of the Guildford Four, Paul Hill. Although the British overturned the Guildford Four's conviction for two pub bombings in England (after they had all served fifteen years in jail), Hill's separate conviction for the killing of a former British soldier, Brian Shaw, still stood. Hill's lawyer argued that the same series of tainted confessions that led to the Guildford Four's conviction in the pub bombings had also led to Hill's conviction in the murder of Shaw. Since leaving jail, Hill has become a media light in Ireland, not only as a member of the Guildford Four but also as the husband of one of Robert and Ethel Kennedy's daughters, Courtney. The pro-unionist press and much of the British press have seen in Hill an example of radical chic; they have mocked Hill's claims of innocence and have remarked unfavorably on the looks of Courtney Kennedy. Shaw's widow was furious when half a dozen Kennedys arrived in Belfast in February for the appeals hearing. "Who are they to come over and try to make an impression?" Maureen Shaw demanded of reporters outside the Chichester Street courts. "Kennedy is just a name. After all, they have had their scandals as well."

Hill grew up in West Belfast and came of age at a time when Ian Paisley was leading unionist marchers through the Falls Road district because some republican headquarters had dared show the banned Irish tricolor in the window. Hill and his working-class mates were aghast in 1968 when middle-class students demonstrating for civil rights for Catholics got beaten up by the police. By the time he was a teenager, most of his friends were on the streets, rioting.

"I would riot the same way that anyone else in West Belfast would riot," Hill told me one night after a day of hearings. He and his wife and Ethel Kennedy were staying at a Catholic retreat on the edge of the city. "If I saw someone on the street I knew the British army wanted, I would tell him, 'Don't go around there, the British are around the corner.' Everybody would do that. Old ladies would stop you on the street and say, 'Don't go down that street, son, the soldiers are down there.' That was the community we came from, and I was an extension of the community. Community didn't fall apart when the British army came in. It carried on in that same close-knit way that it always had. That's how it survived.

"I was certainly never involved in armed resistance. Of the close friends around me, several were, several weren't. From the class I grew up with in school I can name at least ten people who have been killed, dying valiantly in what they saw as armed struggle. Six or seven others are in prison. And the rest of the class—maybe a third—would have been involved in nothing, but they would have rioted, like the rest of us."

Gerry Adams grew up on roughly the same streets, in a working-class housing project in the Ballymurphy area of West Belfast, and he saw the same riots. But while Hill's family was not especially political, the nationalism of the Adams family was a legacy. His parents' marriage was a republican aristocracy. Adams's father, Gerry, was in the IRA, had been shot, and spent time in prison in the forties. His mother, Anne Hannaway, was from a prominent republican family; her father, William Hannaway, was a labor official who knew well two of the patriarchs of the modern nationalist movement—James Connolly and Eamon De Valera. Adams's uncle Dominic Adams was chief of staff of the IRA during the Second World War, and another uncle, Alfie Hannaway, had done time in jail for republican activities.

Adams, like so many republican leaders, is a writer. Under the pseudonym Brownie, he wrote a series of articles for a republican newspaper while he was in jail in the seventies, and under his own name he has written dozens of other articles and many speeches. But far more interesting are his autobiography, *Falls Memories,* and his collection of short stories, *The Street*. The memoir and the stories seem to converge at a certain blarneyish point: the memoir is too misty to be entirely true; the stories are too much like the memoir to be entirely fictional. The two books are much the same, presenting a fable of community, of West Belfast, of the republican striving. Whenever he meets with reporters, Adams is eager to talk earnestly about current politics, rehashing old speeches, but at the very start of *Falls Memories* he means to charm in a more timeless way, evoking a sentimental Belfast in which "the boys" (the IRA) were harmless legends and the old streets were an Arcadia since ripped away by time and urban-renewal plans:

> Here I used to live, spending an uneventful childhood playing rally-oh, kick-the-tin, handball and football, sprinkled with occasional forays against the Getty Street lads who were foolhardy enough to venture into our territory. It appeared to me at the time that our gang had a fearsome reputation, though I suppose by today's standards we weren't really at all fearsome. . . . I passed Harbinson's corner and memories came flooding back. . . . Whispers about "the boys" or an occasional witness to meetings of pale-faced earnest young men who, we gathered disinterestedly, had just "got out." Being chased by "the wackey" while fleeing gleefully after hours from Dunville Park or after disturbing old men playing marleys at the shelter. Later still, but with less glee, being pursued by RUC [Royal Ulster Constabulary] riot squads and, later again, by the British Army.

Later on, he writes:

> No doubt, then as now, there were broken marriages, drunken husbands and great poverty but we were unaffected, by and large, by such mundane things. They were nothing to do with us and we were too busy to have anything to do with them. That

this would change was inevitable but the loss of innocence which comes with the arrival of maturity was staved off by the many diversions which each new day brought. Our front doors, with their little scrubbed half moons of pavement, the wee streets beyond and the mountains behind were our playground. But now the wee streets are gone and with them whole generations of childhood games and customs.

Adams was one of ten children; he was above average as a student, ambitious but not quite excellent. A childhood acquaintance (too nervous to let me use his name) recalled him as "the kid who was always eager to be Irish, to learn Irish, to play the Irish sports, but he was never tops." Adams, like Hill, was deeply struck by Paisley's horrifying march through the Falls Road, and the clashes between the unionists and the Catholics that followed. According to a biography by Colm Keena, Adams became deeply political when he was still a teenager. In 1964, he joined Sinn Fein, which was outlawed at the time, and later Na Fianna, the Boy Scouts of the republican movement. He went to lectures on British colonialism and on the history of Ireland. In 1967, he was arrested for selling an outlawed newspaper; he was soon released without a trial.

Instead of pursuing his education, Adams went to work as a bartender, first at a mainly Protestant pub, called the Ark Bar, and then at the Duke of York, a downtown pub that was a gathering place for journalists and local politicians. People who used to go to the Duke of York remember Adams as friendly, smart, happy to talk politics. In August of 1969, as the Troubles were beginning to boil, he left the pub carrying brown paper bags filled with empty stout bottles—material for petrol bombs.

In *Falls Memories* he sounds rather more like a spectator:

In 1969 I stood behind a barricade of burning tyres at the corner of Albert Street and watched petrol bombs showering into the mill at Northumberland Street. The enormity of it all frightened me a wee bit as the huge place began to blaze. I didn't really understand then what was burning. I know now. And so undoubtedly did the person who threw the first molotov.

The tone is a wee bit disingenuous. By the mid-sixties, according to Keena, British intelligence sources, and various experts, Adams had become a member of the IRA, and by 1969 he was one of the young militants intent on returning to a more uncompromising strategy for the republican movement. He and associates like John Kelly, Joe Cahill, and Martin MacGuinness were urging the republican movement to go "beyond" calls for civil rights and begin a violent destabilization of Northern Ireland. That, these new leaders were convinced, was the only way to attain victory. According to Keena and others, British intelligence sources and former IRA members say that Adams was an ascending star in the IRA, and had become the commanding officer of the Second Battalion of the Belfast Brigade by 1971 or 1972, and later attained even higher military and organizational posts.

Adams, though he denies any military role, began a life on the run. "I don't sleep in my own bed," he told me. "I sleep in my own *beds.*" In 1971, he married Colette McArdle, who also came from a family with a distinguished republican pedigree. They had a couple of days' honeymoon in Dublin and then it was back to the underground life. In 1972, at the height of the violence, at a time when the British had decided they had the right to intern Northern Irish without trial, Adams was arrested at one of his safe houses, on Harrogate Street, and was imprisoned, though he was never convicted of any crime. It was, and remains, the culture of West Belfast to "do your whack"—serve your prison term—without complaint. As he told the writer Tim Pat Coogan, "you faced the wall for hours at a time, supporting yourself only with your fingertips. You'd be waiting all day for something to happen. Sometimes they came up behind you and dropped a tray with a crash. It would scare the living daylights out of you."

During interrogation, Adams followed the republican code. He gave up no one and nothing. For days, he would not even admit he was in fact Gerry Adams. Like many other prisoners, he was beaten mercilessly. One of the threats the police used was to tell Adams that they would throw him in the backseat of a car and take him on a series of raids of the IRA; that would surely "expose" him as an informer and bring an automatic death sentence from the IRA. Adams said only, "I'm sorry, I can't help you." After that period of interrogation, which took place at the Palace Barracks, he was moved to the *Maidstone,* a British navy ship docked in East Belfast, and then to a prison camp called Long Kesh, which he refers to as a "concentration camp," but which proved easier than the days of interrogation. He was returned here in 1973. In *Cage Eleven,* his collection of prison essays, Adams understands his "whack" at Long Kesh to be part of his legacy:

Almost twenty years have passed since Long Kesh was opened and through the years it has been a constant element in the lives of all the members of my family. On any one of the many days since then at least one of us has been in there. My father was one of the first to be imprisoned there when he and my Uncle Liam and a couple of my cousins were interned without trial in August 1971 in Belfast Prison and transferred to Long Kesh when it opened to its unwilling guests in the following month. My brother Dominic, who was only six when our father was first interned, has been in the Kesh for the last few years, and this year our Sean endured his first prison Christmas. Our Liam did his time a few years ago and Paddy A, our eldest brother, has been in and out a few times. That's all the male members of our *clann*—apart from me, of course, and a handful of brothers-in-law and several more cousins.

Those who knew Adams during his stints at Long Kesh remember him as the promoter of discussion sessions—the jailhouse professor who talked for hours about the Cause, about strategy, about Irish history and the perfidy of the British. He was inclined toward Marxist thought in those days and was an avid reader of the prison diaries of Ho Chi Minh.

By 1983, Adams, at the age of thirty-four, had become the president of Sinn Fein and that year was elected to the British Parliament. Even as he justified one ruthless act of terrorism after another, his rhetoric now had to become softer, more statesmanlike. His colleagues, however, were not similarly hamstrung. That year, his friend Martin MacGuinness made clear the strategy of the movement during a meeting of republicans at a graveyard in Londonderry. "We recognize the value and the limitations of electoral success," he said, according to Keena. "We recognize that only disciplined revolutionary armed struggle by the IRA will ever end British rule. . . . Without the IRA, we are on our knees. Without the IRA, we are slaves." The next year, another friend, Patrick Magee, checked into room 629 of the Grand Hotel in Brighton, under the pseudonym Roy Walsh, and planted a bomb in the bathroom. A few weeks later, during a Conservative party conference, the bomb was detonated, killing five people and injuring thirty. The prime minister, Margaret Thatcher, was lucky to survive the blast. The world watched as firemen and police sifted through the wreckage with the help of television lights. Despite killing a few politicians and their wives, the IRA felt it had scored only a partial success. The leaders issued the following statement: "Today we were unlucky, but remember, we only have to be lucky once. You will have to be lucky always." Among the people arrested and sentenced to life imprisonment for the bombing was Peter Sherry. Seven months before the blast, Sherry had run for the Dungannon town council—on the Sinn Fein ticket. Adams called the bombing "a blow for democracy."

On a Sunday evening, I went to hear Ian Paisley preach at the Martyrs' Memorial Church, on Ravenhill Road. Paisley has been an international presence—the enraged face of the loyalist Protestants—for nearly thirty years. He is known as the Big Man, and bears a distinct resemblance to a tribal leader. His power is physical—more particularly, vocal. He is enormous, and is possessed of the vocal equipment that, if he were more graceful, would allow him to sing Wagner. The structure of his church, it seems, has been designed around the power of that presence. Paisley preaches from an immense pulpit. He is so high in the air that to see him from the front rows you must tilt your head back as if you were in a planetarium. His tone, even at sixty-eight, is a marvel: a great rumbling; the sound of terror, it seemed to me—the voice that sentences the damned. Paisley is a southern-style evangelical, a friend of Bob Jones and a frequent visitor to Bob Jones University, which awarded him an honorary doctorate; only certain rolls and gutturals in his accent make it plain that he lives in a different part of the world. Flanked by the Union Jack and standing near a sign that read "We Preach Christ Crucified," Paisley slashed on about the evils of "popery," about "treachery" and "treason in government," and that was just the opening blessing. In his sermon he said, "I have survived! And I will continue to survive because I speak the truth! And the truth shall set you free!" The organist played in the style of the skating rink, and the people sang their hymns in registers shrill and adamant.

Paisley's Democratic Unionist party and James Molyneaux's Ulster Unionist party are the dominant Protestant parties—they hold a majority of Northern Ireland's seats in Westminster—and neither man has any inclination to transcend the old rejectionist politics. Both believe deeply that a united Ireland would invite the hegemony of Rome, the obliteration of Protestant culture. No speech of theirs embodies better the paranoid spirit of their politics than the closing lines of Kipling's poem "Ulster, 1912":

We know when all is said,
We perish if we yield.
Believe, we dare not boast,
Believe, we do not fear—
We stand to pay the cost
In all that men hold dear.
What answer from the North?
One Law, one Land, one Throne.
If England drive us forth
We shall not fall alone!

In public relations terms, the Protestants are hopeless. Paisley and Molyneaux feel no compulsion to soften their language. They feel under assault not only from militant republicans but from all sides: from the SDLP, from Dublin, from London, from the pope of Rome. They have no de Klerk, no politician who seems capable of breaking the old mold. What makes the unionist stand even fiercer is the growing sense that the British departure from Northern Ireland is coming, and soon. Their illusion of permanence is all but gone.

The IRA has no monopoly on terror. There have been Protestant paramilitaries in the region for centuries: the Hearts of Oak, the Whiteboys, the Peep o' Day Boys date back to the seventeenth century. In the 1970s, the Ulster Defence Association, which is the biggest of the modern groups along with the Ulster Volunteer Force, would claim credit for acts of terror using an alias that the Hearts of Oak employed centuries ago: Captain Black. But, despite their long tradition, the Protestant paramilitaries have scarcely tried to conceal the fact that they have organized themselves and behaved as mirrors of the IRA. They strive for the republicans' sophistication, and they have army councils and codes of secrecy. Just as the IRA has got its arms from Libya, the Soviet Union, and the Bronx, the Protestants have built stockpiles courtesy of South Africa. And, like the IRA, the Protestant paramilitaries keep themselves functioning by running any number of racketeering schemes. In Belfast, the Protestants are not known to be as well schooled ideologically as their enemy, but lately they have been killing more people, and that's something.

One afternoon, I drove out to the Protestant suburb of Lisburn to meet with Ray Smallwoods. In 1981, Smallwoods took part in the UDA's attempted assassination of Bernadette and Michael McAliskey. When Bernadette McAliskey was still Bernadette Devlin, she was an internationally known figure in the civil rights movement, and she has become one of the most militant republican voices. One January morning in 1981, while Smallwoods waited outside in a car, two accomplices of his broke into the McAliskey home, in the Derryloughan townland, with sledgehammers and shot Bernadette eight times and Michael four times in front of their three young children. Both McAliskeys survived, and the three-member UDA hit team was convicted of attempted murder. Later, Bernadette McAliskey said that the assassination attempt could have occurred only with the collusion of the British military in the area; hers was a familiar charge of UDA–British collaboration, and one made convincingly over the years not only by republicans but by a number of British politicians and investigators as well.

Smallwoods had given me his address in Lisburn as 21-A Market Place: headquarters of the tiny Ulster Democratic party. "Can't miss it," he said. It turned out to be an unmarked door between an ice-cream parlor and a chip shop. A surveillance camera above the door scanned the sidewalk. A guy no more than twenty years old, a few tattoos on his arms, came running down the stairs. After I explained who I was and what my business was, he blinked once slowly, turned, and ran back up the stairs. I followed. He led me into a freezing room furnished with a couple of plastic chairs.

"Sit here," he said. "Wait."

I waited an hour and a half. Clearly, this side of the war did not have the same sense of stroking the press that the republicans had.

"Here," another UDP kid said. "Read this." He handed me a couple of magazines, *New Ulster Defender* and *Captive Verses*. They were filled with loyalist agitprop, greetings to prisoners, and wretched poetry. There were several pictures of armed men wearing ski masks.

Finally, Smallwoods arrived, and announced that he was hungry. I bought him lunch at a pub nearby, and we talked. Smallwoods is forty-four and grew up in Londonderry. He is short and trim, surprisingly calm in argument, and, like Adams, well-spoken. In fact, in my time in Belfast I came to be amazed at just how articulate everyone was; even kids whose business it was to shatter kneecaps had the gift of fluent speech.

"Look," Smallwoods began. "I won't say I was UFF"—Ulster Freedom Fighters—"but I was an active UDA man. I was never convicted for being UFF." I told him that this was a distinction of interest to the law courts of Belfast, but that it was probably beside the point, at this late date, for him to argue his case as a man of tranquil nature.

"Well, fair enough," he agreed.

Smallwoods said that he was one of eight children and grew up in a two-bedroom prefab bungalow in a decent section of Londonderry. "We were the have-nots surrounded by the haves and a nice park," he said. "If you could, you moved away. Some got a job and the rest joined the army. I joined the UDA instead. Lots moved to England. I didn't. You see, I've always had a political bug in my head. While everyone was into sports, I was into politics—and the opposite sex, of course."

Smallwoods was working in a textile mill when the Troubles began, and he was deeply offended at hearing the protests of the republican demonstrators. "The world from Day One was being told that we, the Protestants, were guilty of persecuting Catholics," he said. "I just got sick of being told that the people who were looting and bombing and rioting were innocent people and I was persecuting them. The only way to strike back was to adopt their tactics. What put me over the line was seeing these people portrayed as victims." I asked how he came to join the Protestant paramilitaries.

"How did I join? One of my mates comes to me and says to me there's a meeting at some hall. This was 1972. There were twenty-two people there. In Lisburn. And we were there to form a battalion for the Ulster Defence Association. There was a time in the early days when the UDA put thousands of men on the streets. Most of those did not cross the line into the Ulster Freedom Fighters, the armed resistance. I was a vigilante. Well, that's an emotive word. Let's say I patrolled the streets.

"We've felt total betrayal by Britain, from 1969 on. They've tried to find accommodation with the nationalists and the Republic of Ireland, just so they wouldn't be called by the world a colonial power. Instead, they should have fought in their own corner for our rights." Even the main unionist leaders are not to be trusted. Molyneaux "is a well-intentioned waste of space" and "the same goes for Paisley," Smallwoods said. "We are under threat. We have no one to look after us. The government deals with Sinn Fein, the IRA, and Dublin. Our politicians are no good. From 1985 on, there has been an almost total alienation of the Protestant working class." Smallwoods did not pretend to be innocent of his assault on the McAliskeys. "I believed I'd done the right thing at the time," he said. "Please understand the context. The world believed that my community was guilty of hatred and repression. They were telling our children that we had no future in this country. The decision to go after McAliskey was an organizational decision."

Was he chosen for the plot?

"Let's say I was a 'volunteer.' The way it worked was that there was a decision to carry out an operation, and 'Do you want in on it?' Suffice to say that nobody had to coax me. It was all very clear and self-explanatory. The whole thing speaks for itself. There was a particular situation in the country then, and you responded to the social conditions you found yourself in. We exist in society. The situation was not of my making."

Smallwoods was convicted, and sentenced to fifteen years at Maze Prison, outside Belfast. He served eight. Like others I had talked to, Smallwoods told me of his great personal transformation in prison, how he came to see the "complications" in violence, and how he is now aloof from the outlawed paramilitary groups. To say otherwise, of course, would put him in jail once more. "But look," he was quick to add. "I'm not a pacifist. If my country were to be absorbed into another against the wishes of the majority—well, we have the right to self-defense."

"What if the Provisional IRA finally renounced violence?" I asked. "Wouldn't that be time for the UDA and the UVF to stop as well?"

"The loyalist paramilitaries will not stop, will never stop, so long as Dublin has an involvement in this country," Smallwoods said. "If the Provos stop, you'll get the Protestant violence shifted against Dublin. It will go on. Don't worry."

In the British press, especially, republican militants, and even their Protestant opposites, have been portrayed as homicidal maniacs, psychotic butchers who relish bloodshed. Ever since the Troubles began, a Belfast psychiatrist named Alec Lyons has been studying its psychological impact, including making a comparative study of domestic and political killers. He has seen victims and offenders in his office in Belfast, in Maze Prison, and at the local hospital, and he has published a number of papers on the subject in medical and legal journals. He has concluded that while the domestic killer often is a psychopath, the political killer is, in his terms, normal.

"The two types are different in nearly every respect," Dr. Lyons told me one morning at his office. "From the psychological aspect, the politicians may use the word 'psychopath' to describe the political murderer, but these people are not psychopaths, by and large. A psychopath enjoys his aggression, he does not learn by his past. Certain political murderers were like this. For example, the Shankill Butchers"—a notorious Protestant gang that was involved in at least a dozen gruesome murders. "But usually the people I saw were stable, without drug or alcohol problems, without histories of psychiatric problems. The domestic murders were at close range, maybe with a knife, a hammer. They tend to be at night, often drunken acts. The political murders are different: bombs, snipers, at a distance. They feel no remorse. They believe in their purpose, what they see as the 'justice' of their actions. Afterward, they rarely suffer from stress disorders. It is just entirely different."

Dr. Lyons spoke for quite a while in this vein and then, unprompted, veered into an analysis-at-a-distance of the republican leadership.

"I don't find it hard to understand a person like Gerry Adams. He's been the leader of a republican movement that's been successful. And if you've attained fifty percent of your goals with a certain method—namely, violence—you are reluctant to give it up. Before 1969, this was a Protestant state, for Protestant people. The Protestants have lost their hold on the government, their police force. They are unsure of power now. Civil rights abuses—inequality in housing, gerrymandering—all that's been done away with. The point is that Gerry Adams has achieved a lot by violence and it is naive to expect him to give it up. He's an intelligent man, a good leader. The IRA's propaganda side is very good. He's got international support and sympathy that the Protestants do not have."

Did that mean that he supported the Adams strategy?

"I said I understood the strategy and the psychology," Dr. Lyons said. "But I can't support violence. I have probably seen ten thousand victims over the years—a vast number of them. I see the usual symptoms: fear, anxiety, insomnia, nightmares, flashbacks, replays stimulated by television or for no reason at all, irritability, a lack of concentration. And much worse. How can I support the violence? I am picking up the pieces every day."

If the political violence of Northern Ireland rarely warrants more than a couple of paragraphs in the newspapers, the more common "punishment shootings" get even fewer. Both republican and unionist paramilitaries say they can no longer trust the police to do their jobs. Although the Royal Ulster Constabulary claims to have a high rate of arrests and convictions for common street crime (it is higher than in American cities, certainly), the IRA and the UDA long ago decided to take on the job themselves.

Geoffrey Maxwell, a Protestant in his thirties who was a community organizer in North Belfast before coming to work at FAIT, grew up in Lisburn when the infamous (and since murdered) UDA leader John McMichael was a formidable presence. Maxwell is intimately familiar with Belfast and the suburbs around it, and one morning at the FAIT offices he described the world of the paramilitaries—young thugs operating with all the insouciance and brutality of the Mob fifty years ago. In the poorer sections of Belfast and Londonderry, and in many of the towns and villages of Northern Ireland, members of the IRA or the UDA act as cops, enforcers, racketeers, and thugs. And what is more, for young kids in those areas, joining a paramilitary group is a career path, a way out of unemployment.

"These kids look around, and the only people with power, money, and prestige are in the paramilitary groups," Maxwell said. "You've grown up with this sense of siege. If you are Protestant, you grow up believing that all Catholics support the IRA and want you to come to harm. At thirteen or fourteen, in school, you'll write 'The Red Hand' or 'UDA' or 'UDF' on your schoolbooks. The same in the Catholic areas, where you'll begin to write 'IRA' and 'Brits Out' on the walls.

"You never see the other side until it affects you directly. As kids in Protestant Lisburn, we never heard that there were these Prod paramilitaries, the Shankill Butchers, going around killing Catholics. We had selective propaganda. The UDA recruiting was easy, because for a long time it was a legal organization. You could recruit openly at school. When you reached sixteen or so, it was clear: either you were in the organization or you were crossing the organization. Extreme loyalists tried to ally themselves with Israel or South Africa. That's the way they see themselves, under siege. Paisley thinks he's Daniel in the den of the lion. He believes God gave them Ulster, God's little acre, and the pope is the Antichrist."

The paramilitaries on both sides expend endless labor on their self-appointed policing operations. By comparison, political assassinations are far less frequent and far less strenuous. The parents of a neighborhood "joyrider"—a car thief—might get a visit from the local IRA or UDA man. They are given a warning that their child should cease his larcenies or expect the paramilitaries to take matters into their own hands. If the paramilitaries decide that the next step is required, someone will be found the next morning severely beaten, or with a bullet in his knee. The kneecappings sometimes come by surprise but often by appointment. Sometimes the IRA, in particular, will inform the offender that he has a day or two to leave the country. If he is wise, the offender is on the next ferry to Liverpool.

"The IRA says that kneecapping and exiling are forms of justice it has to use because police have no right to do the job, but really it is a method of social control," Maxwell said. "The process is not always so orderly. Punishments are usually random. Sinn Fein will tell you that there is a set list—that this offense means a beating or that means a knee. It's not true. A few guys in a bar decide what to do, and they do it—beat someone with iron bars or planks or baseball bats, or chase the guy out of the country. The message to the community is 'We do what we want.' In a dispute between a husband and a wife, the woman's father may be in the paramilitaries, and so 'justice' will come down that way. There is a lot of talk about the Troubles, but the biggest war is the war between the paramilitaries and their own communities. In 1993, the IRA pumped more bullets into Irish Catholics than they did into the army.

"The loyalists are the same way, but, as far as kneecappings are concerned, they tend to make a bit more of a mess than the Provos. But the Provos of late have been more sinister—more multiple shootings, both knees, both elbows, and so on. You might get a six-pack—both knees, the ankles, the elbows. They used to shoot people in public, and the victim would be seen and taken to a hospital. Now the victim is taken farther away, and after he is shot he loses a lot of blood before anyone finds him. Or they'll make sure to shoot the victim behind the knee, straight into the popliteal artery, and the blood flow is tremendous. We had someone in Derry in 1993 who was shot in both legs. No ambulance was called for a while, and both legs were amputated and he died a few days later. He was a Catholic shot by the Provos. They accused him of being a sex fiend. He had no criminal record. There was a guy in the IPLO"—the Irish People's Liberation Organization, which is out of business now— "shot by the IRA. They shot him in both ankles, both hands, both knees, both thighs, both elbows: a tenner. Or they might have you bend over and shoot you in the spine. That's a fifty-fifty.

"There are also punishment beatings. Very often with baseball bats. Or they'll use planks with nails sticking out, iron bars, hammers. In Newry, a guy was beaten with a fire ax. Usually, informers get worse. They call it a 'kneecapping in the head.' "

Maxwell went on to say, "You see, this is not the sort of thing you hear much about abroad. Even in South Belfast, on the Malone Road, they don't really know that this is the day-to-day level of intimidation. People are more likely to dismiss it. Even in the areas affected, people will say, 'Well, the victim deserved it.' Saying that makes it more palatable. You can live with that. To know the person was really innocent, that is harder to digest.

"It just never ends. Guys have been kneecapped three or four times and they keep on joyriding. It becomes a challenge. They might drive up to the IRA leader's house and beep the horn and give him the finger. Look, they get kneecapped not because they stole but because they stole without permission from the paramilitaries. The paramilitaries have no conscience. On the same night the IRA told a woman to take better hold of her eight-year-old after he was throwing fireworks in the street, they drove a two-thousand-pound bomb to High Street."

It would be comforting to think that FAIT is a growing organization and that it is making great inroads in Northern Ireland. Neither is the case. Its annual budget is roughly $45,000, and its main success has been in focusing the attention of the media and human rights groups on the extrapolitical abuses of the paramilitaries. Until recently, groups such as Amnesty International paid attention almost exclusively to the abuses of governments against their own people. If a victim comes to FAIT for help, the group will offer counseling and the possibility of publicity, but it will not try to negotiate a settlement with a paramilitary group.

"For intimidation to be successful, people have to be isolated, and we try to break the level of intimidation," Maxwell said. "We try to get the person out of immediate danger. But we refuse to deal with the paramilitaries. It's an issue of human rights. People have a right to the presumption of innocence, to a free trial. Human rights are not up for negotiation. The paramilitaries have no moral or political mandate. We don't want to legitimate them or their right to judgment."

The strangest figure working alongside Maxwell at FAIT is a young man named Henry Robinson. In his youth, Robinson was a paramilitary, a kneecapper. "Now I'm a vegetarian," he told me over lunch. "I learned not to eat meat in jail. It's cruel to animals." Robinson is from a Catholic suburb, Downpatrick, and is one of eighteen children. The family lived in a three-bedroom house, "so it was a wee bit crowded at times," he said. His father drove buses and ambulances. He himself was a poor student—"at the very bottom of the slowest classes"—and left school at sixteen.

"I couldn't wait to start killing British soldiers," he said. "I was in Catholic schools, where we'd recite the names of the thirty-two counties of Ireland (counting the six of the North) as indoctrination. You got the impression in school that Cromwell was still roaming the streets doing evil things to the Irish, or something. When the riots started, the Catholics felt under attack, and so did the Protestants. A lot of recruiting went on. It would be a long time before I'd ever think that sending British soldiers home in coffins was not the whole answer.

"When I got into the whole thing, I was working as a barman, and it was the secretness of the paramilitaries that was the appeal. You know—boys as kids like meeting in secret and talking about secret things. Now, with the paramilitaries it was the same thing, only they were talking about sinister things. I joined up with something called the Official IRA—a splinter group that had a more socialist-type tinge to its nationalism. It still exists, but off on the fringe, really.

"I shot a guy who'd been IRA. He'd just been released from prison. There'd been a fight between him and a guy from our group. He was throwing his weight around. Our group met and decided the shooting would take place. I'd already been shown how to use a gun in some kitchen somewhere. It was a pretty simple thing. You don't have to be a genius to learn how to fire a pistol into some guy's face. I was nineteen at the time—my first time. I had a .38 revolver. It was a really strange feeling, a rush. A lot of adrenaline goes through your body. It's a macho thing, a feeling of utter control. That's what guns are all about, I guess—the feeling that people are going to do what you say. That's how you advance your argument, sticking a gun at someone.

"So there he was, standing at the bottom of the hill on Stream Street. It was the middle of the day. I had a mask on, and there was another guy with me. The guy was with two of his mates. I walked up to him and said I was with the Irish Republican Army. When his mates saw the gun, they scattered. I shot him three times, hit him in both legs. If I'd been told to kill him, I'd have done it. Paramilitaries are like fundamentalists. They don't question, they just do it.

"I ran for our ghetto, but a guy I knew in school saw me. I had my mask off by that time. (I didn't say I was a bright paramilitary, did I?) And so he told the police. I'm glad he did, too, because if he hadn't I'd be in hell by now."

A few weeks ago, Sinn Fein sponsored so-called Peace Commission hearings at the Conway Mill. A panel of cheerful, nodding Sinn Fein leaders listened all day to a series of individuals and groups who had come to plead their case: republicans, unionists, community workers, academics. The press was invited, and that was very much the point. Sinn Fein, we were to believe, has a humane side. The peace side. But neither the press nor the participants seemed much deluded. A young woman, a Protestant minister, came to speak, and she refused to give her name. "If I were to use my name, I'd be in trouble," she told me afterward. Her hands were vibrating. "It's not considered exactly squeaky clean to be with Sinn Fein," she said. "I'm petrified who could see me here and who could know."

The most astonishing moment of the day came when a spindly old gentleman, a surgeon, arrived to give his own testimony. He was William Rutherford, retired after nearly twenty years as an emergency-room physician at the Royal Victoria Hospital, in West Belfast. One of his patients, back in 1984, was Gerry Adams, who had been shot by a team of Ulster Freedom Fighters after leaving a Belfast court. One of the bullets that hit Adams barely missed his spine. His wounds were so severe that it can be fairly said that Dr. Rutherford, a Protestant, saved his life.

Adams showed up at the Peace Commission for a few minutes, but rushed off before his rescuer spoke. He might have done well to stay. Like the psychiatrist Dr. Lyons, Dr. Rutherford had been picking up the pieces all his professional life, and he spoke with a quiet passion of the need for the most obvious and difficult things: the laying down of arms; an agreement that has the consent and cooperation of all sides.

A few days later, I drove out to Dr. Rutherford's house, in a prosperous development in South Belfast. He is still healthy at seventy-two. He described the varieties of gore he had seen in his career.

"I saw my first bullet wound in 1969, when I was already quite an experienced doctor," he said. "I was stunned. Disbelief. I knew that this did not happen in Belfast. I'd never even seen a gunshot wound. It was as if a red-hot needle had bored through the flesh, so small and yet . . . significant. It was so definite, so real, and yet something inside me said, 'No, this cannot be.' The corrupting effect of armed struggle and warfare! Sure, people had robbed banks and stores before the Troubles started, but they were quite happy to do it without shooting anybody. But now, even if the political struggle fades from the scene, we'll be left with a Belfast of guns.

"When it started, you had people on either side getting worked up. The poor Protestants had so little, but if the Catholics, who had even less, grabbed their share, what would they, the Prods, be left with? That was the conflict. At first, the mass of injuries was cuts, bruises, broken bones, broken noses. Then the guns came out. The next great phase was the bombings in pubs, in streets, bombs left in the boots of cars. There was a period when we used to get these all the time. From one bomb you could get a hundred people coming through the door. The IRA was largely the initiator at that point, but sometimes the Prods would do it and pretend the IRA had done it. In the early stages, the bombs were mostly homemade explosives, so you were seeing a lot of people torn up by flying glass. It depended on your proximity to the bomb. They lost legs. Sometimes, when they were killed they were blown to bits, and you couldn't even tell how many corpses you were dealing with, exactly. It was strange, but when you are working as a professional in these circumstances you have got technical problems to overcome. You are taking care of blood loss, making sure you are setting up the right IV fluids, alerting the right people to do this and that.

"I remember people started coming in in 1970 tarred and feathered—an old American pastime, I believe. When that happened, we would call the hospital painters in to advise us. They were the only ones who understood what substances we were dealing with and how to clean them off. And then later in the 1970s we started getting the kneecappings. A lot of the shootings were around the kneecap but did not destroy the kneecap. How much disability depended on precisely what damage had been done, and this may have been linked to the 'crime' involved. I never knew whether the people involved had any knowledge of anatomy, so they could calibrate the degrees of punishment. I suppose they did. But the point is, you have a lot of arteries, veins, and nerves behind the knee. Our surgeons eventually got very good at repairing these injuries. We learned to create a new artery to replace areas where arteries had been torn apart by bullet wounds. There was the 'breeze-blocking'—dropping construction blocks on someone's back or limbs or head. And there were 'romper rooms' where a person would be taken to be 'breeze-blocked.' Oh, God, it was awful. Sometimes the paramilitary group might leave a calling card on the flesh by 'writing' their initials using electrical terminals.

"I remember the day Gerry Adams was shot. I think we got a message before he was actually wheeled in that he was coming. It was within a couple of minutes of City Hall where he was shot. I remember coming into the resuscitation room taking charge of his case. I remember putting the chest drain into his chest, because there was a lot of bleeding around the lungs, and the blood can exert a lot of pressure down on the lung. That made the breathing easier. I remember thinking how his speeches had needled me, got under my skin in the most annoying sense. It seemed to me there was a lot of bitterness in him, though he was possessed of great powers of logic. I suppose I even blamed him, in a way, for escalating things. I was unsure if he was a politician or really a paramilitary commander, but he was definitely a stir-it-up sort of figure, one that kept it all going. I was born and bred on the other side of the fence from Adams, but when I was looking after him I treated him like any other patient. I never had to struggle with my emotions. As a doctor, if you tried to empathize with your patients you'd go berserk. We have to concentrate.

"I wrote to Gerry Adams about a month ago, because I think that now he may really want peace and want politics. I can very well understand that some people on the military end of the armed struggle find it very difficult to stop. These are people whose lives have little meaning outside the war. These are people whose money and power and status and wherewithal are dependent on the status quo. I think Gerry Adams does not want the republican movement to split over this issue. He'd like to achieve more through direct politics, but he knows the risks that have been taken and what there is to be lost for the people who have taken up arms. He wants to be sure he has a good deal before he persuades them.

"I am an unusual man, a Protestant who wants a united Ireland. But the Catholics must understand the Protestants and their fear. The fear is the fear of death, of communal death. If there were an externally imposed united Ireland within, say, eighteen months, a violent war would be likely. But if it is my kind of united Ireland people must be prepared to spend decades. If they want it in a year or two, they'll reap the whirlwind."

• • •

I was able to see Adams alone the day I was to leave Belfast for London. The press office set the time and the place—noon, at No. 51-55 Falls Road, the Sinn Fein press center. It seemed a propitious time to ask the old questions once more. The IRA had lobbed mortar shells into Heathrow Airport. The shells, as it turned out, did not explode, and there were no injuries. What there was was fear, uncertainty, confusion; in short, the IRA, without killing anyone, had accomplished what it set out to do. It was once more destabilizing Britain—the same strategy that Adams and the class of '69 had worked out at the start.

Once I was buzzed into the Sinn Fein building, a friendly greeter led me into a small waiting room. A dour-looking woman sat next to me as her daughter played "Twinkle, Twinkle, Little Star" on a plastic pennywhistle. They were from the neighborhood and had come by for advice. A large percentage of the Falls Road area is on the dole—in fact, IRA members make it something of a point of honor to draw weekly from the trough of England—and Sinn Fein acts as a surrogate community adviser. In the waiting room, I found forms for free health care and information on arranging for a funeral if you could not afford one. On the walls were posters and plaques in honor of IRA men who had been killed in the line of duty—a commemoration that seemed to give the lie to the public position that Sinn Fein and the IRA were wholly separate. Here, inside, no one bothered with the pretense.

I was summoned upstairs to meet Adams. We sat together in a room not much bigger than an elevator: it had just enough space for two folding chairs. Adams was, as usual, in jeans and a tweed jacket, and was friendly, as always, on a first-name basis from the start. He had, in fact, a friendly way of saying very little: "As I have said many times, David," and so on. His talk about his own life was as sweet and as remote as *Falls Memories;* his answers to political questions were little tape loops he had reeled off a thousand times. His rhetoric is still very much rooted in the sixties: he spoke of the need for a "people's revolution," and of his vision of a more or less socialist, "non-sexist" united Ireland. He spoke of the "regrettable" punishment shootings, the need to sympathize with the "legitimate" worries of the Protestant majority. And, while he denied once more any links to or influence on IRA operations, he admitted that it was "very important that anyone in leadership shouldn't get ahead of the pace."

Adams is a seductive performer. One cannot imagine that the republican movement and its terrorist army possess his better. But his seductions are limited. When I asked him what he meant by "socialist" and "economic democracy," he began with "I don't know" and wandered off into a dismal soliloquy, the sort of schoolboy ramble that usually ends with "Sweden," or words to that effect. The truth is that after an hour with Adams you begin to see that under his considerable powers as a front man, under his veneer of learning, he is a secret. Or a protector of secrets. His talent is his ability to be the appealing face of a repellent organization, an army that has soldiers but meager popular support.

After my meeting with Adams, I flew from Belfast to London. At Heathrow Airport, I learned that the IRA had shelled the runway for the second time in a week (with duds again). When I returned to Heathrow, two days later, to catch a flight to New York, there was a third shelling. To restart negotiations, the British demanded a permanent cease-fire. The IRA said that it would grant only a three-day stay. It did, and then, on April 9, the attacks began again in Belfast. This is what Gerry Adams calls the peace campaign.

———✵———

Several months later, Sinn Fein, the British, and the rest of the parties involved in the Troubles arranged a cease-fire. For seventeen months, the truce held, until finally the IRA, impatient with the British negotiators, returned to their customary strategy. The bombers returned to London; people were slaughtered; and Gerry Adams expressed his "regret," but not his condemnation.

5

Unforgiven

(October 1986)

> Alger Hiss charmed everyone because he was so corrupt that he
> could tell anyone a lie and he could brazen out any lie. No one
> wants to believe that such a one could be a spy also.
>
> —Delmore Schwartz, journal passage, 1949

The demon of modern conservatism lives in the Hamptons. On
a summer morning, he steps out of his red clapboard house to
take a walk past the graveyard and into town. His legs wobble. He
stumbles sometimes over roots and curbs he cannot see. His breath
is wheezy and short. His eyes are blue as cornflowers, but they have
failed him in old age, giving him only the cloudy curve of the head-
stones, the weary bending of the trees in the wind.

"As you can tell," says Alger Hiss, "I'm a very old man."

Even in his dotage, Hiss is as spindly and bird-sharp in his features as he was the muggy morning of August 3, 1948, when he
appeared before the House Committee on Un-American Activities
to deny everything a man named Whittaker Chambers was saying
about him: that he was an active agent of the Communist party in
the thirties, that as a State Department official he frequently passed
copies of secret documents to Chambers, who was working then in
the Communist underground. Unlike other men who are provided
by time with a pillowy, self-satisfied bulk, Hiss, with his razory jaw
and knobby arms, is still as thin as the day in 1950 when he was

handcuffed and carted off to Lewisburg Federal Penitentiary wearing a three-piece suit, a snap-brim fedora, and a Mona Lisa smile.

Hiss was convicted of two counts of perjury—for lying about the documents and the length of his relationship with Chambers. But Hiss has always maintained his innocence. He once said that by the time he turned eighty, he expected to be "respected and venerated." He is eighty-one. And though he continues to search for more evidence, he has exhausted every avenue of judicial recourse. Four years ago in New York, U.S. District Court judge Richard Owen rejected Hiss's petition of coram nobis to set aside the original verdict on the basis of new evidence. Owen said he saw nothing of merit in documents Hiss had obtained under the Freedom of Information Act.

"He was crushed, like any man would be whose lifelong dream had ended," says his son Tony Hiss. But he never showed it. "Stiff upper lip, that's my father's way, his training." There are so many coats of polish, so many layers of courtesy and calm, on the man that little else shows. Not only was Hiss schooled at Johns Hopkins and Harvard Law, not only had he been the brilliant young student described by his mentor Felix Frankfurter as "first rate in every way," he was also a man who had faced an extraordinary trial in childhood and another in adulthood. He met both with steely denial, with masks of patience, serenity, and cool. "When Alger was a child, his father killed himself by slashing his throat from ear to ear," says his friend William Reuben. "Then as an adult he endured the HUAC hearings, a trial, a hung jury, then the second trial and jail. He went through all that with WASP reserve. Never cracked. He has spent his whole life building that shell. He wasn't about to lose it all of a sudden."

"It's my way," Hiss says. "I am an objective man."

To take a walk with Alger Hiss along a country road in 1986 is at once remarkable and eerily ordinary. Remarkable because you cannot help but be aware of the acts he was accused of, the perjury he was convicted of, aware of all the lives he changed, the political careers he made, the bloody, lifelong feuds he caused, the family that struggled around him. Ordinary because he is also a man—an old and ailing man with a wife, a son, a simple home in a grand town. Like Trotsky in Mexico, like Kerensky on the Upper West Side, out of time and out of place, Alger Hiss is an unextraordinary man, a stick figure. He is the eye of a strange and endless storm, a dispassionate man with passions of history and personality still swirling around him.

As he walks, Hiss says he is still "interested" in finding other FBI files that would discredit Chambers or J. Edgar Hoover. But the urgency is gone, the fire is out. Hiss knows it's over, at least for now. He compares himself to Dreyfus, to Sacco and Vanzetti, and insists his "vindication is inevitable"—but "not in my lifetime." And still there are only the slightest fissures in his shell. When he talks about death, his tone betrays a lack of the peace that others his age so often have.

"You know one of my best friends here on Long Island was Alden Whitman, the legendary obit man for *The New York Times*," he says. His vocal cords have bowed with age, giving his voice a quavering, underwater sound. "Alden interviewed me for my obituary about ten years ago. We joked about it a good bit. I suppose back then I could be more lighthearted about an imminent obituary than I can today."

Whitman, for his part, says the obituary is ready to run. "It's in the morgue, but I'm not sure it even has my name on it anymore. It's an important one. Three or four columns—almost half as long as a Stalin or a Churchill."

Hiss stops under an elm and gestures to the boneyard. "The morgue, at least it's quiet. All you hear is the birds. I've always liked birds, of course." He laughs at that. It seems that everything about the man took on legendary dimensions. Alger Hiss was even a legendary birder. As a young New Dealer in Washington, he once saw a prothonotary warbler on the banks of the Potomac. It was a rare, thrilling find, and he told his friends about it. During the HUAC hearings—when Chambers was trying to establish his long intimacy and political complicity with Hiss—Chambers privately informed the committee of Hiss's enthusiasm for birds, for the warbler in particular. When Hiss was asked, seemingly in passing, about the warbler at a hearing, he responded that, yes, he had seen one and wasn't that remarkable? Yes, it was, thought young Richard Nixon and the rest of the HUAC members, indeed it was. From there the Hiss story began to unravel.

His vision is so clouded now that when his visitor, dressed in gray slacks and a sport shirt, asks if Hiss can see him, Hiss says, "I cannot see your features, only the outline. You seem to be wearing jeans and a striped shirt. I think I see stripes." Near-blindness stopped him from driving a car long ago, and several years back he quit his job hawking paper clips for the small New York stationery firm of Davison-Bluth. Friends now take him to the Long Island woods where Hiss "birds by ear."

His sight is a touchstone for him, a way of defining his life and age, his plainness as a man. "It's gone full circle," he says. When he was a boy in Baltimore, his Aunt Lila read the English classics to him. Then, as a young legal aide to Oliver Wendell Holmes, Hiss read aloud to the aging justice. Now Hiss invites friends over to read to him. A recent selection was Gabriel García Márquez's novel *One Hundred Years of Solitude*.

When he returns to the house after his walk, there is a rustling in the grass.

"What's that? A rabbit, no?"

He aims his eyes in the general direction of the sound. "Oh, yes, it must be a squirrel. It must be a squirrel."

In fact, it is a pair of robins near the bushes.

"Robins?" he says. "It looked more mammalian than birdlike to me."

The urgency of present events has a way of stripping history of its full narrative, leaving behind only scraps of half-remembered details. The Greek historian Thucydides wrote that in time only "a few irreducible facts will remain; no more, perhaps, than the names of persons and places." To most, the Hiss-Chambers case is a distant affair, a confusing haze of circumstances somehow involving a Bright Young Man lying about his past, a brooding senior editor of *Time* celebrated by the right as the Former Red Who Saw the Light, an ambitious first-term congressman from California named Nixon who made his name by pressing the case, mysterious documents hidden in a pumpkin, an elusive typewriter. The details blur. And yet the images of Hiss and Chambers are imprinted firmly in the memories and souls of some of the present moment's most crucial figures. The President, for instance. Like so many conservatives, Ronald Reagan credits Whittaker Chambers with helping him find the true way, helping him see the struggle of modern history as a Manichaean one, a contest between the forces of light and darkness, between the Christian democratic West and the godless Communist East. Reagan is not known as a great reader, and yet to this day he quotes from memory passages out of Chambers's dark memoir, *Witness.* Chambers's conviction that liberals, particularly the generation of Roosevelt's New Dealers, were tied willy-nilly to the forces of totalitarianism became the psychic and political force behind Reagan and much of the American conservative movement. "Chambers is a crucial figure to a lot of people in the administration. He's talked about by the president and a lot of others," says White House speechwriter Tony Dolan. "Around here Alger Hiss is thought of like Quisling or Benedict Arnold and the other great traitors of history." William F. Buckley, the ringmaster of the right, joined Reagan in praising Chambers as a hero at last year's thirtieth-anniversary celebration of the *National Review*. Chambers, who died in 1961, was awarded a posthumous Medal of Freedom by the president in 1984. George Will, another acolyte in the Church of

Chambers, calls his rumpled hero "an ungraceful man touched in the end by the blinding grace of painful truthfulness."

Conservatives owe a lot to Hiss, too. Without him there would have been no Richard Nixon. Every Halloween a group of conservatives known as the Pumpkin Paper Irregulars gathers in one city or another to celebrate the conviction of Hiss. Last year in New York the Irregulars invited Nixon and presented him with a cryptic scroll making him an honorary member. In his speech Nixon remarked on how the case affected his political career: "The presidential election of 1960 was one of the closest in United States history: a shift of twelve thousand votes in Illinois and one other smaller state would have changed the result. A friend of mine, postmorteming the election a few days later, blamed the journalistic antipathy directed against me during the campaign: 'If it had not been for the Hiss case, I think you might have been elected.' I replied that without the Hiss case, I would probably not have been nominated."

The case was the first and most formative of Nixon's "six crises." John Dean says that in the Watergate years, Nixon used to urge his aides to read and reread his account of the first crisis. Charles Colson proved himself the loyal soldier, reading it fourteen times. Colson was ignorant of many things, but he knew how crucial the case was to Nixon. Hiss also opened the door for Joseph McCarthy. Just a few weeks after Alger Hiss was sentenced to jail, McCarthy made a Lincoln Day speech in Wheeling, West Virginia, claiming the State Department was "thoroughly infested with Communists"—205 of them, to be exact.

The case was the *Rashomon* drama of the Cold War. One's interpretation of the evidence and the characters involved became a litmus test of one's politics, character, and loyalties. Sympathy with either Hiss or Chambers was more an article of faith than a determination of fact. "I came to believe in the guilt of Alger Hiss," John Kenneth Galbraith said.

Once a litmus test, always a litmus test. As late as 1975, *Harper's* magazine polled eminent journalists, historians, and others on where they stood on Hiss's guilt or innocence. Hiss has had his core of supporters, and they are almost uniformly old acquaintances and friends or on the left: columnist Alexander Cockburn, *Nation* magazine editor Victor Navasky, American Communist party leader Gus Hall, playwright Lillian Hellman, Institute for Policy Studies cofounder Marcus Raskin, Supreme Court justices William O. Douglas and Abe Fortas. Obviously, most conservatives side with Chambers—Buckley, *Commentary* editor Norman Podhoretz, Clare Boothe Luce, authors Russell Kirk and Sidney Hook. But Chambers also has won the support of liberals such as Arthur Schlesinger, Jr., and Galbraith. "Everybody comes to it with values and preconceptions," says Navasky, who has defended Hiss in his magazine. "It's not surprising that in a case that is forty years old—where many of the principals are dead, where the charges of espionage introduce a whole world of lying, deception, and code—it's not surprising that you are left with ambiguity."

The passions and the ambiguities are endless. Historian Allen Weinstein spent years suing the government for documents, tracking down old defense files, and interviewing people from Hungary to Mexico to Baltimore. A former professor at Smith College and now a kind of one-man think tank with an office in Washington, Weinstein says he started out "inclined to believe that Alger was innocent." But with the publication of *Perjury* in 1978, he concluded that "the body of available evidence . . . proves the jurors in the second trial made no mistake in finding Alger Hiss guilty as charged." Once more the case came alive, once more the passions were stirred.

Alger Hiss has read *Perjury*. Indeed, his face tightens into a walnut when the book is mentioned. He calls it a "mendacious piece of work" and prefers to keep on his shelves in the Hamptons a friendlier biography, John Chabot Smith's *Alger Hiss: The True Story*. But the reviewers, including many on the left, sided with Weinstein. One of the most forceful reviews in favor of *Perjury* came from Irving Howe, the critic and democratic socialist. On that score Hiss becomes a political arbiter. "Howe? Howe? I don't consider him on the left."

When Weinstein was finishing his book, he asked to meet with Hiss one last time at the office of their mutual publisher, Alfred A. Knopf. "I told him that I thought it was only fair that he should know that I would conclude that he was guilty," says Weinstein. "Before we parted at the elevator, Hiss turned to me and said, 'Do you really believe this is going to make me suffer? You can't hurt me, you know. You can't hurt me.' And in a way he was right. He has his little group of people around him who believe in him. For Hiss, generations come and go, and since his accusers were Hoover, Chambers, and Nixon, he can always revive his own myth. Maybe he's persuaded himself at some psychological level that he's inno-cent, or maybe he stays the course out of loyalty to those around him. They've been working for him for so many years. To insist on his innocence—he owes them at least that much."

William Reuben has dedicated much of his adult life to vindicat-ing Alger Hiss. The rest of it he has devoted to clearing the Rosen-bergs and handicapping horses. Reuben is seventy-one, a jovial fellow with muttonchops and a series of chins. He is more passion-ate about Alger Hiss than Alger Hiss. Reuben lives alone in a tiny New York apartment crammed to the gunwales with books, docu-ments, and court records. While Hiss himself concedes the futility of vindication in his lifetime, Reuben has never stopped working, pushing for more evidence, wiring and rewiring the jalopy of an FBI conspiracy. He has never given up and does not plan to.

"It frustrates me sometimes that Alger isn't angrier, that he isn't more passionate," Reuben says. "You asked me if it were an obses-sion? It is, it's an obsession. It's like when someone opens a closet and there's a murdered person inside. You have to find out the answer.

"Alger still has a certain sense of naïveté. When people ask me, why did Alger go through with it, why didn't he just take the Fifth, why did he testify in front of a grand jury, I say, 'Did you ever hear of the word *schmuck*?' "

Reuben describes himself as "to the left of Alger and just about everyone else" on the case. He believes that neither Hiss nor Chambers was ever a Communist. "Chambers told lie after lie. He changed his story all the time, and there was never any corroboration. The whole story, top to bottom, is pure bull."

Asked how he would feel if Hiss on his deathbed told the world that it was true, that in the thirties he had worked as an agent for the Party, Reuben says simply, "I wouldn't believe it."

Reuben started out in life a rich kid: school in Switzerland, a nice job working at *Vogue* "with all the beautiful models," bridge games at the home of Condé Nast. After fighting in Europe and earning three Purple Hearts, he returned home radicalized and "looking for something meaningful to do." He wrote for left-wing papers and published a book on his own about Nixon's role in the Hiss case. "I knew the bastard would become president," he says. "I was way ahead on that. I made my living lecturing, huckstering around with my book. I would've loved to have been named by McCarthy so people would have known about the books. No such luck."

Reuben reveres Hiss as a victim, but there are times when he is frustrated by how "distracted Alger can be by all the parties in New York. Sometimes I think he doesn't know how important he is. The case is bigger than he is. There were thirty-one duels fought over the Dreyfus case! Thirty-one! I wish Alger were angrier. All he'll call Nixon is 'an opportunist'! He's too polite, as if it were a private argument or something. He doesn't have a Marxist or socialist view of it like I do. I think Alger is a little like Roberto Duran when he fought Sugar Ray Leonard that last time. '*No más, no más.*' "

. . .

Alger Hiss answers the door wearing a tattersall shirt, gray slacks. He asks about my flight, the drive out from La Guardia, the hotel. His courtesy is formal. "Would you like to use the facilities?" "Would you like a glass of water?" "Let me know when you're hungry." This is the same man of whom Richard Nixon said, "If the American people understood the real character of Alger Hiss, they would boil him in oil."

The house is simple and sparse: a few books on birding and the Hiss case, a poster print of a typewriter, framed photographs, a row of ceramic, lettered blocks on the windowsill spelling out "Liberal Sage." There is a fine garden in the back and a boxy American car in the driveway.

Hiss has one ground rule for these interviews: "You can say I live in the Hamptons, but please don't say which one." A few minutes away are the "cottages" of rock stars, beach-novel millionaires, and thirty-year-old investment bankers. "If you were expecting a mansion like the ones near the beach, you must be disappointed," Hiss says. His modest income has come from a variety of sources: his work selling stationery, Social Security, a trust fund set up by friends that yields about five thousand dollars a year. "I have always lived modestly," he says. "I have no financial anxieties. I just have to live carefully." Since being restored to the Massachusetts bar in 1975, he has "practiced a little law. I have one client, a small foundation. But I have to have all the documents read to me."

To be with him is to always feel unsure. Profoundly so. For if Hiss has succeeded at anything, it is to make certainty impossible. Even the most ardent partisans on either side sense the ambiguity. Weinstein, who must feel he knows all he can or wants to about the case, says he "at least reserves the doubt every historian must have." John Lowenthal, an intimate friend of Hiss's who made a film supporting him, says, "Anyone who has known Alger must entertain it: 'Might he be lying to me, his good friend?' "

"People believe what they want to believe," says Hiss.

And then he proceeds to do what he has done hundreds of times before. He maintains his "complete innocence of the charges." He does so with a terrible evenness, pulling out old anecdotes and character sketches with the ease of an aging vaudevillian. So cool. No one wants to believe that such a one could be a spy. In interviews and even in conversations with friends, Hiss denies himself the passions one associates with the falsely accused: "I do not stoop to the gutter."

Of Richard Nixon, who did more than anyone else to push the case against him, Hiss says, "If I needed a confirmation of my judgment of his moral stature, it was obviously supplied by Watergate. People have marveled, or been surprised, that I am not more bitter at Nixon. He didn't seem worth it." And of Chambers, who tended toward lying, bizarre behavior, and wicked swings of mood and political persuasion, Hiss is equally restrained: "I am not bitter at him because I honestly think he was not responsible for his actions."

Objectivity: Hiss uses the word a dozen times in an hour. He talks about the "Kafkaesque" texture of his life, "the element of entrapment in the social setup and in the nature of K. Whichever way K. turned, he found inimical elements in the world around him. But objectivity tells me that Kafkaesque elements are a part of the social fabric." Hiss says he was a victim of J. Edgar Hoover's FBI, which wanted to discredit the New Deal by tying it to Communist espionage and the Soviet Union. He believes that the famous Woodstock typewriter on which he or his wife supposedly copied secret State Department documents was a fake, an FBI forgery. And the Pumpkin Papers that Chambers unearthed from his farm on the Eastern Shore of Maryland—"It was all trumped up," Hiss says.

At the hearings and trials, Hiss was an imperious representative of the old Eastern Establishment whose courtesy seemed at times stiff and arrogant. But he has never lost his bearing, his calm. If he has been lying, it has been with an eerie cool; if he is telling the truth, it is with untold grace. Either way it is hard to see how he maintains his reserve. "Actually," he says, "you're asking me how it is possible for me to be natural. This comes naturally to me. You see, I am not obsessed. I have only been trying to correct the injustice to me, to my family, to the record and the general public. With objectivity. I would hope that I have also lived a full, vigorous life, unwarped, with other interests, coping without being obsessed. The other day I saw someone who I hadn't seen for eight or nine years and he asked me, 'Do you see yourself as a symbol?' A common question. And I said, 'Certainly not.' 'Well,' he said, 'how do you avoid it?' Well, simply by regarding myself as an ordinary man who has had some extraordinary experiences. Like people who climb mountains. Like Edmund Hillary or something."

In 1948, Alger Hiss was heading toward a refined ordinariness, a privileged obscurity. Whittaker Chambers changed all that. When Hiss volunteered to testify before HUAC, he had already left government service and was president of the Carnegie Endowment for International Peace. Although almost every article or book on him describes him as headed toward an ever more glorious public career, Hiss says that he was already planning to leave all government and foundation work and return to the Boston law firm of Choate, Hall and Stewart where he began his legal career. He would have preferred the privacy and comfort of State Street over public life. Then it began, the days in front of the committee, the weeks in the courtroom, the headlines and newsreels. It could only have been pure agony for a self-described "private" man.

And yet there is nothing so striking in meeting Alger Hiss as the impression that he is grateful for his experience, grateful, on some level, for the disdain as well as the admiration. He seems grateful for the passions evoked, for the unexpected exceptionalness of his life. He was not, after all, the only one accused of such things in those days, but unlike so many who refused to cooperate with HUAC, grand juries, and other investigatory bodies of the era and merely became footnotes to history, Hiss, against the advice of almost everyone around him, volunteered testimony at every level until the quagmire consumed him. He became, with Chambers, a chapter in history, a lead character in a national passion play.

Is he at all sorry he answered the charges? Why didn't he ignore Chambers or take the Fifth?

"With the hindsight I have now, well, who would want to undergo the deprivation that I have?" he says. "I only hope that I would do the same."

Of course, his first leap out of privacy was the decision to answer Chambers's charges publicly. Hiss says he "never had any choice but to testify. At the time of the HUAC hearings, I thought my testimony would clear the whole thing up. I soon learned it wasn't that kind of committee. I felt, too, a sense of relief when I came to court. I felt perfect confidence in that court."

But then all that confidence was dashed. By the truth, say his opponents. By a conspiracy, say his supporters. He settles in his chair, and his eyes wander. The room and all its objects have lost their sharpness.

"I've spent a great deal of time on the issue of 'Why me?' I came to the conclusion that it's largely accident, that I was well down the list of those who were selected in order to bring about a change in American politics. I believe the trend of McCarthyism and the adoption of an official stance close to McCarthyism was a deliberate attempt to break the hull of liberalism. The people that were picked ahead of me were Harry White, who held a higher position in the State Department than I did. But he died. Then there was Larry Duggan, who was similar in outlook and background to me. But he died in a fall. It's clear that they had collected a dossier on my boss, Francis Sayre, but he was too big. I was the right size. The

Rosenbergs and I and others who had been picked were the right size. So fairly early on I disposed myself of the incubus of 'Why me?' It was purely accidental, like a sniper who starts shooting people at random. I got hit."

His life and public image change with the flow of political events. "There are times I get letters in the mail saying, 'You've got a nice capitalist house in the Hamptons, don't you, you Communist. Why don't you just shut up and go to hell.' I still get them." Then the pendulum swings. During the Watergate years, Hiss seized the anti-Nixon feeling as an opportunity to clear his name. He wrote a piece for *The New York Times* in 1973 called "My Six Parallels"—a parody of Nixon's sacred memoir and a comparison of his behavior during Watergate to the HUAC hearings. Then it swings again. Now in the Reagan era, when Whittaker Chambers is the martyr of conservatism, Hiss senses that "the enmity has risen against me once more." Nineteen eighty-six is a Chambers year. The letters arrive again at the little red house in the Hamptons.

"I don't spend all my time dwelling on the case," Hiss says. He could not have more friends or go to more parties. He is a popular fellow. In the Hamptons and in New York, Hiss is a fixture on a certain level of the social circuit. His friends are editors, artists, musicians, civil liberties attorneys. He goes to concerts, dinners, theater, even the movies, "though the subtitles are impossible to see." "Alger is all over the place out here," says Alden Whitman, who lives in Southampton. "He gets around. You see him all the time at parties, not at Kurt Vonnegut's or at Mort Zuckerman's place, not on the fast track, but around. He has always been a charming man."

Victor Navasky remembers first meeting Hiss at a social event in the sixties and being "awed": "People can delude themselves, I guess, but he didn't strike me as living in fantasyland. He struck me as a sad and noble man who was trying to vindicate himself. The more I know him, the more I like him. He has friends in what I'd call 'the Old Left set' and the sort of cultural bohemian set."

In the end Hiss sees very little deprivation in his situation at all. "As a matter of fact, I've gained friends because more people sympathized with me and I've come to know more people than if I'd stayed a purely private person."

Hiss still talks of himself in an automatic way as a "private person." But that rings false. He has appeared on the Mike Douglas show between Neil Sedaka and the Fifth Dimension. He was on the college lecture tour in the seventies, ostensibly speaking on the New Deal, but inevitably answering questions on his trials. In his own book on the case, *In the Court of Public Opinion*, Hiss chose not to answer Chambers's *Witness* with an equally personal testimony. He stuck to "objectivity," to "the facts." "A lawyer's brief," he calls it.

In the months he spent in jail, Alger Hiss made a few friends, mostly mobsters. His best friends were named Vincenzo and Angelo, two "racket men" who had been prosecuted, ironically, by Joe McCarthy's old confrere the late Roy Cohn. Hiss admired his cellmates' "strong sense of loyalty and family ties." Hiss worked in the stockroom and read books in jail that would have "made Joe McCarthy scream"—the memoirs of Lenin's widow, the autobiography of a Canadian doctor who joined the Chinese Red Army, a radical interpretation of American slavery, texts of Eastern philosophy. "Those books kept me in touch with progressive, humane aspects of my life so that I didn't feel cut off from the normal flow of things."

But he was cut off from his family. Tony Hiss remembers the monthly visits to Lewisburg with his mother, Priscilla, whom Alger always called Pros or Prossy. "I think the inmates earned around two hours of visiting time every month," Tony Hiss says. "It was a long trip and they took us into a huge room with lots of bamboo furniture. I especially remember the big Italian families who had warm reunions. Alger explained that for them jail was nothing to be ashamed of. It was an occupational hazard."

When Hiss was released from prison in November 1954, his fellow inmates crowded around the windows and cheered him. Hiss later described his friends in organized crime as "the healthiest inmates of the prison. They had absolutely no sense of guilt."

Separation was painful for the family. Priscilla struggled at home. "She bore the brunt of it," says Tony. "She supported us on next to nothing. She went to job interview after job interview and nothing." There had been difficulty in the marriage before the case, but the pressure never subsided for Priscilla. She felt almost as embattled as her husband. Some people, including Eleanor Roosevelt, stood by Alger but believed he was covering up for Priscilla. She was the real "red hot," they felt. Hiss denies she ever did anything wrong. "The case was a terrible burden to her. I think it hurt her in ways it hadn't hurt me." They began fighting more and more, and in January 1959, Alger left Prossy. He spent much of the year on unemployment. "That was the low point," he says. "I think I had actual depression."

Within a year, though, Hiss met a tall, beautiful woman named Isabelle Johnson who was a kind of siren of the left. She had once been involved with author Howard Fast and was briefly married to screenwriter Howard Cole, one of the Hollywood Ten. Though Hiss soon asked Priscilla for a divorce so that he could marry Isabelle, she would never grant him one. "I think it was her sense of propriety, loyalty," he says. "She once said she wanted to go down in history as Mrs. Alger Hiss. Of course, she would have even if she had granted the divorce, but that would have been a kind of separation." Alger never forced the issue, says Tony, "probably in the mistaken idea that it would cause her more pain. He hates to inflict pain on people." Priscilla alternately cursed Alger and carried the torch. "She always called him 'my dear Alger,' " says Alden Whitman. "She always told me that she kept the latch open for him." But Alger never came home. Priscilla Hiss died in 1985, and Alger married the woman he has loved for a quarter century.

During interviews, Isabelle would say a quick hello, then go off shopping in town, work in the garden, or stay in the bedroom. She would not be interviewed or photographed. "She doesn't believe in publicity," Hiss says.

Tony Hiss, a staff writer for *The New Yorker,* is the only child of Alger and Priscilla. (Priscilla had another son by a previous marriage, Tim Hobson, a doctor who lives in California.) Tony's memoir, *Laughing Last,* is unlike any other work that he has published. It is deeply confessional, marred by a strangely casual, brash tone—"Before Al went off to the jug . . . he started boning up on what he was in for." Tony writes intimately about incidents of his own impotence and homosexuality. Tony, who was married last year, says, "I don't know if I'd write it that way now." The book was a blow to the Hiss family, but Tony and Alger have grown closer in recent years. There is something moving in the son's loyalty to the father: "Just going about his business is his way of exemplifying his innocence. Instead of being broken by his troubles he's found a sweetness in adversity. He endured. From Job onward the test is who will be a whole person, who will be broken."

There are pictures of Tony accompanying his father as he left Lewisburg. The little boy is smiling, proud, oblivious to all he would endure in the years ahead as the son of a man so many regarded as a traitor. Now Tony says, "I wouldn't have asked to live through this. It was painful in many ways. But I learned more than I might have about how our minds operate, what sort of pressures we're given to. The case involves every possible emotion: rage, bewilderment, despair. But there still remains the question of what happened."

One of the most suspect memories in history has finished writing a series of "memoiristic sketches." "I never kept a diary," says Hiss. "My vision is so poor I really can't do research. I've had some help with dates, but I've really had to do it all from memory."

What a strangely cheery and selective memoir Alger Hiss has completed. As he describes it, the book begins with an account of his aunt reading to him from children's books and the English classics, a summer spent in the French countryside with his brother Donald. The son of conservative Maryland Democrats—a family that columnist Murray Kempton has described as "shabby gentility"—Hiss says the Depression "radicalized" him. "The Depression led me to question my own social and political outlook and to decide that I had eschewed politics as something gentlemen didn't sully their hands with. I changed." Hiss remembers a generation when the political spectrum was so wide and change so rapid that Roosevelt would greet his junior New Dealers with "Good morning, fellow socialists!"

Sweet days, days with Roosevelt and Marshall and the rest to Yalta, where he noticed that Stalin doodled while he talked and where Hiss managed to pocket one of the general secretary's doodles. Did he admire Stalin?

"Oh, yes," says Hiss over a sandwich at a restaurant in East Hampton. "In spite of knowing the extent of his crimes, he was very impressive. . . . He was decisive, soft-spoken, very clear-headed. He spoke almost always without notes."

But for Nixon, Hiss cannot muster the same admiration. "I think *Newsweek* exaggerates when it says 'He's Back.' " He gives Kissinger all the credit for opening relations with China and establishing détente with the Soviet Union.

Hiss says his view of Russia in the thirties was "quite sympathetic. I certainly regarded the Hitlerian threat as paramount and regarded the Soviets as potential allies." After the Hitler-Stalin pact, he says, "it was difficult to be as sympathetic, but I was convinced, looking at it from the point of view of power politics, that they were driven to it by the appeasement policies of Britain. It was every man for himself. And now, in terms of American policy, what I think is good for the United States and the world, I have not changed my belief that we should avoid confrontation."

Hiss criticizes Reagan at length, especially for his policies in Nicaragua.

"My hopes are with Mario Cuomo," he says. But then with fantastic understatement Hiss adds, "Of course, my endorsement would be of no help."

During lunch, people stare at our table, not quite sure who this old man could be. Who is that eating the blueberry pie and talking so casually about "Dean" and "Averell" and "Franklin"? They seem to know he is somebody. Perhaps they would know him by his ancient courtesies: "I insist on making this lunch dutch. That was the way with us New Dealers. We paid our own way." Or maybe they heard something in the way he described the action of the Walker spy ring: "It wasn't a proper way of behaving."

But they do not know him, not without a hint: a pumpkin, a typewriter, his accuser. In this way Alger Hiss, the man, has become a half-remembered face, a ghost. Hiss mentions that his friend the psychiatrist Meyer Zeligs regards Alger's objectivity as a neurosis. "Isn't that stunning?" Hiss knows that many people believe he is so outwardly serene because, while guilty of a crime committed many years ago, he has come to believe himself innocent. He speaks not of delusion, but of the ways the whole affair may have drained him. "How can one judge one's own sanity? I don't think I'm mad. And as I look back at what's happened to me and what's happened to other people, I think I have nothing to justify self-pity. I suppose every person has had his momentary feelings of wanting to jump off a high place . . . but a feeling of a thought-out, rational sense of despair? Never! There is too much going on in the world."

We are walking along the road. Hiss is tired and has to stop every fifty yards or so to catch his breath. One of these days we will pick up a newspaper and read his obituary. It will probably begin on the front page next to a photograph circa 1948 of the young Alger Hiss—handsome, trim, and accused. It will be a long and prominent obituary—almost half as long as a Stalin's or a Churchill's. Once more the puzzle pieces, the Pumpkin Papers, the typewriter—all of it will seem familiar again. But it will end in ambiguity. For that has been the triumph of Alger Hiss's dotage. His persistence gives him the possibility of martyrdom, even if he is probably not a martyr. It has helped him win friends, loyal defenders. It has made him more important than he ever could have been, either as a loyal servant to Franklin Roosevelt or to the Communist party. Ambiguity has been a savior to him. Could there be a surprise in his obituary? Could death be the opportunity to tell the world a secret?

"Will we learn anything more about you?" I ask him. "Do you have a secret to tell?"

Hiss stops near the graveyard and leans against a tree. "I have none," he says. "No secrets."

———

In the aftermath of the Cold War, the Hiss case, amazingly, persists. Not long after the collapse of the Soviet Union and the opening of various Soviet-era archives, Hiss and his supporters proclaimed victory when Russian army general Dmitri Volkogonov said there was nothing in the archives indicating Hiss had been a spy; in a matter of days, however, it turned out that Volkogonov had searched only a fraction of the archives and he had to admit that his announcement had been meaningless. In 1996, historians and journalists combing through National Security Agency documents claimed there was evidence that American intercepts of Soviet transmissions showed that an American agent known as "Ales," who was "probably Alger Hiss," spied on the United States for Soviet military intelligence, the GRU, at least through the Yalta summit in 1945.

6

The September Song
of Mr. October

(June 1987)

In the last weeks before spring training, Reggie Jackson drove down the freeway from his home in the Oakland hills to the ballpark where he began his career in 1968. He ran sprints across the outfield, fielded fungoes, and took batting practice with players half his age, boys who looked at him with the same slack-jawed regard he once had for Mantle, Maris, and Mays. They studied his easy looping warm-up swings, his murderous slashes at the ball, even the vicious way he spit through his teeth after every pitch, and as they watched him, they may have remembered seeing the same motions a decade ago on television or, if they were lucky, from a seat in the upper deck. Jackson was a part of their boyhood. Now they were professional ballplayers and an audience for the September song of Mr. October.

The youngest of them could hardly imagine Reggie Jackson in gold, green, and white; for them, he was born in pinstripes. But all knew him as a man of swaggering qualities, a name as resonant in their imagination as Ali, Elvis, or even the Babe. At least a dozen players in Reggie's era, from Clemente to Schmidt to Mattingly, were better players, more complete and consistent, but he was the Promethean among them. He defined an Age of Jackson.

Statistically, he is king only of strikeouts, the all-time leader in that category, but his legacy is the big stroke, the electric moment. He won three championships with the Athletics, two with the Yankees. He played in the postseason in eleven of his nineteen years. No player ever had a single day greater than his October 18, 1977. On the cool night when the Yankees won their first World Series in fifteen years, Jackson hit three home runs on three swings. No one else had ever done that. Likely, no one would again. "I have been to the mountaintop, and I have seen the promised land," he said. "I've seen it more than any man alive."

The brilliant light was out. It was like watching the movements of a shadow on the grass. His swing—which often left him screwed into the clay, his helmet falling over his eyes, his number, 44, stretched grotesquely across his back—his swing still had the old ferocious look. But something was wrong. The eyes, the concentration, the reflexes, something. Jackson was not past heroics—he could still send the ball screaming into the outer dark—but he was past the *expectation* of heroics. His home runs now had the quality only of nostalgia and accident. He was forty years old.

In the fall of 1986, he seemed sure to play in another World Series. "I might have gone out on that," he said. His California Angels were one strike away from beating the Boston Red Sox. Horribly, the Angels let go their grip, and the Red Sox advanced instead. It mattered little to Jackson that in the Series against the Mets, Boston would imitate California's collapse, and, somehow, surpass it. Only one thing resonated in his mind. His last at-bat had been a strikeout, and his team had lost. "Of course, you can't blame the Angels," he said. "They'd never won anything. They didn't know how. I was a different story. I'd been there." When it was over, California no longer wanted him. They had already forced one of the game's most superb batsmen, Rod Carew, into a ragged, undigni-

fied end. Now to the sixth-leading home-run hitter of all time, the
Angels said, in no uncertain terms, find another team, quit. Suddenly, Reggie Jackson was just an overpaid .240 hitter without a
glove. Jackson waited for offers. Thirty-six hours after the owners
of the A's called him, he signed a one-year contract with them for
$525,000, little more than half his old salary. He was already worth
millions in stocks, real estate, and other investments. He had homes
in Carmel, Oakland, and Los Angeles; his own Cessna jet; and a car
collection worth two and a half million dollars. He had a china
collection featuring a six-hundred-dollar teacup. The money was
meaningless. He would not go out on strike three. "It wouldn't be
right," he said. "Someone like me is supposed to leave the game in a
different way. That's not how it ends for Reggie Jackson."

A couple of days before his next workout at the Coliseum, Jackson
flew in his private plane to Las Vegas. A Canadian auto-painting-
supply company called Spraybake had invited him to the auto show
there, where they were displaying Jackson's favorite, a 1955 Chevrolet Bel Air. The license plate read R JAX 55. Normally Jackson gets
ten to fifteen thousand dollars to lend what he himself calls the
Reggie aura, but Spraybake was one of his "best relationships,"
he said, and he would do it for expenses. "They like me. They're
Reggie guys."

Jackson walked in a half-hour late, wearing a blue sweatshirt and
faded, pressed jeans. His hair, which he used to wear in a woolly Afro
style, now had the patchy look of a putting green on an abandoned
course. There were flecks of gray in his beard. More than one visitor
noted that he seemed shorter than his "official height" of six feet. "I
thought he'd be a giant," said one young girl. "He's just plain."

Jackson found a central spot on the carpet, spread his legs, folded
his arms over his chest, and waited. Warily, all the Spraybake men
formed a circle around the star. They made small talk about Jack-

son's hundred or so cars, about his feelings on having just joined the Oakland A's. And as their nerve increased and their imagined sense of fraternity took hold, they asked his opinion of a passing girl in silver tights. They had seen the photographs through the years of Reggie with dozens of beautiful women, mostly blondes. "Not bad," Jackson allowed. "Not bad."

Clubhouse talk with Reggie: even fifteen thousand dollars would have been a small price to pay. Still, the men were uncomfortable. They appeared to concentrate very hard on what they said before they said it. If Jackson does not care for a question, he will often ignore it. If he thinks a query too obvious, he will say, "You mean you don't know?" Disgust is one of his moods. They shift easily, inexplicably. But he was in a good mood now, and he received even banalities with cheer.

After a while, the crowd thinned out and Reggie was almost alone. There were no balls to sign, no absurdities to answer. And so he picked up a soft towel and began polishing the fingerprints off his Chevrolet. "I hate fingerprints," he said. "Why do people put their fingers all over something like this?" As he buffed the chrome, he said, "It's like I've lived a dream. If you're talking about a standard for success, they're Steve Jobs in computers, Lee Iacocca in cars, and Reggie Jackson in baseball. I was the standard in clutch situations for ten years. I wasn't the best hitter, but I was the most feared. I was the baddest motherfucker on the block. I was Jesse James, Wyatt Earp. But even they slow down. Even they deteriorate.

"From 1972 to 1979, when you needed a home run in the ninth, and the pennant was riding on it, I was going to the plate to hit that cocksucker over the fence. And not just hit it over. I mean, like forty rows deep. You know what I'm saying? But it didn't last forever. It wasn't just last year or the year before that. It goes as far back as the 1981 Series against the Dodgers. I was out hurt at the beginning. I got back in it, but I couldn't turn it around. I couldn't do it anymore."

Jackson sat down on a couch and drank a cup of orange juice. The crowds returned as quickly as they had gone.

"Hi! I'm a Ziebart girl!" said an almost-blonde in a pair of white hot pants. "I thought you were giving balls out."

"Reggie. Hey, Reggie! I just want to shake your hand. No questions asked. Is that okay?"

"Hey, Reggie Jackson. You're always selling something, aren't you?"

One after another. The strangeness of being Reggie. In public, he is like a ferocious animal in a zoo cage: people admire him, poke him, measure themselves against him. Then they go away, perhaps frightened, disappointed, or thrilled. Usually Jackson endures it. Sometimes he snaps back. It depends on his mood.

Once, when all of New York wanted to know when Reggie would recover from an injury and return to right field, a young boy said to him in an elevator, "Hey, when are you gonna play, Reg?"

Jackson grabbed himself by the crotch and said, "Play with this."

Sometimes it is not his fault. In bars, people try to pick a fight. In New York, someone took a shot at him with a pistol. It is part of the idiocy of being that famous.

Finally, Jackson rose from the sofa and told the Spraybake men, "The crowds are a little thick. I'll be back in fifteen minutes." He said he'd take a walk and let them thin out. He was gone for hours. When he finally returned, it was time to go.

Jackson left the convention center that evening with Everett Moss and Ted Kay, two of his buddies from California. Moss is Jackson's closest friend and one of six people on the Reggie payroll. Ted Kay is a scarred former football player from Kent State who met Jackson in a pickup basketball game. Ted told Reggie he was out of work, and the next day he had a job caring for the "L.A. division" of Reggie's car collection. "Reggie saved me," Ted said. "Now I live over the garage."

As they left the hall, 1984 Playmate of the Year Barbara Edwards, who was at the convention selling Snap-on tools, caught up to Jackson. A calendar photo of Edwards wearing a farmer's-daughter outfit and clutching a Snap-on tool hangs near the desk in his L.A. garage. In Las Vegas she wore fur.

"You ever see anything that gorgeous?" Ted said to Everett as they kept a respectable distance behind their man.

"Yes, I have," Everett said. He has been with Jackson for twenty years. "Sometimes even a bit better," Everett added.

The streets were clogged with conventioneers, and Jackson and Barbara Edwards could not get a cab. One cabdriver slowed, as if in response to Jackson's signal, but then he drove away. All he wanted was a closer look.

"My Gawd," said Barbara Edwards. "What kinda town is this?" Jackson ran across the street in an attempt to flag a cab, but it was filled, and defiantly sped away. Finally, he gave up and took a place in line at a nearby hotel. He was reduced to the sort of patience required of bunters and long relievers. It hurt. When Barbara Edwards climbed into her cab, Reggie leaned into the backseat and kept his face very close to hers for almost a minute. Then he said goodbye.

Someone mentioned that perhaps her beauty exceeded her intellectual strengths. "It's true. She doesn't seem too sharp," Reggie said, "but it's probably the whole thing of meeting Reggie Jackson for the first time. If I spent time with her, she'd get over it."

The next cab was supposed to be Jackson's, but a woman in the line insisted otherwise. Exasperated, he offered to split the ride with the woman, who called herself Roxanne. In the front seat, Roxanne turned to Jackson and said, "I drive eighteen-wheelers. Whadda you do?"

Ted and Everett laughed nervously. Then Reggie laughed, too. He knew it was just a joke, but when he dropped her off he made no motion to let her skip the fare. As the cab rode toward the airport he said, "Fuck her. She wasn't too impressed with me."

Then, to the driver, he said, "You like this job? It's not bad, is it? Six months from now I'll be out here in Vegas with a checker cab, cigarette breath, and a T-shirt. I'll be great. Won't I?"

As the car pulled up to the airport gate, Reggie had one more question for the driver. "Hey, you ever get a blowjob in the cab?"

The walls of Reggie's plane are covered with Ultrasuede. The seats are deep and embracing. Before he fell asleep, Reggie put his feet up on a seat and said, "This plane doesn't make economic sense. It's seven thousand eight hundred dollars an hour. But I'm buying time. I'm buying solitude."

That winter he needed quiet more than ever. His father was very sick. Several times in the weeks before spring training, Reggie flew to Philadelphia to visit him in the hospital. "For a while we weren't sure if he was gonna make it," Reggie said.

Martinez Jackson ran a cleaning store when Reggie was growing up, and brewed corn liquor in the basement to make a little extra money. To keep the cold out of the house, they draped blankets across the doors.

One day when Reggie was around six, he was riding with his father in the delivery truck when he noticed his father was crying.

"What's wrong?" Reggie asked.

"Your mom and I are splitting up," he said. "She's leaving today." In his autobiography, written with Mike Lupica, Jackson put it this way: "The next thing I knew, my mother was just kind of gone. Her other three natural children went with her. I stayed with my dad. . . . There are things that happen to you in your life that you don't question, maybe because you're afraid of what the answer will be. My mom leaving me behind is one of those things. I never asked her why."

Martinez and Reggie grew closer. Then, when he was a senior at Cheltenham High School and the best athlete in the Philadelphia area, Reggie saw police cars parked in front of his house. A court sentenced Martinez Jackson to six months in jail for making liquor illegally. For a while, Reggie was as alone as a boy can be. With his father gone, Reggie helped run the business, finished school, handled the recruiters, and, finally, left for Arizona State. He visited his father only once in prison. He could not stand the sight of the old man in prison grays.

And now Martinez Jackson was worn out. Reggie did not know what more he could do for his father. He had been a good and grateful son. Long ago, when times were tough, his father dreamed of owning a red Cadillac. Reggie bought him one. He helped him build his cleaning business. So his dad could make some extra money, Reggie even got him a "job" as a scout for the Angels. ("The only scouting he's got to do is scout the mailbox for his check every month.") He had always done for his father what every son hopes he will be in the position to do. But he could not make it all right, not with fame or money or words.

In feeling his own decline, Jackson was himself learning a little of what it is to grow old. "You don't retire at your convenience. You don't die when you're ready," he said. Below, the lights of Los Angeles blurred through the fog. "It's an inconvenience to die. You don't retire at the top. There are no announcements. There are no invitations. You're just gone."

He had a date in town that night, but by morning he was alone. He woke at 6:00 A.M., made a few business calls, and rode a stationary bike for twenty minutes. At seven-thirty he drove his garnet Porsche to Super Bodies, a storefront gym near Newport Beach. Another "Reggie guy," a hulking blond named Walt Harris, met Jackson on the sidewalk, and the two men went inside to stretch. "I used to tear my muscles up all the time," Reggie said. "Now I don't run fast enough to tear nothing."

Jackson worked harder than anyone else in the gym. "When I quit I'll become a body builder," he said with a load of weights on his back. "Just for the hell of it. For vanity." He worked his quadriceps, his calves, his triceps and biceps. Between sets, he ran in place with the quick, short steps of a shadowboxer. He wore a baseball cap, sweatpants, and a blue rubber shirt. Sweat washed over his face and dripped off the point of his chin. He had always looked more like a heavyweight fighter than a ballplayer.

To strengthen the muscles that power his baseball swing, Jackson took a twenty-five-pound barbell and mimicked the motions of batting. Many players disdain heavy weight training, saying it makes them bulky, but Reggie was not lifting for singles or doubles to the opposite field. He was training his muscles for a last season of all-or-nothing.

Jackson climbed on a computerized exercise bike to get his heart beating faster. "When I was twenty-eight years old I didn't have any of this," he said over the whir. "I did nothing. I did, like, a million five hundred thousand dollars in the off-season just hustling business."

He finished his workout with a series of abdominal exercises. Some days he did thirteen hundred sit-ups.

At last he rested and drank a glass of blended fruits. A few friends dropped by the gym to say hello, including a young woman named Anne Appleby, who brought her one-month-old daughter, Kimberley Nicole. Reggie cradled the baby in his arms and stood in front of a mirror. "How do I look?" he said. "Like a daddy?" The mother laughed. Kimberley cried. Reggie gave the baby back to Anne. "Hey, so it's only Reggie Jackson," he said. "Who cares, right?"

Before every game at Yankee Stadium, old clips of Ruth and Gehrig, DiMaggio and Mantle flicker on the big screen above the bleachers.

When he visits the stadium, Jackson sometimes tries to take his batting practice while his own image—younger, faster, reliably heroic—is on the screen. Once, while warming up on an August afternoon with the Angels, he belted one ball straight at his own looming icon. Afterward he told *The Washington Post,* "I'm still Reggie, but not as often."

Inevitably, the stadium's film shows Jackson's performance against the Dodgers in the sixth and final game of the 1977 World Series. As he hits his three home runs, the PA system plays the old rock standard "Lightnin' Strikes (again and again and again)."

"It was the worst year of my life," Jackson said behind the wheel of a van. "I was a walking-around mental case." It began with a disastrous interview in which he said that he, and not the team's gritty catcher, Thurman Munson, was the "straw that stirs the drink." Every morning in the *Times,* the *Post,* and the *News,* the protagonists continued their *opéra bouffe.* Billy and George and Reggie. Thurman and Graig and Sparky. That one season generated more books than the Korean War. Though he never avoided the clubhouse and dugout madness, Jackson would spend hour after hour that year sitting on the terrace of his Fifth Avenue apartment, depressed and weary. "I used to read the Bible and take little sayings out of it because I needed support, I needed help," he said. "Sounds like I was nuts, huh?"

Then the autumn came. In the postseason most hitters do not perform nearly as well as they do in the spring or summer. It is not only the pressure that oppresses them, it is the cold air, the truncated and superior pitching staffs, the constant night games.

Reggie Jackson lived for October. That he could focus so clearly on a speeding ball amid all the turbulence—that was always his gift. After five games, the Yankees had a 3–2 lead over the Dodgers. Reggie left Los Angeles on his second homer of the Series, a long shot off Don Sutton. He wanted the season to end, and, somehow, he had an idea of just how it would.

Driving toward a body shop where he often hangs out, Jackson turned down the oldies station he listens to and let it all roll back over him like a wave.

"The day of game six, well, everybody has asked me, what did you do? And I just kinda said I relaxed and listened to the radio. The truth is I spent the afternoon relaxing with a lady. Relaxing, baby, I was relaxed.

"I knew I was swinging the bat good in batting practice. I probably hit two dozen balls out. The crowd in right field was going crazy.

"I was on the money. I was like a guy rolling a three hundred game. I was like a basketball shooter, and when he lets go you know it's gonna be all net. So I was ready. Sometimes you just know.

"The first time up against Burt Hooton, I didn't get to swing. Got walked on four pitches. The next time up, Thurman was on base and they had to give me a ball to hit. It was the first pitch he threw. It felt like I'd hit it hard enough to go five hundred feet, but I hit over the ball because I thought it was going to sink. But Yankee Stadium has a short right field, and the ball stayed up just long enough.

"The next time up, in the fifth, Hooton was out of the game and Elias Sosa was in. Sosa was a hard thrower, and I knew he was going to try to bust me with a pitch inside. That's always been the thing to do. Even when I was on deck I was saying to myself, Please, dear God, let him hurry up and get ready so I can get it.

"I knew as soon as Sosa let go of the ball I was going to hit it out of the ballpark. It was the best ball I hit all night, like a one-iron shot. Now I could hear the crowd starting to chant my name. 'Reggie. Reg-gie.' Jesus.

"I knew I was going to get up again, and I figured I might as well go for another one. It wouldn't matter even if I struck out. No matter what I did I'd still get another ovation.

"And so they brought in Charlie Hough. We were up seven–three in the bottom of the eighth. A knuckler! I probably have more career home runs off knucklers than any pitchers I'd ever faced. I couldn't lose. All I wanted him to do was throw a strike. And, man, he threw a cookie."

The second-base umpire, Ed Sudol, could not believe it. "Hough threw him a tremendous knuckleball," he said. "I don't know how Reggie even got his bat on it, let alone hit it about four hundred and twenty feet." The Dodger first baseman, Steve Garvey, began to applaud in his glove. In the dugout, all the year's tensions melted. Munson hugged Reggie, and so did Martin. Graig Nettles, who would later get in a fistfight with Jackson at a party, said, "It was magic. And it didn't matter in the slightest whether you liked him or detested him. After the third home run, I walked out to the on-deck circle as the crowd was cheering and cheering, and I took my helmet off and waved at everybody as though they were cheering me, and I enjoyed my little fantasy as the noise swirled over the whole stadium."

When Jackson trotted out to right field, they chanted his name, louder and louder, *Reg*-gie . . . *Reg*-gie . . . *Reg*-gie. Confetti, most of it torn flecks of programs, napkins, and toilet paper, showered over him. For once, the sound was clear and unanimous. No one who appreciated the difficulty of what he had done could withhold his admiration or affection.

He never grew bored remembering his perfect night. He pulled the van off the highway, turned off the engine, and gripped the wheel with both hands. A hard sun shone through the window, and Reggie put his face in the light. He was quiet awhile. Then he said, "When all is said and done, people like me. They like me. That's something."

Reggie drove back home. His condominium was packed with Reggie memorabilia: a wood clock with Reggie's image carved into the face; a gilt baseball, a tribute to the home run that propelled Reggie past Mickey Mantle; two copies of his autobiography, *Reggie;* a videotape labeled REGGIE JACKSON, POSITIVE AT-BATS, 1985; a batch of Reggie clips stacked on a director's chair emblazoned with its owner's name.

Earlier he had read with evident sadness a story about George Foster, a once-extraordinary hitter for the Reds and Mets who had squandered his fortune. "You see it all the time," Reggie said. "Sometimes it's the player, sometimes it's these agents who are telling them what to do. They're just a bunch of white guys with Samsonite briefcases and bad suits." He was in his bedroom, dressing while he watched the Financial News Network on cable. His eyes fixed on the stock ticker that ran across the bottom of the screen. Every few minutes or so he stopped to place a call to his lawyer in Oakland, his agent in New York, his real estate partner in Phoenix, a car dealer in Los Angles. He seemed to love this part of being him.

"Are you in?" he asked his broker. They were talking about a "very hot" jeans company. "It was up to three and heading toward four. You in? Hang in there, at least today. If it gets hairy, I'll call you."

He got up from the bed and began to sway to the electronic bounce of FNN's theme songs. "I'm a capitalist," he said. "And I'm a Reagan supporter. But mostly in politics I'm a fence-sitter. I don't want to put myself in a position to say too many controversial things, because a lot of the people I'm in contact with are CEOs. They can affect my future." He shimmied during the bond report, hopped during the NASDAQ index. When the report on the top ten stocks of the day came on, Reggie sat perched on the edge of his bed and watched every second.

"I think you're getting to see that there are all sides to Reggie," he said after it was over. "I may not necessarily be better than anyone, but I'm unique. There's Reggie the ballplayer and Reggie the media guy and Reggie who's into cars. But Reggie's also meeting with the main players of the eighties. I call Boone Pickens for advice on high-end economics. I look hard at what Steve Jobs is doing. Tonight I'm supposed to have dinner with John Sculley, the head of Apple. You think I won't come away with any wisdom?"

A report came on the television about the scandals on Wall Street. "Boesky just got caught," Reggie said. "I'm not condoning what he did. It's just not wrong. They say that pigs get fat, hogs go to market."

Jackson made a few more calls. Then he pulled out his suitcases. The next morning he had practice at the Coliseum in Oakland. He stepped into a walk-in closet filled with dozens of shirts, and fingered sleeve after sleeve. When he emerged with the chosen shirts draped across his arm, Jackson's whole expression had changed. "Let me ask you something," he said. "What kind of story are you doing?" There was a painful, nervous pause. "Is it a Reggie profile? A 'Reggie retires' kind of thing? See, I think the media get some kind of weird enjoyment out of asking, 'What are you going to do when you're not the center of attention anymore? What are you going to do when all the adulation is dried up and all the cheers die down? Huh?' It's like they want you to say, 'I'll collapse. I won't be able to make it in society. I'll end up in a halfway house.' Well, you can see that baseball is just a part of me. Reggie Jackson is not your average baseball player."

Reggie cannot get over the completeness of himself, his multi-faceted self. "I guess I underestimated the magnitude of me," he has said. No one, he is convinced, has told his story adequately. He has already written two autobiographies and is considering a third. When he contracted Lupica to write *Reggie* with him, there were hermeneutic debates of every sort. *Reggie,* Jackson believed, did not contain all that is Reggie. "It was on the best-seller list, but it could have been a huge book, you know what I'm saying? It could have been something. It could have been another fucking Hemingway, but for that I would've needed a . . . James Michener."

He checked his watch, a chunky gold Rolex. "It's getting late," he said. "We've got a couple of things to do before we fly to Oakland, and I've got that dinner with John Sculley tonight. Did I mention that? He's the head of Apple."

· · ·

At lunch, Reggie, Ted, and Walt stood in front of a big-screen TV that was playing old baseball highlights. As the tape rolled they quizzed each other on averages, plays, nicknames—all the ephemera of the game. Jackson never missed a question.

"You're the king," Walt said.

"Yes," Reggie said.

They drove back to the garage—Ted and Walt on motorcycles, Jackson in one of his vintage "muscle" cars. There to greet them was one of Reggie's girlfriends—a young, blond student from Golden West College. ("About the ladies. Keep the names out of it," Reggie said. "I don't want one of them getting mad about another. I mean, they know, but, well, you understand.")

"I thought we were going to lunch," she complained. "I've been here for like an hour."

"I said one o'clock, didn't I?" Reggie said.

"I was here early," she said. "You guys were gone."

"*Ahh,* well," Reggie said, and he enveloped her in his arms.

For the next hour or so Reggie watched Ted hose down a buddy's Oldsmobile. They talked carburetors and camshafts. Jackson walked from one car to the next, admiring the Corniche, perusing the Corvette, checking out the "fat fender" on the custom Mercedes-Benz. The blonde looked for something to do. She helped Ted polish the hood of the Oldsmobile. Reggie watched her while he spoke once more on the phone to his broker.

"Honey!" he said when he hung up. "It's long strokes. Not across. Not short. *Looong* strokes."

"I didn't—"

"I know, honey, you're learning."

Reggie and the blonde drove back to his condominium, leaving Walt and Ted to work in the garage. "I've got the plane set to go in a couple of hours," he told them. "I've got some packing to do."

Jackson was once married to a woman named Jennie Campos. They were divorced, after four years, in 1972. Since then he has come close to marrying once, lived with at least one other woman, and has dated "a lot." "Reggie's girls all look pretty much the same," Walt said. "Blond, pretty, twenty-one or twenty-two, perfect bods, kind of beachy." He said he wants a family "after baseball sometime," but for the moment one of the biggest portraits in his house is of Reggie and his Chevrolet. "So I'm not married," he said. "Whoopee shit. The only thing about not being married is I don't have children, or I don't have someone to share my life with all the time. So I'm missing a couple of things, but I'm not exactly . . . I don't need a goddam psychoanalyst."

Walt checked his watch, smiled, and said, "That should be enough time." He drove Jackson's van back to the condominium. When Walt arrived, Reggie was standing outside surrounded by his bags. He was fidgety, scowling. He was in a panic. Once more the mood had shifted.

"You see a little white sack?" he asked Walt.

"No, what's in it? What are you talking about?"

"I can't find the thing," Reggie said, louder now. "I hid it and now I don't know where I put it."

"What's in it? How big is it?"

"It's a little bank sack with ten thousand dollars in it, that's what it is, and now I can't find it. Jesus."

"Maybe you hid it in the garage."

For the next couple of hours, Reggie, Ted, and Walt looked everywhere in the garage, in the condominium. They shuttled back and forth following one false lead after another. Finally Jackson went back home and emptied his bags all over his driveway. A neighbor named Heather walked over from the condominium next door.

"Hi! What's goin' on?" she chirped through her gum.

"Oh, I just misplaced something," he said. The sun was getting dim, and the appointment four hundred miles away with John Sculley, one of the main players of the 1980s, was drawing close. "It's driving me crazy," he said.

Then Heather began laughing. "Hah, hah, hah." It was inexplicable.

"Yeah, well . . ." Reggie said, containing himself.

"How's that ball team up in California?"

Reggie blinked. Wasn't he in California?

"Oh, they're all right," he said.

Heather just stood there.

"Well . . ." Reggie said hopefully.

"Well," Heather replied. Then, after a cruel silence, she added, ". . . see ya 'round."

"See ya 'round, Heather."

Reggie drove once more to the garage, where he leaned on his Chevrolet. "Ten thousand bucks," he said. "Ten thousand bucks." He called San Francisco and canceled his dinner with John Sculley.

"All right, now, we're not going home until we find it," he announced. Ted and Walter never stopped looking, no doubt out of good fellowship, but also, one could not help thinking, in an effort to obliterate suspicion. They were Reggie guys.

"Wait," Jackson said. "I think I know where it is." Jackson's relief was considerable, though nothing compared with Ted's and Walt's. Walt drove Jackson back to the condominium. Reggie opened the trunk of his garnet Porsche and found a black box used for holding compact disks. Inside was the sack, and inside that was the ten thousand dollars.

On February 26, 1935, the Yankees released Babe Ruth. He played two months for the Boston Braves, hitting just .181. Fat, tired, and looking for an exit line, he hit three home runs one afternoon at Forbes Field. But those home runs had the quality of nostalgia and accident. Ruth retired that June at the age of forty. For the rest of his life he tried to win a job as a manager. No one would hire him.

Twelve years later, Ruth was dying of throat cancer. Commissioner Happy Chandler declared a "Babe Ruth Day" at Yankee Stadium. Wearing a camel's-hair coat, Ruth stepped slowly up to the microphone and spoke in a rasp. "You know, this baseball game of ours comes up from the youth," he said to the crowd. "That means the boys. The only real game in the world, I think, is baseball."

Yogi Berra was there, and he later said, "When he finished talking, the Babe waved a salute and turned around and walked back to the dugout. Nobody made a move to help him. I remember one of the ballplayers saying, 'Do you think we ought to go out and give him a hand?' And somebody said, 'Leave him alone. He knows where the dugout is.' "

In his last days, Ruth still had a strong appetite, but he could no longer chew. Some days Babe would eat a mound of chopped meat. As he grew worse he ate soft-boiled eggs. At least the cancer had not robbed him of his memory. He could summon pleasure in an instant. One day shortly before he died Ruth looked down at his egg and said, "To think of the steaks . . ."

"You compare me to Babe Ruth and I'll look silly," Reggie said, driving the Oakland freeway. In athletic terms, he is right. It is as a folk hero, not as a player, that Reggie reaches across time to Babe.

Now Reggie was trying to end a little better than the Babe. He would be a designated hitter, he would play first base. He would change if he had to. But he could not humiliate himself. He would not go out on .181. That would be torture to him. "I'm not going to embarrass myself," he said. "You talk about the way Ted Williams went out on a home run. Who wouldn't want that?"

As he sat now in the Coliseum's dim and tiny clubhouse, Jackson looked around at all the kids. Who had worked as hard as he had? Who among them understood the importance of the game, and the short time they had to play it? Jackson saw players with better reflexes but with rolls of fat around their middles; he saw young men charged by the pleasures of their game but ignorant of its subtleties. Even their lack of financial savvy annoyed him. He saw young Tony Phillips dressing and joking about the "great salary deal" he was going to make. That did it.

" 'Great'? How great?" Reggie said. "What did you make last year?"

"Three-fifty, four hundred thou with incentives," Phillips said.

"And now you're in arbitration?"

"Yeah."

"What are your numbers? How many hits did you have last year?"

"I don't know exactly."

"How many runs?"

"I'm not sure."

"You don't know?"

"Not sure."

"You've *gotta* know," Reggie said. "If you're in arbitration how can you *not* know? You have an agent?"

"Yeah, sure I do." Phillips was getting more and more defensive. He wanted out, he wanted to hit and run and get out of the jaws of Reggie Jackson.

"Who is he? Your brother? Your best friend? Why don't you do your own deal?"

To Phillips's astonishment, Reggie began to explain the way "agents can cut you," the sort of studying he'd better do, the interest-free loans he could ask for. "You have to make the deal that's good for you," Jackson said. "Are you gonna have any left when you're done? Can you buy your own home? Can you structure a bank loan? I'm giving you the third degree, man, because you gotta know what you're doing."

Phillips was silent. Vaguely, he understood that Jackson, of all people, knew what he was talking about. Still, he wanted out.

Reggie smiled. "Hey, man, don't listen to me. I'm just an old shit. I don't know nothing."

"No, brother, what have you been around? Twenty years?"

"Don't mean nothing. I'm just an old man."

The other players left for the field, Phillips included. Reggie waited until the others were gone before he put on his jade-colored Athletics jacket, his shades, and his shoes.

"You think Phillips will listen?" someone asked him.

Jackson spit through his teeth as he walked through the shadowy hall toward the field. His spikes clicked on the concrete. "I don't give a shit if he listens or not, to be honest," he said. "I just don't care."

The morning was clear and cool, and the grass brilliant in the hard winter light. So direct was the sun that it burned off the previous day's rain in a couple of hours. Only twenty players came to the optional workout. The manager, Tony LaRussa, was out of town, and most of the veterans had better things to do. Spring training was still weeks away. The emptiness of the seats made an echo chamber of the Coliseum, so that a sharp line drive sounded like the report from a .22.

In the dugout, a young outfielder named Michael Williams slammed a ball into his glove. He played awhile for the Cleveland Indians in 1986, but they released him. Now he was hoping to land a job in the A's system. "Class A would be fine with me," he said. "I've gotta start somewhere." Williams grew up in Hayward, California, just a short drive from the Coliseum, and when he was six or seven years old he and a friend came to the ballpark to see their first game.

"Just about the second I walked into the park, Reggie put one over the fence. Right over there," Williams said, pointing to left center field. "It was incredible, the way he hit it, and he'd just drop his bat at home plate and watch the ball and admire it going over the wall. Man! I followed every move he made. I didn't watch any-one else."

After the players did a few stretching exercises and ran laps around the grass, Jackson seized the privilege of seniority and took the first turn at bat. His own bats had not yet arrived in Oakland, so he selected a thirty-four-ounce Adirondack of white ash from a heap on the grass. "I used to use a thirty-six or a thirty-seven. Biggest bat in the league for five years," he said, taking a few warm-up swings. "Now I use a thirty-three or a thirty-four."

With his old Yankee teammate Bob Watson watching him, with nearly everyone in the park watching him, Jackson stepped into the cage. He tapped his bat on home plate, then bunted three pitches to the left, three more to the right.

"Okay now, Reg, let it rip," Watson said. It was unlikely that the A's would ask him to do any bunting.

Jackson took the first pitch, then hit three pop flies to short right field. They were too shallow for the outfielders to bother with them.

Jackson tapped once more on the plate, then cracked a line drive to center field.

"Better," Watson said. "But you're lifting that back foot."

"It's February," Jackson said, and he stepped in once more. He hit another drive, which echoed through the empty park, then a dozen pops to center and right. He smacked a foul back into the cage. At the finish of his swing his body had dropped close to the dirt and his arms and bat described a pretzel. "Damn," he said.

Jackson unwound himself and took on a more determined air. Sweating freely now, he kicked the dirt and nodded to the pitcher. He hit a couple of drives that would have been singles, then another series of shallow fly balls that were sure outs. "That's slow hands right there," he grumbled. The big hits were just not coming: foul, foul, fly, single, fly, single, single. No numbers on the board. "It takes a while for my hands to get ready," he said.

"Keep that back foot down," Watson said.

Then the pitcher grooved one in, chest-high, medium-fast. Reggie cocked his elbows and lunged at the pitch. The ball exploded off the bat, arcing into the cloudless sky and sailing over a group of fielders who were chatting in center field. Reggie dropped his bat and, along with everyone else, followed the flight of the ball. It was beautiful what the man could do. Finally, the ball cleared the fence and smacked sharply off the empty seats. A lovely, lonely sound. A home run in wintertime.

TWO

ARTISTS AND SCHOLARS

7

Hamlet in Hollywood

(November 1995)

It was a broiling morning in late August, a day so hot that all the palms and Freon in Bel Air could not cool it. There was no telling what tensions had come to overflow inside the gated mansions off Sunset, but it is a fair surmise that the heat was most intense at Bob Newhart's old place on Strada Corta, now the home of Steve Sohmer, a writer and independent producer who was once the president and chief operating officer of Columbia Pictures. A thick-set, balding man of fifty-three, Sohmer sat in his backyard office and glared across his desk at a young Shakespeare scholar from Boston University named Mary Ann McGrail. Sohmer felt deceived, betrayed. McGrail, in his eyes, was laying claim to his "intellectual property." More specifically, she was laying claim to his theory of *Hamlet*—a theory that the life of Martin Luther is the hidden source of the play—and he would not allow it. Sohmer had won a battle over writing credits for the NBC miniseries *Tom Clancy's Op Center* just a few months before. Did she doubt he would fight this, too?

In middle age, Sohmer had revived a long-standing interest in Shakespeare, and in 1992, to help him pursue that interest, he hired a tutor, Mary Ann McGrail. Their arrangement was friendly and simple: Sohmer flew McGrail out from Boston to Los Angeles and paid her a hundred dollars an hour—plus, in the fourth summer, a thousand dollars a month for expenses. They met every weekday morning for two hours at the Bel Air estate. For four summers running, there had been no clash between their two worlds—between Hollywood and the academy. Instead, Sohmer and McGrail intersected at a common passion: the plays of Shakespeare.

But now, in his anger, Sohmer no longer cared to play the role of the passionate amateur scholar; he became once more the studio head, the proprietor. McGrail had suggested that they could publish companion articles, he on the part of the theory that was his, and she on what was hers. The *Times Literary Supplement,* in London, might be interested in publishing both. But Sohmer would not accept the arrangement; both names would have to appear on both pieces. He also wanted to collaborate on a book; he'd give her "top billing"—that was the phrase he used. McGrail wanted to work on her own.

In court documents, McGrail claims that Sohmer told her, "If you fuck with me on this, you will regret it. What's in the past will be irrelevant. And you'll be in a very, very unpleasant fight with me in which I have nothing to lose."

Sohmer denies that he ever made this threat, but he and McGrail agree that their meeting ended in a bitter impasse and a rapid exeunt. Have your lawyers get in touch with me, she told Sohmer, and, with that, she walked out of the office, got into her car, and drove away.

That was August 31. For nearly six weeks, Sohmer and McGrail communicated only through legal counsel and stacks of papers filed in the courts of Los Angeles County—claims, counterclaims, applications for temporary restraining orders. They did not meet again until depositions began, in mid-October.

Until August, Sohmer and McGrail had formed a satisfying, if somewhat odd, team. After Sohmer was fired from Columbia Pictures, in 1986, he became what is known in academe as a "mature student." For a long time, he had felt a certain hole in his life—a sense that he was "wasting" himself, as he put it—and so, in 1989, while juggling a new career as an independent television producer and writer and an author of Washington thrillers, Sohmer enrolled in a master's-degree program at Boston University. He took McGrail's Shakespeare course there and thrived. After receiving his M.A. from Boston, he started a doctoral program at Oxford—he spent two full terms in England—and in the summers he worked with McGrail.

Sohmer had made his fortune grinding out what might be called the opposite of Shakespeare: *Leonard Part 6, La Bamba, Bloodknot, Mancuso, FBI.* He spoke the hermetic language of participation points and grosses. And yet he indulged his passion for Shakespeare, took it very seriously, despite the ribbing he endured for it at the Bel Air Country Club. He plunged into the Latin grammars, the concordances, the black-letter texts, all the stuff of Renaissance studies.

McGrail was a creature of the academy, a denizen of the library carrel and the faculty meeting. She was a highly promising scholar and popular teacher, but she was thirty-seven and was virtually unpublished. She faced the specter of imminent tenure review, and to pass she would have to write something of moment. The job in Los Angeles gave her time, money, and proximity to good libraries and friends. It also provided her with someone to talk to who was as enthusiastic about Shakespeare as she was.

It was true that some of McGrail's friends were wary of her arrangement in Bel Air. One of McGrail's closest friends in Los Angeles, a Dead Sea Scrolls scholar turned screenwriter named Bob Davis, thought Sohmer was just another Hollywood egomaniac craving intellectual respectability. "From the first time I met him, I thought he was a fake," Davis told me. "But Mary Ann always defended him as a good student. She'd say he had his faults, he had his pompous aspects, but as a student he was one of the brightest she'd run across. . . . The first two years she was out in California, I had more contact with Steve—usually as Mary Ann's escort to one occasion or another at his place in Bel Air. I remember one particularly surreal afternoon when there was a picnic by the pool and the guests were me, Mary Ann, Steve and his wife, Gene Simmons, from the rock band Kiss—the guy with the huge tongue, I think—and his companion, a former Playmate of the Year, or something, who was so pregnant I thought she was going to burst. Gene Simmons and Steve sat discussing medieval Jewish legends. Meanwhile, the Playmate and I listened and Mary Ann kept watching me, hoping I wouldn't say anything improper."

Odd as the Bel Air arrangement may have seemed to some of McGrail's friends, it had its distinct appeal. McGrail got along well with both Sohmer and his wife, Deidre Hall, who is an actress and plays a troubled (and occasionally demon-possessed) psychiatrist on the soap opera *Days of Our Lives.* The study sessions were more than civil; they were friendly and intense. After the morning meetings, Sohmer went to what he laughingly calls his "real job"—his production company in Burbank—and McGrail was free to pursue her own academic research. She usually drove up to San Marino and worked at the vast and luxurious Huntington Library.

This summer had looked as if it would be no less ideal than the three previous ones. In July, Sohmer had earned his doctorate from Oxford, and a few weeks earlier, he and McGrail set out to work their way carefully through *Hamlet.* That was when their problems began.

Both of them believe that the play has buried within it an ingenious and highly subversive reading of Martin Luther's rebellion against the Catholic Church. How and when each of them came to that conclusion was the crux of their dispute, but they were united in their feeling that the idea itself is of great importance. In the improbable event that this theory of *Hamlet* were to prove correct—if it should indeed turn out that Shakespeare wrote a play in complicated support of the religious reformer who dared oppose the popes of his era—it could alter, even revolutionize, our understanding of the loftiest figure in the history of English literature and the play that is probably his best-known work. To say nothing of what it would do to the Shakespeare-criticism industry.

Within days of that last August meeting, both sides rushed to establish a paper trail for any possible legal battle. Sohmer's work emphasized Shakespeare's use of the calendar in *Hamlet,* and how it might provide hints of the character's relation to Luther. McGrail, who acknowledges the originality of Sohmer's work on the calendar, was working out textual parallels between *Hamlet* and various biographies of Luther—particularly a long passage on Luther in the sixteenth-century Protestant martyrology *Actes and Monuments,* by John Foxe.

In early September, academic journals from California to England began getting query letters and phone calls from Sohmer and McGrail. On the advice of his lawyers, Sohmer even issued a press release claiming a new, "unrecognized source" for *Hamlet,* though he neglected to say what the source was. A week later, Sohmer sent an article on *Hamlet* out over the Internet. Not long after that, Sohmer's lawyers filed an ex parte application for a temporary restraining order that would forbid McGrail to engage in any public discussion of or to arrange any publication of a theory that was not in fact her own. A judge granted the temporary restraining order; it expired after two weeks. The next step was a full-blown lawsuit.

In court documents filed in September, Sohmer said McGrail was a kind of assistant "hired for the sole purpose of working for my benefit." In a sense, he acted as if McGrail were a contract writer at his own backyard version of Columbia Pictures. Sohmer also claimed, in a letter to McGrail's lawyers, that the ideas about *Hamlet* were the "intellectual property" of Steve Sohmer and his independent production company, Steve Sohmer Incorporated. He demanded that McGrail cease her attempts to publish any work on *Hamlet* and Luther, turn over to him any of her writings on the subject, and "forthwith deliver to Plaintiff all notes taken by her in the course of her employment with Plaintiff."

In a letter laying out the demands necessary for a settlement, Sohmer said that McGrail would have to apologize for her alleged misdeeds and curtail any publication on *Hamlet* and Luther for eighteen months. He planned to pursue the case with little regard to time or expense. Sohmer realized that the battle might cast him in the villain's role—"I know that this might seem like a David-and-Goliath story," he told me, "and I ain't gonna be the Jewish guy"— but he did not care. He wanted what he believed was his. "This is a matter of principle," he said later. "I am not a vindictive man."

McGrail, for her part, continued her research on *Hamlet* but was profoundly frightened that the battle with Sohmer would wipe out her savings, bury her in debt, and ruin her career in academe. "I can see twenty years of work going down the drain," she said. "And for what?"

I first heard about this strange theory of *Hamlet,* and the even stranger dispute, at the end of August. An old friend of McGrail's called an editor at this magazine to say that McGrail was in the early stages of working on what could well turn out to be a singular discovery in the history of Shakespeare scholarship. After talking to McGrail a couple of times on the phone, I made plans to go to Los Angeles on Labor Day weekend—just a few days after Sohmer and McGrail held their last meeting.

Before I left, I reread the play and then went over the historical and mythological background of the *Hamlet* story. The leading scholars all provide roughly the same account. While living an intensely active life in the theater, Shakespeare wrote his plays at the rate of nearly two a year. He relied heavily, and unapologetically, on other dramas, poems, tracts, and chronicles. As if to prove T. S. Eliot's saw that immature poets imitate, mature ones steal, Shakespeare stole wholesale. He grabbed up facts, narratives, imagery, and vocabulary, and then transformed those materials for his own use, always transcending the power of the original sources. For the Roman plays, for instance, he went to Plutarch; for the English-history plays, he combed Holinshed's *Chronicles.*

The standard explanation of *Hamlet* is that it is based mainly on two sources: a twelfth-century history (not published until the sixteenth century) called *Gesta Danorum,* by Saxo Grammaticus, and a retelling of Saxo's tale by the French writer François de Belleforest. A prince called Amleth, murder in the court, incestuous marriage, philosophical introspection, feigned madness, a voyage abroad, and an altered letter—Shakespeare clearly dug these elements out of Saxo and Belleforest and fitted them to his own design.

Scholars have also made arguments, with varying degrees of speculation, that Shakespeare used a wide range of other texts to develop particular episodes or characters in *Hamlet:* Thomas Kyd's *The Spanish Tragedy,* Thomas Nash's pamphlet *Pierce Penniless His Supplication to the Devil,* Timothy Bright's *Treatise on Melancholy,* and Montaigne's *Essays.* It is also possible that Shakespeare saw a play based on the Hamlet legend. Although scholars have not been able to identify this so-called *Ur-Hamlet,* there are references to such a play in the writings of Thomas Nash. Thomas Lodge, writing in 1596, four or five years before Shakespeare probably wrote his play, refers to the "ghost which cried so miserably at the Theatre, like an oyster-wife, *Hamlet, revenge.* "

There is very little in the mainstream criticism—almost nothing in nearly four centuries of commentary—to suggest that Shakespeare used the life of Martin Luther as essential source material for

Hamlet. But scholars have not overlooked the matter. Roland Mushat Frye's book *The Renaissance Hamlet* (1984) is just one of many that have puzzled over the echoes of Reformation theology and history in the play.

Through the years, beginning in the late eighteenth century, *Hamlet* commentators have repeatedly cited two details in particular that are suggestive of Luther. The first, and more obvious, detail is Shakespeare's use of Wittenberg as the university where Hamlet has been studying abroad. In Act I, Scene 2, Wittenberg is mentioned four times, and we learn that it was there that Hamlet met his friend Horatio. Wittenberg, a provincial university founded in 1502, became famous when Luther nailed to its church door his revolutionary Ninety-five Theses in 1517, decrying the abuses of the Roman Church. If Shakespeare did not mean to highlight this link with his *Hamlet,* why did he not send the prince to some other university?

The second Lutheran suggestion comes in Act IV, Scene 3, when Hamlet, who has killed Polonius, is asked where the body is. Hamlet replies:

> *A certain convocation of politic worms are e'en at him. Your worm is your only emperor for diet: we fat all creatures else to fat us, and we fat ourselves for maggots.*

The import of the pun will elude most contemporary readers, but Elizabethans, critics have argued, would very likely have heard the echo of the Diet of Worms. In 1521, after Luther refused to disavow his writings, the council, or diet, of the German city of Worms, headed by Emperor Charles V, pronounced him an outlaw. This was a pivotal moment in the history of the Reformation— even in England, where Calvinism and the Church of England eventually prevailed over Lutheranism.

Various editions of the play—the Arden, the Oxford, the Cambridge—all take notice of one or both of these Lutheran moments in *Hamlet,* but there is little to be found on their implications. They are remarked on as wordplay, puns, winks at the Reformation, and not much more. Shakespeare was an incessant punster, and no amount of scholarship could cover all his puns in detail. According to Samuel Johnson, punning was Shakespeare's "fatal Cleopatra for which he lost the world, and was content to lose it."

And yet Shakespeare was a deeply intentional poet, an artist who wasted nothing, who layered his language and meanings with unsurpassed complexity and wit. What if the two moments hinted at a far more elaborate architecture of puns and references? What if Shakespeare, writing around 1600, had been able to divert his critics (and monarchs) with an already complicated story based on Saxo's narrative, and had at the same time been, sotto voce, playing out the drama of a religious revolutionary who had dared to defy Henry VIII, the father of the reigning queen, Elizabeth? Is it possible that no one has ever noticed this? These were the questions that Mary Ann McGrail, for one, was asking herself this summer. When I asked her what her discovery would mean if it turned out to be legitimate, she did not hesitate to answer. In fact, she had created for herself, and her theory, a heightened sense of drama.

"It means that I'm telling four centuries of scholars, including Samuel Johnson, that they either have not disclosed this, which is entirely possible, or have missed it," she said when we met. "And, if I'm right about this, it means editors who have spent their careers, their lives, editing the text will have to rethink their work and reedit the whole thing. It means that scholars will have to rethink a central work of Western literature. And that there will be other reactions, too. Negative stuff. Someone will say, 'Well, if this is true, why the hell have four hundred years' worth of commentators missed it? And why is it that this unheard-of academic from Boston is claiming to find something so outrageous? Who is she? Some kind of lunatic?' "

On the telephone, McGrail sounded jittery, humorless—especially when we talked about her falling-out with Sohmer. I expected to meet an academic eccentric of the type familiar to readers of the university novels of David Lodge: fragile, bookish, and a little off. McGrail, it turned out, is a tall and attractive woman of almost self-defeating confidence. Time and again, she cautioned that she would have to subject her work to critical readings by all sorts of experts, but she nevertheless had a quality of certainty about her. "I think you're going to be amazed when you see what I've put together— what *Shakespeare* put together," she said.

The night before we were really going to get down to work, McGrail met me for a drink at the bar of my hotel. As a jazz trio played softly, she talked awhile about her career. McGrail's father is a retired lawyer, and the family—her parents and a tribe of four daughters—lived outside Washington, D.C. After getting an under-graduate degree from Harvard in 1980 and spending a year as a vol-unteer worker for Mother Teresa in India, she returned to Harvard for a doctorate in English literature.

McGrail worked on her thesis with the resident Shakespeare spe-cialist, Marjorie Garber, but, as a political conservative, found herself drawn less toward Garber's feminist readings and more toward the views of Harvey C. Mansfield, Jr., a leading figure in the government department and a conservative follower of the late political philoso-pher Leo Strauss. Even as she was studying classics and the languages and literature that dominated the English Renaissance, she also grew interested in Shakespeare's political thinking and in the idea of a writer working under—or around—the complicated political pres-sures of his time. After writing her dissertation, on tyrants in four of Shakespeare's plays, McGrail embarked on the typical *Wanderjahre* of young humanities scholars in the age of the cutback. She taught at Kenyon College and Catholic University, and finally wound up in the University Professors Program at Boston University. All the while, McGrail taught a number of courses on censorship and literature—with reading lists that included Plato, Milton, Lawrence, Joyce, Bulgakov, and Solzhenitsyn—and, most of all, on Shakespeare. In McGrail's thinking, Shakespeare wrote about a controversial figure like Luther with some of the same conscious stealth as a Soviet writer trying to sneak criticism of Stalin past the Politburo.

Shakespeare wrote *Hamlet* at a time when Elizabeth's reign was reaching its end, and James, the son of a Catholic—Mary, Queen of Scots—was the likely successor. England was still feeling the aftershocks of the Reformation. Elizabethan audiences would still have had in their memory the notorious Ridolfi Plot, for example, in which James's mother, together with a Florentine banker who had ties to the Vatican, schemed to topple Elizabeth. They would also have remembered the Catholic slaughter of Protestant Huguenots in 1572, memorialized in Christopher Marlowe's play *The Massacre at Paris*. At the same time, if Shakespeare wanted to write a play celebrating Luther and admonishing a new king to avoid a return to Catholicism and the power of Rome, he had to do it without insulting James. He clearly succeeded. James so prized Shakespeare's troupe that upon taking the throne, in 1603, he brought it to court as the King's Men.

"Remember, Shakespeare was the most successful commercial playwright of his time," McGrail said. "He had the support of the two monarchs and was careful about staying at the top of the heap. He didn't want to get shut down. He waited until the very end of his career to write about Henry VIII, who was closer to his time, and generally wrote about figures who were more safely in the past. I think he knew well that it would have been impossible to stage an overt play about the life of Martin Luther. He was writing *Hamlet* at a very delicate time, when it seemed likely that the inheritor to

Elizabeth would be James. Shakespeare had to be conscious of this. He also had to be painfully aware that Elizabeth was the daughter of Henry VIII, who had come into severe conflict with Luther. Henry VIII won the title Defender of the Faith from the Vatican after he denounced Luther. Then, amazingly, Henry VIII asked Luther to endorse his marriage to Anne Boleyn, and Luther refused. Maybe Shakespeare wouldn't have been beheaded for staging a play on Luther, but it would have been enormously risky."

The next morning, McGrail arrived at my hotel carrying a bag bulging with books, charts, photocopied manuscripts, and notes, and plopped herself down across from me. She began at once to go through her research, starting with the origin of her idea.

She said that she had been thinking for a long time about Shakespeare in relation to "esoteric writers"—a term that Leo Strauss and his followers often applied to, say, Plato or Maimonides, who used oblique strategies to express their insights when they were under political and social duress. As part of that thought process, she said, she began to ponder the two Lutheran clues in *Hamlet*—the four mentions of Wittenberg and the pun on the Diet of Worms. Two years ago, she said, she pointed them out to Sohmer. (Sohmer says he cannot remember that but concedes that it's possible.)

Sohmer wanted to read *Hamlet* this summer, and he was specifically interested in Shakespeare's use of the calendar in the play. He said that this spring he had come to think of *Julius Caesar* and *Hamlet* as companion pieces, with *Julius Caesar* representing the advent of Christianity and *Hamlet* the Reformation. McGrail had intended to use 1995–96, a sabbatical year for her, to write a book for the Duckworth Press, a small English publisher, on Aristotelian and Platonic theories of the artistic imagination, but as the summer wore on she started to concentrate on that lingering notion: the life of Luther as a direct source of the play. McGrail says that she then came across a translation of Philipp Melanchthon's Luther biography—Melanchthon was a close friend of Luther's. (Sohmer says they discovered the biography together at his direction.) Then, McGrail claims, working on her own at the Huntington Library, she began studying John Foxe's *Actes and Monuments.*

McGrail's argument, as she sketched it out for me, is that, although Shakespeare certainly used Saxo and Belleforest for his account of the Hamlet legend, he also used Foxe as a direct source. (Melanchthon's biography, she said, informs Foxe but doesn't have nearly the same direct bearing on *Hamlet.*) *Actes and Monuments,* perhaps the most popular book of the time after the Geneva Bible and *The Book of Homilies,* contains a sixty-five-page passage called "The History of Doctor Martin Luther, with His Life and Doctrine Described."

In a draft of an article written for—and eventually rejected by—the *Times Literary Supplement,* around the time of the breakup with Sohmer, McGrail opens with a characteristically bold proclamation. After declaring that Foxe is the key to unlocking *Hamlet,* she writes, "This source should be regarded as a transparency, to be laid over the play, which gives new depth and shape to it. The play is a play of riddles to which the Foxe provides the answers. To date, no one has bothered to hunt the fox."

Shakespeare was so playful and, at the same time, so cautious about highlighting the Lutheran theme, McGrail maintains, that he may even have teased his reader about his source, dropping a single tremendous hint. In the First Folio version of the play, published in 1623, seven years after Shakespeare's death, the editors added a line that had been left out of the Second Quarto and other editions published while Shakespeare was still alive.

HAMLET: *The body is with the King, but the King is not with the body. The King is a thing—*
GUILDENSTERN: *A thing, my lord?*
HAMLET: *Of nothing: bring me to him, hide Fox, and all after.*

For McGrail, the half line "hide Fox, and all after" is an incredible "teaser," and one that Shakespeare might have thought too obvious for publication in his lifetime. "Hide Fox, and all after" refers to a children's game, but in McGrail's thinking it is Shakespeare or the Folio's editor playfully hiding John Foxe and his life of Luther within the text of *Hamlet.*

In a general scheme, McGrail sees Luther, like Hamlet, as a man in a world "out of joint," who is commanded by a ghost of a father to "set it right." According to Foxe's account, Luther saw the world as "out of frame" (a phrase that Claudius uses, in Act I, Scene 2), and Luther's mission was to battle the decadence of the Church of Rome, its drift from Scripture into ornate ritual and corruption. He struggled against the Church's practice of selling indulgences, for instance—the practice of papal representatives promising shorter terms in Purgatory for a fee. Hamlet is commanded by his father's ghost to set right the natural order of the Danish court: he must kill Claudius and avenge his father's murder. The Danish court is like the decadent Church.

Foxe and Shakespeare open their texts in literal and metaphysical gloom. In Foxe, those with intelligence and judgment or "eyes to see" can note "in what blindness and darkness the world was drowned," thanks to a corrupt and powerful Church immersed only in "outward observations, ceremonies, and idolatry." Foxe continues, "Instead of the only living Lord, we worshiped dead stocks and stones: in place of Christ immortal, we adored mortal bread." *Hamlet,* too, opens in darkness, at midnight on the battlement of a castle, the kingdom plunged in a state of corruption and war. Foxe says the priests of the Church "make battle" on Europe, exacting tribute, in the form of indulgences, all over Europe in order to build St. Peter's; Shakespeare's Denmark is a "warlike state," exacting tribute from Britain and occupying the Norway of Fortinbras.

McGrail notes that Foxe begins his account of Luther by emphasizing Luther's immersion in the Bible, in St. Augustine, and in the writings of his early intellectual influence St. Bernard, from whom the monk began to understand that "man is freely justified by faith" rather than works—a principle that would form the core of Luther's theology. And the first character to speak in *Hamlet* is "the sentinel, Barnardo—an Italian form of the name Bernard," McGrail notes, and says, "Reading St. Bernard, Luther begins to ask who is guarding the Church."

Acting on the reported testimony of Barnardo and the other sentinel, Francisco, Hamlet himself sees and speaks with the ghost of his father. (Incidentally, McGrail points out, Hamlet addresses him as "old mole" and "pioner." Both "mole" and "pioner" were terms for a miner, and Foxe notes that Luther's father was a miner.) Hamlet's conversation with his father's ghost is, in McGrail's reading, a search into the knowledge of past authority, a reenactment of Luther's reading of St. Augustine, a staging "of what it means to read ancient texts."

McGrail also sees a link between Luther's urge to reform the Church—for it to reemphasize its core commandments and texts—and images in *Hamlet* of a backward movement in time. The first three characters who appear in the play, in the scene on the ramparts, are Francisco (whom McGrail cites as St. Francis), Barnardo (St. Bernard), and Marcellus (St. Marcellus the Centurion). They are, McGrail says, "introduced in reverse historical order, which sets the clock of history going backward in the play." And there are two more such metaphors of moving backward even while looking ahead. The first comes when, in Act II, Scene 2, Hamlet remarks to Polonius, "Yourself, sir, shall grow old as I am, if like a Crab you could go backward." Then, in Act II, Scene 1, Ophelia recounts for her father Hamlet's bizarre behavior, ending with his crablike exit:

> *That done, he lets me go,*
> *And with his head over his shoulder turn'd*
> *He seem'd to find his way without his eyes,*

For out o' doors he went without their helps,
And to the last bended their light on me.

McGrail sees Luther's character, as it is portrayed in Foxe, and in later biographies as well, as not unlike Hamlet's. Both Luther and Hamlet are on a spiritual journey and, in their respective ways (in theological writings and in dramatic soliloquy), are given to extended rumination on issues of the soul, existence, and action. The spiritual journeys that Luther and Hamlet make are similar, from doubt to a belief in faith over works. In his first soliloquy, Hamlet questions God's "canon," but, finally, in a remark to Horatio late in the play, he says, "There's a divinity that shapes our ends, / Rough-hew them how we will."

The two men are also similar in disposition. "Remember," McGrail said as we finished a long session over her notes, "like Hamlet, Luther was a very strange guy. He was given to what is called *Anfechtungen*—periods of spiritual turmoil. He was a very tortured soul. The Foxe biography talks of Luther's 'astonyings'— his fits. In debate, Luther would appear very staunch—'Here I stand!'—and to others his actions looked like insanity. Luther looked like a crazy man." Hamlet's strategy throughout the play is to feign madness, and even in private contemplation he is also touched with *Anfechtungen*.

Early the next morning, McGrail picked me up at my hotel and we headed north on the San Diego Freeway. She wanted to take me to the Huntington Library, where she had been reading various editions, some quite rare, of *Actes and Monuments* and an even rarer version of *Hamlet,* a Second Quarto edition, circa 1604–1605—one of eight originals in the world. (The Second Quarto is generally recognized as the "good," more accurate version of Shakespeare published in his lifetime—a corrective to the First, or "bad," Quarto.)

"I think when you get there and you actually hold this text in your hands you'll get a better idea of how excited I am," McGrail said as she accelerated into the passing lane.

The library was the gift of a California railroad magnate, and it has the vernal magnificence of a health spa for the rich. One expects to see the shade of Gloria Swanson being wheeled around, her face caked in curative muds. Surrounding the library is a vast botanical garden, a kind of Disneyland for the green-thumbed. It includes a cactus garden with every imaginable species, a Japanese garden, a rose garden. There was a baking breeze. The only moisture came from the sprinkler system. The gardens glistened. Tropical birds twittered in the museum of trees.

Once we were inside, it took a while for McGrail to convince the librarians that her guest could be trusted to sit with her in the reading rooms. She told them that she wanted to show me the Foxe manuscript and the Second Quarto of *Hamlet* but that she would be there the entire time, monitoring the situation.

"The Huntington has a reputation as a stuffy place, but they're nice once you get to know them," she assured me. "In fact, it's a pretty strange place. A lot of weird regulars. There's one guy here who comes dressed in a white turban and a blue tutu."

McGrail led me into a rare-book reading room and ordered the Foxe and the *Hamlet*. The librarian looked me over and narrowed her eyes. Then she stared at my breast pocket.

"No pens," she said. "Pencils. No pens."

I removed my pen and laid it out like a gun on the desk between us.

"I'll call you when the books are ready."

The Foxe, an enormous artifact, arrived first. In the Renaissance, nearly every Protestant church had a copy of *Actes and Monuments*. I enjoyed going through it, but I already had a Xerox copy of the Luther section and was really more eager to see the Second Quarto.

When it arrived, I was a little surprised at how small it was. The pages of the original had been sliced out and pasted onto clean pages and bound in green leather. The frontispiece asks for the reader's confidence, declaring this version of the play to be "according to the true and perfect Coppie."

I picked up the book. The librarian, twenty yards away, shot me a dark, lids-low glance.

"Here, you'd better let me hold that," McGrail said. "She's nervous you'll do something."

McGrail began flipping to some of her favorite "correspondences" in the play—the links between Hamlet and Luther. She turned to a moment in Act II, Scene 2 when Hamlet, reading a book (the Bible, McGrail ventures), gets into a verbal duel with Polonius, all the while feigning madness:

HAMLET: *For if the sun breed maggots in a dead dog, being a good kissing carrion—Have you a daughter?*
POLONIUS: *I have, my lord.*
HAMLET: *Let her not walk i'th' sun. Conception is a blessing, but as your daughter may conceive—friend, look to 't.*

Then she moved on to the end of the play. In the climactic scene, which ends with a pile of corpses, the King drops a pearl into a goblet of wine.

"What you're seeing there is Shakespeare playing with the two sacraments that spell out the key differences between Catholicism and Protestantism," McGrail said. "With Polonius, Hamlet is playing around with the Immaculate Conception, which Luther questioned. And then the King is performing some sort of Communion. For Catholics, Communion is actual—the wine becomes Christ's blood, the bread his flesh—but it is symbolic for Protestants. These are central debates."

McGrail flipped to the gravedigger scene, which begins Act V—a scene that we had examined earlier, at the hotel. In that scene, two gravediggers talk about what constitutes a proper burial for a suicide like Ophelia: "What, art a heathen?" one gravedigger asks the other, who has just displayed biblical ignorance. "How dost thou understand the Scripture? The Scripture says Adam digged. Could he dig without arms?"

"That's central for Luther," McGrail said. "Remember, even Luther wasn't able to read the Bible for himself until he was practically a grown man. That was typical for that time. Luther wanted the common man to read Scripture for himself in vernacular translations. . . . Here the gravedigger shows that he has done it, and his interpretation is literal. This is a more interpretative point, but Shakespeare is bringing out one of the consequences of Luther's Reformation."

Then we turned to a central moment in McGrail's argument. In Act III, Scene 2, just before the court players are about to perform "The Mousetrap"—the play within the play—Hamlet coaches them to avoid "o'erdoing" their roles:

HAMLET: *Be not too tame neither, but let your own discretion be your tutor. Suit the action to the word, the word to the action, with this special observance, that you o'erstep not the modesty of nature. . . . O, there be players that I have seen play—and heard others praise, and that highly—not to speak it profanely, that neither having th'accent of Christians, nor the gait of Christians, pagan, nor man, have so strutted and bellowed that I have thought some of Nature's journeymen had made men, and not made them well, they imitated humanity so abominably.*
FIRST PLAYER: *I hope we have reformed that indifferently with us.*
HAMLET: *O reform it altogether.*

McGrail pointed out that for Elizabethans, Protestants of rather recent vintage, theater had in large measure replaced some of the high ritual and ceremony that went missing with the diminishment of Catholicism and the rise of Calvinism. Hamlet, then, is speaking ostensibly of theater but metaphorically of religion. For McGrail, the line "O reform it altogether" is a pivotal moment. "An Elizabethan audience can't fail to hear the resonance," she said. " 'Reform' would ring in their ears."

But that was still not why we had driven out to the Huntington. McGrail leafed through the little green book, pointing out the places where Shakespeare names animals: Moles in Act I, Asses in Acts II and V, a Deere and a Hart in Act III. Many more: an ark.

"Will you look at these?" McGrail said. "I found out from Luther biographies that he was interested in Noah. I thought, Well, I have finally lost it. I've gone crazy." Shakespeare, she argued, capitalized the names of the animals to emphasize their presence not only to those who would see *Hamlet* but to those who would read it.

"Luther was deeply attracted to the story of Noah," McGrail went on, "and that's because it was with Noah that God made his Covenant. Luther identified with Noah's position and his place in the world. The Church had become so corrupt and worthless that it had to fall. Luther was in a place analogous with Noah's, in a sense. When I saw that, I felt as if I were reporting back from four hundred years ago, saying, 'Just look at what this guy was capable of!' "

It wasn't until we were driving back from the Huntington and cruising along the hills on Sunset Boulevard that I realized just how shaken McGrail was about her dispute with Steve Sohmer. Their fight had not yet reached the deposition stage, and she kept saying that she wanted to keep our talks, as much as possible, on the subject of Shakespeare. Never mind that the reason she was rushing her work, the reason she was talking to me at all, had everything to do with Steve Sohmer. "If this turns out to be a duel, a scandal, it'll ruin me and my ideas," she said.

Although McGrail said that the ideas we had run through were her own, she also said many times that Sohmer had made "an important contribution" by figuring out how the life of Luther and *Hamlet* were linked through Shakespeare's manipulation of the calendar. In his doctoral dissertation on *Julius Caesar* and in his writing on *Hamlet,* Sohmer tries to prove that Shakespeare created a series of resonances—between Caesar and Christ, between Hamlet and Luther—through an intricate use of mathematics and the calendar. The action in *Hamlet,* for example, falls on the same dates that marked particular festival days in 1517, the year Luther nailed his Ninety-five Theses to the church door in Wittenberg. McGrail, in the piece she wrote for the *Times Literary Supplement,* refers the reader to only one other scholar—Steve Sohmer.

"I mentioned the business of Luther to him a couple of summers ago, and this summer he came up with the 1517 material," McGrail told me. "I said, 'You should pursue that, it's elegant work.' That is work that is original with him."

As we were driving along Sunset, McGrail casually pointed out the gates of Bel Air. I asked her if we could drive by the Sohmer house.

At first, McGrail's eyes widened, then narrowed, as if she had gone from shock to determination. She pulled into a side street and made a U-turn. Then her eyes filled with tears.

"I can't do it," she said.

"There's no reason we have to."

"I'm sorry. I can't do it," she said, and we drove on, past Bel Air and into the heart of the Sunset Strip.

Not long after arriving in Los Angeles, I had left a message with Sohmer's production company, in Burbank, asking if it would be possible to get together with him to talk about Shakespeare. When we finally hooked up and I said I'd met with Mary Ann McGrail,

Sohmer said, well, fine, that was interesting, we'd talk. "Come on over later, around five-thirty," he said. "We'll have a good glass of port. You like port?"

The *Los Angeles Times*, which covers the real estate market with impressive zeal, reports that Sohmer's house, on Strada Corta, for which he paid three million dollars, is just under six thousand square feet; there are four bedrooms, seven baths, maids' quarters, a guest apartment, an office, and "a motor court." (Sohmer also owns a four-bedroom wing of a "condoized" seventeenth-century manor house seventy miles northwest of London, in Shipton-under-Wychwood.)

I eased my car up to Sohmer's gate and, with a camera eye staring at me, announced myself to a fizzing intercom. Then came the buzz, the yawning gate, the "motor court": a Rolls-Royce, a mini-van, a red Mercedes sports car, a Lincoln Town Car, an ancient bulldog sleeping in the late-afternoon sun.

I rang the front doorbell and waited for a while. Waited and shuffled, but no one came. Then from around the side of the main house came Sohmer. He wore a faded blue work shirt, tennis shorts, white socks, and sneakers.

"Come on back to the office," he said.

Sohmer uses a small house behind the pool as his office. He gets up at five and spends at least the first half of the day working at home, first on Shakespeare and then on "something productive," which is to say his work in television and movies. Later in the day, he drives to his production offices "to check in." After studying writing at Columbia in his early twenties, Sohmer published a book of short stories, *The Way It Was,* which won for him the sort of reviews that lead to a promising career. But the pressure to earn money, he said, led him to eighteen years in television production and then the movies. Since he was fired as the head of Columbia Pictures in 1986, he has made his living writing and producing television shows, including a miniseries made from his novel *Favorite*

Son. One of his latest projects is *The Deidre Hall Story,* a television movie that tells the story of how Sohmer and his wife struggled with infertility problems and finally had two children with the help of a surrogate mother.

Sohmer led me into his office and sat behind a huge glass-topped table. He was surrounded by a vast library dominated by Shakespeareana, and, above the bookcases, walls decorated with posters from his own past in books and shows. His computer was on, and an article he was writing about *Hamlet* and Luther throbbed on the screen. Just as we were settling in and starting to talk about his doctoral dissertation, he took a phone call that had something to do with the details of a miniseries.

"From the sublime to the ridiculous," Sohmer said, smiling and covering the receiver with his palm.

Sohmer does not apologize for making a living in low- and middlebrow entertainment; in fact, he seems to thrive on his dual role. In each of the two worlds he inhabits—Hollywood and Stratford-upon-Avon—his other identity gives him a certain panache. "Steve is an extraordinary character, with all the self-confidence associated with Hollywood, but now directed toward this other unusual area, toward Shakespeare," I was later told by Lawrence Danson, a Shakespearean at Princeton University who once stayed at Sohmer's home in the Cotswolds. "He goes about his work sometimes in a sort of Hollywood way, consulting, taking a meeting with this or that professor. He is a fascinating figure in a sacred-monster sort of way. You are tempted to laugh at his autodidact ambitions, but when I looked at his dissertation I was skeptical of its conclusions and yet I saw that it was the product of enormous labor and considerable scholarship."

After Sohmer finished his call, I said that I was fascinated by the notion of Hamlet as Luther but dumbstruck to see that two people, both deeply immersed in Elizabethan culture, were now engaging lawyers and preparing to go to war over what amounted to a highly speculative theory about a play written nearly four hundred years ago.

As Sohmer listened, he puffed peacefully on a cigar. Yet, more often than not, he gazed at a large television screen above his desk and its ghostly image of the security gate in front of his house. When I finished, Sohmer took a last drag on his cigar, blew a long plume toward the ceiling, and looked across the desk at me. "You have come at a propitious time," he said. "We sent out a press release announcing a new source for Shakespeare."

Sohmer dug out a copy of the release that his lawyers had advised him to write. It was dated September 1 (the day after his breakup with McGrail) and headlined "Unrecognized Source of Shakespeare's *Hamlet* Discovered by California Scholar." The first paragraph read:

> Dr. Steve Sohmer, the internationally known novelist who holds a Doctorate in English from Oxford University, announced the discovery of a previously unrecognized source of William Shakespeare's play, *Hamlet*. While the title of the obscure 16th century biographical book remains a closely guarded secret, a small circle of specialist scholars already believes the book may deserve recognition as a source of the play.

In two following paragraphs, Sohmer paraphrases the discovery that McGrail was quick to credit him with: that Shakespeare, by setting the action on certain Catholic holy days that were considered dubious by Protestants, hinted at his theme—Luther's conflict with the Church. What Sohmer leaves out—but makes clear in an eight-page article that he posted on the Internet—is the real point of interest: that those holy days would have come up in the Church calendar on identical days in 1601, the possible year of *Hamlet*'s first performance, and 1517, the year Luther nailed his theses to the church door. The release itself is otherwise opaque.

Sohmer then began to give his version of how the summer with McGrail had started as an intellectually exciting discussion and ended in argument, threats, and legal action.

"On July second, Mary Ann came here, and I said that I had decided to spend time on the calendrical design of *Hamlet,*" Sohmer said. He went on to tell me that the search for that design had led to a biography of Luther that was available in English in Shakespeare's lifetime—a translation by one Henry Bennett of a Latin book, as Sohmer, late of Oxford, put it, "by a chap named Philipp Melanchthon." McGrail, in her work, had all but abandoned Melanchthon as a central source, and had concentrated on Foxe's *Actes and Monuments.* Several times in more than three hours I spent with Sohmer, he mentioned Foxe, but only in passing. He seemed far more comfortable talking about the calendar and, to a lesser degree, Melanchthon.

According to Sohmer, an Elizabethan audience would have been aware of the nuances of the calendar. By studying hints given in the play about various dates, Sohmer thinks he has also discovered what he calls "the single greatest mystery in Shakespeare"—that is, why Hamlet did not succeed to the throne after the death of his father. And the answer, which Sohmer explored even in his dissertation on *Julius Caesar,* is that Hamlet was born before his parents married. He was illegitimate. Similarly, according to some accounts, Luther's mother could not remember the year of his birth—a notion "that stretches credulity," Sohmer says. "She can remember the hour and day of the birth, but not the year?" In one biography, written by Cochlaeus, a virulently anti-Luther Catholic priest, it is even suggested that Luther's mother coupled with a devil in a bathhouse. "I want to write a whole book about the calendrical aspects of *Hamlet,*" Sohmer said. "A couple of months before Mary Ann showed up on July second, I'd started writing a book called *Luther at Elsinore.*"

Just as McGrail had been quick to credit Sohmer with doing the principal work on the calendar, Sohmer was quick to credit her with helping him on textual issues. But, like her, he had no doubt about who was in the lead. Both in conversation with me and, six weeks later, in deposition, Sohmer made several of the same general points about the parallels between Hamlet and Luther which McGrail had and claimed them as his ideas: namely, that Shakespeare's character makes a spiritual journey much like Luther's, that Shakespeare uses some of his characters to represent figures (such as Henry VIII) who take part in the Luther drama, and that Shakespeare raises some of the key religious debates of the Reformation in the play, including the debate over various sacraments and the existence of Purgatory. But Sohmer rolled his eyes at my suggestion that McGrail, whom he had been paying a hundred dollars an hour just a week before, was in any way his teacher, his tutor, or his superior.

"Mary Ann *started* as a tutor," he told me, leaning back in a huge upholstered desk chair. "Then there is an old saying: A student who does not surpass his master fails his master. I was the one who was really conducting the seminar on *Hamlet.*"

"So then you are ahead of her on the study of *Hamlet?*" I asked.

"I'm ahead of her—oh, by miles, on this subject." Later, he added, "The whole essence of the process shifted away from a tutorial process into a very equal and collegial sort of relationship."

"If it was equal, then why pay her?"

"Because I thought she could use the money and I think she likes coming to California." For anyone to have failed to see that their relationship had changed, Sohmer said—well, that person would have to be "brain-dead."

This seemed curious to me. Sohmer's academic career, to put it mildly, was only a budding one. His Oxford D.Phil. was of a few months' vintage. Sohmer has never taught Shakespeare. Where McGrail was defensive about her publishing record and determined to accelerate it, Sohmer, at fifty-three, seemed to consider himself a kind of boy wonder, able to take on the career of original scholar as a kind of entertainment, a lark. Sohmer seemed to be saying that it was as if his motives and interests were somehow purer than the average scholar's because he, as a wealthy man with "a real job," had no need to impress anyone but himself.

"After all, what do I get out of this?" he said. "I get bragging rights at the Bel Air Country Club, that's all it means to me, and they think I'm crazy over there anyway. I don't need the publication. I don't need the work. The other party does."

I could not quite fathom how Sohmer viewed McGrail's role. When I asked him, he struggled with an answer. "Mary Ann has been here as an employee," he said. "I don't think there is any dispute about whose intellectual property this is. What we're disputing is whether she could write about these things without sharing credit. The task I set out for us—and the kind of work I've been doing—is my intellectual property, not hers. I view her as a paid— I guess you'd say she was— I can't think. She wasn't a consultant or a researcher, although she did some of the grunt work."

When the subject turned to Sohmer's life, he stopped and said, "You want a bio? I got a bio!" He handed me a two-page, single-spaced document headed "Dr. Steve Sohmer," which began this way:

> Steve Sohmer leads multiple careers as a writer-producer, entertainment industry executive, novelist, and Shakespearean scholar. *As a writer-producer:* Since 1986, Steve has served as president of his own television production firm based in Los Angeles. In 1988 Steve created, wrote, and produced the NBC miniseries *Favorite Son,* starring Harry Hamlin and Linda Kozlowski. In 1989–90, Steve wrote and produced the high-rated NBC telefilm *Bloodknot,* starring Jaclyn Smith.

Since Sohmer was most completely the creator of *Favorite Son,* I ran through some old reviews. The plot, in both the novel and the telefilm versions, concerns a dark-horse vice-presidential candidate who becomes a national hero when he is wounded during the assassination of a Nicaraguan contra leader. While the *Times* television critic John J. O'Connor called it a "hard-driving political thriller," Tom Shales, the critic at *The Washington Post,* was less impressed: "One reason to watch the NBC miniseries *Favorite Son*—and there really aren't that many—is to play a game of 'which scene is the ickiest?' A top contender comes early in the three-part, six-hour opus, when two FBI agents investigate a crime site. A dead woman is lying in a large pool of blood on the kitchen floor when a dog comes into the room and begins to lap at the puddle. The younger FBI agent vomits into the camera. The older one says he remembers a dog once urinating on a corpse. The younger man vomits again."

Sohmer mentioned more than once that *Favorite Son,* the novel, had been translated into more than a dozen languages. He went on to say that reading Shakespeare had made him "a better writer," explaining, "I try to use the minor characters to mirror the major characters. Obviously, I can't do it as well as Shakespeare. No one can."

Sohmer seems to waver between an outsized ego and a disarming gift for self-deprecation. Even in his résumé he sees himself as a Renaissance man and does not hesitate to point out lesser literary accomplishments ("Steve created and wrote *Where the Fun Is,* Pan American Airways' annual student travel guide"). As a scholar who makes television shows for his fortune, he once told *Newsday,* he resembles "a man with a cholesterol problem who is running a cheese factory."

After talking to me for a while about his life, Sohmer described— as he would in his initial application for the temporary restraining order—the collapse of his collaboration and friendship with Mary Ann McGrail, what he saw as the series of betrayals that led to anger and heartbreak. In his telling, he was the generous patron betrayed, McGrail the ungrateful deceiver.

Sohmer said that as he was finishing his doctoral dissertation on the calendrical structure of *Julius Caesar* and the play's relation to the life of Christ, he began to focus, in May of 1995, on *Hamlet* and similar issues of time, festival days, and religious conflict.

The court papers lack none of the confidence that Sohmer reveals in personal conversation, and they benefit from greater concision. In his statement attached to the request for a temporary restraining order, he says that prior to McGrail's arrival in Los Angeles he "quickly realized that the play (Hamlet) had a calendrical structure that had never been detected by . . . scholars before." He goes on,

I also recognized that Shakespeare was writing about Martin Luther and reformation theology and the conflict between the reformers and the Catholic church. Although Edmond Malone first recognized . . . a connection between Hamlet and Wittenberg, Germany, which was Luther's university, I was the first to recognize that Shakespeare was examining Luther's theology of conversion and his relationship with the English King Henry VIII with whom Luther and his colleague, Phillip Melanchthon, corresponded in 1522–25. My recognition of the depth to which Shakespeare was exploring the life and theology of Luther through Hamlet is a significant and new theory which has never been recognized by Shakespearean scholars before.

Sohmer then describes how McGrail was hired and paid "to assist me in my research into the calendrical and religious dimensions of Hamlet as I have discussed above." His statement then turns to the personal, an epic of disintegration: "This revelation that I made to Dr. McGrail," Sohmer says of his theory, "was conveyed in complete confidence outside of the presence of any other person or individual." He claims he told McGrail, at their first session this summer, that the theory was his own, and was confidential. The two then began to work their way through the play, line by line. Sohmer says he wrote an article on *Hamlet* and the calendar, completed by mid-July, for a British journal, *Notes and Queries,* and "as a courtesy to Dr. McGrail, I included both of our by-lines" before sending it off to Oxford.

I asked Sohmer when the conflict over articles and publications came up.

"When we identified this Melanchthon and the passages in Foxe, Mary Ann proposed we write an article for the *Huntington Library Quarterly,*" he said. "I thought that was a wonderful idea. A couple of days passed, and Mary Ann said, 'I think I should write this piece for the *Huntington Library Quarterly.*' I said, 'Why's that?' She said, 'Well, you don't want to do text editing, do you?' I said, 'Why not?' A couple of days later, she walked in and said, 'I've got a wonderful idea. Let's write a piece for the *Times Literary Supplement.*' I said fine, I'd write the part about the calendar and she'd write about the Melanchthon book or Foxe, or whatever. Then she said, 'It's got to be done by Tuesday.' This was all two and a half, three weeks ago— mid-August. I said, 'Why Tuesday? You've talked to someone about this, haven't you?' "

All the while, Sohmer testifies in the court document, he was growing more and more suspicious that McGrail was withholding information from him. He claims that at one point she said of herself that a collaboration wouldn't do her any good—meaning, he assumed, that it would not benefit her standing in the academic world or her quest for tenure at Boston University.

McGrail, for her part, told me she never wanted to collaborate with Sohmer and never led him to believe otherwise. In fact, she said, she never proposed an article to the *Huntington Library Quarterly;* she did invite him to submit a companion piece to her *TLS* submission. In her court filings she denies Sohmer's claims on nearly every point.

"I wasn't castigating Mary Ann. I was pleading with her," Sohmer told me, in a wounded voice. "We have a unique working relationship—a professor and someone with no ax to grind, with no need of tenure or publications. I recognized this publication would be important for her. I said, You can have top billing and write the introduction. But to take work done in this room and at the Huntington—I paid you, I accepted you as a friend and as a member of the family, and then to take this idea and exploit it for your own benefit—well, the word might be 'ingratitude.' "

Sohmer sat for a while in silence. He stared at the television monitor above his desk. He puffed on his cigar. There were no unusual movements at his gate.

"You know something?" he said. "I wish we hadn't found this stuff. I wish we had worked on *Antony and Cleopatra* instead of *Hamlet*. Because if we had, we'd still be sitting here talking about Shakespeare. Mary Ann would still be walking in here at eight o'clock with her coffee and we'd talk. You know, the journey is everything and the destination is nothing. Working on Shakespeare, it's also true. The destination means nothing. It's the pure excitement of study. The stakes for me have always been small. I never see the *TLS*. We don't take that. I've never even seen the *Huntington Library Quarterly*. What's it to me? If she had walked in and said, 'Please let me do it alone,' it would never have been an issue. How could I say no to a friend? But that's not how this happened. It happened after being told one thing and then another."

What, I asked, could have been McGrail's motive? Why would she possibly have betrayed him?

"My hunch is that this publish-or-perish thing may be at work here," Sohmer said. "There's an x factor here. That may be it."

I suggested to Sohmer that perhaps the dispute was unreal, even preposterous: while the two parties were agreed that there were Lutheran aspects to *Hamlet,* the specifics of their work were not so much overlapping as contiguous. Sohmer was deep into his research on the calendar, and McGrail was working mainly on Foxe's *Actes and Monuments*.

Sohmer replied that, if that was the case, it would come out in litigation.

Then Sohmer said he would soon be going out to the Huntington Library to work on the various editions of *Hamlet*—the First and Second Quartos, the First Folio—"if I ever get around to it. It's very tedious work."

I asked if he was working hard on the Luther biographies.

"I have started on the text, but I'm a long way from anywhere," Sohmer said. "The answer is, I'm nowhere on it."

Scholars have been combing through Shakespeare's works for centuries. The growth in Shakespeare criticism is exponential. Thousands of articles, monographs, and books on Shakespeare are published every year. Critics of all schools are still searching for an answer to the question "Who is Shakespeare?" Is he primarily a man of the theater, as he is in Bernard Beckerman's *Shakespeare at the Globe*? Is he a closet Catholic, as Eric Sams believes? Was he gay, as a number of critics of the sonnets hold? Is he a writer obsessed with his position at court, as Alvin Kernan writes?

While it is certain that every age will produce its own interpretations, its own Shakespeare, it grows less and less likely that someone will come up with some sort of archaeological find, a riddle answered. But still people try. Scholars are still poking around the question of authorship, the possibility that someone else—Bacon; or De Vere, the Earl of Oxford; or someone quite obscure—wrote one or more of the plays now attributed to Shakespeare.

Once in a great while, a scholar believes he has added to the existing Shakespeare canon by discovering a lost manuscript attributable to the Master. In 1985, Gary Taylor, now a professor at Brandeis University, did that when he found a poem in Oxford's

Bodleian Library called "Shall I Die? Shall I Fly?" Taylor was convinced that the poem, though not an especially good one, was Shakespeare's. His discovery sparked much dissent and at least as much jealousy in the academic world—especially after it was publicized on the front page of the *Times*. A few years later, after the furor had subsided, he wrote an article for the *Times* recalling the strange interplay between scholarship and its interpretation in the press. "Literary scholarship, like journalism, is a competitive business," Taylor wrote. "New theories do not, and should not, win instant unanimous acceptance. So whenever a new theory is propounded, in literature or science, rival experts will leap to attack it. Every newborn theory has to fight for its life. That war of theories goes on all the time, whether or not journalists become involved. The press simply accelerates, exaggerates and personalizes the struggle."

For whatever reason, accelerating the struggle was undoubtedly McGrail's intention. It was McGrail's friend who, with McGrail's permission, had called *The New Yorker* in the first place. Had there been no dispute with Sohmer, she would have worked, written, and published at a more ordinary pace. Sohmer said he would have preferred that the matter stay private. "With all due respect, I wish you had kept your nose out of it," he told me.

After returning home from California, I asked some Shakespeare scholars what they thought of the idea of *Hamlet* under Luther's shadow. I thought, for example, that Berkeley's Stephen Greenblatt, founder of the New Historicism school of criticism, might not endorse such a reading, but in fact he was intrigued.

"Luther? I've been working on a little of that myself," he said. "I'm fascinated by Shakespeare's invoking Wittenberg, and I've been working on the theological implications of the use of the Eucharist: 'Not where he eats, but where a is eaten.' That moment after the killing of Polonius. It doesn't seem really new. It seems pleasantly old. People have been noodling around for years with phrases like 'hide Fox' and what they mean and what secrets they might possess, chewing on old bones and seeing what sort of marrow we can eke out."

Lawrence Danson, the Shakespearean at Princeton who had stayed at Sohmer's place in England, told me that McGrail and Sohmer, in their separate ways, were flirting with a potentially reductive theory. "Yes, of course Hamlet went to Wittenberg, but Marlowe's Dr. Faustus lived there, too. What then? The same with the calendar. With a capacious enough text, like *Hamlet,* you can find almost anything you're looking for. If this kind of study is not done well, it runs the risk of bearing a resemblance to the ciphering of the text that some scholars do to 'prove' that Shakespeare never wrote the plays—that it was Bacon or someone else. It's like conspiracy thinking: you take a series of details—a fox, a series of dates—and you make a case. But how does that jibe with the rest of the play? Shakespeare does not operate that way. Why would he have shifted tactics this way? I'm skeptical, at best, but I look forward to reading their actual work."

I told Peter W. M. Blayney, a resident fellow at the Folger Shakespeare Library, in Washington, whose specialty is the printing trade in the age of Shakespeare, about McGrail's notion that Shakespeare wanted the animals capitalized in the Second Quarto as a way of emphasizing the Noah story and thus the link with Luther. He was not impressed. In Elizabethan printing houses, Blayney told me, capitalization was up to the compositor, and "personified abstractions"—the names of animals, plants, rocks, or minerals—were capitalized all the time. "Capitalized animals are virtually standard in printing houses of the time," Blayney said. "I don't know Mary Ann McGrail, but this is extremely far-fetched. It just doesn't sound as if she were within her area, here at least. . . . If there were any running imagery of Luther, I don't think it would be conducted in this manner."

Finally, I visited one of the leading young Shakespeareans, James Shapiro, who teaches at Columbia. He has spent a lot of time on *Actes and Monuments* and the religious atmosphere of post-Reformation England. We met at his apartment, on Riverside Drive, and he had ready a number of editions of *Hamlet*.

As I went through points of the argument as McGrail had laid it out for me, Shapiro was both curious and skeptical. Because he is a scholar deeply interested in the religious aspects of the play and of the culture, he seemed to want the theory to make sense. But more often than not he shook his head and demanded that McGrail "put more pressure" on her own points: he wanted her to ask herself *why* Shakespeare would drop certain hints, use certain names. Too many points seemed contrived or coincidental, he said. McGrail, for example, argues that when Polonius gives Reynaldo money to take abroad and give to his son, Laertes, and, incidentally, see what sort of sins he is up to ("drinking, fencing, swearing, / Quarreling, drabbing"), the scene is an echo of the Church's sending priests all over Europe to sell indulgences—Luther's great bugbear.

"There's just no evidence for that," Shapiro said. "Or not enough. So far, what I see is Polonius giving Laertes money for expenses."

As we went on, Shapiro was more interested in other points, such as "O reform it altogether." But overall he seemed dubious. McGrail, he concluded, was in far too early a stage of scholarship to be talking about theories with any confidence.

"Certain questions aren't being asked here," he said. "The first is about Shakespeare's handling of source material. Why is he dealing with Foxe differently from the way he dealt with Holinshed or Plutarch? In the history plays, he compresses dates, uses other sources, and so on, but here he seems to use it differently from the way he uses other historical biographies. Why? If he is using the Foxe—and I do believe Shakespeare was familiar with Foxe, at least some of it—I don't think he is using it as a source. But even if I did accept the argument, this is still not the way Shakespeare works through a plot. Shakespeare usually takes whole phrases, sentences—not just key words here or there. You can see the way he'll transform things wholesale. Why would he have to hide the Foxe? Is it because Shakespeare was more closely aligned with Lutheran than with Calvinist theology? If Shakespeare had been interested in Luther, he would have looked at a variety of sources. He was never satisfied with the first version that crossed his path."

What worried Shapiro most about McGrail's approach was its emphasis on riddles and hints. He said that there has always been a tendency in Shakespeare studies for certain scholars to see what they wanted to see in a play, finding buried puns and anagrams to "prove," say, that Francis Bacon wrote the work. "With enough inventiveness," Shapiro said, "almost anything can be argued about Shakespeare's plays—and most of it has been." Just this year, he noted, two highly respected scholars, Alvin Kernan and Eric Mallin, have published separate books arguing that the story of Hamlet parallels not the Luther story but, rather, that of James himself, the king-in-waiting.

"Don't get me wrong," Shapiro said. "*Hamlet* comes at the height of Shakespeare's powers, and so that Reformation context would have to be there. People are reading Foxe now, and it is a serious topic that has been overlooked for a long time."

Even if McGrail's work is finally dismissed in its particulars, it represents a renewed interest in the religious dimensions of Shakespeare. The New Critics—the generation of Cleanth Brooks, Harry Levin, and Robert B. Heilman, who dominated the forties and fifties—emphasized language above all; the text as a self-contained unit, the well-wrought urn. The New Historicists and their British cousins, the Cultural Materialists, came of age in the sixties and seventies and now tend to dominate Shakespeare studies; their focus is on the mediating factor of history, and they are especially attuned to race, class, gender, and power relations. Members of that generation have been more secular in outlook and less focused on religion. Scholars of McGrail's generation—the generation from twenty-five to forty-five—are adding religion to the historical view of the plays. Shapiro said he hoped that both McGrail and Sohmer would give up the hunt for the "holy grail" of a lost biographical source and concentrate more on the way Shakespeare may have been taking a position on the religious controversies of Elizabethan England. McGrail's theological hunches have the "strong ring of truth, but rewriting cultural history is a slow, laborious affair," Shapiro said. "There are no shortcuts, no huge discoveries. It's not about individuals like Luther, but about more complicated cultural shifts."

About Sohmer's work on the calendar, Shapiro was no less skeptical. If too much of Sohmer's work depends on establishing that the first performance of *Hamlet* was in 1601, then "it's like building oceanfront property in California: sooner or later the whole edifice will be washed away." As Sohmer himself acknowledges, there is still a great controversy over the dating of the play.

Shapiro and I walked up 116th Street and across the Columbia campus to his office. As we passed the library, I told him about the conflict between Sohmer and McGrail.

"An intellectual-property dispute over this is hilarious," he said. "In fact, it's sad." The norm in Shakespeare studies, he added, is to circulate ideas, to discuss things openly, to collaborate—and may the best scholarship prevail.

"You know, it's funny, but Shakespeare was litigious himself," Shapiro said. "He was a killer businessman who never cut anyone any slack on loans or business arrangements. This was an especially litigious period of history, and Shakespeare was completely wrapped up in that. He moved from Stratford to London, but he was very careful about keeping up with his real estate interests in the country. Even the creation of the Globe Theatre involved a huge legal battle, which had workmen dismantling the theater at night and dragging the pieces across the frozen Thames because the lease on the land had run out. Rather than let the landlord reuse the timbers, they took them across the river and constructed the Globe. So this is not the first time the Shakespeare world has been recorded in the annals of law."

In the weeks that followed, I spoke with McGrail and Sohmer periodically, both to talk about Shakespeare and to follow the course of their dispute.

McGrail had neither the resources nor the ability to affect an aura of calm. In the first days of the case, she had spent more than ten thousand dollars on legal costs. Scared and broke, she stayed with friends for a while and then left Los Angeles for nearly a week in mid-September, in part to avoid being served with an injunction by Sohmer's lawyers.

She traveled first to Vancouver, to lecture on *Hamlet,* then to Boston, to get advice from Lloyd Weinreb, a professor of copyright law at Harvard Law School, and then to Washington to visit her parents and friends. Weinreb recommended a lawyer named Michael Doyen to represent her pro bono in Los Angeles and told her that Sohmer's case was completely groundless. (Doyen, who took on the case after my reporting began, recently represented *The New Yorker* in a lawsuit.) Weinreb said in an affidavit, and in a conversation with me, that Sohmer's lawyers were improperly regarding McGrail as an employee who had betrayed commercial secrets, whereas in fact she was, strictly speaking, an independent contractor, working part-time. The ideas at issue were just that—ideas, not trade secrets. The key legal point, Weinreb continued, is that ideas are not intellectual property, and no court would consider them so. Sohmer's suit, he said, was "frivolous." McGrail said that Sohmer was waging against her an "effective campaign of intimidation."

As the autumn wore on and the lawsuits lingered, McGrail seemed to feel the burden of her scholarship almost as much as the burden of the legal case. In a field as vast and passionate as Shakespeare studies, she could not expect a warm and easy welcome. What she considered daring could well end up condemned as marginal, a failed attempt. Not long ago, in a critical review of yet another reading of Shakespeare, the veteran critic Frank Kermode wrote, as much in sympathy as in reproach, "Finding something new, true, and useful to say about Shakespeare is a task so formidable that one can only wonder why so many keen and eager spirits compete for the privilege of attempting it."

When I asked Sohmer what sort of reaction he got to his work after he sent it out over the Internet, he said, "I've gotten the electronic equivalent of blank stares."

After a month of legal wrangling between the lawyers on both sides, with the case shifting between courthouses, Sohmer showed no sign of letting up. One of his lawyers, Ronald Lewis, told me that the case was a rather simple matter. "Look," he said. "If Albert Einstein comes up with $E = mc^2$ and then he asks a couple of professors to go to the blackboard and work out a proof, who's the one who thought up the formula?"

In letters to McGrail's side, Sohmer and his lawyers said that a settlement would have to include an apology and a promise not to publish for eighteen months. Then Sohmer made another offer. When McGrail's lawyers deposed Sohmer in mid-October 1995, he faced his antagonist. He offered to drop his lawsuit if McGrail agreed to collaborate with him on a book about *Hamlet* and Luther. She angrily rejected the offer.

At one point in the deposition, Doyen, McGrail's lawyer, suggested on his client's behalf that Sohmer and McGrail have a private conversation. McGrail and Sohmer agreed. After the conversation, McGrail declined to talk about the meeting, other than to say it was "unpleasant."

Sohmer said that when the two of them were left alone McGrail seemed "distraught."

"In a loud and desperate voice, she said, 'What is going on here?' I said, 'What do you mean?' And she said, 'What are we doing in this lawyer's office?' I said, 'Mary Ann, I told you when you pursued this course of action what would ensue.' She then told me a story about how she discovered the Melanchthon biography, which is completely false. I listened to her, and when she finished, I said, 'Do you really believe what you are saying?'

"Suddenly she went through what seemed like an enormous mood swing. She clutched her hands together and said, 'I've been such a good teacher, I've been so generous. This is *my* world.' I said, 'I can't continue this conversation.' And I got to my feet. Now, the geography of the room was such that I was on one side of the table and she was on the other, with the doorway to the hall behind her. I took a step to my left to get to the door. She got to her feet and stood in the doorway. I was alarmed. I said, 'Mary Ann, I'm leaving the room. Get out of the doorway.' She kept talking, some kind of vitriol. I said again, 'Mary Ann, I'm leaving the room, get out of the doorway.' And with that she tore the door open and ran down the hallway.

"Later, I told Doyen, 'Look, I appreciate your letting me talk to Mary Ann. I had no idea how this was affecting her. I want to reconsider the matter.' "

McGrail said that she never blocked the doorway, and that she did not run—she "walked quickly."

In late October, I asked Sohmer if he had indeed reconsidered. He said he had thought it through and could see "no other course" than to pursue the case. "Look, this is my hobby," he told me at one point. "These are my boats and bottles, and someone's thrown my boats and bottles on the floor. It's like when I was growing up and going to some bar in Queens and there would be guys there arguing passionately about the merits of Johnny Mize and they'd have a lump in their pants. They loved it! That's how I feel about arguing about *Hamlet*."

· · ·

In the first week of November, Sohmer reconsidered once more. He decided to drop his suit, and McGrail, in turn, dropped hers. Sohmer said he had his reasons but did not want to discuss them. The terms of the agreement were simple: no further action, with both sides free to publish. McGrail, who had lost her savings and two nerve-shattering months, would have preferred vindication in court, but she was relieved, all the same. "Mr. Sohmer, caught in a mousetrap, clearly realized he was wrong," she said. "What's of genuine interest is the discovery about Shakespeare."

As for Sohmer, he was reading various biographies of Luther, but mostly he was trying to write television programs. "It's the pilot season, and pari passu"—he says "pari passu" more often than William F. Buckley, Jr.—"and pari passu I'm trying to work on the material about *Hamlet*." Sohmer said he was now rebuilding his scholarly team. He had hired a Latinist to do some translating. Someone on his staff was already doing library work for him. And now he was on the lookout for a new Renaissance scholar. "I need someone to replace Mary Ann," he said.

8

The Devil Problem

(April 1995)

Sixteen years ago, Elaine Pagels, who was then a professor in her mid-thirties at Barnard College, shattered the myth that early Christianity was a unified movement and faith. It is a rarity for a scholar so young to alter even slightly the historical view of something as vast and essential as the Western world's dominant religion. Ordinarily, only the physicist or the mathematician can hope to enter early middle age having made a scholarly mark; indeed, for such a scientist a glide into the thirties without distinction can be cause for despair—or a job in university administration. The historian, by contrast, cannot rely on intuition or mental speed. History is an art not only of imagination but also of accumulation—of languages, reading, travel, perspective. Pagels, who is now the Harrington Spear Paine Professor of Religion at Princeton, had accumulated thousands of hours in the library, the classroom, and the archives, and a working command of Greek, Latin, German, Hebrew, French, Italian, and Coptic as well—an appropriately full quiver for a specialist in early Christianity. She had also, at this preposterously early point in her career, hit the academic bull's-eye. In

1979, Pagels published *The Gnostic Gospels,* a brief and elegant analysis of a series of ancient documents known collectively as the Nag Hammadi Library. Just as Edmund Wilson illuminated for a wide audience the importance of the Dead Sea Scrolls, Pagels explained the value and meaning of a trove of manuscripts unearthed in 1945 in the upper-Egyptian desert by a peasant named Muhammad Ali al-Samman. While digging near the village of Nag Hammadi for *sabakh,* a soft soil used as fertilizer, Muhammad Ali found a red earthenware jar. Thinking there might be gold inside, he smashed the jar with his mattock, and found instead thirteen papyrus books bound in leather. That night, his mother burned much of the find in the oven as kindling. What she did not burn ended up in the hands of black marketeers, antiquities dealers, and, eventually, scholars of first- and second-century Christianity.

Through a careful reading of the fifty-two sacred texts that survived—they are Coptic translations of Greek originals, some as old as the four Gospels—Pagels made it clear that early Christianity was far more complicated than anyone had ever imagined. A wildly diverse compendium of poems, chants, myths, gospels, pagan documents, and spiritual instructions, the texts are distinct evidence of fierce theological debate and of an alternative tradition within early Christianity—a kind of mystical variant, much like the Zen tradition in Buddhism, Kabbalah in Judaism, Sufism in Islam. What was more, Pagels argued, the early Church Fathers, in their attempt to eliminate this more experiential Christianity in favor of building an orthodox institution—a universal, or catholic, church—declared the texts to be heretical. The Gnostics may well have buried the texts to avoid brutal purges being led by the notorious Bishop of Alexandria, Athanasius, in the year 367. Although many of the stories in what became the New Testament—the Virgin Birth, the Resurrection of Christ—are at least as strange as anything in the Gnostic texts, the Church leaders canonized the Gospels attributed to Mark, Matthew, Luke, and John as a reliable basis for a social organization with mass appeal. Gnosticism, with its emphasis on individual divinity and unmediated personal communion, was a threat to the authority of bishops and priests. Its suggestion, for instance, that the Resurrection of Jesus was a mythological vision, rather than, as the Synoptic Gospels assert, a historical event, was intolerable, and so was the Gnostic notion that God was both father and mother of Jesus. Thus, in the second century an orthodoxy began to take shape—and, with it, a temperament. Irenaeus, the orthodox Bishop of Lyons and one of the leading crusaders against the Gnostics, declared that, while certain heretics "boast that they possess more gospels than there really are," no Church leader may, "however highly gifted he may be in matters of eloquence, teach doctrines different from these."

The Gnostic Gospels won the National Book Award, the National Book Critics Circle Award, and the praise of Pagels's professional colleagues. Harold Bloom, a literary critic with a minor in Gnosticism, credited Pagels (in *The Washington Post*) with "devoted and sound scholarship"; reviewers remarked on her skills as an artful, concise explainer. She had, remarkably, delivered a complicated argument to a popular audience without cheating the demands of scholarship.

In the years that followed the success of *The Gnostic Gospels,* Elaine Pagels seemed to lead a life of invariable good fortune. Her professional future was limitless, her personal life a source of pleasure and vitality. Her marriage, to the physicist Heinz Pagels, was a match of intellect and spirit. Heinz Pagels was a research scientist, a writer, the executive director of the New York Academy of Sciences, a human rights activist, and a famously charming raconteur. "In a way, they were a perfect couple," Elizabeth Diggs, a playwright and one of Elaine's closest friends, recalls. "Heinz was tall, blond, fabulously good-looking. He was brilliant, and he was good. He had flaws—he could be a name-dropper—but he was a good, deeply moral man. Heinz had more passion and love of the world than almost anyone else I've ever known. He was a perfect foil to Elaine. He adored Elaine and completely supported her. He more than supported her—he championed her."

In 1980, Elaine gave birth to a son, Mark. When Mark was two, he was diagnosed with a respiratory ailment that would inevitably shorten his life; this knowledge haunted the family, yet they lived a nearly ideal existence. Elaine began work on a study of the Adam and Eve story and the way Augustine of Hippo had reinterpreted it in the fourth century as a parable of inherent sinfulness rather than of human freedom. Heinz became increasingly involved in writing popular books about physics and in studying the emerging field of complexity theory. Mark grew up a radiant and preternaturally intelligent little boy, who went everywhere in New York with his parents (often on Heinz's shoulders): to the Hayden Planetarium and the Museum of Natural History, to the ships docked along the Hudson, to the galleries in the East Village. In 1986, Elaine and Heinz adopted a second child, a girl named Sarah.

On April 10, 1987, Mark Pagels died, at the age of six and a half. As he got older, his lungs had failed to grow properly and had lost their elasticity. By the time Elaine finished the manuscript of *Adam, Eve, and the Serpent* and Heinz finished his study of complexity theory, *The Dreams of Reason,* they found themselves dedicating their books to the memory of their son. Friends remember coming out of the funeral service, at the Church of the Heavenly Rest, on Fifth Avenue, and seeing men and women weeping openly as they went down the steps. "I've been to God knows how many funerals and yet this one seemed to break everyone's heart," one friend said.

For the next year, Elaine and Heinz plunged into an unthinkable grief, an ache worthy of Job. "Raw absence, sadness, dumb grief," Elaine called it later. But they refused to succumb to despair. They still had their daughter, Sarah, and after about a year had passed they adopted a son—David. Heinz, especially, provided a spirit and a perspective that helped move the family forward. In *The Cosmic Code,* a study of modern physics, published in 1982, he concluded with a joyful meditation on the pleasure of understanding, even in the face of death, some of the structures and the logic of the universe:

> I used to climb mountains in snow and ice, hanging onto the sides of great rocks. I was describing one of my adventures to an older friend once, and when I had finished he asked me, "Why do you want to kill yourself?" I protested. I told him that the rewards I wanted were of sight, of pleasure, of the thrill of pitting my body and my skills against nature. My friend replied, "When you are as old as I am you will see that you are trying to kill yourself."
>
> I often dream about falling. Such dreams are commonplace to the ambitious or those who climb mountains. Lately I dreamed I was clutching at the face of a rock but it would not hold. Gravel gave way. I grasped for a shrub, but it pulled loose, and in cold terror I fell into the abyss. Suddenly I realized that my fall was relative; there was no bottom and no end. A feeling of pleasure overcame me. I realized that what I embody, the principle of life, cannot be destroyed. It is written into the cosmic code, the order of the universe. As I continued to fall in the dark void, embraced by the vault of the heavens, I sang to the beauty of the stars and made my peace with the darkness.

By the beginning of the summer of 1988, friends began to think that Heinz and Elaine were starting to emerge from the shock of their first child's death. That June, the family went to Aspen, where Heinz could work at the Center for Physics, Elaine could read, and they and the children could relax together. Seth Lloyd, a young physicist who was working with Heinz on complexity theory, recalled that the summer started out with an aura of promise. "Elaine and Heinz were really looking happy," he said. "It seemed as if they'd finally made it to the other side."

In Aspen, Heinz and, sometimes, Elaine took long hikes in the hills and the mountains. On the morning of July 24, Heinz and Seth went for a long trek up Pyramid Peak, a fourteen-thousand-foot mountain in the Elk Range, outside the town. Elaine stayed behind. Seth was an experienced climber, but he had never been up Pyramid Peak. Heinz had, and he took the lead. "The only reason there is any danger on Pyramid Peak is that there is the danger of crumbling, falling rock," Lloyd said. "Otherwise, it's really more of a hike than a climb. It's only in the last thousand feet that you have to use your hands. At around midday, we made it to the top and hung around there for about an hour. It was a nice day, with long, clear views. We ate our lunch. Then we started down."

As a child, Heinz had suffered from polio. The condition had left him with weakened ankles, but outward signs of that weakness were slight. Once in a while, climbing or just walking down the street, he would stumble, but not very often. He wore ordinary hiking boots on the climb up Pyramid Peak. "We'd come down a half mile, maybe four hundred vertical feet from the top, and then we came to a tricky bit on a ledge with a deep drop below," Lloyd went on. "Heinz was in front. At the end of the ledge, there's a spot where you have to hop onto a saddle, a little ridge. It's a hop of a couple of feet—nothing that a kid couldn't do, really—but Heinz had those weak ankles, and as he landed on the ledge his ankle gave out. He slipped and he fell. That's all it was—a slip. Heinz slid down a kind of rock chute into a narrow ravine and out of sight. He was trying to save himself, but there was nothing for him to grab onto." Three hours after the fall, a mountain-rescue team found Heinz Pagels's body two thousand feet below the point of his fall. He was forty-nine years old.

Soon, Elaine Pagels will publish a new book, *The Origin of Satan*. Characteristically brief and lucid, it is an attempt to describe the evolving shape of the Devil in the sacred Judeo-Christian literature and the rise of demonization, a practice that has haunted two thousand years of history. For Pagels, demonization is a crucial and terrifying component of Christianity. What began as a minority sect's rhetorical strategy, a way of defining and asserting itself, became a majority religion's moral, and even psychological, justification for persecution: first of Jews, then of Romans and of heretics—of all opponents, real or imagined.

Pagels, like many other scholars, begins with the observation that, although all kinds of angels frequent the Hebrew Bible, demonic beings are nearly absent; there are agents of obstruction in the Book of Job and in Numbers, for example, but they are still members of the heavenly court. This changes with the rise of sectarianism. To two first-century Jewish sects—the Essenes (who died out and became a historical curiosity) and the followers of Jesus (who flourished)—figures called, variously, Satan or Belial or Beelzebub, who would shatter the unity of the heavenly court, appear as the great Other in a cosmic war. Pagels outlines the way the four Gospel writers, who probably wrote between the years 60 and 70, just after the Roman destruction of the Temple of Jerusalem and the dispersion of the Jewish people, shaped their stories and imagery to unify the Jewish followers of Jesus. The typology of God and Satan, Us and Them, appears. Although the Gospels tell a story of the moral genius of Jesus—his lessons of charity, redemption, and love—they also tell a parallel story in which the enemies of Jesus threaten tribal unity on earth and are, moreover, incarnations of Satan. This second story, in which the Gospel writers create a psychology of cosmic war, has influenced the course—the tragic course—of Western history.

Pagels begins with the details of the text to chart the appearance of Satan. The Gospel of Mark, for example, deviates from Jewish tradition and describes (3:23–27) the ministry of Jesus in constant battle with the "kingdom" of Satan. For the Gospel writers, the first enemy was "the intimate enemy"—the majority of their fellow Jews, who did not follow Christ. The creation of such a powerful Satan in the orthodox Christian cosmology becomes not only a foundation for anti-Semitism but also a pattern of viewing the world. "Such visions have been incorporated into Christian tradition and have served, among other things, to confirm for Christians their own identification with God and to demonize their opponents—first other Jews, then pagans, and later dissident Christians called heretics," Pagels writes. This apocalyptic vision, in which victory is assured to those who stand on the side of Christ, "has taught even secular-minded people to interpret the history of Western culture as a moral history in which the forces of good contend against the forces of evil in the world." Demonization is crucial to the language and thinking of fundamentalists, from Pat Robertson to the ayatollahs; during the Gulf War, it was present in the rhetoric of both Saddam Hussein and George Bush. Demonization is also present even in secular fundamentalisms: Lenin's rhetoric, his prediction of a global victory over the capitalist infidels, borrows from the religious tradition he promised to bury.

Curiously, *The Origin of Satan* begins with a nakedly personal moment, a hint of the way Pagels transformed pain into scholarship: "In 1988, when my husband of twenty years died in a hiking accident, I became aware that, like many people who grieve, I was living in the presence of an invisible being—living, that is, with a vivid sense of someone who had died." It is a tantalizing moment, but, just as quickly as Pagels opens the curtain on her creative process in *The Origin of Satan,* she rings it shut.

When I first met Pagels, she reminded me of a caricature Einstein—the dreamy academic heading down Nassau Street, his keys falling out of one pocket, a pen leaking in the other. Pagels, too, presents a deceptively absentminded face to the world. Because she is forever rushing from one commitment to another, she is often late, forgetting things, dropping things, a little helpless. Her acquaintance with the world of the ordinary seems, at times, unsure. When we traveled together from Princeton to Harvard, train schedules and airport gates seemed to baffle her. In a retro sort of way, she invites help. You can't resist carrying her bag, or checking her forehead to see if she has a fever. And yet she is enormously strong. Pagels not only survived two tragedies in the space of fifteen months but since then has written another book, reared her children, taught her many students. She is, by all reports, a good colleague, a devoted friend. Her mind is quick and generous. At fifty-two, she has a mild, earnest appearance (a rounded, friendly face, windblown blond hair), and yet in conversation she is absolutely fierce, focused, picking apart the careless question, delighted by the unexpected one. When she delivers her lectures for an undergraduate course on the New Testament—Monday and Wednesday mornings at ten—she does not so much pace the room as prowl it. Pagels radiates so much intensity that you somehow imagine a fast-burning cigarette in her hand. There is none. She does not smoke. She smolders.

"At one point in my life, I had to make a decision," Pagels told me one day as I raced after her, past a "Don't Walk" sign and into the street. (We narrowly missed being hit by a maroon minivan doing about thirty miles an hour.) "I had to decide whether to have too little or too much in my life," she went on. "Study, children, friends, travel—all of it. That was an easy one. I chose too much."

After reading the manuscript of *The Origin of Satan,* I asked her how the death of her husband and her child could possibly have led her to a study of the Devil.

"The tragedy—the *tragedies*—were absolutely devastating, unimaginable," she began. Her voice was even, deliberate. "You're just beginning to think you can get through one tragedy and start again and then this hits—Heinz's death. David was three months old and Sarah was two and a half when Heinz died. The thought of raising these children without him was inconceivable. But the question was: Can you get through? I found that in times of grief the Church has little to say. It's just too remote. The meditation techniques I'd learned from Trappist monks in Colorado were more useful. But just to imagine doing anything was so hard. I withdrew from teaching and went for a year to the Institute for Advanced Study. Mostly, I spent time with my children and my friends, reading, listening to music."

After a brief pause, she went on, "When two things like that happen, you wonder, How can I cope? You wonder, What ever happened to a sense of proportion in the universe? But the universe, of course, is not about that. Heinz had a sense of all this. His work was all about chaos—chaos theory. But in me—even in me, who was raised by a nonbeliever—there was a subliminal perception of a morally ordered universe. Look at the story of Sodom and Gomorrah in the Hebrew Bible. It is a story about how a feature of the natural universe, a volcano, destroyed two towns. The writer tries to describe how every one of the men in these towns was evil and therefore they were all destroyed by this volcano. But in fact erupting is simply what volcanoes do. They erupt, regardless of whether anyone in their path is good or evil. So I began to think about these stories and these questions, and move myself out of a position of subliminally accepting a position in which a moral order is so present. I began to see and become aware of the extent to which I perceive things through this idea of a universe of good and evil. It didn't matter that I was not a believer in the traditional sense. These stories, whether you believe them literally or not, are shadow images, the mental architecture we live in, and they are pervasive.

"The kind of response that most of us would have to such an event would be as though the event itself were part of a morally ordered universe, as if God had planned it to punish someone. This to me seemed impossible and strange. Nevertheless, it is a pattern that works on you psychologically. The impulse is to ask, Why me? It just couldn't be meaningless, any more than the birth of a wonderful child could be meaningless. I began thinking of how the Greeks and the Romans thought about the forces of nature as powerful forces that were benign or malevolent. They either graced your life or destroyed it, but it was not a matter of intention. Zeus and Apollo and all the rest affected your life, but without thinking about it, without intending to."

After the deaths of Mark and Heinz, Pagels said, she wondered how people dealt with catastrophe, where they focused their anger. "For people more religious—well, some might get angry at God, but that made no sense to me," she said. "In the ancient Church, they got mad at Satan. That seemed to make more sense. And so I had to ask, What is Satan? What's the Devil?"

Elaine Hiesey Pagels grew up in a world in which the idea of such questions—or of studying the history of religion as an academic discipline—was faintly comic. Her father, a professor of biology at Stanford, was Protestant but almost aggressively nonobservant. He considered religion obsolete. In his view, there had been in human history a line of progress from magic to religion and on to science. Partly out of curiosity, partly out of a teenager's search for the precise way to drive her parents crazy, Elaine began going to a local evangelical church when she was thirteen. She succeeded in her rebellion, but stopped going to church a couple of years later, when she decided that the stories and the instructions of the Bible were being understood too literally. Her ambivalence, which persists, is the familiar modern one: a constant wavering between spiritual need or interest and the unwillingness to heed the orthodoxies of any church. Even now, when Pagels is asked whether she is a believer she will answer, "Not exactly," or "Not in the sense that believers mean it," or something of the kind. She is deeply attracted to religious ritual: she has visited a Zen center in San Francisco, watched Hopi snake-dancing rituals in the Southwest. (Nowadays, she even goes regularly to an Episcopal church, "though at first it ran counter to my self-image.") After long thought, she decided, upon graduating from Stanford, to apply for graduate study in religion at Harvard.

"At that time, in the sixties, religion was not considered a fit subject for study by most of my peers," Pagels said when we met at her office in Princeton one afternoon. "Even Heinz, when I got to know him, thought it was a little strange. But I was determined. When I applied to Harvard, they said, 'Wait a year. We've had bad luck with women students. They always quit and get married.' But I wanted to go, so I got my master's degree in Greek in the meantime and then entered the doctoral program in religion at Harvard in 1965. My parents, needless to say, thought this was all a little strange."

Pagels is interested in a range of subjects—poetry, music, modern dance—so I asked her if she had decided to study religion as part of a spiritual quest or as an academic pursuit.

"Well, both, really," she said. "For so many people like me, who are put off by the shape the modern church can take, there is the idea that if you go back to the early Christian Church you'll find some pure golden age, some clear and much simpler version of what later became more complex and amplified. Christians look around the world today and they see Christian Scientists, Roman Catholics, Greek Orthodox, Southern Baptists, Methodists, right-wing Presbyterians, Pentecostalists—and they say that this is a tremendous cacophony of voices, an impossible situation. When I went to graduate school with that rather naive idea, one of my teachers—Krister Stendahl, a former Lutheran bishop—asked me, 'Why have you come?' I said something about finding the essence of Christianity. And he looked at me in a very penetrating way and said, 'How do you know it has an essence?' Then I knew why I had come to graduate school—to be asked that kind of question. But I was looking for some phenomenon that would account for both my fascination with Christianity and my disaffection with its various institutional forms. I thought that it would be way back in the beginning, something pure in its divine revelation. What I found, first of all, is that one cannot get back to that revelation in any form we would agree is pure. In just a generation after Jesus of Nazareth, there are all kinds of refractions, and even more later than that. Not only that but there were refractions and differences in the Gospels themselves. It was a much more complicated picture than I had ever imagined."

Nothing proved to Pagels the complications of early Christianity more decisively than her first encounters with the Gnostic manuscripts. Gnosticism was not by any means unknown in scholarly circles: early Christian orthodox thinkers wrote extensively about Gnosticism, mostly by way of debunking it; writers as diverse as Gibbon, Blake, Melville, and Jung were aware of Gnosticism and interested in it; between the World Wars, the German-born scholar Hans Jonas (among others) wrote about the sources of Gnosticism. But when the Nag Hammadi manuscripts were discovered, in 1945, the concrete proof of Christianity's complications, its diverse forms in those first generations after Christ, became inarguable.

As had been the case with the Dead Sea Scrolls, study of the Nag Hammadi Library languished for years because of confusion, bureaucracy, and academic turf battles. For several years after Muhammad Ali found the manuscripts, they were mainly in the hands of antiquities dealers, who tried to make their fortune from them. Some papers slowly became available to scholars, but mostly they remained scattered. In 1952, the Egyptian government declared the manuscripts national property, yet in that same year a dealer managed to sell an important codex to the Jung Institute, in Zurich. Eventually, this and the rest of the Nag Hammadi Library were returned to Cairo and put in the Coptic Museum. Throughout the fifties, some scholars were allowed to examine the papers, but there was still no formal system of access or publication. Finally, in 1961, the director-general of UNESCO called for the publication of the papers and proposed the establishment of an international scholarly panel to prepare an edition of photographs of them. The first volume of that edition appeared in 1972, and the series was completed in 1977. James Robinson, the director of the Institute for Antiquity and Christianity, who was a member of the UNESCO committee, played an especially heroic role, circulating copies of all the manuscripts privately, so that many scholars had access to them well before official publication.

Pagels was one of the scholars who won access to the Gnostic samizdat. She was thrilled to be among the favored few. Twenty years after the find in upper Egypt, the texts were still a loosely held secret. The first she had heard about the Nag Hammadi find was when she began her graduate studies at Harvard. With the encouragement of her mentor at Harvard, Helmut Koester, she learned Coptic in order to study the manuscripts. In 1970, she completed her doctoral dissertation on the struggle between Gnostic and orthodox Christianity, and in 1975 she went to Cairo to study the documents at first hand. Her experience there was amazing. In the Coptic Museum, she worked at a table, hunched over papyri that seemed to her far more beautiful than any of the photographs she had seen circulating among scholars in the United States; children played nearby and a cleaning woman mopped the floor as Pagels made her way through the Dialogue of the Savior, the Interpretation of Knowledge, the Gospel of Mary, and all the other strange texts of the Gnostics—myths, mystical instructions, creation epics, alternative gospels. Pagels joined an international team of a few dozen scholars which, under Robinson's direction, issued an English edition of the manuscripts—*The Nag Hammadi Library*—in 1977.

"It's funny," she said. "I remember reading that novel by Irving Wallace, *The Word*. It's about someone finding a secret gospel. At the end, it turns out to be something trivial—some sort of Protestant truism, totally boring and disappointing. But when you open the

Gospel of Thomas, which was hidden for so many centuries, it's not trivial at all. You find Jesus speaking cryptically, as in a Zen koan. In the Gospel of Thomas—this is one of my favorite passages—Jesus says, 'If you bring forth what is within you, what you bring forth will save you. If you do not bring forth what is within you, what you do not bring forth will destroy you.' " Many of the Gnostic texts are thought to have been written later than the canonical Gospels. According to Helmut Koester, however, it is quite possible that the Gospel of Thomas, or part of it, may have been written somewhere between the years 50 and 100—that is, as early as, or earlier than, the Gospels of Mark, Matthew, John, and Luke.

To some degree, Pagels's title, *The Gnostic Gospels,* is too loose. Not all the Nag Hammadi papers are Gnostic in origin, and not all are, strictly speaking, gospels. The variety of the texts makes a synthetic analysis quite difficult. But there are texts, such as the Testimony of Truth, that are clearly rivals to the canonical biblical literature. In the Testimony of Truth, for example, the Garden of Eden story is told through the eyes of the serpent—a symbol, in Gnostic literature, of divine wisdom. In this version, the Lord threatens Adam and Eve, while the serpent prods them toward eating the fruit of knowledge. Perhaps the most important feature of the text is that it denies the actuality of the Passion of Christ and attacks the canonical enthusiasm for martyrdom. (In fact, several of the Nag Hammadi texts—the Apocalypse of Peter, the Second Treatise of the Great Seth, the Treatise on the Resurrection—tell the Passion story in far different ways, which suggest that Jesus was not an ordinary human being and that his suffering is not a model for emulation.) The Testimony of Truth mocks "empty" martyrs for their delusions of redemption and mocks thinkers such as Ignatius and Tertullian for welcoming martyrs as an offering to God; such a God, the text says, would be a cannibal.

And yet the orthodox vision of martyrdom, and of Christ as human, prevailed. Why? Pagels writes that the orthodox emphasis on martyrdom was essential to the building of the Church institution in the second century. Church leaders like Ignatius wrote letters about martyrdom to various Church groups at a time of terrible persecution of Christians, for distributing accounts of martyrdom was a way of warning others, closing ranks, and lifting spirits. The Gnostic vision of Jesus as a purely spiritual being, in this case, could serve no such purpose. The Church Fathers were rightly convinced that ordinary human suffering is better validated through the orthodox Christian version of the Jesus story: an ordinary man martyred by his enemies.

Another text that fascinated Pagels was "Thunder: Perfect Mind," a mystical poem spoken in the voice of a female divine:

> *For I am the first and the last.*
> *I am the honored one and the scorned one.*
> *I am the whore and the holy one.*
> *I am the wife and the virgin. . . .*
> *I am the barren one, and many are her sons. . . .*
> *I am the silence that is incomprehensible. . . .*
> *I am the utterance of my name.*

Pagels suggests that this passage represents a tendency in the Gnostic literature to provide for a female aspect in the representations of God. In the Gospel of Philip, the birth of Jesus derives from the unity of the Father of All, a masculine divinity, and the Holy Spirit, a distinctly feminine presence. The text mocks the orthodox notion of Mary's conception of Jesus independent of Joseph: "They do not know what they are saying."

The early-Christian movement showed great openness toward women—Jesus himself flouted Jewish tradition by talking freely with women; women sometimes acted as prophets, apostles, and teachers—and the Gnostics generally affirm that tradition in their texts. But orthodox Christians struck back—and decisively. Once more, Pagels says that the reason for the orthodox victory was as much political as theological. The Church leaders simply would not tolerate what they saw as a feminine interest in Gnostic literature or a position in the Church hierarchy. Tertullian, a great enemy of the Gnostics, was outraged at the idea of women flocking to heretical sects. "These heretical women—how audacious they are!" he wrote. "They have no modesty; they are bold enough to teach, to engage in argument, to enact exorcisms, to undertake cures, and, it may be, even to baptize!" By the year 200, Christian feminism was clearly brought to an end by the text known in the New Testament as Paul's First Epistle to Timothy: "Let a woman learn in silence with all submissiveness. I permit no woman to teach or to have authority over men; she is to keep silent." This consensus of masculine hegemony "has continued to dominate the majority of Christian churches," Pagels wrote. "Nearly 2,000 years later, in 1977, Pope Paul VI, Bishop of Rome, declared that a woman cannot be a priest 'because our Lord was a man'! The Nag Hammadi sources, discovered at a time of contemporary social crises concerning sexual roles, challenge us to reinterpret history—and to reevaluate the present situation."

Pagels determined as she read the Gnostic texts that the Church Fathers feared their strangeness and variety—especially the way they gave individual knowledge and transcendence priority over obedience to a patriarchal orthodoxy. Some of her critics, however, including Raymond E. Brown, a Catholic theologian, believe that Pagels went overboard in her claims for the importance of the Gnostic texts. In a mostly negative assessment in the *Times Book Review,* Brown said that in *The Gnostic Gospels* Pagels gives more than "about nine-tenths" of her discussion to the Gnostics, "which will leave the reader cheering for them and wishing that the narrow-minded orthodox had not won." But in fact, Brown argued, the Gnostics were elitist, and thought of other Christians as ignorant. "Read the texts themselves," Brown wrote, "and you may emerge 'conservative-chic,' concluding that crusty old Irenaeus"—the orthodox Bishop of Lyons—"was right, after all, to regard the gnostics as the crazies of the second century."

For the most part, though, the critical reception was positive, and most accepted Pagels's assurance in the book that she did not intend to proselytize for or celebrate the Gnostics but, rather, to underline the complexity of early Christianity and explain some of the social and political reasons for the rise of an orthodoxy.

"One of the real reasons Elaine's book was a blockbuster was that it shattered the entire premise of the ecumenical movement," Malcolm Diamond, a professor emeritus in the Princeton religion department, has said. "There was this idea that you could get back to the presumed unity of the early Church, get away from the fragmentation in Christendom. What Elaine showed was that there was more fragmentation in the early Church than there is today. That was startling—and it was just one point of many. She wanted to show, through the Gnostic manuscripts, the active role of women in early Christianity and how they were forced out of the governance of the Church. She gave such perspective on the established Gospels and the diverse traditions they competed with. It was her point to go back to that time when you have it all up for grabs and take the competitors seriously and are not just dismissive of it. Her achievement wasn't a matter of discovery so much as it was a novel attitude to noncanonical material."

Not only did *The Gnostic Gospels* gain wide academic and popular audiences but Pagels herself became, through no choice or desire of her own, a kind of spiritual sage for some of her readers. She still gets letters from religious seekers describing their encounters with the Gnostic Gospels; some of the letter writers approach Pagels not as a scholar of ancient texts but as the texts' evangelist or author. "Once in a while, it all gets a little weird," she said, laughing. When *Vogue* asked the actor Harvey Keitel for an interview before the release of *The Piano,* Keitel asked that the interviewer be Elaine

Pagels. *The Gnostic Gospels,* he said, had changed his life. (Pagels, for her part, refused the assignment—"I don't know how to write that way," she says—but she did sit in on the interview, at Keitel's request.) Not long ago, Pagels met a woman who was the head of a Gnostic church in Palo Alto. "I was quite enchanted by her and delighted by her," Pagels told me. "She said she met some people at Orly Airport who told her about an ancient order—the Order of Mary Magdalene.

"But this is serious stuff," Pagels said. "It's fermenting. People are beginning to think about incorporating into the canon elements of Christianity that were lost. There are many people, of course, who have abandoned Christianity altogether and have gone out in search of more experiential modes of access to the divine, like chanting, channeling spirits—you name it. Gnosticism isn't a matter of belief. It's not about that. That's why I think the analogy is with Zen Buddhism, or Buddhism in general. It has to do with dimensions of experience and meditation. It's about practice, spiritual discipline, and the religious imagination. If you look at one of the Gnostic texts, the Discourse on the Eighth and the Ninth, it's a dialogue between a teacher and a student. The student has read all the books, and the teacher says, 'Now you have to go beyond what you've read in the books.' And he tries to take him to a higher level of contemplation, to an ecstatic state through mantras, chanting, and so forth. It's about leaving belief behind; *gnosis* means knowledge, or understanding. I'm not a missionary for Gnosticism, but what interests me about it is that it opens up dimensions other than the ones usually available in churches or on the basis of a statement of faith, which is often a series of propositions that many people do not believe."

Adam, Eve, and the Serpent, which was published in 1988, grew out of *The Gnostic Gospels* and elaborated on the idea of an early pluralistic Christianity. According to Pagels, the Creation story and Adam's defiant decision to eat of the Tree of Knowledge, as it appears in the second and third chapters of Genesis, was widely understood by early Christian thinkers as a parable of human freedom. Such an understanding had a profound influence on behavior: sexuality was without stigma, marriage was considered no less holy than celibacy, divorce was considered a regrettable but tolerable event. In Christianity's early manifestation, as a dissident Jewish sect, Pagels writes, its adherents championed the notion of free will. "So long as Christianity remained a persecuted movement," she wrote, "the majority of Christian preachers proclaimed the plain and powerful message of freedom that appealed to so many people within the Roman world—perhaps especially to those who had never experienced freedom in their everyday lives."

With the conversion of the Roman emperor Constantine in the year 313, and the rise of Christianity as a majority religion, the interpretation of the Creation story—the self-image of Western Christianity itself—changed radically. When the monk Jovinian argued that celibacy was no holier than marriage, he was denounced by the fourth-century theologians Jerome, Ambrose, and Augustine, and was excommunicated. Augustine, whose pagan father had encouraged his youthful sexual adventures, gave up a Christian marriage that would have guaranteed him wealth and social status and adopted a life of asceticism. He wrote about sex in the language of the addict, and, like some recovering addicts, he took an absolutist position: there is no middle ground on the question of lust; self-mastery is impossible; all men and women are fallen. In his interpretation of the second and third chapters of Genesis as the fall of all humankind, Augustine rejected the idea of free will and recoiled from human sexuality as innately sinful. It was Augustine's interpretation, Pagels writes, that became the orthodoxy of the Western church, displacing theologians as prominent as Justin Martyr, Clement of Alexandria, and John Chrysostom. Augustine's interpretation was linked not only to personal experience and thought but to the politics of his day: it proved useful to the emperor. Where once the revolutionary church had preached a message of human freedom in the face of the Roman oppressor, now, as Rome's official religion, it described human nature as inherently sinful, fallen, infirm, and in need of the absolute authority of the state's moral institution, the Church.

One afternoon in Princeton, I asked Pagels why either Augustine's reading of Genesis or the New Testament versions of Satan still matter.

"It's true that many Christians today would say, 'Oh, the Devil, who believes that?'—as if it were a throwaway part of Christianity," Pagels said. "Liberal Christians would say the Devil is irrelevant. But that's not so. The dramatic tension of the whole Jesus story would not work without this figure, because, after all, the story is about the defeat of the Lord. Why did Jesus fail if his failure wasn't due to an enormously strong and evil force? The shape of these stories matters so much to the way we think. The details are essential. Just imagine, it was only about twenty years ago that people began to think that the use of 'he' as a general pronoun might be exclusive of women. At a certain point, one realizes that it does make a difference. It might be a trivial example of the way a culture is formed, even without malice, but it points to the shape of the social order. In the case of 'he,' it points to the efficiency of patriarchy. In my own work, I've never been concerned with changing the language but, rather, with identifying the language—in this case, the language about the Devil—and seeing its effects on the social order. When I was thinking about *Adam, Eve, and the Serpent,* I took notice that there had been all these recent changes in attitudes toward divorce and homosexuality, and yet for a very long time these sexual attitudes of Western culture were just built into the universe. Why? Where does all this come from? Much of what seems to be written into nature itself is a matter of cultural patterning. You don't have to believe in these religions for them to have an effect.

The work is exciting because you begin to uncover what Jungians would call the cultural unconscious.

"What I'm interested in is how these images and stories relate to the way we live. How do we interpret our own lives and understand ourselves through them? How does that imaginative process affect our dreams, how does it appear in our metaphors? How does our imagination of the invisible relate to the way we act and feel and think? With Adam and Eve, it is clear that the social attitudes we have as children are shaped by the story. Satan is a way of perceiving opponents. You may not believe the mythology of such a universe, but it's in you, a background perception."

Pagels lectures at universities all the time, but few appearances have meant more to her than her recent talk on the Satan book at the Harvard Divinity School. Parts of the book have appeared in academic journals, and she has shown the manuscript to some colleagues, but here was a chance to rehearse her arguments in front of a room filled with graduate students and, most important, her former mentors—Helmut Koester, Krister Stendahl, and several other scholars of the New Testament and of early-Christian history. That day, Pagels was getting over a cold passed along to her by her children, and by the time our cab reached Newark Airport she was thinking about turning around and going home. But a few hours later, at the divinity school lectern, she seemed miraculously transformed: healthy and ready for cosmic battle.

Pagels gave her reading of the development of the New Testament Satan and its role in the development of Christian anti-Semitism. The New Testament Gospels, she said, identify Satan not with the Romans (despite the dominant Roman role in the trial and execution of Christ) but, rather, with their Jewish contemporaries—"the intimate enemy." In the Gospel of Matthew (23:13–15), for example, Jesus accuses the Pharisees, the Jewish majority, of being demon-possessed and sons "of hell"; similarly, in the narrative of the Passion, Mark (14:53–64) makes it plain that "the chief priests and elders and the scribes" assembled and "condemned him as deserving death." Mark concludes that the Jewish court, the Sanhedrin, as well as "the crowd"—the Jewish majority—was responsible for the death of Jesus.

The figure of Pontius Pilate, the Roman governor, grows increasingly benign with each successive Gospel; the Jewish enemy is framed in ever more hostile rhetoric. While historical testimonies of the time, from Philo and Josephus, describe Pilate's cruelty in detail, recounting that he would routinely round up Jews suspected of anti-Roman activity, he becomes in the Gospels a nearly sympathetic character, the better to depict the Jews as the satanic agents of Jesus' execution. The social result of this interpretation in the Gospels is that, as the Christian movement became more Gentile, its followers could find canonical justification for the hatred of Jews. At one point, Pagels looked up at the packed auditorium and said, simply, "This material is painful."

By the end of *The Origin of Satan,* it becomes clear that while Pagels does not consider herself an evangelist for Gnostic wisdom, she does in some cases show a clear preference for a Gnostic interpretation over a canonical orthodox one. After expressing her profound regret about how the figure of Satan has distorted human perspective and heightened aggression among peoples, she turns to the Gnostic Gospel of Philip, which, she says, offers a more subtle and promising discussion of good and evil. In the Gospel of Philip, Satan never appears. The message taught is not that there exists an eternal clash between good and evil but, rather, that each individual needs to know his potential for doing evil. "Instead of envisioning the power of evil as an alien force that threatens and invades human beings from outside, the author of Philip urges each person to recognize the evil within, and consciously eradicate it," she writes.

At the conclusion of the lecture, someone made the point that while Satan is a critical figure in the four Gospels, he is almost absent from the other great New Testament literature, the Epistles of Paul, for example. Pagels had no argument with that, but she said to me later on that the Gospels, as literature, have an extraordinary narrative power that the Epistles, for all their theological importance, cannot match. *The Origin of Satan* is, in fact, a one-sided book. Pagels admits as much. Balance is not really her intention; in all her books, she is best at shaking up and rearranging set ways of thinking. She leaves the intellectual tidying up for others. Once the graduate students and the guests had left the hall, Pagels went off to dinner at the faculty club with her mentors and colleagues. She heard a fair amount of criticism. Koester told me later that he saw "loose ends" in the book; Pagels, he said, finds evidence of Satan in texts "where it really isn't there." Stendahl wished that Pagels had covered Paul's Epistles, but he was more enthusiastic. "When the book comes out, there will, of course, be a certain amount of defensiveness," he told me. "People will say she is overdoing it. But I don't think so. Demonization is one of the plagues of religious tradition because you are dealing with an intense rhetoric intensified to the voltage of the divine. My only comments would be that she has not taken account of the countervailing rhetoric and traditions in Christianity: love your enemies, and so on." In fact, at the end of her book, Pagels does mention a tradition of generosity of heart in Christianity that runs from St. Francis of Assisi to the Reverend Martin Luther King, Jr.

After dinner, Pagels felt like talking some more. It was late, and I figured that, what with her cold, the trip, and the long day, she would be exhausted. On the contrary, she said that she felt cured, even charged up, by the lecture and the arguments over dinner.

"After my son died," she said, "I went to the Church of the Heavenly Rest, up on Fifth Avenue, just to see if I could stand to walk in there for the funeral service that would be held a couple of days later. I was with an Israeli friend. It was the Easter season, and I stood there listening to the Good Friday liturgy, all about the death of Jesus, and, probably because my friend is Jewish, I became intensely aware of what was being said. I was taken aback, really distressed, because within that story are these terrible accusations against the Jews about the execution of Jesus. It struck me so deeply, this demonic language. Animosity between groups is a human universal, but what's different here is the moral and religious dimension of the animosity. The Greeks had certain jealousies of the Jews, the Romans had their resentments, but Christianity added this moral and religious dimension."

Back in Princeton a few days later, I asked her if she thought that by publishing *The Origin of Satan* she would have an effect beyond the academy—whether the laying bare of the demonic language in the Gospels would make any change at all in demonization in the modern world.

"When I was talking at Harvard about trying to dislodge the inherited assumption of a structure of right and wrong in the universe, that was something I needed to do because of events in my life," Pagels said. "That doesn't mean I'm relativistic about good and evil. The book is a meditation on the issue of how we *perceive* good and evil. For me, the book moves from a consideration of the social patterning about good and evil to an awareness of the individual's capacity for evil.

"When I read the Gospels now and I come across the figure of Satan, instead of gliding over it as part of the story, I see it as raising a sort of warning flag, and I think, Ah, what is this writer doing now? What is the clue? What group of people are we speaking about and who is saying this? I became really interested in the structure of who is being demonized and who is doing the demonizing. It's a question of awareness instead of just reading the story by rote. When that happens, it changes the way we read our own history. There was a time, for instance, when very few people who didn't suffer from it were aware of racism as an idea. Now this question is a part of our culture. It's not undone, but most people find it impossible to be unaware of racism. The same is true of sexism or homophobia. So that, too, is what the work on Satan and demonization is about. It's about being aware."

Now that Pagels has finished going over the proofs for *The Origin of Satan,* she is starting to consider her next project. This time, she is thinking about the problem of religious participation—the contrast between how people can participate in religious traditions and rituals quite apart from accepting basic propositions of the Church. "What happens with Christians—people brought up nominally as Christians, as I was—they ask themselves, Well, do I really believe that?" Pagels said. "Do I believe that Jesus was the son of God, or whatever. And if they answer the question in the negative, they tend to abandon the tradition. That's quite different from Judaism. You can go to a seder and it doesn't matter if the person next to you is observant or is just home for the holidays. Everybody can participate in the seder, or go to a service. What you think about it or believe about it is not necessarily important. Rather, it's a kind of connection with a community. In a Christian community, that doesn't exist as much. Many people, if they don't believe, leave the religious traditions behind."

Sometimes, in our conversations, I got the feeling that the invisible world is still very much a presence for Pagels. She talks about Heinz often. He is there in her talk and, it seems, in her being. The loss must still be unbearable. At the same time, she told me that for the past few years she had been seeing "a wonderful man," a prominent law professor at Columbia named Kent Greenawalt. Like

Pagels, Greenawalt was widowed six years ago; he has three sons ranging in age from twenty-four to seventeen.

"When you're seeing Elaine now, you're seeing someone who has gone through horrible stuff," her friend Elizabeth Diggs said. "If something terrible happens to you, you can either become heroic in the face of the awfulness of it and end up a better and stronger person or become diminished by it, become a victim and give in to self-pity and rage. After a time, Elaine came out on the other side. She's come out larger and more generous, kinder and more mature."

At the end of my last meeting with Pagels in Princeton, I mentioned what Elizabeth Diggs had said—that she had changed in the years since the deaths of Mark and Heinz. Pagels smiled. "At first, what I really felt had changed was that I unwillingly had to take on many of the tasks that Heinz had taken on in our life together—as a parent, as a provider, as a taxpayer, as an organizer, as the person who takes care of the car," she said. "There are certain ecological structures in any marriage—some with a traditional gender bias and some not. Simply, people take on certain roles. In a way, I had to do everything. But, most of all, I also wanted to take on the challenge of not giving up, of not despairing. Because Heinz was on the side of life. He loved life. He was full of explorative excitement, interest, passion. I realized that it would be no honor to him to say, 'I can't take this, I can't go on, it's too hard.' Somehow, I wanted to take on something of what I'd learned from him, the way he embraced life, with all its dangers and difficulties. I was challenged to do that. I can't say I've done it, but that's what I wanted to do."

The Origin of Satan *was published in June 1995 and was dedicated to the living: "To Sarah and David with love." That same month, Pagels married Kent Greenawalt in an Episcopal church in Princeton. "It's like the beginning of a different life," she said.*

Perfect Pitch

(February 1996)

What gets left of a man amounts to a part.
To his spoken part.
To a part of speech.

A few weeks ago, I turned on the television in Moscow and channel-surfed. A Bruce Lee movie, dubbed. News. All of it bad. A bank ad with a bimbo stroking cash. Joseph Brodsky: bliss.

I'd spent a long day on the campaign trail following Gennady Zyuganov, the witless leader of the Communist party, and, since every poll showed the Reds leading the color war, I had the vertiginous feeling of drifting into a time machine that was tugging me—and, more to the point, Russia—back to what the Party used to call "the shining future." Zyuganov spoke in the cadences and the language of the Central Committee man. Television proved, as it rarely does, a restorative. Brodsky read his poems in a kind of dream voice, the same nasal incantation that stunned his great teacher, Anna Akhmatova, half an age ago in Leningrad. All day, I had been caught between two constituencies: Communists who railed against everything that had changed since 1991 and democrats who argued that nothing had changed. Now here were the face and the voice of a man at liberty: passionate, ironic, weary, not at all well—heading toward one more heart attack, inevitable as Christmas—but free, absolutely free. The tragedy was that he was so far away and was never coming back.

Brodsky died at the criminally early age of fifty-five and will be buried in Venice. A few days before, he had finished work on the galleys of a new collection of poems in English, *So Forth*. He left behind a grown son, Andrei, in St. Petersburg, and, in Brooklyn, his widow, Maria, and their two-year-old daughter, Anna.

Ever since the day in 1972 when Brodsky bowed to the official "request" to leave the country for the West (he had been charged with "social parasitism" and branded a "drone of literature"), people had been constantly asking him about Russia—above all, about his visiting Russia, or even returning home for good. They asked him the same questions on Russian television. They asked him everywhere. He always answered more or less the same way. "I find it hard to imagine myself a visitor and performer touring the country in which I was born and grew up," he said once, in Paris. "That will be one more of the absurdities that my existence, as it is, already has in abundance. While it may still make some sense for a criminal to return to the scene of the crime—if he has some money buried there, let's say—it's basically senseless to return to the scene of love. Of course, I could go there and smile, and say, 'Yes,' and accept congratulations, but the idea of that sort of thing I find terribly unpleasant. I've never allowed—and never will—a lot of fuss to be made about my life. That is, I'll always be opposed to it. . . . If I could just show up there quite suddenly as a private individual and see two or three people . . . On the whole, though, I doubt it."

Brodsky's nonreturn to Russia was in distinct contrast to Aleksandr Solzhenitsyn's return, more than a year ago: his journey began in the Russian Far East and proceeded, via specially outfitted railway car, to Moscow. But while Solzhenitsyn's life is perhaps his greatest work, Brodsky resisted dramatics and mythmaking. He admired Solzhenitsyn, and even called him the Soviet Union's

Homer, but he could not bear that level of political engagement. That was not the issue for him.

A few weeks before Brodsky won the Nobel Prize, in 1987, I met him at his basement apartment, on Morton Street in the Village. It was the start of glasnost. His poems were being published in Russia for the first time in more than two decades. He did not betray an ounce of joy about it. For the regime to publish his work, and the work of all the other banned writers, was to return stolen property to its rightful owner. There was no need to be grateful to the thief. To the Russian language he was loyal, a great lover and craftsman; of Russia he was suspicious to the end.

"I don't believe in that country any longer," Brodsky said as he cradled his cat, Mississippi. "I'm not interested. I'm writing in the language, and I like the language. I really don't know how to explain it to you. Country is . . . it's people, basically. And I'm one of them. And I'm more or less enough for myself. What's happening in Russia now is devoid of autobiographical interest for me. Maybe it's egocentric. Whatever it is, feel free to use it. When Thomas Mann arrived in California from Germany, they asked him about German literature. And he said, 'German literature is where I am.' It's really a bit grand, but if a German can afford it, I can afford it. Now I am quite prepared to die here. It doesn't matter at all. I don't know better places, or perhaps if I do I am not prepared to make a move."

Russian readers—that is, the broad swath known as the intelligentsia—are famously contentious; mention the name of nearly any poet or prose writer and someone at the table will pronounce his work unimportant, or worse. In years of living in Russia and traveling back and forth, I have never heard Brodsky dismissed. Solzhenitsyn, yes; Voinovich, Bitov, Tolstaya, yes; never Brodsky. A few might complain that Brodsky was insufficiently Russian, as much a part of world literature as of the Russian pantheon, but that was all. The literary critic Andrei Zorin once told me, "I think I have memorized more Brodsky than I have Pushkin, which is saying something." Zorin is not alone.

The shame of it is that in English, a language that Brodsky loved and mastered, his poems are too often ruins of their real selves, or, at best, simulacra. Here and there are well-rendered translations, but very few even hint at his technical skill, his internal rhymes and wordplay, his wit. Yevgeny Rein, a distinguished poet himself, said one afternoon in Moscow, "America will just have to take our word for it: Brodsky is the great Russian voice of his time. He came from the generation that followed the camps and the blockade, the generation that fed itself on literature when there was nothing but a void. And he was always the best of us."

Brodsky was born in Leningrad in 1940. His father was a news photographer. His parents were Jews—assimilated, but not sufficiently so to make anti-Semitism any less a feature of life. The family lived in one and a half rooms of a communal apartment, the same place where the Symbolist poet Zinaida Gippius lived, and from which she shouted out abuse at the revolutionaries on the street. During the nine-hundred-day siege of the city in the Second World War, Brodsky's father was fighting the Nazis, and he and his mother, like so many Leningraders, nearly starved.

As a schoolboy, Brodsky was bookish and sullen, a red-haired rebel, though his anger was directed less at ideology than at the sheer drabness of Soviet culture and the ubiquity of the image of the Leader. "There was baby Lenin, looking like a cherub in his blond curls," Brodsky wrote in a memoir of his youth. "Then Lenin in his twenties and thirties, bald and uptight, with that meaningless expression on his face which could be mistaken for anything, preferably a sense of purpose. This face in some way haunts every Russian and suggests some sort of standard for human appearance because it is utterly lacking in character." Trying to ignore those images, he wrote, was his "first attempt at estrangement."

Stalin died in 1953. Brodsky was twelve. He and his schoolmates were called into the auditorium, and the "class mentor" gave them the news. "She began a funeral oration," Brodsky told the writer Solomon Volkov, "and suddenly cried out in a wild voice: 'On your knees! On your knees!' Pandemonium broke out. Everyone was howling and weeping and it was somehow expected of me to cry, too, but—to my shame then; now, I think, to my honor—I couldn't. When I got home, my mother was also crying. I looked at her with some astonishment, until my father suddenly gave me a wink. Then I realized for sure that there was no particular reason for me to get upset over Stalin's death."

Brodsky's estrangement from the state ripened in adolescence, and at fifteen he dropped out of school. Between 1956 and 1962, he held thirteen jobs. He worked as a milling-machine operator at a defense plant and as a stoker in a boiler room; he traveled with geological expeditions to the Chinese border, to Siberia, to the top of a glacier. He even worked as an assistant in the dissecting room of a hospital morgue, slicing up corpses, scooping out the organs, and stitching up the skin. "You know, I rather liked that job," Brodsky told me. "It was a shame to quit that one, *ya?*"

In his late teens, Brodsky started writing poems, and he fell in with a group of young writers that included Yevgeny Rein, Dmitri Bobyshev, and Anatoly Naiman. "The idea of individualism, of a man on his own, all by himself, was our proud property," Brodsky wrote many years later. "But the possibility of realizing it was minuscule, if it existed at all." The only path was literature and the private experience of reading. The poets' rebellion against tyranny consisted of almost total submersion in language—in Pushkin and Baratynsky, Mandelstam and Tsvetayeva, Pasternak and Akhmatova. Brodsky learned Polish and, in particular, English. It was not easy to get hold of English-language books, and two that he eventually managed to find, poetry anthologies edited by Oscar Williams and Louis Untermeyer, were precious; both contained tiny black-and-white photographs of his heroes—above all, Auden, Frost, and Hardy—and from those tiny images he tried to imagine them, their personalities, their voices.

In 1961, Rein, the eldest of the group, brought Brodsky to see Akhmatova, who at the time was the greatest living poet in Russia, a *grande dame*—"the keening muse," he later called her. Brodsky recited some of his poems for her, and she took a liking to him. She practically adopted the group—her "magic choir"—and was especially adoring of, and worried about, Joseph. Akhmatova, writing in 1962, foresaw a tragic fate for him:

> *I don't weep for myself now,*
> *But let me not be on earth to witness*
> *The golden stamp of failure*
> *On this yet untroubled brow.*

By 1963, Khrushchev had reversed the thaw. Sensing the suicidal implications of an open society, the Soviet leadership began a neo-Stalinist phase that lasted twenty-odd years. Even now, some historians wonder why the regime began its cultural crackdown by arresting a little-known twenty-three-year-old poet. But it is a mystery only if one doubts tyranny's instinct for sniffing out its greatest threat.

Following a Supreme Soviet decree to "intensify" the "struggle" against those without "socially useful work," the Leningrad KGB arrested Brodsky and locked him up in Crosses, a transit prison. According to Efim Etkind's book on the trial, *Protsess Iosifa Brodskogo* ("The Trial of Joseph Brodsky"), the charges included holding a "world view damaging" to the state; "decadence and modernism"; a failure to finish school; and, of course, "parasitism . . . except for the writing of awful poems." An article in the local paper, the *Evening Leningrad,* described Brodsky as a "semiliterary parasite whose pornographic and anti-Soviet poetry" corrupted the young. The article also provided its readers with the information that Brodsky had once tried to steal an airplane and wore "velvet trousers."

A number of artists and writers came to Brodsky's defense, not least Akhmatova, Etkind, Lydia Chukovskaya, and Dmitri Shostakovich. But Brodsky's most important ally was a rather obscure and owlish journalist named Frida Vigdorova, who assigned herself the dangerous task of attending the trial, transcribing what went on, and then spreading the news in samizdat. Her transcriptions are a marvel of the antitotalitarian genre, superior to any of Havel's plays:

THE COURT: What is your work?

BRODSKY: I write poems, I translate. I believe . . .

THE COURT: There will be no "I believe." Stand straight! Don't lean on the wall. Look at the Court. Answer the Court as directed! Now, do you have full-time work?

BRODSKY: I thought that I had full-time work, yes.

THE COURT: Answer precisely!

BRODSKY: I wrote poems. I thought that they would be published. I believe . . .

THE COURT: We are not interested in "I believe." Answer: why were you not working?

BRODSKY: I worked. I wrote poems.

THE COURT: This does not interest us. We are interested in what firm you were connected to.

BRODSKY: I had agreements with a publishing house.

THE COURT: Did your contract provide you with enough to feed yourself? Name them: provide dates, sums.

BRODSKY: I don't remember precisely. My lawyer has the contracts.

THE COURT: I am asking you.

BRODSKY: In Moscow, two books of my translations were published.

THE COURT: What is your work experience?

BRODSKY: More or less . . .

THE COURT: We are not interested in "more or less."

BRODSKY: Five years.

THE COURT: Where did you work?

BRODSKY: In a factory. With geological expeditions . . .

THE COURT: And in general, what is your specialty?

BRODSKY: Poet. Poet and translator.

THE COURT: And who deigned that you are a poet? Who put you in the ranks of the poets?

BRODSKY: Nobody. Who put me in the ranks of mankind?

THE COURT: Did you study for this?

BRODSKY: Study for what?

THE COURT: To become a poet. You never tried to finish college where they prepare . . . where they study . . .

BRODSKY: I didn't think that this was a matter of education.

THE COURT: How is that?

BRODSKY: I thought . . . well, I thought it came from God.

The judge did her best to keep to her script. She badgered Brodsky. She called to the witness stand comrades who, in the style of 1937, were more than willing to testify to Brodsky's sins. One man claimed that his son had fallen under Brodsky's evil spell—had quit work and decided that he, too, was a genius. The same man said that Brodsky's poems—meditations on time and death and love—were somehow anti-Soviet. "Which one?" Brodsky interrupted. "Name one!" Of course, the man could not. No one had prepped him for that.

Vigdorova wrote a letter to Chukovskaya about Brodsky's trial. "Perhaps one day he will become a great poet," she said, "but I will never forget how he looked—helpless, with an expression of astonishment, irony, and challenge all at the same time."

"The lot had fallen on him by chance," Etkind wrote. "There were many other talented poets at the time who might have been in his place. But once the lot fell upon him he understood the responsibility of his position—he was no longer a private person but had become a symbol, the way Akhmatova had been in 1946, when she was picked out of hundreds of possible poets to be punished and became a national symbol of the Russian poet, as Brodsky had become that day. It was hard for Brodsky—he had bad nerves, a bad heart. But he played his role in the trial impeccably."

In the end, Brodsky was sentenced to five years in internal exile. He worked in the northern village of Norinskaya, in the bogs near the White Sea. Only Akhmatova, who had been through so much more, who had lost so much family, so many friends, in the meat grinder of the Lenin and Stalin years, could manage a smile and the crack "What a biography they're creating for our redhead! You'd think he hired them."

When I asked Brodsky about his time in internal exile, he told me that he had actually enjoyed it. He enjoyed pulling on his boots and working on a collective farm, enjoyed shoveling manure. Knowing that everyone else across Russia was shoveling shit, too, he felt a sense of nation, of kinship. He was not kidding. In the evenings, sitting in his shack, Brodsky had time to write his "awful poems" and indulge himself in the "bourgeois formalism" of his idols. Two stanzas of Auden struck him to the core:

> *Time that is intolerant*
> *Of the brave and innocent,*
> *And indifferent in a week*
> *To a beautiful physique,*
>
> *Worships language and forgives*
> *Everyone by whom it lives;*
> *Pardons cowardice, conceit,*
> *Lays its honours at their feet.*

Brodsky was affected not merely by the way Auden imparted wisdom—tossing it off as if it were folklore—but by the wisdom itself, the idea that language is superior, is more ancient and enduring than everything else, that even time bows before it. Brodsky made that a dominant theme of his poetry, and a central principle of his prose and his teaching.

Sitting in his shack, smoking, his back aching from the pitchfork, dung on his boots, the reek of the bog still on his clothes, Brodsky could not imagine that twenty years later, dressed in fine and odorless cloth, he would step to the lectern at the Swedish Academy, in Stockholm, and, by way of accepting the grandest prize in literature, declare the primacy of literature, not as entertainment or instruction but as the concentrated moral imperative of mankind. If his life's work had a singular message, it was what he learned in the stanzas of Auden:

> The revulsion, irony, or indifference often expressed by literature toward the state is essentially the reaction of the permanent—better yet, the infinite—against the temporary, against the finite. To say the least, as long as the state permits itself to interfere with the affairs of literature, literature has the right to interfere with the affairs of state. A political system, a form of social organization, like any system in general, is by definition a form of the past tense that aspires to impose itself upon the present (and often on the future as well); and a man who works in grammar is the last one who can afford to forget this. The real danger for a writer is not so much the possibility (and often the certainty) of persecution on the part of the state as it is the possibility of finding oneself mesmerized by the state's features, which, whether monstrous or undergoing changes for the better, are always temporary. . . .
>
> Every new aesthetic reality makes one's experience even more private; and this kind of privacy, assuming at times the guise of literary (or some other) taste, can in itself turn out to

be, if not a guarantee, then a form of defense, against enslavement. For a man with taste, particularly with literary taste, is less susceptible to the refrains and the rhythmical incantations peculiar to any version of political demagogy. The point is not so much that virtue does not constitute a guarantee for producing a masterpiece as that evil, especially political evil, is always a bad stylist. . . . It is precisely in this applied, rather than Platonic, sense that we should understand Dostoevsky's remark that beauty will save the world, or Matthew Arnold's belief that we shall be saved by poetry. It is probably too late for the world, but for the individual man there always remains a chance.

When the Soviet authorities grew tired of the flow of telegrams from abroad, they sent Brodsky home, cutting short his sentence by more than three years. Back in Leningrad, Brodsky began writing some of the strongest poetry of his career. By thirty, he was assuring for himself a permanent place in the Russian—and international— pantheon. The KGB, a keen critic but a poor judge of character, offered to arrange a publication deal for Brodsky if he would collaborate. He refused. He was not published. In May 1972, the visa department of the local police suggested that he apply to leave the country immediately, according to Volkov's book *St. Petersburg*.

"And if I refuse?" he said.

"Then, Brodsky, in the very near future you will have a very hot time."

Before leaving, Brodsky wrote a letter to the Party's general secretary, Leonid Brezhnev. "I am bitter to have to leave Russia. I was born here, grew up here, lived here, and everything I have in my soul I owe to it," he wrote. "Once I stop being a citizen of the USSR I will not stop being a Russian poet. I believe I will return; poets always return—in the flesh or on paper. . . . We are all condemned to the same thing: death. I, who am writing these lines, will die, and you, who are reading them, will die, too. Our work will be left, but even that will not last forever. That is why no one should interfere with another in doing his work." There is no evidence that Brezhnev read the letter. There was no response.

Brodsky left Russia on a plane for Austria with his typewriter (which the KGB kindly disassembled for him at the airport), a change of clothes, a volume of Donne, and a bottle of vodka—a present for Wystan Auden. In Austria, he met his hero, who was kind to him and happily drank the vodka. A young professor of Russian literature at the University of Michigan, Carl Proffer, the only Virgil Brodsky would ever need in the West, suggested that he come to Ann Arbor. Brodsky thought, What the hell, let the change be one hundred percent, and agreed:

> *And as for where in space and time one's toe end touches,*
> *well, earth is hard all over; try the States.*

Brodsky tried the States, first Michigan, then New York. He may well be the most successful exile of his time. As a poet, he was not slowed down or disoriented by the English in the air. He said that he rejected the bravura multilingualism of Nabokov, but ("What the hell, *ya?*") he wrote most of the essays in *Less Than One* and *On Grief and Reason* in English. He said that it was faster that way. He taught at Michigan and Mount Holyoke, and, despite an outer shell of put-upon irony, proved generous to young writers. He fell in (and sometimes out) with, in no particular order, Derek Walcott, Seamus Heaney, Susan Sontag, Richard Wilbur, Mikhail Baryshnikov, Anthony Hecht, Isaiah Berlin, Mark Strand, Robert Silvers, Roger Straus. He married Maria Sozzani, a younger woman, half Italian, half Russian, a serene beauty out of Fra Angelico. They moved to Brooklyn Heights and had a daughter. In 1991, Brodsky was Poet Laureate and, in an address at the Library of Congress, suggested that the government help subsidize the publication of an anthology of American poetry to be sold door to door or in drugstores, to be placed in motel rooms next to the Gideon Bible. (Such a program, in nonprofit form, has begun, if more modestly.) "American poetry is this country's greatest patrimony," he said. "It takes a stranger to see some things clearly. This is one of them, and I am that stranger. Fifty million copies of an anthology of American poetry for two dollars a copy can be sold in a country of two hundred and fifty million. Perhaps not at once, but gradually, over a decade or so, they will sell. Books find their readers. And if they will not sell, well, let them lie around, absorb dust, rot, and disintegrate. There is always going to be a child who will fish a book out of the garbage heap. I was such a child, for what it's worth."

Brodsky was unlucky with his health, and more than a little foolish about it. He had open-heart surgery twice and was facing a third operation. He smoked more cigarettes than Bogart, drank more coffee than Balzac. When I was with him one afternoon, interviewing him for *The Washington Post,* a photographer arrived. "Do you have cigarettes?" Brodsky said by way of hello. "I am dying for cigarettes."

He refused the role of celebrity-martyr and did his work, but in those moments when he was called on by fate to step forward—in the courtroom, in exile—he did so with perfect pitch. Nadezhda Mandelstam, in her memoir *Hope Abandoned,* wrote that Brodsky was "a remarkable young man who will come to a bad end, I fear." Joseph Brodsky is ended, it is true, but Mandelstam was wrong. He died with his work finished and published in the languages that mattered to him, and he died in a place that was home, or home enough. It was language, not biography, for him: the lyric, not the epic. There was never any reason to return to St. Petersburg:

> *Having sampled two*
> *oceans as well as continents, I feel that I know*
> *what the globe itself must feel: there's nowhere to go.*
> *Elsewhere is nothing more than a far-flung strew*
> *of stars, burning away.*

—⟨⟨⟩⟩—

Visible Man

(March 1994)

In a modest apartment overlooking the Hudson, at the weld of northern Harlem and southern Washington Heights, Ralph Ellison confronts his "work in progress." He has been at this for nearly forty years, and rare is the day that he does not doubt his progress. He wakes early, goes out to buy a paper on Broadway, returns, and, when he has exhausted the possibilities of the *Times* and the *Today* show, when the coffee and the toast are gone, he flicks on the computer in his study and reads the passage he finished the day before. "The hardest part of the morning is that first hour, just getting the rhythm," Ellison says. "So much depends on continuity. I'll go back to get a sense of its rhythm and see what it will suggest, and go on from there. But very often I'll start in the morning by looking back at the work from the day before and it ain't worth a damn." When that happens, as it does more frequently than he would like, Ellison will turn away and stare out the window, watching the river flow.

Ralph Ellison turned eighty on March 1, 1994, and his peculiarly modern burden, the burden of a second act, grows heavier with age. The man is far too composed, too regal, to betray the weight of it, but the soul must weary of its persistence. So great was the celebration in 1952 for his first (and only) novel, *Invisible Man,* that the sound of critical applause, rattling medals, and whispered expectations took years to fade. Few novels have ever entered the canon so quickly. Ellison won the National Book Award, the Presidential Medal of Freedom, the Chevalier de l'Ordre des Artes et Lettres, a place in the American Academy of Arts and Letters, and a position at New York University as Albert Schweitzer Professor of Humanities. Here and there, critics' and readers' polls would declare *Invisible Man* the greatest American novel of the postwar period or of the century. Ellison's rite-of-passage novel absorbed everything from black folklore to Dostoevsky's *Notes from Underground,* creating something entirely new, lasting, and American. It was translated into seventeen languages, and the Modern Library produced an edition. But at the end of all this lingered the nervous, American question: What's next?

Ellison did not intend to distinguish his career with such an austerity of publication. By 1955, he had begun a novel set mainly in the South and in Washington, D.C. At the center of the story—as far as we know it from a few published extracts—are the community and the language of the black church and the relationship between a black preacher and a friend who eventually becomes a senator and a notorious racist. After a few years of writing, Ellison was not shy about showing excerpts to friends like Saul Bellow and the novelist and cultural historian Albert Murray. He was not reluctant to publish a piece here and there in literary quarterlies.

For a while, expectations for the book soared. "I shared a house with Ralph in the late fifties in Tivoli, New York, along the Hudson in Dutchess County," Bellow says. "At that time, he was hard at work on the book, and he let me read a considerable portion of it—a couple of hundred pages, at least, as I remember. We were running a magazine at the time called *The Noble Savage,* and we published an excerpt of Ralph's manuscript called 'Cadillac Flambé.' But all of it was marvelous stuff, easily on a level with *Invisible Man.*"

A couple of weeks before his birthday, I called on Ellison at his home. The apartment was lined and stacked with books. Here and there were African sculptures and piles of papers, mostly correspondence. As he and his wife, Fanny, showed me around, a small cloud of cigar smoke still hovered over his computer in the study. Slender and graceful, with the courtly elegance of his friend Duke Ellington, Ellison looked fifteen years younger than he was; a man of old-fashioned southern grace, he was polite in the high style, careful in conversation almost to the point of deliberate, if ironic, dullness. I said that his friends have often remarked on the gap in style between the turbulence of *Invisible Man* and the reserve of its author.

"Well, one inherits a style from the people one grows up with," Ellison said, referring to his childhood in Oklahoma, which was segregated at the time but had never been a slave state. He studied composition at Booker T. Washington's Tuskegee Institute, in Macon County, Alabama—and was the intellectual star of his class—before coming to New York, in 1937. "I am rather passionate about some of the inequities that are part of the country," he went on. "But why should a writer be different? No one asks a surgeon to be different. He has to be a surgeon first. He has to know the techniques and traditions of surgery. That's how I approach writing. I would do the same thing if I were an opera singer. Black opera singers have to master the tradition. We all have at least double identities."

For a while, Ellison skated amiably, and elliptically, around various questions of the day, but when the subject turned to his work in progress, the book that Bellow had remembered so vividly, the one that Albert Murray used to hear Ellison read aloud from, he seemed, at first, a little startled. Then, as he described a fire two decades ago at his old summer house, in Plainfield, Massachusetts, he slumped back in his chair, resigned, his voice lowering into a growly whisper. "There was, of course, a traumatic event involved with the book," he began. "We lost a summer house and, with it, a good part of the novel. It wasn't the entire manuscript, but it was over three hundred and sixty pages. There was no copy. We had stayed up in the country into November, in the Berkshires. We went to do some shopping and came back and the house was burning. An electrical failure. And, being in the country with a little volunteer fire department—well, they were off fighting another fire and didn't make it. They never got it put out. It all burned down. They came and tried, but in the country it's difficult to get water, especially there."

Ellison's friends say that it was years before he went back to work on the novel; some say three or four, others five or six. Albert Murray, who lives across town, off Lenox Avenue, and has known Ellison since they were students together at Tuskegee, had told me, "Ralph was just devastated. He just closed in on himself for a long time. He didn't see anyone or go anywhere. At a certain point, you knew not to say much about it. A wall, Ralph's reserve, went up all around him." Ellison was reduced to trying to summon up his novel from memory or from the memories of those who had read it or heard him read it.

When I asked Ellison how much time he lost, he was quiet for a while, and then he said, in a tone that suggested we were talking about someone else and the question was merely *interesting,* "You know, I'm not sure. It's kind of blurred for me. But the novel has got my attention now. I work every day, so there will be something very soon. After the fire, I had certain notes here in the city and a pretty good idea of where I wanted to go. Snatches of it had been published. And I did a lot of teaching after that. Let's say I was disoriented, but I worked on it. I don't know how long the interruption was. Maybe four or five years. It wasn't as if I weren't working. I was trying to reimagine the situation. The characters are the same and the mixture of language is the same. But nuances are different. After all, when I write I am discovering things. One development suggests another, a phrase will reveal things. You just try to get through it.

"Letting go of the book is difficult, because I'm so uncertain. I want it to be of quality. With *Invisible Man,* I wasn't all that certain, but I had friends like Stanley Edgar Hyman, who worked on *The New Yorker,* and who was invaluable to me. There's a photograph of Stanley reading *Invisible Man* in Francis Steegmuller's office. I'll always remember: he looked up at me and said, 'Say, this thing is funny!' When you are younger, you are so eager to be published. I am eager to publish this book. That's why I stay here, and not in the country. I'm eager to finish it and see how it turns out."

Ellison's readers can be greedy and hope for more novels and essays—come to think of it, a memoir would be nice, too—but what's done is done and, in a sense, is more than enough. On the occasion of his eightieth birthday, it was clearer than ever that *Invisible Man* and his two collections of essays, *Shadow and Act* (1964) and *Going to the Territory* (1986), are the ur-texts for a loose coalition of black American intellectuals who represent an integrationist vision of the country's history and culture. Ellison's books are a foundation for talents as various as the novelists Charles Johnson, John Edgar Wideman, Leon Forrest, and James Alan McPherson; the critics Shelby Steele, Henry Louis Gates, Jr., and Stanley Crouch; the poet Michael S. Harper. When Johnson, for instance, received the National Book Award, in 1990, for his novel *Middle Passage,* he devoted his entire acceptance speech to a celebration of Ellison. Johnson said he hoped that the 1990s would see the emergence of a "black American fiction" that takes Ellison as its inspiration, "one that enables us as a people—as a culture—to move from narrow complaint to broad celebration."

The publication of *Invisible Man* predates the civil rights movement of the 1960s, the drama of Malcolm X, and the rise of Afrocentrism, and yet it anticipates, or answers, all of these. The dema-gogic figure of Ras the Destroyer in the novel is based, no doubt, on Marcus Garvey, but it turns out to be a prescient depiction of the Farrakhans to come. The lancing portrait of the Brotherhood was modeled on the Communist party of the 1930s, but it stands for all the doctrinaire utopianism and fakery to come. The metaphor of the paint factory and the mixing of black paint into white antici-pates a sane multiculturalism, a vision of American culture as an inextricable blend. Unlike so much fiction labeled somehow as eth-nic, *Invisible Man* is a universal novel. From the first lines to the very last ("Who knows but that, on the lower frequencies, I speak for you?"), it insists on the widest possible audience.

In Ellison's view, America is not made up of separate, free-floating cultures but, rather, of a constant interplay and exchange. In the essays, he describes slaves on a southern plantation watching white people dance and then transforming those European steps into something that is American; he speaks of what Ella Fitzgerald has done with the songs of Rodgers and Hart, what white rock bands did with the blues; he watches the black kids in Harlem in their baggy hip-hop gear walking down Broadway, and on the same day he sees white suburban kids on television affecting the same style. What Ellison has called the "interchange, appropriation, and integration" of American culture is evident in the music we hear, the games we play, the books we read, the clothes we wear, the food we eat. For him, integration is not merely an aspiration but a given, a fact of cultural and political life. Without pity or excessive pride, Ellison also sketches the facts of his own life—especially his self-discovery, first through music, then literature—to describe the American phenomenon. *Invisible Man* itself looks not only to the experience of Ralph Ellison at Tuskegee Institute or in Harlem but to Ralph Ellison in the library, the young reader that Albert Murray remembers as "always looking to the top shelf." When Ellison finally came to New York, Richard Wright and Langston Hughes became literary mentors and friends, but their influence was secondary, following a youthful tear through Eliot, Pound, Faulkner, Hemingway, Stein, and Dostoevsky. Out of many, one.

Ellison's vision of American life and culture has not always sat well with critics, black or white. For the Black Arts Movement of the 1960s and 1970s, *Invisible Man* and its author lacked the necessary rage. Amiri Baraka (LeRoi Jones) and other nationalists denounced Ellison from platform after platform. And that had its wounding effect, especially in the academy.

In 1969, Charles Johnson dropped by the library at Southern Illinois University's new black studies program. "Where can I find a copy of *Invisible Man?*" he asked the librarian.

"We don't carry it," came the answer.

"Really? Why not?"

"Because Ralph Ellison is not a black writer," the librarian said.

An extreme example, no doubt, but it suggests the climate of the time. "When Ellison got an award in 1965 for the best novel since the Second World War, people were still under the sway of the vision that came from Martin Luther King," Stanley Crouch, the author of *Notes of a Hanging Judge,* told me. "Once the black-power separatist agenda came along, and once white people showed that they preferred some kind of sadomasochistic rhetorical ritual to anything serious, Ellison's position began to lose ground. That's been the central problem in Afro-American affairs since the black-power-cum-Marxist vision took over the discussion. We have had to deal with one or another intellectual fast-food version of that these last twenty-five years or so. What it comes down to is that Ellison perceives Afro-American history in terms of the grand sweep of American life, not in terms of sheer victimhood. And that has been very difficult in the wake of the whole Malcolm X 'You didn't land at Plymouth Rock, Plymouth Rock landed on you' thing."

"Let's face it," Henry Louis Gates, Jr., the chairman of the Afro-American studies program at Harvard, said. "Ellison was shut out, and Richard Wright was elected godfather of the Black Arts Movement of the 1960s, because Wright's hero in *Native Son*, Bigger Thomas, cuts off a white girl's head and stuffs her in a furnace. For Ellison, the revolutionary political act was not separation; it was the staking of a claim for the Negro in the construction of an honestly public American culture. Wright's real message was not that different, but no one wanted to see that."

The resistance to Ellison's vision was by no means limited to black critics. In "Black Boys and Native Sons," an essay published in *Dissent*, Irving Howe adopted a strangely patronizing tone to celebrate Richard Wright's authenticity and to reprimand James Baldwin and Ellison for failing to possess a similar sense of rage. Howe declared himself astonished by "the apparent freedom [*Invisible Man*] displays from the ideological and emotional penalties suffered by Negroes in this country."

Ellison's passionate reply, "The World and the Jug," was published in *The New Leader*, and can be read as a manifesto, a defense of his vision and art, and of the life that created them:

> Evidently Howe feels that unrelieved suffering is the only "real" Negro experience, and that the true Negro writer must be ferocious. But there is also an American Negro tradition which teaches one to deflect racial provocation and to master and contain pain. It is a tradition which abhors as obscene any trading on one's own anguish for gain and sympathy; which springs not from a desire to deny the harshness of existence but from a will to deal with it as men at their best have always done. . . . It would seem to me, therefore, that the question of how the "sociology of his existence" presses upon a Negro writer's work depends upon how much of his life the individual writer is able to transform into art. What moves a writer to eloquence is less meaningful than what he makes of it. . . . One unfamiliar with what Howe stands for would get the impression that when he

looks at a Negro he sees not a human being but an abstract embodiment of living hell. He seems never to have considered that American Negro life (and here he is encouraged by certain Negro "spokesmen") is, for the Negro who must live it, not only a burden (and not always that) but also a discipline.

Ellison's answer to Howe was, in a sense, an elaboration of the first paragraph of *Invisible Man,* with the hero's demand to be seen as himself, as "flesh and bone, fiber and liquids—and I might even be said to possess a mind." The mind of Ellison has been deeply influential. Even if Leonard Jeffries and Molefi Kete Asante have been successful in imposing dubious Afrocentric programs on the City College of New York and Temple University, even if such ideas have trickled into school systems as far-flung as Portland's and Atlanta's, Ellison's godchildren have been at least as influential in stating their case. His integrationist position has shaped black studies programs at Harvard, Princeton, Yale, Stanford, and many other leading universities.

"Ellison grants blacks their uniqueness without separating us from the larger culture," Shelby Steele, the author of *The Content of Our Character,* said. "After reading Ellison, you realize that talk of a 'white culture' or 'black culture' is simplification. In the academy, identity politics is often the thing, and people would prefer to deal with finite categories: 'black culture,' 'white culture,' 'Hispanic culture,' and so on. Nationalist politics gets more attention, because it's more flamboyant, more glamorous, more controversial. It's better press. But the vast majority of black people in this country are not nationalist. My sense of the problem has to do with the nature of black politics, an oppression-based politics since the 1960s. People like me, who believe that there are some difficulties of black life that are not the result of oppression, are just branded conservatives, no matter what the range of opinion."

Stanley Crouch sees the ambivalence toward Ellison as a symptom of the separatist drift represented by Ras the Destroyer. "Ellison knew a long time ago what the dangers were," Crouch said. "All the dangers are in *Invisible Man*. The dangers of demagoguery. The dangers of trying to hold up a rational position in a country that can become hysterical about race, from either side. You see, the race hysteria that was dominated by white people for the bulk of time Afro-Americans have been in America was overtaken by the black-power, Malcolm X–derived, pro–Louis Farrakhan, anti-American, romantic Third World stuff that came up in the sixties. You had thugs, like Huey Newton, who were celebrated as great revolutionaries. You had West Indians, like Stokely Carmichael, who were calling for the violent overthrow of the country. You had LeRoi Jones ranting anti-Semitism from one coast to the other, and black students on campus cheering and howling. And that's going on now. If people had paid more attention to what Ellison had to say in 1952, we might have got beyond some of the stuff we're in."

Leon Forrest, a black novelist Ellison took time to praise in our meeting, told me, "Ralph goes back to a fundamental tradition in African-American life. He's what we used to call a race man. Areas that seem conservative, supporting businesses in the community, respecting the workingman, the family—that's part of it. A race man means you're in a barbershop conversation, and there might be a nationalist, an NAACP man, whatever, but they're all concerned with getting African-Americans ahead in the community. I know Ralph had a lot of respect for many of the things Adam Clayton Powell stood for at first, the way Powell broke the back of Tammany Hall, though not the shrill things he said at the end of his life. Ralph is for a robust onslaught against racism but, at the same time, for building within the race. What's happened is that there hasn't been enough building within the race: our families, our businesses, the inner strength of the people.

"What disappoints him today is that not enough black Americans are learning from the possibilities of the book. We don't read enough. His own literature is informed by a vast library, and yet we are cutting ourselves off from that. You've got a problem in Afro-American society these days: if a woman has a niece and a nephew, she'll give the niece a copy of a Toni Morrison book and take the nephew to the Bulls game. We don't do nearly enough to enrich our kids in the middle class in our body of literature—the body that fashioned Ralph Ellison's imagination and scholarship."

Sixteen friends and associates gathered on March 1 at Le Périgord, on the East Side, to celebrate Ralph Waldo Ellison's birth. Once the food and not a little wine had been consumed, Albert Murray, by way of toasting his friend, recalled his youthful admiration for Ellison as the smartest, and smartest-dressed, upperclassman at Tuskegee. It was, of course, impressive to Murray that Ellison always seemed to check out the best books in the library, but it was at least as daunting for him to set eyes on the nascent elegance of Ellison, a slender concertmaster in his two-tone shoes, bow tie, contrasting slacks, and whatever else the best haberdasher in Oklahoma had to offer. "I even remember the poetry Ralph wrote," Murray said. " 'Death is nothing, / Life is nothing, / How beautiful these two nothings!' "

"Thanks for remembering so much," Ellison said, smiling and rising to his feet. All evening long, he had been reminiscing at the table, about his friends in jazz, his ill-advised attempt to play the trumpet not long ago in the presence of Wynton Marsalis, his pleasure in everything from the poems of Robinson Jeffers to the liturgy of the Episcopal church. And then, turning to Murray, he said, "Isn't it interesting and worth a bit of thought that from Booker T. Washington's school, which was supposed to instruct youngsters in a vocation, two reasonably literate writers emerged?

Isn't that just part of the unexpectedness of the American experience? It behooves us to keep a close eye on this process of Americanness. My grandparents were slaves. See how short a time it's been? I grew up reading Twain and then, after all those Aunt Jemima roles, those Stepin Fetchit roles, roles with their own subtleties, here comes this voice from Mississippi, William Faulkner. It just goes to show that you can't be southern without being black, and you can't be a black southerner without being white. Think of LBJ. Think of Hugo Black. There are a lot of subtleties based on race that we *will* ourselves not to perceive, but at our peril. The truth is that the quality of Americanness, that thing the kids invariably give voice to, will always come out." And to that everyone raised a glass.

———

Ralph Ellison died a couple of weeks later of pancreatic cancer. Naturally, only a few people even knew he had been sick. He is buried in a vault not far from his apartment building uptown. At the funeral, Michael Harper read from Invisible Man; *at a memorial service, Wynton Marsalis played a blues. From everything I have heard, there really is a second novel, filed on dozens of computer disks, and Random House will publish it sometime in the future.*

Dr. Wilson's Neighborhood

(April–May 1996)

Chicago is the "*known* city," Richard Wright once wrote, and the black neighborhoods of the South Side, especially, have probably been the scene of as much academic scrutiny in this century as Gettysburg or the cave of Lascaux. More often than not, the scholars have come from the University of Chicago's Department of Sociology. Wright never studied at the university, but he said that, thanks to "the huge mountains of fact" assembled by the department's scholars, starting with the great innovator in the field, Robert E. Park, he had been provided with his "first concrete vision of the forces that molded the urban Negro's body and soul"—a vision that led to *Uncle Tom's Children, Native Son,* and *Black Boy.*

The inheritor of the Chicago-school tradition and the keenest liberal analyst of the most perplexing of all American problems— race and poverty—is a grave and courtly academic named William Julius Wilson. While the early Chicago scholars influenced, among others, a great novelist, Wilson has influenced, among others, the President of the United States. During and after the 1992 campaign, Bill Clinton told all who would listen that the most recent of

Wilson's books, *The Truly Disadvantaged* (1987), "made me see the problems of race and poverty and the inner city in a different light." Wilson's emphasis on the social isolation of the urban poor and the link between joblessness and the "pathologies" of the inner city has continued to influence Clinton's thinking on welfare reform, affirmative action, race, and other key social issues. Just as the right wing used Charles Murray's laissez-faire critique in *Losing Ground* as a justification for saying that welfare led to dependency and indolence, Clinton has looked for a rejoinder in the works of William Julius Wilson. Clinton often calls on Wilson for advice, inviting him to dinner and soliciting memorandums.

Wilson will soon publish his magnum opus, *When Work Disappears: The World of the New Urban Poor.* Based on a survey of the ghetto poor in Chicago, and also of employers who regularly decide whether or not to hire inner-city African-Americans for jobs, Wilson's book provides an unflinching view of unemployment and its symptoms. Unlike some on the left, he does not look away from the behavioral problems of the ghetto—the fatherless children, the levels of crime and abuse—but, unlike many conservatives who focus on what they see as an inbred and irredeemable "culture of poverty," he emphasizes the structural obstacles to bringing about mainstream behavior and social mobility. Joblessness in the inner city is the root of the problem, Wilson says, and the only way out is a panoply of "race-neutral" government interventions, including universal health care, educational reform, and a welfare reform that would feature time limits for able-bodied recipients but also the promise of a last-resort, public-sector job modeled on the New Deal–era WPA.

For Wilson, work is all-important. "Regular employment provides the anchor for the spatial and temporal aspects of daily life," he writes. "It determines where you are going to be and when you are going to be there. In the absence of regular employment, life, including family life, becomes less coherent." The book builds on a lifetime of study, and scholars in the field are looking forward to it with edgy impatience. "Bill Wilson's work is the work everyone has to answer to, one way or another," says one of the leading sociologists to Wilson's left—Herbert J. Gans, of Columbia University. "He is our unignorable thinker."

Wilson is sixty years old and looks forty-five. He has been teaching at the University of Chicago since 1972. In an era of denimed sympathy with the kids, he comes to class in full regulation gear: horn-rimmed glasses, a tweed jacket with leather patches on the elbows, a white button-down shirt, a tie flecked with dull diamonds, flannel slacks, cordovan loafers, a Burberrys trench coat. (He used to smoke a pipe.) Although he has been the object of fierce criticism—and, indeed, of accusations of racial betrayal—he does not have the bearing of a controversialist. His manner, like his writing style, is cool, even, correct; he does not seem to trust passion, and does not indulge in it. He prefers a telling statistic to a rhetorical flourish. "At Chicago, formal is the style," Christopher Jencks, a sociologist from Northwestern University, says. "Bill is formal even for Chicago."

One drizzling morning this winter, I set out with Wilson in his maroon Toyota for a ride through the same neighborhoods of the South Side—Douglas, Grand Boulevard, and Washington Park—that had been the turf of perhaps the greatest of the early Chicago studies, St. Clair Drake and Horace R. Cayton's *Black Metropolis,* published in 1945. A comprehensive survey of the South Side and its structures and miseries, *Black Metropolis* described the city of Bigger Thomas, in *Native Son,* Richard Wright said.

Now, half a century later, Wilson steered past abandoned lots and abandoned brownstones, the crack dens of Sixty-second and South Greenwood, the check-cashing stores and the barbecue joints, and past some of the worst housing projects in the country: the low-slung Ida B. Wells Homes, the endless string of sixteen-story towers that is the Robert Taylor Homes. In the vast Taylor project, only 3 percent of the adult residents have jobs, according to the Chicago Housing Authority. "Look at all this," Wilson said. His tone demanded concentration. "Keep looking."

Wilson has been driving through the South Side for twenty-five years, and, without romanticizing the segregation of the forties, he says that the people left in those neighborhoods today are immeasurably worse off than the residents in the pre–civil rights era. "The people populating *Black Metropolis* had it hard—we shouldn't minimize that," Wilson said as he drove. "But this is an incomparably more difficult world. If the authors of *Black Metropolis* were to come back and look at the South Side today, they would be shocked to see all these vacant lots, the boarded-up buildings, the way the shopping districts have gone from vibrant places to places that are barely operating. They'd notice a relatively new sense of resignation, of demoralization."

In the forties, the streets of the South Side were lined with stores, banks, churches. Cottage Grove Avenue and East Sixty-third Street, the strip running along under the elevated tracks, were commercial and bright, places to be seen on a Saturday night. Nicholas Lemann describes in *The Promised Land* how tens of thousands of southern blacks in the forties left their lives as sharecroppers in places like the Mississippi Delta and headed for the South Side. There were jobs to be had. With the end of the Harlem Renaissance, the South Side became known as the capital of black America. Joe Louis lived here. Mahalia Jackson lived here. The Savoy Ballroom was here. A majority of the adults worked. There were poor folks, tenements, and slums, to be sure, but also working-class and middle-class, and even upper-middle-class, residents nearby—models of economic and social mobility. "For all the difficulties, there was also hope, some sense of possibility," Wilson said.

But as the factories and steel mills and meat-packing plants started to shut down, in the sixties and seventies, the jobs dried up.

City governments could offer businesses all the tax breaks in the world, but in the end they could not compete with the lure of the suburbs. In a twenty-year period, from 1967 to 1987, Chicago lost 326,000 manufacturing jobs, New York more than half a million. The pattern was the same throughout the cities of the industrial Northeast and Midwest. In Chicago, the working and middle classes left the South Side and moved out to create suburbs of their own, mainly southwest of the city. For those left behind, poverty rates rose higher and higher—by 1990, often to more than 40 or 50 percent. Stores closed. Banks moved out. Churches, recreation centers, restaurants boarded up their doors and windows. In North Lawndale, a West Side neighborhood that is part of Chicago's contiguous Black Belt, a population of around 66,000 now has at its disposal, at last count, exactly one bank and one supermarket, but it does have forty-eight state lottery agents, fifty currency exchanges, and ninety-nine licensed liquor stores and bars.

"The social organization of these neighborhoods changed radically," Wilson said as we headed down Grand Boulevard, which has been renamed for Martin Luther King, Jr. "In those days, the overwhelming majority of the population was employed—at least seventy percent of the males. There were all kinds of factories, and now all that's really left is service jobs. If you're lucky, you can be a hospital orderly, a janitor, or a fast-food worker earning poverty-line wages." As the poverty rate went past 40 percent—a real threshold of misery, many social scientists agree—the population became more uniform. There were thousands of single mothers on welfare, out-of-work men hustling on the streets, drugs, gangs. Of the eight and a half million people considered to be in the nation's "underclass" (or, to use a less loaded term, the ghetto poor), about 50 percent are African-Americans.

"You can walk into any maternity ward in these areas and look at the rows of babies and predict with almost unerring certainty what their lives are going to be," Wilson said later. "Chances are they've been born to a family in which there is no steady breadwinner and whose lives lack the organization that work provides. Usually, the adult present will be a young woman, the mother, who is in such difficult straits that odds are she is suffering from real depression or is angry, with little capability of coping with her situation. The child will be exposed almost entirely to families like his or her own—an almost total social isolation. Most middle- and working-class families are long gone. Those role models left town. So his exposure to mainstream behavior is slight, if it exists at all.

"Most of these kids have practically no contact at all with white people, and when they do encounter white people they are intimidated. They have no sense of how to interpret the behavior and manners of this new world, and so they react badly. On the contrary, they are exposed to an environment that provides a vast opportunity for crime, drugs, hustling, illicit sex. The child might arrive at school full of hope, but that hope is soon dashed, because of the schools themselves. Most of the teachers have become demoralized; principals have given up. The kid comes in bright-eyed in the first grade, and by the fourth grade he is completely turned off. In *Dark Ghetto* Kenneth Clark wrote that the longer the kids stay in these schools the *lower* their test scores go. In high school, if these kids are still thinking about college, they have no idea of how to get there, no information and guidance on how to prepare, how to submit an application. There is an abysmal lack of information for these kids. Sooner or later, these kids come to the realization that they should expect to be walking the streets without jobs."

At this point in his explanation, Wilson's voice became almost inaudible. Wilson is a supremely confident man, especially when he is talking about his field, but it is not hard to see when he is moved either to indignation or, as now, to utter sadness at the world he studies and lives so close to. "Well, you know what it is," he said finally. "It goes on from there. The whole sorry picture."

. . .

One night when we were having dinner at a restaurant downtown, I asked Wilson to tell me about what he does not write about—the course of his own life.

"I am very wary about talking about my own past, because I'm afraid of people drawing unreasonable comparisons and conclusions," Wilson said. "They'll say, 'Well, he pulled himself up by his bootstraps, why can't these kids? See? Anyone can make it in American society.' But look: in any population, you'll find some extraordinary individuals or families who make it one way or another. You can't generalize on the basis of the experience at the far end of the bell-shaped curve—to coin a metaphor."

Wilson grew up in Blairsville, Pennsylvania, a town of a few thousand people in a mining district about an hour east of Pittsburgh. The family lived in a two-bedroom house: one bedroom for the parents, the other for six children. When Wilson was twelve, his father died of lung disease. For a while, the family lived on relief; then his mother found part-time work cleaning houses. "We used to go hungry a lot. It was real poverty," Wilson said. "We were struggling all the time. We lived on an inadequate diet. For a family of seven, we had one quart of milk a week. Thank God, we had a garden and could grow string beans, carrots, corn, tomatoes, squash, and can them all for winter."

The Wilsons were one of a handful of black families in town. "I was called 'nigger' by the older boys, and I got into some fights triggered by racial slurs," Wilson said. "We experienced some discrimination in stores—I remember a restaurant wouldn't serve us once in Blairsville. But I didn't feel especially deprived. I've never lived in a segregated community. We were poor, but we didn't feel *trapped* in poverty. 'Poor' did not have the same meaning in those days. I experienced life in a wholly different way from the way a poor kid in the inner city does now. My parents worked. Our lives were organized around work. Even though my parents didn't go past the ninth and tenth grades, it never occurred to me that I wasn't going to college—that I wouldn't have a bright future. There was never that feeling of hopelessness, of despair. There were no signs of chronic social pathology. I never saw anyone shot. Our teachers never gave up on us. I remember a white teacher calling me in and telling me that I had a very high IQ and it was time I started living up to my potential." All the Wilson children expected to go to college, and they all did.

Wilson got an extra boost from his father's sister, Janice Wardlaw, who was a social worker in New York. He was sent off to spend summers with his aunt, and she took him to museums, gave him books to read, and talked to him constantly about the importance of ambition and creativity. Even when Wilson began to compete at higher and higher academic levels, Janice Wardlaw gave him the confidence he needed.

"She was always bragging about me, always making me feel I was smart and worth something," Wilson said. "You *have* to have someone like that in your life. I remember her when she was dying of cancer, in 1980. There was a piece in a magazine on race and class, all of it centered on me and my work. Aunt Janice was on her deathbed, she barely had the strength to stay awake for long, but she asked her daughter to read her the magazine piece aloud. She could barely summon the strength to stay awake, but she did. And when it was over she grabbed my hand and said, 'Billy, you've made it now.' "

With a small scholarship from his church and some further financial help from his aunt, Wilson went off to Wilberforce, a predominantly black university in Ohio. A sociologist there, Maxwell Brooks, captured his interest with courses in social problems and race; Wilson started reading Robert Park, Ernest Burgess, E. Franklin Frazier, W.E.B. Du Bois, Charles S. Johnson. His politics began to incline toward the left, his ambitions toward the academic. After spending a couple of years in the army and earning a master's degree at Bowling Green State University, in Ohio, Wilson turned down a chance to earn his doctorate at Columbia and went instead to Washington State University, where a white liberal southerner named T. H. Kennedy had been recruiting black graduate students. "I became a star out there and came into my own," Wilson said. "It was a real ego boost."

Wilson's first academic job was at the University of Massachusetts at Amherst. His specialty in those days was sociological theory and methodology. It was the mid-sixties, the thick of the civil rights era. Although Wilson was not much of an activist, he was deeply interested in the movement and read many of the new books on race in his field. He discovered that with rare exceptions (*Dark Ghetto*, for one) the work had more to do with polemics than with scholarship. Out of sheer frustration with those books, Wilson began working on a project of his own—*Power, Racism, and Privilege,* a comparative study of race relations in the United States and South Africa, which was published in 1973. In the end, that book may turn out to have been more significant for what it lacked than for what it contained.

"Right after it went to press, I realized I had failed to take into account the class changes in the African-American community," Wilson said. "The black experience is not monolithic, and I had not captured that. I would drive around various areas in Chicago—I'd moved here on a temporary appointment in 1971—and I would go through some middle-class neighborhoods in South Chicago, like Kenwood, and you'd see a Mercedes in the driveway, lawns that looked like putting greens, and then you'd drive a few hundred yards west or south and you'd be in a ghetto area. You had to live in Chicago to appreciate the changes that were taking place. I felt we had to start thinking about the black class structure and the extent to which public policies can deal with racial equality. One segment seemed to be improving, with higher incomes, better lifestyles, while the rest were falling further and further behind."

For the next several years, Wilson devoted himself to that very dilemma, to the shifting balance between class and race, and in 1978 he published *The Declining Significance of Race.* In that book

Wilson argued that, owing largely to the civil rights movement but also to the dramatic rise of a growing black middle class, problems of class had become more central to the black poor than racial discrimination. He expressed support for affirmative action, yet he noted that such programs tended to help mainly the educated middle class, while those left behind by a changing economy had begun to form a disadvantaged class in real danger of becoming permanent.

Wilson took pains in the book to point out that racism had not disappeared, but, like Bayard Rustin before him, he was convinced that the main problems facing poor blacks had more to do with economics than with race. For many of Wilson's readers, this was a dangerous heresy. There were attacks in the New York *Amsterdam News* and the Chicago *Defender*. Kenneth Clark wrote an op-ed piece in the *Times* calling Wilson's thesis mistaken. When the American Sociological Association gave Wilson the Sydney A. Spivack Award for *The Declining Significance of Race,* the Association of Black Sociologists filed a protest, saying that the book had completely overlooked the realities of racism in American life. The group was "outraged over the misrepresentation of the black experience."

Charles Willie, a black sociologist at Harvard's Graduate School of Education, carried on what he told me was a "ten-year war" with Wilson, blaming him—a prominent *black* sociologist—for giving "aid and comfort" to a society that would quite happily "blame poverty on poor people" and ignore the inner city altogether. "By identifying the poor as cut off—as an underclass with no relation to anyone else—it absolved the rest of society of responsibility," Willie said of Wilson's book. Wilson had to endure not only the condemnation of some of his colleagues but also the far less civil opprobrium of the Chicago activist Steve Cokely, who publicly called him a "nigger."

Nowhere does Wilson dismiss racism or absolve society of responsibility in any way for poverty. In fact, he was paying a price not only for the title of his book, which—by academic standards, anyway—was inflammatory, but also for his timing. Wilson's book came out during a period of liberal skittishness. By the early sixties, two liberal writers—Oscar Lewis, an anthropologist, and Michael Harrington, a leading democratic socialist—had advanced the idea that a dysfunctional culture, in opposition to mainstream culture, develops in conditions of poverty and is then handed down, from generation to generation. As Nicholas Lemann observes, the "culture of poverty" idea was an attractive one for the liberals around Lyndon Johnson, "because the obvious cure for it was for the government to act as an agent of acculturation." Conservative scholars and politicians, however, adopted the notion and widened it by saying that such a culture is beyond repair—immune to the best efforts of any social program. The "culture of poverty," therefore, quickly became an incendiary phrase among liberals—a subject to avoid at all costs.

In that context, Daniel Patrick Moynihan, in 1965, when he was an assistant secretary of labor in the Johnson administration, issued his famous report, *The Negro Family: The Case for National Action.* In it Moynihan said that poverty was now "feeding upon itself," and explained, "At the center of the tangle of pathology is the weakness of the family structure. Once or twice removed, it will be found to be the principal source of most of the aberrant, inadequate, or antisocial behavior that did not establish but now serves to perpetuate the cycle of poverty and deprivation." Much that was in the Moynihan report had appeared decades earlier in E. Franklin Frazier's books on the black family in Chicago and in the United States generally, but Moynihan was vilified, much as he was a few years later when he served as an adviser to Richard M. Nixon and urged a policy of "benign neglect." He was accused, in the phrase of a white psychologist and civil rights activist, William Ryan, of "blaming the victim." In the aftermath of the Moynihan report and its attendant controversy, many liberals were wary of describing behavior in the ghetto in harsh terms. And into that still-charged atmosphere came *The Declining Significance of Race.*

"Maybe Bill should have called the book *The Rising Significance of Class* and saved himself a lot of trouble," Columbia's Herbert Gans said. "I think one reason black people were so upset is the fear that if the problem is class, and not race, then the political clout of the race, and black leaders, will somehow be less."

As a result of *The Declining Significance of Race,* Wilson, who considers himself a social democrat, was now hearing himself described in some quarters as a neoconservative. And not only in academe. At one point, he got a call from the White House asking him if he would come meet with President Reagan. The president, the aide said, wanted to meet with some black conservatives.

"Where did you get the idea that I'm a conservative?" Wilson said. "To the contrary, I'm a member of the Democratic left." The White House staffer apologized for his error.

The controversy surrounding *The Declining Significance of Race* was painful for Wilson. Like Ralph Ellison, he was being denounced in some quarters for insufficient loyalty to the race. "It was extremely unpleasant," he says, to be abused, to have one's status as a "race man" called into question.

As a public figure, Wilson has maintained his customary reserve. At home, he is not quite so buttoned up. He is a huge White Sox fan and a NordicTrack addict. One black colleague, who sees a lot of him, says, "Bill is a get-down brother behind closed doors. But remember—this is a man who comes right after the generation of John Hope Franklin. It's a wonder he's not *more* buttoned up in public."

Christopher Jencks is one of Wilson's closest white colleagues, and I asked him one day how much of a role he thought race has played in the reception of Wilson's work. "His race has to have a meaning," Jencks said. "His work wouldn't have had the same meaning if I had written it—not in impact or in the size of audience.

He's got a lot of rewards for what he's done, but it took terrific courage—there was a lot of flak to take."

Wilson told me he agreed with Jencks that a small part of the authority of his work comes from his race. "I think my race gives me a little more credibility when I talk about these questions. There are still a lot of people (and I'm not one of them) who believe in the insider-outsider doctrine—that, say, only blacks can understand the black experience."

Throughout his academic life, Wilson has worked constantly and easily with white colleagues. His wife, Beverly, is white. Wilson said that discrimination had not been his experience. "In the academic world, give me two equal individuals, equal in training and talent and motivation and work, one white and one black, and I'll take my chances with the black in terms of social mobility," he said. "Black talent in academe is in short supply, and those of us who make it have our pick of jobs, whether we want to admit it or not." He added, "But I've encountered problems that all blacks encounter. One professor here at Chicago, now dead, was editor of the *American Journal of Sociology*. Another professor appointed me an associate editor. The then editor asked, 'Can Wilson read?' Someone else said, 'My God! He's a tenured member of the faculty.' The editor said, 'Well, you know how those people are.' Several years later, that same man had to approach me when I was chairman of the department. I was sorely tempted to deny him whatever it was he wanted. But I didn't."

By the mid-eighties, when Ronald Reagan was in office, liberal scholars had lost the initiative on race and poverty. Conservative thinkers like Thomas Sowell, Lawrence Mead, George Gilder, and, above all, Charles Murray filled the academic and policy vacuum. Murray may be best known now for his collaboration with the late

Richard J. Herrnstein on *The Bell Curve,* but his 1984 book, *Losing Ground,* was far more influential. The underclass, Murray argued, was expanding thanks to the very programs that were intended to help it. Poor women were giving birth to more and more babies out of wedlock because welfare benefits had become more lucrative than getting a low-wage job; crime rates were rising because the probability of punishment had become so slight. Murray proposed the end of welfare—the social-Darwinist solution—and a rhetoric and policy of tough love. He crystallized the idea among conservatives that liberal social policy had actually worked against the poor, by creating a culture of dependency, and that the libertarian solution—to do nothing—was the true act of grace.

Wilson had a hard time finding the love in Murray's toughness. He also questioned Murray's numbers. Among Murray's many sins against fact, Wilson argued, was that *Losing Ground* simply failed to account for the overall negative trends in the economy when the rise in the poverty rate was being calculated. Murray failed to note that between 1968 and 1980 the unemployment rate had doubled.

Wilson questioned not only Murray's numbers but his motives as well. "I think a lot of Charles Murray's conclusions are ideologically driven and he doesn't let facts get in the way of his beliefs," Wilson told me. "Somehow, I'm more charitable toward Reagan than I am toward Murray. Reagan was naïve. Charles Murray is not, and he is extremely selective in the way he interprets his material. I think the man is. . . . Well, I think he's dishonest. He plays to conservative fears, and I think he knows better. A lot of what he says he doesn't really believe, but it's conservatively popular. It's politically driven. I get the sense that Murray would rather keep looking for something to prove his case that blacks would rather be hustling in the streets than working."

The most painful and lasting influence was Murray's effect on the conservative rhetoric and, consequently, on the popular notion of poverty; the changed notion lingers even now. "What bothers me is that a lot of conservatives blame the individuals and pay no mind at all to the structures that create those cultural styles and habits," Wilson said. "Bill Bennett has a vision that places primary emphasis on culture as an explanation for everything but says nothing about the source of that culture. If Bennett tries to explain the problem of family values and responsibility, he isn't likely to take into account the overwhelming problems of living up to these values when you grow up under different circumstances and with near-impossible obstacles."

Wilson's answer to Murray and the Reagan rhetoric came in 1987, with the publication of *The Truly Disadvantaged,* in which he took on the vexed question of "the culture of poverty." In private conversation with colleagues, Wilson admits that inner-city poverty has, of course, given rise to a set of styles, attitudes, and habits that might loosely be considered a culture of poverty. But the way the term has often been used, in both scholarship and politics, is anathema to him. "It's just too loaded a term and too given to extreme notions," he told me. In his book Wilson did not shy away from describing the maladies present in the inner city—out-of-wedlock births, welfare dependency, crime—but he described them only in the context of their having grown out of a set of very particular and trying circumstances: joblessness, segregation, and oppression among them. One of the many findings of Wilson's research is that, contrary to much conservative thinking, the ghetto poor generally support such "mainstream" values as hard work, initiative, and honesty; what prevents their being adhered to is the difficulty of establishing and sustaining the social structures and circumstances needed to help carry them out.

Wilson describes how the triumph of so many African-Americans—the great rise in the number of working-class and middle-class blacks and their migration from the inner cities to the suburbs—changed the ecology of the urban neighborhoods they left behind. Since the departure of the middle class, and of the commerce and the institutions it once supported, the remaining population has been suffering from the "concentration effects" of poverty: joblessness, crime, fatherless children. With no jobs around, young men make "rational" decisions to hustle on the street; with so few "marriageable" young men around, young women decide to have children on their own. Without working-class and middle-class role models around, "mainstream" behavior begins to weaken. There are now fewer churches, community groups, and after-school programs to help parents teach their children the sort of values and behavior that will help them get jobs and survive in a world beyond the inner city. Kids learn styles of bearing and speech that might help them survive in the ghetto but will sink them at a job interview. "For one reason or another," Wilson told me, with a hint of disdain in his voice, "conservatives find it convenient not to factor all this into their discussion."

Christopher Jencks said of *The Truly Disadvantaged,* "What Bill had done was create a political space for talking about things people had agreed not to talk about. Within academic sociology, people went around walking on eggs, basically. The field had been largely abandoned by white scholars, because of the feeling that it wasn't appropriate for white people to tell black people what's wrong."

According to David Ellwood, a professor of public policy at Harvard and a former Clinton administration official, the publication of *The Truly Disadvantaged* was "the defining moment" in the debate. "What it did, was, for the first time, to acknowledge real and significant problems in central cities and then provide a coherent and comprehensible theory or structure to understand what was going on," Ellwood said.

In Chicago, community activists influenced by Wilson's work even began a successful program called Jobs for Youth. A nonprofit group, Jobs for Youth has made sixteen hundred placements, mainly of black men and women between the ages of seventeen and twenty-four, in a wide range of businesses in the metropolitan area.

"What we are trying to do fundamentally is de-ghettoize the kids that come to us from public housing projects, isolated places," Jack Connelly, the executive director, told me. "One of the fundamental tenets of Bill's writing is that the isolation has sustained the poverty over time. What we find is that when the kids start doing well they leave their neighborhood and go somewhere safer and more diverse. A trick for some of the kids is just trying to figure out how to get downtown to the Loop. A girl might never have left the ten-block radius of her house on the South Side, except maybe for a trip to the Delta in Mississippi to see her relatives."

The critics of *The Truly Disadvantaged* came, once more, from all sides. Adolph Reed, Jr., a political scientist at Northwestern, wrote in *The Nation* that Wilson—"who exemplifies the limits of the liberal technocratic vision"—focused on "disorganization" and "deviance" using a vocabulary of pathology that unjustly implied a model of social health elsewhere. "What is that model?" Reed asked, and he added that Wilson's view was "abominably sexist, not to mention atavistic." In a book entitled *Turning Back,* Stephen Steinberg, a sociologist at the Graduate Center of the City University of New York, wrote that with *The Truly Disadvantaged* Wilson had become little more than "a black reincarnation" of Moynihan, and that Wilson's book "quietly served as President Clinton's exculpation for the administration's failure to develop policies to deal with the plight of the nation's ghettos." Wilson legitimated a "retreat from race," Steinberg went on to say, and "this is the significance of Wilson's elevation to national prominence and even to celebrity status."

Neither Reed nor Steinberg treated Wilson's claim to being on the liberal left with anything other than derision. When I called Reed and asked him why he had attacked Wilson so fiercely when Wilson was offering policy recommendations that made him a "social democrat," Reed laughed. "I don't know where Wilson is politically," he said. "He's proclaimed himself to be a social democrat. I don't know what that means. I can call myself the king of France but that doesn't mean I am one."

In other words, in the view of his critics on the left Wilson had once more overlooked the problem of race and racism as an autonomous element of poverty. Wilson is, as I said, courtly, but when he is attacked on that level he is not exactly defenseless. Neither Reed nor Steinberg, he said, is a serious scholar, and he left it at that.

Charles Murray's critique has more to do with the European-style social programs that Wilson recommended as solutions than with his analysis of the problem itself. "I remember when I read *The Truly Disadvantaged* I was struck by how the first chapters were so similar to *Losing Ground*—the damning statements about the problems associated with the social pathologies, and so on," Murray told me. "My main reaction is that he then gets to the end, where he says we need a more progressive social democracy, and I say, 'Where did that come from?' There is a disjoint between the analysis of the problem and the analysis of a solution."

Murray has a point: there *is* a disjunction between the analysis and the prescription. It's just not the one Murray has in mind. Wilson's problem—and he faces it even more squarely in *When Work Disappears*—is that he is prescribing a kind of expensive medicine that Americans show no sign of wanting, or wanting to pay for. With the new book, he has ventured even further into the practical realm of policy, and the criticisms of his solutions are bound to be even sharper than they have been so far.

Wilson's life will change drastically in the fall of 1996. After twenty-five years at the University of Chicago, he is moving east. Wilson has been feeling isolated at Chicago for several years—cut off, especially, from the national policy debates. The break came after Henry Louis Gates, Jr., the chairman of the Department of Afro-American Studies at Harvard, threw a dinner for Wilson at which many of the most important black scholars in Cambridge—Anthony Appiah, Orlando Patterson, Leon and Evelyn Higginbotham, Charles Ogletree, and Cornel West among them—gathered around the table and tried to persuade Wilson to come join them.

"That was one of the most exciting evenings of my life," Wilson told me. "Not because of the flattery but because of the intellectual level of the discussion. Harvard has somehow collected this critical mass of black intellectuals, and I found I could no longer resist it. No matter what Chicago could still offer, I had to make the change. I had to come."

When Wilson announced his decision, the news set off a flurry of articles in *Time, Newsweek, The Washington Post,* and elsewhere declaring that Harvard had now officially become the mecca of black intellectuals—a focus, much like what the offices of the *Partisan Review* were for the Jewish intellectuals (and their *goyishe* cousins) of the fifties. For Chicago, the change will not be easy: the most prominent sociology department in the field has lost its singular scholar, and the Center for the Study of Urban Inequality will probably shut down within a year or so, he says. "It will be difficult for a while, but I think Chicago will rebound," Wilson said one day as we were walking to class. "I just had to do this now—something really new, as a last stage of my work."

At about the same time Wilson shows up at Harvard, *When Work Disappears* will show up in the bookstores. The manuscript, which Wilson gave me to read, is more ambitious and more accessible than anything he has published before. His survey of the South Side and of Chicago employers gives an empirical heft to the speculations of *The Truly Disadvantaged.* Because of his prominence in the field, Wilson has become a magnet for grants, and he has funneled that money into the fieldwork necessary for such a project. A few of his students have become so involved in Wilson's even more recent work that they have moved into working-class neighborhoods on the South Side; one graduate student, who did much of his interviewing at a gym, has become an amateur boxer—a rare feat in sociology.

How top-level academics view poverty and race, and even the language they use to talk about it, can have serious consequences out in the greater world. Wilson knows that as well as anyone, and once more he is publishing in a highly charged, politicized atmosphere. The static will come not only from the obvious names on the right, for in the last few years a number of liberal social scientists have been trying to present a view of the ghetto that is somehow more optimistic than Wilson's portrait of the South Side. A young sociologist named Mitchell Duneier, for example, now at the University of California at Santa Barbara, won several awards and a lot of attention in 1992 with *Slim's Table,* a profile of a group of working-class black men who gather every day at a South Side cafeteria. The book suggested that the inner city was not nearly as bleak as it had been portrayed—that there was still a prevalent, healthy sense of hard work, pride, and self-sufficiency.

Wilson was annoyed that *Slim's Table,* which lacks a systematic sample of the local population, tries to make a few men stand for more than the real evidence allows. "Of course there are Slims in this world. The tragedy is that there are so few of them," Wilson told me. "We have a problem with political correctness in sociology. There is an urge to skim over the facts in the interest of not making a community look bad somehow. . . . People get sick and tired of hearing about the problems, and so when someone can come along and say the problems are not so bad, they are relieved and happy. Unfortunately, it doesn't do anything to change the reality of the problems."

In *When Work Disappears,* the landscape is still one of "depopulation," "concentration effects," "ghetto-related behavior," the lack of "soft skills"—the same sorry picture that was on display in *The Truly Disadvantaged*—but this time Wilson has widened his scope. For one thing, he has used the voices of some of the hundreds of people who spent time with his team of researchers. Although what they are saying is familiar from journalistic accounts like Alex Kotlowitz's *There Are No Children Here* and Darcy Frey's *The Last Shot,*

Wilson puts those voices in a scholarly context that makes them extremely powerful and indicative of an entire world. To set the scene, for example, he quotes a seventeen-year-old college student and part-time worker from a poor neighborhood on the West Side, who says that about 40 percent of her neighbors are alcoholics:

"They live based on today. You can ask any of 'em: 'What you gonna do tomorrow?' 'I don't know, man. I know when [it gets] here.' And I can really understand, you know, being in that state. If you around totally negative people, people who are not doing anything, that's the way you gonna be regardless."

As Wilson and his assistants worked with more and more residents in Black Belt neighborhoods, he uncovered a rapid increase in concentrated poverty. Of the ten communities that represent the Black Belt, eight had rates of poverty exceeding 45 percent, including three with rates higher than 50 percent and three higher than 60 percent. Twenty-five years ago, only two of these neighborhoods had poverty rates above 40 percent. This sort of poverty is something new. "For the first time in the twentieth century," Wilson writes, "most adults in many inner-city neighborhoods are not working in a typical week." Today, more than half of all African-American men between the ages of twenty-five and thirty-four either are not employed or do not earn sufficient wages to support a family of four above the poverty level. Moreover, nearly one in three black males in their twenties was either in prison, out on parole, or under the supervision of the justice system in 1994. Wilson's numbers and polling also suggest that class makes the essential difference in behavior and opportunity: blacks with a middle-class income show no greater tendency toward violence, drug use, or joblessness than whites of the same income level.

Wilson's interviews reveal how circumstances breed an extraordinary degree of suspicion between men and women in the black community. In Chicago's inner city, 60 percent of the black adults between the ages of eighteen and forty-four have never been married, and that rate is much higher down the economic scale. When one inner-city black woman was asked why she had never married, she said, "I don't think I want to get married but then . . . see, you're supposed to stick to that one and that's a fantasy. You know, stick with one for the rest of your life. I've never met many people like that, have you?" A twenty-five-year-old unmarried father from the West Side said, "Well, most black men feel now, why get married when you got six to seven womens to one guy, really. You know, 'cause there's more women out here mostly than men. 'Cause most dudes around here are killing each other like fools over drugs or all this other stuff. And if you're not that bad looking of a guy, you know, and you know a lot of women like you, why get married when you can play the field the way they want to do, you know." Wilson's data reveal, in other words, that these men and women believe that since marriages will inevitably disintegrate, it is better to avoid wedlock altogether.

When Work Disappears explores why it has become harder than ever for residents of the inner city to find work. By interviewing potential employers at 179 Chicago-area firms, Wilson discovered that almost three quarters of them tended to avoid hiring blacks from low-income neighborhoods, because they saw such blacks as too often lazy, unreliable, dishonest, mixed up with drugs, or lacking in language skills, or as having a "bad attitude." Some respondents seemed to speak out of racism, others out of wearied experience. One manufacturer said:

> I think that today there's more bias and prejudice against the black man than there was twenty years ago. I think twenty years ago, fifteen years ago, ten years ago, white male employers like myself were willing to give anybody and everybody the opportunity, not because it was the law, but because it was the right thing to do, and today I see more prejudice and more racial bias in employers than I've ever seen before. Not here, and our employees can prove that, but when we hear other employers

talk, they'll go after primarily the Hispanic and Oriental first, those two and . . . I'll qualify that even further, the Mexican Hispanic, and any Oriental, and after that, that's pretty much it, that's pretty much where they like to draw the line, right there.

The black potential employers were often more nuanced in their comments, but they, too—80 percent of them—expressed a negative attitude toward hiring inner-city blacks. Wilson quotes this exchange between one of his field workers and the black president and CEO of an inner-city wholesale firm. The CEO says:

> So, you put . . . a bunch of poor people together . . . I don't give a damn whether they're white, green or grizzly, you got a bad deal. You're going to create crime and everything else that's under the sun, dope. Anytime you put all like people together— and particularly if they're on a low level—you destroy them. They not, how you going to expect . . . one's going to stand up like a flower? He don't see no reason to stand up. . . .
>
> INTERVIEWER: So, you understand this wariness of some employers?
>
> RESPONDENT: Sure.

Wilson is well aware that there are many points in the book which, if they were to be dumbed down to the point of absurdity, his opponents could exploit (Mexican immigrants good, black males bad, etc.). And yet he will not hold off. In one passage he writes about the way ghetto kids who no longer have recreation and entertainment centers in their own neighborhood come into conflict with other classes when they go beyond their usual locales. Without passing judgment either way, Wilson uses the example of how middle-class moviegoers resent inner-city black kids who talk through the film. This is a conflict of "style"—the "communal" style of moviegoing versus the silent one—and one of many details in the overall conflict between races and classes in the American city.

"I know I may get clobbered, but this is descriptive work," Wilson said. Conservatives, he went on, will pick up some of these details of personal behavior and use them for their moralistic purposes, but ignore the connection Wilson makes between those behaviors and structural factors—especially joblessness. The American politics of poverty invariably centers on the management of individual behavior, Wilson writes. "From the building of almshouses in the late nineteenth century to President Johnson's War on Poverty, Americans have failed to emphasize the social rights of the poor."

Most sociologists do not dare go much beyond description and analysis and enter the realm of policy. In *When Work Disappears* Wilson elaborates on his recommendations. To untangle the web of joblessness, family disintegration, welfare dependency, violence, and all the other problems of the inner city, the government needs to follow the lead of Western Europe, and promote social welfare policies that make it possible for ghetto residents to work and thus end their social isolation. The United States devotes a far smaller percentage of its gross domestic product to social expenditures than Germany, England, France, or Sweden, and has higher poverty rates than any of them. Wilson is furious because the Republicans in Congress support a welfare-reform proposal without guaranteed jobs, one that would adopt the idea of time limits but would then make welfare the business of the states, with the states, in turn, allocating (or not allocating) benefits as they saw fit. And once welfare recipients are no longer getting benefits, Wilson asks, where will they go for a job, for health care, for anything at all? At the moment, universal health care is dead, and welfare policy is in danger of growing far more draconian. Wilson, however, thinks that the sort of progressive proposals he favors will resurface—and, with better political handling, could even prevail.

Naturally, the biggest question that Wilson faces in terms of policy is money. Who is going to pay for what he suggests? How does a country with an angry antitax electorate, with a Social Security system on the verge of catastrophe, do much of anything for the poor? Moreover, who, exactly, gives a damn anymore?

"For me, lower taxes is a code for not doing anything. That's one of the reasons I was so disappointed in Colin Powell when he talked about his politics before bowing out of the race," Wilson said. "Bob Dole just does not have the vision that Clinton has. He doesn't have the full understanding of what affects the life chances of these kids that Clinton has. Dole is more compassionate than some of the other leading Republicans—he won't demonize whole groups, the way they do—but he doesn't have Clinton's vision. I think if Dole were elected, there just would not be much attention paid to these problems.

"Overall, I fight pessimism all the time," Wilson went on. "But somehow I have a sense that things are beginning to turn. I even get the sense that Americans could be having their doubts, that they are beginning to blame the Republicans. I even get the sense that they are hungry for liberal books. People are waiting for something different—a different message, a progressive, populist message."

Wilson had said that sort of thing to me more than once over the several days I spent with him in Chicago. He tried, as best he could, to end our sessions on a promising note. But then, one afternoon, unprompted by any question of mine, and in the middle of a conversation about something else entirely, he stopped, and said, "You know, I would really hate to be a young person right now. If we don't stem the tide now, the jobless percentage I'm talking about now will seem mild. And there is no serious planning going on for this. There will come a day when ignoring the poor is not an option."

12

A Father and His Son

(February 1995)

When the Japanese novelist Kenzaburo Oe was in Stockholm to collect the Nobel Prize in Literature in December he told all who would listen that he would now withdraw from the arena of his success. Over and over, he told his polite audiences and interviewers, "I am going to stop writing fiction." It was such a queer statement, and delivered with such calm and good cheer, that no one seemed to believe it. Oe is just sixty years old, in good health, and recognized as the leading writer of Japanese prose. The prize has accelerated sales of his books in Japan, and sent his foreign publishers racing to translate more of his novels and stories. Oe is neither tired nor depressed. He has never felt more at peace. His decision is more one of closure than of crisis. He is quitting fiction, he says, because the mission he set for himself thirty-one years ago—to speak somehow for his severely brain-damaged son, Hikari—is no longer necessary. Hikari, who suffers seizures, rarely speaks, and must be cared for at all times, has found his voice. He has composed some remarkable music for piano and flute—"like dew glittering on grass leaves" is how his father describes it—and has recently issued his second compact disk, *The Music of Hikari Oe, 2*.

"Sometimes my son thinks it is he who has won the Nobel Prize!" Oe said, delight creasing his face. "When journalists come to my house in Tokyo, they see him first and say, 'Congratulations!' Also, Hikari has just put out this new music, and so, in a way, he *has* won the prize. My own work"—including the novels *A Personal Matter* and *The Pinch Runner Memorandum*—"is based on our life together, the communion with my son. So, if he thinks he has won, then he is right. It's amazing to me that this boy, with such a profound handicap of the brain, can continue to deepen his music. For a long time, I felt that it was my role to express things for him, but now he can do it on his own. It turns out that I overestimated my role."

In the near future, Oe plans to care for his son—Hikari, thirty-one, is the oldest of three children—and turn to study. In 1996, he will be resident at Princeton University. "I intend to read for three or four or five years and, if possible, discover a new style for my literature," he said. "I do not yet have a definite conception of my literary future, the new form, the new types. But I do hope to write for children—or, at least, I hope the new style will be such that even children can appreciate it. I will write for children and for desperate old men—men like me."

Winning a Nobel Prize means, among other things, a pleasant stay of about a week at the Grand Hotel in Stockholm and a flurry of ceremonies, congratulations, and requests. (It also means $930,000.) Oe fulfilled his duties with unflagging charm. When he was asked by an obnoxious television anchor to "look into the camera when I go like *this,* and say, 'Tonight! At quarter to eleven!,' " Oe did what he was told. Although he admits to having slugged writers in bar fights ("But just two in thirty-six years! Not too bad!"), he is a gracious man of good humor, joking with fellow Nobelists in Japanese, English, and French. Oe's work is often elusive, difficult, and dark, but there is nothing forbidding about his physical presence. He wears funky, wheel-like glasses and has a spiky haircut. His fabulous ears flare out magnificently, as if to catch the wind.

As we sat talking in Oe's suite at the Stockholm Grand Hotel one morning, his wife, Yukari, tended to Hikari, washing his face with a cloth, helping him on with a jacket. In the novel *A Personal Matter,* Oe writes that his handicapped son soon began to resemble him, and while Hikari does look a bit like his father, he still bears the marks of his condition at birth: crossed eyes, a misshapen skull. Hikari (the name means "light") is an adult, but the level of his speech, his father says, is as simple as that of a three-year-old child and does not improve. He suffers from epileptic fits. His eyesight is weak. He has trouble walking sometimes. As Oe spoke, he kept glancing across the room at his son and interrupting his thoughts to get up and help him. Like his wife, Oe is a completely devoted parent, and a grateful one: Hikari "illuminated the dark, deep folds of my consciousness," he has said. Hikari saved his life.

Kenzaburo Oe was born in 1935 in Ose, a mountain village on the island of Shikoku; the village was long ago annexed to another town and erased from the map. When Oe was six, the war in the Pacific began. He lost his father and his grandmother. His first major story, "Prize Stock," recounts the war years in a mythologized, almost primeval Japanese village, and the atmosphere is of an Eden disrupted by the shattering sight of a captured American aviator. "To us the black soldier was a rare and wonderful domestic animal, an animal of genius," Oe wrote. "How can I describe how much we loved him, or the blazing sun above our wet, heavy skin that distant, splendid summer afternoon, the deep shadows on the cobblestones, the smell of the children and the black soldier, the voices hoarse with happiness, how can I convey the repletion and rhythm of it all?" The tone is of a lost world—a world of isolation and simplicity that was, in fact, gone forever by the end of the war. When he was eighteen, Oe took his first train trip, a journey to Tokyo, where he would begin his life as a student and as a writer. Oe wrote his first stories while he was studying French literature at Tokyo University and rose quickly to fame around the time of his graduation, after winning the Akutagawa Prize for "Prize Stock" in 1958. That year, he also published his first novel, *Nip the Buds, Gun the Kids,* about the wartime evacuation of fifteen reform-school boys to a village much like Ose. Oe could not have launched his career with greater speed or notice.

"In the beginning, I was a happy enough writer," he said, in clear but hesitant English. "There was the shadow of the war and the American occupation, which caused anxiety in a young man from the periphery, but I was mainly happy. But by the time I reached twenty-five or twenty-six I lost all sense of identity, all the stability of feeling that I might have had before. For several years, suicide became a strong preoccupation. Then, in 1963, my son was born. This little baby was a kind of personification of my unhappiness. He looked like a baby with two heads. There was a huge growth on his head that made him look like that. This was the most important crisis of my life. The doctors made us decide whether or not to operate. Without an operation, Hikari would have died very quickly. With the operation, he might live, but with terrible, terrible difficulties. My son was born on the thirteenth of June, and I went to Hiroshima on August first. Hikari was still in the hospital. I was escaping from my baby. These were shameful days for me to remember. I wanted to escape to some other horizon. I'd been asked to do some reportage in Hiroshima, and so I went there, fled there, intending to talk to politicians and doctors and activists at an international antinuclear conference. I despaired of the political people and their talk, and I quickly went over to the hospital, where the surviving victims of the bomb were being treated. There I met the director, its great doctor, Fumio Shigeto, and we talked for hours and hours. In my hotel room at night, as I edited the notes of what Dr. Shigeto was telling me about the perseverance of the atomic bomb victims, I began to create in my mind a new image of the human being. It is difficult to explain, but my thinking was changing."

Oe interrupted himself to look at his son, who was sitting at a table across the room. Hikari lifted a teapot close to his face and examined it from all angles, watching his own reflection curve, expand, recede, as in a convex mirror. He did this for a while and then looked up. Hikari smiled at his father, and his father smiled back. Oe turned away, finally, and went on with his story.

"And so on a Saturday, as I remember it, I told Dr. Shigeto about the situation with my son. He told me about a young ophthalmologist working under him. In Hiroshima, you see, many people were hurt in their eyes, from the atomic flash, from broken bits of flying glass. This young doctor, who eventually committed suicide, was in despair. He said to Dr. Shigeto, 'What can we do? We know nothing about the effects of radiation. I do not know how to cure these people.' Dr. Shigeto told him, 'If there are wounded people, if they are in pain, we must do something for them, try to cure them, even if we seem to have no method.' He told me this story, and I felt great shame that I was doing nothing for my son—my son, who was silent and could not express his pain or do anything for himself. And so I knew that I must face my baby, ask for the operation, and make every effort to care for him. I returned to Tokyo, and my son was operated on.

"As it turned out, the doctor was successful. Hikari could live on, and in Hikari's presence I began to deconstruct my life. My work began to change, and I discovered a strong standpoint against suicide. Until then, I had been a passive person. My life had been dark and negative, with no thought toward the future. My wife is a deeply strong and independent person, and I was terribly ashamed of myself before her for thinking so darkly. Sometimes a writer will commit suicide despite having such a strong wife, and I was close to that, but with the birth of my son my heart opened."

For more than two decades, Oe examined and reexamined that birth and his own behavior with a pitiless eye, studying the situation, distorting it, turning it over to see all its possibilities. In Japan, where the handicapped are stigmatized more than in many other countries, Oe's voluminous, even obsessive writing on the subject of a father and his damaged son was especially shocking. In a story entitled "Aghwee the Sky Monster" a father kills his deformed baby by feeding him sugar water instead of milk. When an autopsy reveals that the child's tumor was benign, the father is visited by the ghost of his son. In the short novel *A Personal Matter* the father runs not to Hiroshima but to an old girlfriend—a "sexual adventuress," who helps him plot the killing of his infant, the "monster baby." At the last minute, the father abandons the plan and accepts—even embraces—the responsibility of his sick child. ("In life," Oe told me, "I chose the path of *A Personal Matter*.") And in a short story entitled "Teach Us to Outgrow Our Madness" Oe describes the father's unspoken communication—his absolute, even physical sympathy—with his son. The enormously fat father in the story experiences every hurt of his son's, and tries, through speech and touch, to penetrate the shell of the boy's outward silence, to nourish and protect him: "The fat man was convinced that he experienced directly whatever physical pain his son was feeling. When he read somewhere that the male celatius, a deep-sea fish common to Danish waters, lived its life attached like a wart to the larger body of the female, he dreamed that he was the female fish suspended deep in the sea with his son embedded in his body like the smaller male, a dream so sweet that waking up was cruel."

Unlike in that fictional dream, Oe and his wife have been unable to protect their son from unending ailments and indignities. "In these thirty years there have been many crises for my son," Oe said, "but always we—Hikari, my wife, and I—try to meet the difficulties and transcend them. Every time we surpass one difficulty or another, we feel as though we are a little higher than we were before. We are ascending—like a staircase, somehow. When he is sick, we are all sick, and when he is cured we are cured."

Oe and his wife are now able to talk with their son, and the development of that communication has been much as it is in some of the stories and novels—a slow and inexplicable process. "We created our communication step by step," Oe said. "At first, Hikari was completely negative about communicating with me or with my wife. It was as if he were trapped inside his body. But we were always trying to reach him. When Hikari was four years old, we bought a recording of various birdsongs and played it over and over again. There would be a bird singing and then an announcer's very neutral voice saying 'This is a water rail' or 'This is a pigeon,' 'This is a blue jay.' This went on for more than two years. We played it for him all the time. One day when Hikari was about six years old, we went to our cottage in the mountains. I was walking in the woods with him on my shoulders, and I heard a bird chirping. I didn't know what kind of bird it was. Then I heard a voice saying—in Japanese, of course—'This is a water rail.' I thought I was hallucinating. There were no other people around. It was like a phantom. Then came another chirp and, again, 'This is a water rail.' It was Hikari! And he was right! So it seemed clear then that he was capable of learning. It turned out that when we played the recording he could identify *all* the birds: 'This is a pigeon,' 'This is a blackbird,' and so on. He knew the sounds of seventy birds. A kind of genius. And so my wife and I began to talk to him, at first, through the names of birds.

"Then my wife began to play recordings of Bach, Mozart, and others around the house—mostly for herself. But it became clear that even if we just played a snippet of one of the pieces—a Brandenburg Concerto, say—Hikari could identify it. His speaking has never really developed that much, but even though he cannot mature in speech—in language—his music always develops. Our doctor tells us that the brain is divided into two hemispheres, and the one side takes on the role of speech and the other the role of music. He says that in Hikari's brain the halves are divided, with only the weakest connection between them. His musical side is the strong side."

Hikari's parents hired a piano teacher for him, but they soon discovered that the boy could not master the mechanics of playing. It seemed, however, that Hikari was writing down all the music he heard. At first, the teacher thought the music was fragments of Bach and Mozart, but rearranged, out of order. Then she realized that the music was in fact Hikari's own. Two years ago, with the help of a pianist and a flutist, Hikari put out his first compact disk. His new disk has won an award in Japan—the most important award, his mother says, that the family has won all year. "You know, some Japanese critics say that I have somehow exploited my son," Oe said. "But I have lived with him for thirty-one years. I am the expert in this, not they. I think I can understand him. He is not capable of reading my books, but I believe that, even if he could, he would not be injured. Of this I am sure."

While the theme of the "idiot son" has been the most personal of Oe's literary concerns, he is also known in Japan as a writer of engagement, a political presence. His best-selling book is *Hiroshima Notes,* a collection of essays and reportage published in 1965 on the aftermath and meaning of the atomic bomb attacks of 1945. As a public figure, Oe resembles Germany's Günter Grass, a literary provincial (Grass is from Danzig) lecturing his powerful nation on its authoritarian tendencies and the vacancy of its current politics and its cultural scene. Oe is especially quick to strike at the endurance of Japan's imperial symbols. This fall, not long after greeting with unreserved pleasure the news of his Nobel Prize, he refused the Bunka Kunsho, the Order of Culture—an award bestowed by the emperor. He did so, he told the Kyodo News Service, because "the Order of Culture does not fit well with the postwar democracy." Soon he was receiving threats and public insults.

Oe is the remaining pillar of a postwar generation of writers that included Kobo Abe and Yukio Mishima, artists who came of age in a time of unusual intellectual vitality and political protest. (Abe died in 1993, Mishima in 1970.) That generation witnessed the physical and economic devastation of the country followed by its spiritual reexamination and fantastic economic growth. The most dramatic event in Oe's early political development was, of course, the war and the shock of its aftermath. As a schoolboy, he took turns with his classmates vowing that if they were commanded by the emperor to commit suicide they would do it: "I would die, sir, I would cut open my belly and die." The delusions of the war, of official Japanese culture and cosmology, vanished on August 15, 1945, the day Hirohito announced the unconditional surrender to the United States. In an essay entitled "A Portrait of the Postwar Generation," Oe wrote of that day, "The adults sat around their radios and cried. The children gathered outside in the dusty road and whispered their bewilderment. We were most surprised and disappointed that the Emperor had spoken in a *human* voice. . . . How could we believe that an august presence of such awful power had become an ordinary human being on a designated summer day?" While the emperor was forced to renounce his role as deity, his centrality in Japanese culture did not fully recede. The crisis of psychology and politics continues even now. While Mishima gravitated to a theatrical right-wing nationalism, a pro-emperor position, Oe wished for an end to all traces of imperial Japan. Michiko Niikuni Wilson, the author of *The Marginal World of Oe Kenzaburo* and translator, with her husband, Michael, of *The Pinch Runner Memorandum,* writes that one political event that weighed heavily on Oe came in 1960, when a seventeen-year-old right-wing fanatic, Otoya Yamaguchi, charged a public stage and fatally stabbed the leader of the

Socialist party, Inejiro Asanuma. Oe wrote a story, entitled "Seventeen," that was based on that event, and the complaints and threats against the writer and his publisher were so daunting that the magazine it was printed in, *Bungakukai,* issued "Our Humble Notice," apologizing for the story. "Seventeen" has not been included in Oe's collected works. Oe reluctantly agreed to that arrangement, mainly because he feared for the lives of his publishers and their families.

For a long time, Oe kept quiet about the incident and wrote about other matters—especially his childhood village and, soon, his newborn son. Five years later, however, he used the occasion of an August 15 Memorial Meeting to talk about the imperial system, calling it an effective *kakuremino,* "a magic coat that can make the wearer invisible" and so permits the wearer (the Japanese people) to ignore the meaning of the war. In an article published later, he asked why it was that Japanese writers led a battle for the publication of a translation of *Lady Chatterley's Lover* and yet did not come to the defense of "Seventeen" and its sequel, "The Death of Political Youth." Oe wrote, "It is because both works concern not so much right-wing elements in Japan as everything that the Emperor system evokes."

In the 1960s, Oe was friendly with Mishima, despite Mishima's politics. But in 1970, when Mishima committed suicide—seppuku—as, Oe writes, a kind of aestheticized ritual of devotion to the emperor and a call for a right-wing coup d'état, Oe rejected the act as a useless and vulgar attempt to create a bogus image of the Japanese writer. In 1972, partly as a response to Mishima's suicide, Oe wrote an angry parody, "The Day He Himself Shall Wipe My Tears Away." The story is among the most difficult of Oe's works, and vacillates between its anger at Mishima and a desire for the very sort of unclouded faith and sense of spiritual and national belonging that the suicide dramatized. In the end, Oe saw Mishima's life and death as a botched attempt to embody Japanese identity not to the Japanese but to the world beyond. Later, in a conversation with the novelist Kazuo Ishiguro that was published in the magazine

Grand Street, Oe said, "Mishima's entire life, certainly including his death by seppuku, was a kind of performance designed to present the image of an archetypal Japanese. Moreover, this image was not the kind that arises spontaneously from a Japanese mentality. It was the superficial image of a Japanese as seen from a European point of view, a fantasy."

For Oe, Mishima's suicide was a peculiar form of Orientalism. In Edward Said's study of the phenomenon of Orientalism, the Western colonial-adventurer journeys to the East and returns with a literary image of the Oriental: the Arabs, say, in T. E. Lawrence's *The Seven Pillars of Wisdom* or in Flaubert's memoirs of Egypt. In Mishima's case, it was the Japanese himself who created the distorted image, for a wide and admiring Western audience. When I asked Oe about Mishima, he threw up his hands and laughed at the memory of the Mishima craze in the West. "You know, I am fascinated by Ralph Ellison's great book, *Invisible Man,* and it applies to us—us Japanese," he said. "When I speak of the Japanese as an invisible man, I mean it this way. You can see Japanese technology in Europe, you know all about Japanese economic power, you know all about the quaint tea ceremony; but these are all images, masks of Japanese modesty or technological strength. Mishima and Akio Morita, the head of Sony, are like the two poles of the perception of what is Japanese. The majority of Japanese images are masks. We followed and imitated Western philosophy and literature, but even today, more than a hundred and twenty-five years after our great modernization, the Meiji Restoration, began and Japan opened to the rest of the world, we are inscrutable in the eyes of Europeans and Americans. You can understand other Nobelists, they are available to you in the United States: Czeslaw Milosz, Derek Walcott, Joseph Brodsky. But there is not much of a Western desire to understand the people who make all those Hondas. I don't know why. Perhaps we only imitate the West or are just silent in the face of European peoples."

. . .

While Oe may set aside fiction for a while, he has promised to increase his involvement in the Japanese public arena, if only because that debate, he says, is now a "happy wasteland," self-satisfied, money-crazed, unreflective. These days, Oe's leftish political engagement is, for most Japanese who bother to pay attention, a quaint relic of the fifties and sixties. "When I began working as a writer, there was a great generation of independent thinkers— the postwar generation—but today the scene is empty," Oe told me. The most popular younger novelists—minimalists like Banana Yoshimoto and Haruki Murakami—show little interest in the political engagements and complications of their elders; their fiction tends to have the flashy emptiness of a video game, and often sells in the millions. Oe is not dismissive of either Murakami or Yoshimoto, but is concerned that their work portrays and appeals to Japanese who are politically uninvolved and content to exist within a late-adolescent or postadolescent subculture.

"I know that older generations always complain, but that is not quite it," Oe went on. "The situation in Japan is more serious. My friends in the United States worry about the intellectual atmosphere in their own country, but I find that there are people there of great independence, outspoken, complicated. In Japan, our cultural life is very simplified. There is the mode of mass-media culture, and that is nearly all. We rarely hear from our thinkers and intellectuals. There is only the importation of new modes of philosophy from Europe, and it is rehashed, nothing deeper."

As a reader and thinker, Oe has been immersed in Western literature since his childhood obsession with *The Adventures of Huckleberry Finn* and the Swedish tale *The Wonderful Adventures of Nils,* by the Nobel laureate Selma Lagerlöf. As a writer, Oe hopes to reach a Japanese audience, and yet he works in a style that he calls "peripheral," outside the mainstream that began with *The Tale of Genji* and

runs through Mishima and the previous Japanese Nobelist in literature—the 1968 winner, Yasunari Kawabata. As Michiko Wilson has
said, Oe's long, thorny sentences and his themes of abnormality,
sexuality, and marginality are outside the tradition of Japanese
equipoise. Oe wants Japanese art to drop its tradition of stylized
ambiguity, its vagueness, and help reveal the true faces of its people, without masks. His work has a gritty, grotesque quality, which
makes him seem more akin to Mailer, Grass, or Roth than to many
Japanese novelists. The literary critic who has been most important
to Oe is Mikhail Bakhtin, the Russian Rabelais scholar and theorist
of grotesque realism. Perhaps this is why many Western readers,
seeking in Oe the sort of exoticism found in Mishima's *Runaway
Horses*, go away bewildered, as if they had been cheated of reading a
"genuine" Japanese writer.

It is in politics rather than in literature that Oe hopes for a Japanese
exceptionalism. For many years, he has called for the continued
demilitarization of Japan. He has criticized the government for sending the Japanese Self-Defense Forces on foreign missions, and has
criticized foreign governments for pressuring Tokyo to do so. "The
Japanese chose the principle of eternal peace as the basis of morality
for our rebirth," Oe said in his Nobel lecture—an event that fell, he
was quick to point out, on Pearl Harbor Day. "To obliterate from the
constitution the principle of eternal peace will be nothing but an act
of betrayal against the peoples of Asia and the victims of the atom
bombs in Hiroshima and Nagasaki. It is not difficult for me as a writer
to imagine what would be the outcome of that betrayal."

At the Grand Hall of the Swedish Academy, Oe devoted much of his
lecture, "Japan, the Ambiguous, and Myself," to an analysis of
Japanese inscrutability, a critique of the mainstream Japanese literary tradition, and an indictment of Japanese politics, but he also
managed to incorporate in his speech personal matters, including

a passionate acknowledgment of his debts to his family. Standing before his audience and a bank of television cameras, Oe recalled his boyhood in a "peripheral, marginal, off-center" village in a "peripheral, marginal, off-center" country, and how he had found inspiration in *The Wonderful Adventures of Nils*. As he read about the naughty boy who communicates with wild geese, Oe recalled, he had sensed two prophecies for himself in the book: "One was that I might one day become able to understand the language of birds. The other was that I might one day fly off with my beloved wild geese—preferably to Scandinavia."

With a slight smile, Oe told the audience about his son, Hikari, and the way birdsong had moved him to human speech and, eventually, to music. And so, he said, "on my behalf, Hikari has thus accomplished the prophecy that I might one day understand the language of birds."

Then Oe looked at the attractive woman sitting in the front row. Yukari Oe "has been the very incarnation of Akka, the leader of Nils's wild geese," her husband said. "Together with her, I have flown to Stockholm and the second of the prophecies has also, to my utmost delight, now been realized." Three days later, on December 10, the king of Sweden handed Oe the Nobel Prize medal. Not long after that, the family flew back to Tokyo, and Kenzaburo Oe began the next stage of his career: reading, not writing, and taking up the role of the father of a brilliant young composer.

13

―♦♦♦―

"I'm Back"

(May 1995)

Nearly all the old American basketball arenas have been abandoned or razed, victims of the corporate demand for more
"luxury suites," more room to hawk the beer and the cheese dogs
and the "regulation" Nerf balls. Boston Garden is scheduled for
demolition (the Celtics have played their last season on the exquisitely warped floor), and Chicago Stadium, once a graceful barn
on the West Side, is already gutted—four walls awaiting the wreck-
ing ball. The Bulls play their games now across the street at the
United Center ("United" as in the airline, of course), and the place
features all the new amenities: lots of bathrooms, nice parking, no
rats. The United Center is huge, cool, and white: a mobster's mau-
soleum, the world's largest freezer unit. It is a distant place to watch
an intimate sport; the "luxury suites" are so far from the court that
the plutocrats keep their televisions on during the game. All around
the National Basketball Association, the geniuses who own teams
seem to have no faith in the audiences or in basketball itself. At an
ordinary weekend game at the Brendan Byrne Arena, in the Jersey
swamps, not long ago, I sat through more low-end entertainment

than Liberace knew in a lifetime. It was like Vegas Night at the Chamber of Commerce: fireworks and strobe lights during the introduction of the starting lineups; a karaoke contest; a recorded voice urging us to "stand up and cheer"; a recorded laugh mocking the efforts of a player at the foul line; two guys dressed in mattresses who declared themselves "sumo wrestlers" and jumped on top of each other during time-outs; dancing "Jersey Girls"; pre-pubescent "Junior Jersey Kids"; a mascot called Super Dunk who shot foam-and-plastic sticks into the crowd. It's this way just about everywhere—Chicago included.

Michael Jordan once promised that he would never play at the United Center—Chicago Stadium was his Old Vic, his artistic home—but, with his decision to rejoin the Bulls after his midlife sabbatical as a minor-league baseball player, he has deigned to enter the vulgar hall, and thus transform it. Just when the sports pages had become little more than labor reports and police blotters, Jordan stepped in. He has saved the spring.

Jordan, who is the most self-conscious of performers, began his unretirement from basketball March 19 with a gig in Indiana. Except for some brief thrilling moments—a breakaway dunk in the first half, a ferocious struggle for the ball with Reggie Miller in the second—he proved rusty against the Pacers: errant on the jump shot, winded at times, out of synch with his new teammates, barely reacquainted with the old. The Bulls' Croatian forward, Toni Kukoc, who had been heartbroken two years ago to discover that Jordan was leaving the team just as he was joining it, seemed daunted now by the return of his hero. Kukoc spent much of the Indiana game with his feet glued to the floor, his jaw slack. Like so many millions of others, Kukoc was delighted just to be watching Jordan—even a temporarily mortal Jordan—play the game again.

Jordan's first game in Chicago came five days later, against the Orlando Magic, a first-place team featuring two of the best young talents in the sport: Shaquille O'Neal, a Goliath with grace, and

Anfernee (Penny) Hardaway, a silky guard who, with his preternatural sense for the flow of the game, reminds everyone of Earvin (Magic) Johnson. An hour before tipoff, I was talking with Hardaway in the Orlando locker room. The United Center's locker rooms are, admittedly, very new, very clean, like a suburban den. Ordinarily, teams play tapes of the night's opponents, but the Orlando players seemed determined to convince themselves that it was Michael Jordan who ought to be concerned about them. An episode of *Star Trek: The Next Generation* played on the television. Hardaway, for his part, wore a T-shirt bearing the hermetic logo

Step Up, I Lay You,
Step Off, I 'J' You,
Foul Me, I Trey You,
I Gotta Get P.A.I.D.

In-your-face braggadocio is the lingua franca of the NBA, but where Jordan was concerned, Hardaway did not mimic the rhetoric of his T-shirt. He was worshipful, even wary. To play against Jordan "was something I always wanted," he said. "When he retired before I had a chance to play against him, I felt cheated. It's strange. One guy comes back and everything changes. Everybody's *thoughts* change." It was amazing how readily the players and coaches around the league deferred to Jordan. Indiana's coach, Larry Brown, suggested that Chicago, barely a winning team through mid-March, could now win the NBA championship. Chuck Person, of the San Antonio Spurs, used a mystical vocabulary. "He's like a poltergeist," he said of Jordan. "He's an incident by himself."

Out on the court, a few players were getting limber, taking desultory jump shots, walking through moves they would later attempt at frenetic speed. Unguarded, unhindered by an opponent whacking him in the ribs or waving a hand in his eyes, even a backup player like the Chicago forward Corie Blount hit 70 or 80 percent of his shots. It means nothing. In baseball, players are competing mainly against the difficulty of the sport itself, the almost laughable improbability of hitting a speeding baseball with a flame-tempered twig. Baseball is such a hard game that small children modify it (they hit off a tee) and the middle-aged *enlarge* it (calling it softball). In basketball, the fundamentals—shooting, passing, rebounding—are relatively easy to manage, at least in the solitude of an empty schoolyard; the difficulty comes in competing against the athleticism, the obstructions and wiles, of an aggressive opponent. Anyone can hit a fifteen-foot shot, sneakers to the floor; only a professional can manage it with a leaping lump of muscle in his face. That's why Jordan is so much better than anyone else who has ever played the game. He plays as if in solitude. High in the air, his legs splayed, his tongue flopping out of his mouth, he seems weirdly relaxed, calm, as if there were no one special around and plenty of time to think through his next move, floating all the while. Faced with double coverage, as he almost always is, Jordan finds a way to wedge between defenders, elevate as if on an invisible forklift, his legs dangling, and then drop the ball through the hoop. The ease of his game makes the rest of the players, all of them stars in college, look rough, somehow—clumsy, a step slow. "Scoring is scoring," Jordan says serenely in *Rare Air,* his autobiography. "If I want to average 32 points a game, I can do that easily. It's just eight, eight, eight, eight. No problem. I can do that anytime. That's not being cocky. That's confidence."

In the late eighties, the Detroit Pistons, coached by Chuck Daly, seemed to find a way to stop a Chicago team that was, at the time, so lopsided in talent that it was often known in the papers as "Michael Jordan and the Jordanaires." With a jaunty bounce of pride in his voice, Daly told me, "Michael is a player with no weaknesses—he has all these skills, great intelligence, a bionic physical presence—and so when we played him we devised a strategy called the Jordan Rules. We committed ourselves to double-teaming him and, if we could, steering him to his left, his presumably weaker hand. But you know what? Jordan outgrew the Jordan Rules. He just learned to play through them." Others are more dubious, and remember that it was the Pistons' brutality—their stray elbows and surreptitious shoves—that worked so well. Frank Layden, the former Utah Jazz coach, once said to Jordan's biographer Jim Naughton, "The Jordan Rules? You know what the Jordan Rule is, don't you? Knock him on his ass. They can talk all they want, but the one thing they did—when he got in midair—they knocked him down."

The crowd is desperate to set eyes on Jordan. Four huge video screens above the court are playing a tape loop of his greatest hits—scenes from his career in high school, at the University of North Carolina, and on the Bulls. The screens are also playing his collected commercials—McDonald's, Gatorade, Nike, Coca-Cola —as if these, too, were part of his game. The film will have to do for a while. Jordan, who has been trying to get used to this alien arena's bright lights and tight rims with solitary workouts in the afternoon, is out of sight, hanging back in a room reserved for players having their ankles taped. "No Press Beyond This Point," the sign says. In the open, main part of the locker room, many of the Bulls come and go, dressing, watching film of old Orlando games, wearily answering questions about their returning leader.

The Bulls have handed out hundreds of press passes for this game, and everyone's mandate is the same: Get Jordan—Jordan pictures, Jordan quotes. Both the *Tribune* and the *Sun-Times* published special pullout sections in the morning; the local television stations have been broadcasting live from courtside since late afternoon. The press cannot afford to miss a Jordan sighting. A pack of reporters and half a dozen cameras all cluster near his locker. As a group, we gaze at his open closet and the vestments dangling therein: a mustard-colored sports coat on a hanger, slacks and shirt on hooks. There is, as well, a heap of basketball shoes, a box of Bubble Yum. We all stare, as if doing so would draw Jordan into the room.

It is a strange tableau, and on the other side of the room one of the Bulls' centers starts laughing. At first, it is hard to tell which center: Luc Longley, the Aussie; Bill Wennington, the bearded one; or Will Perdue, who wears a Hannibal Lecter mask to protect his face. All three are big, bulky white guys; they look like bouncers at a very tough club.

"Hey, boys, you never look at my locker that way!" It's Wennington, the one with the beard.

Then, under deadline pressure, one of the cameramen says, "I gotta have something!" He angles his camera lens toward the closet floor. He is filming a jockstrap. Written on the waistband is "Jordan, #45."

Michael Jordan leads one of the grandest and most peculiar American lives since Elvis left the building. His return this spring has been big news in Chicago, and in Chengdu, too. The *China Sports Daily* said in its story, "This flying man, Qiao Dan"—M.J. in Mandarin— "is still the most popular sports star on earth." He may also be the most valuable human commodity in sports. He earns about thirty million dollars a year endorsing products—nearly eight times his basketball salary. Every detail of his return has implications. The mere rumor that he might return to basketball caused Nike stock to soar. Simply by changing his jersey number from 23 to 45, he spawned an industry. Every kid in the country wants the new shirt. Champion, the company that makes the official shirts, has ordered its plant in Winston-Salem to add a midnight-to-eight shift to fill the demand.

At the age of thirty-two, Jordan is the subject of picture books, a shelfload of biographies, and countless videocassettes, and his face appears on lunch boxes, drinking cups, sneakers. In Chicago, his image is everywhere, like Kim Il Sung's in Pyongyang. Every one of Jordan's endorsements is designed to make him (and, therefore, the product) heroic, available, pleasant, elegant, "beyond race." Even academe has turned its eyes to the Air. ("Finally, there is the subversion of perceived limits through the use of *edifying deception,* which in Jordan's case centers around the space/time continuum," the scholar Michael Eric Dyson explains in his essay "Be Like Mike? Michael Jordan and the Pedagogy of Desire.") So that Jordan can get his teeth fixed without causing a commotion, his dentist comes in on a day off; his barber used to do the same, but Jordan shaves his own head these days, giving it the pleasing burnished look of an antique desk. Once, Jordan was out on the golf course and paused to finish eating an apple. He threw the core into the woods, and suddenly a group of kids, who had been following his foursome, ran off in search of the remains. "Please, please don't do that," Jordan said. Jordan receives between forty and fifty letters every week from dying children who tell him that it is their last wish on earth to meet him. He obliges as many as he can; to the rest, he sends a pair of Air Jordans that he has worn in a game. One child, who died of leukemia, was buried wearing the size-13 shoes that Jordan had given him.

On October 6, 1993, Jordan announced that he was quitting professional basketball to spend more time with his family. (Jordan and his wife, Juanita, have three children.) "I'm going to watch the grass grow and I'm going to have to cut it," he said. Basketball fans accustomed to watching aging superstars lurch on until the last possible paycheck were shocked—Jordan's skills had not fallen off at all—but, with time, his decision began to make some sense. The Bulls had won three championships in a row, putting to rest the shibboleth of Jordan as a ball hog incapable of giving up some shots for the good of the team. In the end, Jordan had raised the level of every player on the Bulls, including the mysterious and pouty all-star Scottie Pippen. There was nothing left to prove on that score.

Jordan's decision to retire also had an artistic dimension. His career was his oeuvre, and he refused to tarnish it with an autumnal slide into repetition or self-parody. In the short run, he was depriving us of his presence and weakening the entire enterprise of professional basketball, but in the longer view we would never have to remember him logy and diminished as he closed in on middle age. Jordan had long been a student of the career of Julius Erving—the purposeful flamboyance on the court, the studied grace when dealing with reporters and advertisers—and he did not want to end up as Erving had in his final years, reduced to ordinary standards of play. Jordan's art would know no senescence; our memories would remain pure.

What was more, his closest friend and adviser—his father, James Jordan—was killed in a robbery that summer. It was hard to argue with the decision. The man was just worn out in every way. After so many years of playing the perfect gentleman for the press, after enduring the sanctimonious criticism of his gambling, Jordan revealed in his retirement news conference a Nixonian prickliness, a mock gratitude that he would no longer have to put up with "you guys," the reporters.

Jordan was getting out before his desire or his legs or his grace abandoned him. If fans did not like it—well, then, we would have to learn to live with it. In an issue of *Sport* that appeared at a time when he was already reconsidering his decision to retire, Jordan was asked if it concerned him that he had left behind an "emptiness" in his fans and in the game itself. "I'm sorry, but it doesn't," he said. "Unfortunately, people are going to be thinking that way for years, because I'm through. I'm not coming back. At least, that's my feeling right now. I know there are people who wish I was still playing basketball, but at some point in time, either now or twenty years from now, those people will get over it. I apologize if some people think that's selfish of me, but that's the way it is."

Of course, Jordan's retirement had little to do with his desire to play catch in the backyard with his children. Having satisfied his familial longings in a matter of a few months, he signed on to play baseball for the Chicago White Sox, who assigned him to their Double-A club, the Birmingham Barons. It was something like a lark—Jordan had not played baseball since he was in high school—but not quite. Jordan is a competition maniac—his friends have seen him get hysterical when he loses at golf, poker, or Ping-Pong; he has lost hundreds of thousands of dollars betting with shady characters on the golf course—and he cannot, it seems, live without the rush. James Jordan often said, "My son doesn't have a gambling problem. What he does have is a *competition* problem." Unfortunately, he had chosen for his lark the most impossible of games, and one he had little hope of mastering. In countless feature stories on television and in print we were witness to the spectacle of Michael Jordan as George Plimpton, the amateur at play, and it was not an entirely pretty sight: Jordan fanned at curveballs, he lost fly balls in the sun. He was game and serious, but as a baseball player he was never more than a novelty act—and, in his own way, he had the decency to admit it. "This has been a very humbling experience," he said.

Meanwhile, the vacuum in Chicago was becoming increasingly apparent. The Bulls did well enough without Jordan in the 1993–94 regular season—they won fifty-five of eighty-two games—but, faced with the New York Knicks in the playoffs, they found their limits. They lost, four games to three. This year, the slide was more precipitous: suddenly the Bulls were not much more than a .500 team, a mediocrity. Pippen remained a star, but, unlike Jordan, he could not make stars of his more earthbound teammates. The yearning for Jordan was painful to witness. Every night before Bulls games, fans would come early to the new arena and mill around a statue of Jordan—a soaring construction of the master about to dunk, and, underneath, the inscription "Michael Jordan 1984–93. The best there ever was. The best there ever will be." Even in the worst Chicago cold, fans would trade Jordan stories, remembering particular moments in his career: the change-of-hands-look-I'm-still-up-here-floating layup that blew everyone's mind and ruined an aging Lakers team in the 1990–91 finals; the eyes-closed foul shots; the kiss-the-rim slams.

Jordan's absence from the game left the league with middling champions and no leading man. The NBA is full of young players with fantastic potential: O'Neal and Hardaway may turn out to be the cornerstones for a dynasty in Orlando; a rookie guard in Dallas, Jason Kidd, has made a team out of the beleaguered Mavericks; Glenn (Big Dog) Robinson is a hit in Milwaukee; and Detroit's Grant Hill, a player of rubbery grace and fine manners, is already the league's official answer to the spoiled stars who skip games and practices with bogus injuries and then demand salaries in the tens of millions of dollars. But none of these players was ready to fill the Jordan gap, and everyone in the league office and in the press knew it. The NBA, which had been so ascendant with Jordan, Magic, and Bird in the game, was in a slump.

Late last spring, while the Knicks were attempting to slug, shove, and trash-talk their way past the Houston Rockets in the NBA championship series, I sat in the Madison Square Garden press section with a friend—Michael Wilbon, who is a columnist for the sports pages of *The Washington Post*. Wilbon's life, as far as I have been able to read it, is a nonstop busman's holiday. He is a basketball fan—a basketball *fanatic*—who is paid by his editors to follow the game as closely as he can. He complies. He has racked up a million frequent-flier miles, mainly in the pursuit of basketball games, but he is not likely to use his off-season to hit the beaches in, say, Tahiti. As Wilbon would say, "You can't get no goddam ESPN in no goddam Papeete." And yet, as we watched the Knicks and the Rockets pound up and down the boards in quest of the NBA title that night at the Garden, it was clear that Wilbon was taking no pleasure in this series. He despised its artlessness. He frowned at every collision, sneered at every turnover. For me, as for nearly everyone else at the Garden that night, the possibility of a Knicks triumph was a chance to relive the singular thrill of an age ago: the championship of 1969–70, when Willis Reed, his injured leg shot up with painkillers, limped out onto the Garden floor (El Cid of Louisiana) and led the team to its legendary victory over Wilt Chamberlain and the Los Angeles Lakers. But Wilbon is not of this city—he is Chicago-born—and he was having none of it.

"This game is a dog," he declared.

"Why's that?"

"Michael's hitting .200 in Birmingham and these fools think they're winning a championship."

My illusions were now shot. The Knicks were suddenly there before me in all their limitations—plodding, erratic, hysterical, a squad of lager louts trying to scare their betters by whacking their hands on the bar and talking too loud. The Rockets were more obviously a limited flock, a team with an extraordinary center—the Nigerian Hakeem Olajuwon—and four guys named Ed. In the end, the Rockets won the misbegotten series, and everyone except the participants and their dependents has long forgotten the whole thing.

Michael Jordan's return has rescued basketball from more mediocrity. He reminds us why we buy the tickets, why watching is not a waste of time; and the degree of gratitude is not just great but strange. In early March, while Jordan was merely reconsidering his status, I read a Mike Wilbon column in the *Post* in which he declared, without irony, that he would gladly give two years of his life if Jordan would only return to the Bulls.

Not long afterward, Wilbon, the league, the city of Chicago, even Knicks fans—all of us—got our wish. Jordan announced his intention by sending a fax through his agent's office. "I'm back," Jordan wrote, and that was all. Wilbon, pay up.

The Orlando game was a bust. Jordan shot too much and he shot too long. Seven of twenty-three from the field. His jumpers kept banging off the butt of the rim. Over and over. He was like a man who keeps pumping the gas pedal until the engine floods and the car dies. And then he turns the key again and pumps, just to make *sure:*

106–99, Magic. But, in a sense, Jordan was right to shoot as much as he did. Chicago had no prayer of going far in the playoffs unless Jordan got his timing back. A regular-season loss to Orlando was a small price to pay.

Jordan walked into the interview room trailed by a presidential-size security detail. (He does not do the naked-interview thing. He showers and dresses first, and all await him.) He managed to look spectacular in that mustard-colored jacket, but he could not hide his frustration. He was more bewildered than anything else. "I just can't turn it on," he said. "As much as I want to, I just can't turn it on. It will take time."

Jordan was in a five-week, seventeen-game race before the playoffs to retune himself to basketball. He had been away from the professional game for 636 days—nearly two full seasons—and in that time he had hardly touched a ball bigger than a baseball. "When I was down in the minors, every guy wanted to play me in basketball," he said. "I used to play on Sundays with some of the guys in Arizona. We'd go and rent a gym and play pickup games. And I think these guys thought I'm retired—or maybe they're like me, they think they can be a basketball player just as much as I think I can be a baseball player. But, really, each time I played, my appetite got a little bit greater."

Jordan himself never doubted that he could return and average thirty-odd points a game—in other words, lead the league in scoring—but the *Chicago Tribune,* which chronicles the Life of Michael with definitive attention, pressed some medical experts on the nervous question. "We tested Michael at our biochemical lab during his previous playing days," Dr. Charles Bush-Joseph, of the sports-medicine section of Rush–Presbyterian–St. Luke's Medical Center, told the *Tribune.* "He was off the charts in his ability to generate power in the legs. At thirty-two, he is a bit past a man's physical prime in terms of quickness and explosiveness, but his high level of skills can more than cover any such loss. He just needs time to get back his neuromuscular edge—more commonly known as timing."

For my own peace of mind, I talked with two of Jordan's precursors at the guard position—Bob Cousy and Walt Frazier—and neither had any doubt that Jordan would scrape off the rust in time for the trials of May. Retired ballplayers—especially players of a certain level—are often touchy about the subject of the current crop. They can be grouchy, deliberately uncomprehending, like aging composers whining about the newfangled twelve-tone stuff. But not where Jordan is concerned. Cousy, who led the Celtics in the fifties and early sixties, and Frazier, who led the Knicks in the late sixties and the seventies, would not begrudge Jordan his eminence.

"Until six or seven years ago, I thought Larry Bird was the best player I had ever seen," Cousy, who works as a broadcaster for his old team, said. "Now there is no question in anyone's mind that Jordan is the best. He has no perceptible weaknesses. He is perhaps the most gifted athlete who has ever played this foolish game, and that helps, but there are a lot of great athletes in this league. It's a matter of will, too. Jordan is always in what I call a ready position, like a jungle animal who is always alert, stalking, searching. It's like the shortstop getting down and crouching with every pitch. Jordan has that awareness, and that costs you physically. If you do it, you are so exhausted you have trouble getting out of bed in the morning. Not many athletes do it. To me, he hasn't lost a thing."

"Leapers are usually not great shooters, but Michael is the exception," Frazier said. "If you give him a few inches, he buries the jump shot. When he gets inside, his back is to the basket and he's shakin' and bakin' and you're dead. When he drives, good night. He's gone. Now that the league has made hand-checking illegal—you can't push your man around on defense any longer—it's conceivable that Michael could score even more. I don't think he's even sensed that he has more license now. When he does, he'll be scoring sixty if he feels like it."

· · ·

For the next few weeks after the Orlando game, I followed Jordan, at various arenas and on the tube. Game by game, he was playing his way into condition. He hit a game-winning shot against the Hawks in Atlanta. He iced the Celtics in Boston. Most important of all, even when his shot was off he did enough of the other things—passing, rebounding, defending, and exhorting his teammates, his eyes narrowed with impatience—that suddenly the Bulls were once more a top-rank team. Pippen was getting the ball enough to satisfy his sensitivities; Kukoc was realizing he could play with, and not merely worship, Jordan; even the three amigos—Wennington, Longley, and Perdue—seemed smoother, professional, in the game. Curiously, the only deficiency in Jordan's game was his tendency to shoot poorly at the United Center. "I guess I'm used to playing across the street at the Stadium," he said one night. "This is a new surrounding. But the court dimensions are the same." He had faith in his own powers of concentration. Suddenly his life was strange and cluttered again, a mass of requests and fans and commercials. "But once I step on the court I'm having fun," he said. "That's the good part."

On March 28, the Bulls played the Knicks at Madison Square Garden. No crowd at the Garden had been this jumpy since the playoffs last year. Most of the new arenas diffuse the noise of the crowd—spread it out and turn it into a muffled undertone, a murmur. The Garden on a good night still rumbles, and once Jordan stepped on the floor the crowd kept up a steady roar—half in pleasure, half in fear for the home team. Against New York, Jordan is guarded by the most temperamental of the defenders he faces— John Starks, a young man who is capable of brilliance one night and errant rage another, and then a long, inert period of funk; he is maddeningly inconsistent, more talent than player. To be a Knicks fan is to be forced to live with the moody vacillations of John Starks. It is no way to live. And yet five minutes into his encounter with Jordan I felt for Starks, felt for him deeply. From the opening tap, Starks did the best he could, steering Jordan to his supposedly bad hand (the left), guiding him into other defenders, jumping high with the shot. It was all for nothing. Jordan opened the game with a jumper, shot as casually as tossing a stone into a lake. The next time Jordan had the ball, he palmed it, and waved it up and down, teasing Starks, as if this were a Globetrotters act and Starks were the paid dupe. Another score. Not long after that, Jordan caught a pass on the baseline and, before putting the ball on the floor, did a little trick in which he began arching his back, rocking back and forth, mesmerizing Starks. Suddenly, as Starks fell into the sleepy rhythm, Jordan spun and dashed around him. The layup, of course, was good. Starks trotted up the court on offense blinking, stone-faced, determined not to betray the frustration he was feeling.

From then on, my notes are a mess—a stream of underlinings, exclamation points, hieroglyphs, each centered on another Jordanian amazement. By the end of the first quarter, he had twenty points. What was, secondarily, so thrilling about the game was that the rest of the players on the floor (Starks included) were at their best. I don't know that I have ever seen a better game in the regular season. The Knicks were freed of their psychoses. No one kicked the scorer's table. No one dissed the coach. There were no head butts, body slams, or petty screeds. Derek Harper drew a harmless technical foul. (As usual, he earned it, and then pulled off a theatrical palms-up protest of innocence, the way professional wrestlers do when they are accused of producing a "foreign object" from their shorts.) The Knicks were doing all they could to win. Were it not for Jordan's performance, Patrick Ewing might have been the morning headline.

But, of course, it was Jordan's night, and, as the game went on, Starks—alas, poor Starks!—began to wear the mask of infinite pain. Jordan hit shot after shot. There have been times in the past when his teammates, wearied of their role as supporting players, have rebelled against their leader's dominance. At one point against the Knicks, Scottie Pippen, a player of remarkable talents but delicate ego, seemed to ignore Jordan, who was open for a layup, and instead threw up an absurd bomb from long range, as if to say, "No, Michael, I will not *always* yield to you." Except for that moment, the Bulls meshed as well as they had in two years.

For the Knicks, and for the rest of the teams in the NBA that would face the Bulls this spring in the playoffs, the final play was the most dangerous—the one that sent out a reminder of Jordan's dimensions as an athlete. Part of why we cleave to sports and fandom (besides the sheer escapism) is that excellence is so measurable, so knowable in numbers. The .500 shooter averaging twenty-five points and a dozen rebounds a game is an all-star; the .410 shooter averaging fewer points and boards is a mediocrity. Jordan's numbers—his seven consecutive scoring championships, his stats as a rebounder, passer, and defensive thief—easily identify him as among the best to play the game. The last play against the Knicks shades in the picture; it identifies him as—well, supernatural.

There were fourteen seconds left. The score was 111–111. By then, Jordan had fifty-five points. I was somehow relieved that the game would soon end. Jordan was performing at such a level that it seemed inevitable that he would find a way to score and end it. And to go on watching Starks continue his futile mission had about it a quality of voyeurism, cruelty. Jordan was humiliating a weaker opponent. At times, it was beautiful to witness; at others, it was like watching a man poke a wounded dog with a stick.

Jordan handled the ball. After letting a few seconds melt off the clock, he closed in toward the side of the lane. He drove hard to the right, dipping his shoulder, and then cut sharply to his left and toward the basket. Starks stumbled. He was beginning to lose his man. Suddenly, Ewing, all seven feet of him, stepped forward to help smother Jordan. Now there were just five seconds on the clock. Jordan coiled and jumped, leaving his feet as if to shoot. As he would admit later, shooting had been his intention all along. How can you not shoot with fifty-five points already? ("I'd be lying if I said I came out to pass the ball.") But now the logic of the moment had changed. Ewing had gambled—it was a smart gamble, for there are times when Jordan is sure that he has a better chance of scoring over two men than a teammate has of scoring unattended. Not now. In the huddle, Jordan had advised Wennington, the slow-footed center, that there was a chance—not a *big* chance, but a chance—that he would get a pass if the play broke just so. Which is how it broke. Even in midair, in the tensest moment of a game, Jordan has a look of both concentration and calm, as if he knew he was capable of suspending himself until the proper decision is finally made. Meanwhile, everyone else is frantic, flailing. And now, after passing up what would have been a low-percentage shot, even for him, with Knicks leaping all around him, Jordan shoveled a pass to Wennington. The center gathered the ball in, jumped, and hit the point-blank shot: 113–111. Game.

Afterward, the Knicks coach, Pat Riley, said that yes, of course he admired Jordan's performance, but he betrayed, as well, an over-tired testiness. "You're gonna talk a lot about Michael tomorrow," he told the reporters surrounding him. "But it would have been a hell of a thing if he had scored fifty-five and we'd won. It would have been a different story line." Three weeks later, at the United Center against the Knicks, Jordan did not need to play half as well as he had in New York. This time, he shared the ball with Pippen, and the two of them destroyed New York. Jordan is right. He's back.

———

The Bulls lost to Orlando in the playoffs, but in the 1995–96 season, with Jordan stronger and once more leading the league in scoring, with Pippen adjusted to the return of his master, and with the acquisition of rebounding specialist Dennis Rodman, Chicago was the best team in the league, finishing with an unprecedented 72–10 record. The murderers of Jordan's father were convicted.

14

~oo~

Raging Bull

(June 1996)

Children yearn to read about exemplary lives, and the children of the television age inevitably select the objects of their passion from the little screen. If the doings of Achilles had been televised when I was growing up, I might have memorized the *Iliad* and pursued a career in Hellenic studies, but, as it happened, Channel 9 broadcast the Knicks and Channel 11 the Yankees, leaving me in a state of addiction and with no choice but to read and reread the stories of such noble Athenians as DeBusschere and Reed, Mantle and Ford. Often my friends and I would read these books at the rate of two or three a day—consuming them like literary Cheez Doodles. Each tale had its thematic importance: Bob Gibson's *From Ghetto to Glory* was a Dickensian struggle against modern-day Gradgrinds; Ted Williams's *My Turn at Bat* was, like *Le Morte D'Arthur*, a primer in the art of noble battle; Gale Sayers's threnody for his teammate Brian Piccolo, *I Am Third,* was our version of "To an Athlete Dying Young"; Joe Namath was our Frank Harris, introducing us to sexual delicacies in the masterful *I Can't Wait Until Tomorrow, 'Cause I Get Better-Looking Every Day.*

And then there was the moral instruction of Sandy Koufax's autobiography, *Koufax,* written with the assistance of a greatly underestimated ghost, Ed Linn. (Linn is often overshadowed in literary studies by the suspiciously prolific Maury Allen and Phil Pepe.) In my circle, *Koufax* was known simply as the Talmud. While I was a pupil of dubious standing at the Temple Emanuel Hebrew School, I successfully recycled on an annual basis my classic Linn-lifted dissertation, "Sandy Koufax: Great Pitcher, Greater Jew." By recounting with increasing fervor and commitment the story of Koufax's legendary refusal to pitch a World Series game on Yom Kippur, I sidestepped any need to work up a new paper on the traditional twin towers of adolescent Jewish studies—Rabbi Akiba and Sammy Davis, Jr.

I pull this juvenilia down from the shelf not to riffle through its dusty pages but, rather, to understand the meaning of a current phenomenon. Dennis Rodman's *Bad As I Wanna Be* is No. 1 on the *Times* nonfiction best-seller list. How are we to account for this? Rodman is a certifiable star in a mainstream sport, and yet one is curious about how, as a matter of literary history, we got from the herculean tales of Mantle and Mays to the confessional style of an athlete who poses on the book jacket with his bare *tuchis* flush to the camera and who writes that to "put on a sequined halter top makes me feel like a total person and not just a one-dimensional man." This is not the first athlete confessional. (There are times, in fact, when it seems that the athlete memoir has picked up where *Life Studies* and *Ariel* left off.) So why is Rodman riding (literarily speaking) so high?

It is true that Rodman's team, the Chicago Bulls, is on its way to a National Basketball Association championship. Moreover, Rodman has famously unburdened himself of the details of his romance with Madonna Ciccone. ("She wasn't an acrobat, but she wasn't a dead fish either.") When Rodman first met Madonna, he told her that "I didn't like her music." But, he insists, "that was the one thing about this relationship—we were totally honest with each other. I told her that her house in Los Angeles sucked." In what must surely be the most selling passage in the book, Rodman describes his first night of intimacy with Madonna—more particularly, how he denied her a sexual favor that the lady had said would "get me loose."

"Believe me," our hero said. "I won't do that, darling." And, he duly reports, "I didn't do it. I think she was a little surprised that I said no to her, but I did: I said NO to Madonna."

Admittedly, a scene as gallant as that is also in Rodman's commercial favor, but, still: No. 1?

Before the advent of television, the pivotal sports books were works of inspirational fiction, much like the homiletic prose inventions of Parson Weems. ("Father, I cannot tell a lie. I chopped down the cherry tree," etc.) John R. Tunis's *The Kid from Tomkinsville* and *World Series,* exemplars of the form, were sandlot tales of effort and sportsmanship. Many of the early ballplayers, including Ty Cobb and Babe Ruth, eventually found ghostwriters (Al Stump for Cobb; Bob Considine for Ruth), but only after their playing days were long over. Autobiography existed, but not as the dominant form. I think I know the reason. As Roger Angell has pointed out in these pages, when baseball was the preeminent American sport, before the Second World War, it was a game known mainly through radio, sports columns, and box scores. In order to see a player, one had to actually go to the park, and even at the stadium there was a sense of enormous distance. One was never close enough to begin wondering about a player's wife, his history, his halter top.

The books of my childhood, however, derived from our intimate access to the game through television. We knew the players with the help first of the zoom lens ("Look, there's a fly on Boog Powell's ear!") and then of the biographies. The books themselves followed strict narrative patterns: triumph over tragedy, victory through work, etc. As a result, a thoroughly unpleasant man like Mantle could be portrayed as an archetype. We learned of Mutt, Mantle's doomed and devoted father, and of the way Hodgkin's disease haunted the entire clan, generation after generation. But we were spared the details of ol' No. 7 being hung over in the dugout on game day and of his womanizing on the road.

It's not as if no one knew any better. Ty Cobb, Hemingway once said, was "the greatest of all ballplayers—and an absolute shit." Cobb's ghost, Al Stump, suffered every indignity possible in a literary venture. Old, psychotic, and sick, Cobb hurled empty booze bottles at Stump, and even threatened him with a pistol. Needless to say, none of this unpleasantness was recorded in *My Life in Baseball: The True Record,* published in 1961. The contractual agreement among star, ghost, and publisher was that the publisher would hire the ghost to delineate and glorify the deeds of the star as a noble man: ghosts were meant, as Plutarch wrote of his own approach to the lives of Alexander and Caesar, "to epitomize the most celebrated parts of their story, rather than to insist at large on every particular circumstance of it." The athlete in question was then meant to live up to the chronicle; he was not required to read it. The great Phoenix Suns forward Charles Barkley was once asked about a particular remark he had made in his autobiography, *Outrageous.* Barkley didn't even fake it. "I was misquoted," he said.

Times have changed, of course. Stump eventually did write an independent account of Cobb's life, portraying him in all his ugly brilliance. But that came in 1994, thirty-three years after Cobb died. Wilt Chamberlain, for his part, wrote a book in which he claimed to have slept with twenty thousand women (a scoring record that will stand even after his hundred-point-game mark has been broken). But Chamberlain's confessional was also late: he retired from basketball eighteen years before its publication.

The book that changed everything in the commercial sports-literature field was Jim Bouton's baseball memoir, *Ball Four,* which came out in 1970. Although Bouton had known some winning moments as a pitcher, next to teammates like Mantle he was a pipsqueak. As a writer, however, he was fresh, funny, and irreverent, informing an astonished public that some players cheated on their wives, popped pills, and, during the national anthem, looked up the dresses of women in the stands—a practice known among the Yanks as "beaver-shooting." The book was, at once, elevated to the bestseller list and denounced by everyone from Bowie Kuhn, the baseball commissioner, to Dick Young, the reactionary *Daily News* columnist, who wrote, "I feel sorry for Jim Bouton. He is a social leper. He didn't catch it, he developed it." Trying to imagine the commotion around *Ball Four* now is a bit like wondering what all the fuss was over *Les Demoiselles d'Avignon*. Bouton's younger readers tended to appreciate him; the older ones thought he had "torn down" heroes and betrayed what was inevitably called "the sanctity of the game."

As it turned out, of course, one might as well have tried to resist free verse. Publishers would continue to put out reverent books about sports heroes—the shelves are filled with hagiographies of everyone from Michael Jordan to Joe Montana—but Bouton had changed the form.

The history of the sports autobiography most closely parallels that of the other form of literary junk food, the Hollywood life story. But, since the sports-trash form tends to do its work on a younger and more impressionable audience, it is more important. I don't know of many kids who are terribly interested in the life of Tom Cruise, or are under any misapprehension that what Tom Cruise does is as difficult as hitting a major-league curveball.

I can still remember with a weird clarity hundreds of details from books I read before I was twelve. And, whether I like it or not, I can already see signs of this fascination in my elder son, Alex, who is almost six. Five seems to be the genetically encoded starting point. I made the mistake of once taking Alex to a Mets game when he was not quite four: after he made his way through a hot dog, a pint of Coke, popcorn, another Coke, and a miniature batting helmet filled with chocolate ice cream, he declared his desire to get back on the subway and go home. It was the top of the second. And yet the next year he started drawing pictures of Patrick Ewing and wearing a Knicks road jersey as pajamas.

So far, Alex's loyalties are imitative. He has declared himself a Knicks fan and a registered Democrat. But he has also taken a disturbing interest in the opposition: he has, for example, told me that Michael Jordan is "real awesome" and Scottie Pippen is "also real awesome." He doesn't know quite what to make of Dennis Rodman. Kids are not often scared or offended by the bizarre, but they are deeply curious—they notice everything. Certainly Alex has noticed what there is to notice about Dennis Rodman. "Why is his hair red?" he has asked. Or yellow. Or green. And "Why can't I tattoo my shoulders?" One day, to help him understand, I'll give him *Bad As I Wanna Be*. Like when he's thirty-two.

Rodman is not the only player-litterateur who is selling himself as an antihero, but most of his competitors do nothing to risk shocking the consumer of fast food and sneakers. Barkley's *Outrageous* is full of "controversial" chat, but he still manages to rake it in with McDonald's ads. *Bad As I Wanna Be* ("with Tim Keown") goes well beyond Bouton's *Ball Four*, getting in our collective face with an absolute, and desperate, authenticity. There is no whimsy. Here we are on the edge of a new sports form: autopathography.

The book opens with the scene of Rodman, at the height of his talents, sitting in his pickup truck with a rifle and "deciding whether to kill myself." His championship team, the Detroit Pistons, is being dismantled; his coach and father figure, Chuck Daly, is gone; his marriage is a ruin; he is a tortured mess. Mostly, Rodman was haunted by the undeniable truth—that if he were not six feet eight and a master of the art of grabbing a basketball as it bounces off the rim he would more than likely be dead or back in the hole he came from.

Rodman grew up in Oak Cliff, a dismal housing project in Dallas. His father was the aptly named Philander Rodman. He ran out on the family when Dennis was three years old. As Rodman tells the story, his sisters were successful students, while he himself was slow, homely, and, in general, a disappointment to his mother. He felt rejected by everything and everyone around him. "There have been many times, none of them recent, when I sat back and wished I was white," he writes. "I grew up in the projects, where everyone was black. But I feel I was abused within that culture. I wasn't accepted there. I was too skinny, too ugly, too something."

At nineteen, when so many of Rodman's eventual peers in the game were already assured of multimillion-dollar contracts, Rodman was adrift: homeless at times; working odd jobs at others. He had barely played any organized basketball. "I was a nobody, just bumming around with some hoodlum buddies." He worked the graveyard shift as a janitor at the Dallas–Fort Worth Airport but was fired for stealing fifty watches from the gift shop. Having flunked out after a semester of junior college, he ran across a coach from a tiny school in Oklahoma who thought he had some promise. Rodman became a twenty-one-year-old freshman. (At twenty-one, Shaquille O'Neal was already a bazillionaire and had published an autobiography, *Shaq Attaq!*—a book with all the spontaneity of a Pepsi ad.)

At Southeastern Oklahoma University, Rodman proved himself an eerily tireless player, notable as much for his effort as for his skills. Suddenly, he was accepted in a community; he knew, though, that it all depended on his ability to play ball. "When I was twenty, those people would have crossed the street to get away from me."

Rodman was drafted by the Detroit Pistons as a "project" player; that is, the coaches wanted to see if a twenty-five-year-old rookie could play with men who had been stars since they were in the sixth grade. Rodman more than acquitted himself on the basketball court. What was really difficult was learning to cope with the impossible strangeness (no matter how delicious) of being a poor, lonely kid one day and an impossibly rich object of desire the next.

"Fifty percent of life in the NBA is sex," he writes. "The other fifty percent is money." Rodman is exaggerating only slightly. As a newspaper reporter, I covered the N.B.A. for a season, and wherever the players stayed, the hotel lobby resembled the waiting room at a modeling agency. The women fairly auditioned for them. One reporter told me that a player he covered—one of the greatest in the history of the game—used to have a friend roam the arena for him searching out the best-looking women; the friend would line up the women he had selected, and as the player headed for the bench he would nod his approval or disapproval of the gathered chattel. "This is the ultimate turnaround," Rodman writes. "When I was a kid, the girls made fun of me and didn't find me attractive at all. I was skinny and small and they thought I was funny-looking. Now, they all want me. Too many of them want me." (For the record, Rodman does not believe Chamberlain's boast of having slept with twenty thousand women: "That's three or four women a day for fifteen to twenty years. I dare anybody to keep up that kind of pace.") But while Rodman, like so many of his colleagues, availed himself of his sexual privileges, he did it, he tells us, with a darkness in his soul: "Once you've had a total stranger ask you to fuck his wife while he watches, you're not going to be easily shocked. There's only one thing that shocks me: I'm still here."

Rodman is hyperaware of his mortality, both as a man and as a commodity. Because he's not much of a shooter (the skill that attracts the most attention in the N.B.A., and thus the biggest salaries), he must do the dirty work of basketball: defense, setting screens, and, especially, retrieving the missed shots of others.

About basketball itself, Rodman is a cultural conservative. He despises the "fifty-year-old white men," the executives who crowd every second with bogus entertainment: "You've got guys flying off a trampoline to dunk a ball, you've got dancing gorillas and high-light shows during time-outs." This is the sort of grouchy rant that Michael Jordan, with his awareness of his place on the corporate marquee, would never indulge in.

Rodman not only resists the N.B.A.'s blandishments to be a "role model" (a dubious concept plucked out of the social-science jargon of the fifties) but insists on his own confusions. "Sometimes I don't even know who I am, and these people are calling me their hero?" The sports-addicted American public now has a player willing to describe his sexual anxieties (he fantasizes about making it with another man); a black man who admits that his alienation from black culture is so deep that his favorite band is that icon of Seattle grunge, Pearl Jam; a star who shows up late at the opening of a new arena in San Antonio because he wanted to go as a blond and "the damned bleach job took too long." I am not sure we have ever known a star athlete so eager to tell us that he paints his fingernails and that his pickup truck is pink and white. Whereas Michael Jackson denies up and down his ambiguities in a music world that would be more likely to accept them, Rodman celebrates his in a realm of conspicuous machismo:

> I don't think painting my fingernails is a big deal. It's not like I'm sitting home by myself, trying on lingerie. That's not my style. I don't do lingerie. . . .
>
> When I cross-dress now, it's just another way I can show all the sides of Dennis Rodman. I'm giving you the whole package, I'm becoming the all-purpose person. . . .

I'm not gay. I would tell you if I was. If I go to a gay bar, that doesn't mean that I want another man to put his tongue down my throat—no. It means I want to be a whole individual.

Rodman is right to complain that he is making only two and a half million dollars a year when inferior, lazy players like Derrick Coleman make three times that. But sometimes his insistent honesty is just too much. His insults directed against other players are unappealing and so are his attempts to portray himself as unawed and superior to nearly everyone he encounters. ("I said, 'I'm Dennis,' and she said, 'I'm Madonna,' and we both said, 'Great.' ")

At least one teammate, John Salley, claims that Rodman gives himself an easy ride in the book, but I think our man comes across with some real truth. Jordan's sponsors demand of us that we "Be Like Mike." Rodman wants to be a different kind of hero, a frontiersman of the soul. He is an embodiment of the times: a gender-bender filled with racial anxiety. As Rousseau puts it in his own confessions, Rodman can claim to have "shown myself as I was; contemptible and vile when I was so; good, generous, sublime when I was so." In the end, we like him—or, at least, we don't mind him. Besides, it's hard not to look forward to the future performances of one who says, "I want to play my last game in the N.B.A. in the nude." He gives us a reason to go on living.

———

With his book still at the top of the best-seller lists, Rodman and the Chicago Bulls won the N.B.A. Championship in June 1996.

THREE

THE NEWS BUSINESS

15

Last of the Red Hots

(September 1995)

When I arrived at *The Washington Post* in 1981, in that amphibious state of semi-employment known as a summer internship, Ben Bradlee, the executive editor, was suffering from wounds inflicted on the paper by a young woman named Janet Cooke. Bradlee is the very model of the devil-may-care WASP—his entertaining memoir, *A Good Life: Newspapering and Other Adventures,* gives the lie to Socrates' idea that the unexamined life is not worth living—but it was clear then, in the summer of 1981, that he had seen a life's work nearly destroyed by a rookie reporter he had hardly known. Suddenly, the editor-knight of Watergate, the one newspaperman routinely compared to Errol Flynn, was off his feet.

Cooke, it will be recalled, was a young reporter of considerable potential, and even greater duplicity. Determined to make her mark and make it quickly, she wrote a story about "Jimmy," a "precocious little boy with sandy hair, velvety brown eyes and needle marks freckling the baby-smooth skin of his thin brown arms." Cooke's profile of a child heroin addict, entitled "Jimmy's World," ran on the front page on Sunday, September 28, 1980. The article, so shocking then in its premise, stunned the city; Marion Barry, having arrived at his mountebank stage as mayor, assured the populace that young Jimmy was known to the city and was under treatment. The following April, Cooke's worst and most private fears were realized. She was awarded the Pulitzer Prize.

"Jimmy," it turned out, was a fake, from his hair to his toes. Other papers of stature have committed similar errors—the *Times Magazine,* not long afterward, printed an "account" of Pol Pot's rebels in Cambodia by a freelance who never left his house in Spain and lifted a chunk of Malraux's *The Royal Way* when his own prose failed him—but only the *Post* had won a Pulitzer for a fabrication. Receiving the award, of course, raised the level of embarrassment considerably. Bradlee returned the prize, ushered Cooke into oblivion, and then endured the *Schadenfreude* of peers who had been green of soul ever since Jason Robards played the editor's role with uncanny brio in *All the President's Men.* The sin of newspaper people is almost invariably the sin of envy, and so Bradlee's fall was for many members of the American Society of Newspaper Editors an especially piquant bit of justice.

Bradlee reacted to this colossal institutional failure by assigning the *Post*'s in-house ombudsman, Bill Green, to write an account of just how such a thing could have happened. In a business crippled by self-righteousness, Green produced a fourteen-thousand-word article that was an exception; it was pitiless, independent, and complete. In Green's report, racial politics, personal vanity, bureaucratic miscues, and, above all, Cooke's incredible talent for deception conspired in the disaster. The paper, run mainly by white liberals, yearned to promote a young black reporter and her seemingly authentic dispatch from across the Anacostia River. Green was unsparing in his criticism. Bob Woodward, who had been running the Metro section with an eye out for what he called "holy-shit stories," and Milton Coleman, who, as the city editor, had been in direct charge of Cooke, endured brutal scrutiny.

As editors do dozens of times every day, Bradlee had trusted a young reporter, and Cooke, as it turned out, had duped him from the moment she came calling, armed with a résumé (Vassar College, *magna cum laude;* speaks two foreign languages fluently, etc.) that was no less a pipe job than "Jimmy's World." Her letter, Bradlee writes in his memoir, "stood out because she produced clips that showed she could write like a dream; she had top-drawer college credentials; and she was black. The answer to a modern editor's prayers."

Cooke had succeeded where Nixon & Company had failed. She laid Bradlee low with a direct hit to his most celebrated organ: his instincts. Since he came over to the paper from *Newsweek,* in 1965— he had told Katharine Graham at lunch that he would give his "left one" to be managing editor—Bradlee had guided the *Post* with the most exquisitely tuned set of nerve endings in the business. Possessed of a mind not much cluttered with rumination, he had a talent for forceful and uncanny judgment. He had arrived at a mediocre paper and, with Katharine Graham's money and support, had made it great: it is still the only real competitor of the *Times.* He not only made the right decisions (to urge Graham to print the Pentagon Papers, in 1971; to back "the kids," Woodward and Bernstein, during Watergate) but made them almost instantly, from his gut. Bradlee had standards and principles and, above all, instincts; it seemed he was constitutionally incapable of letting the *Post* down.

But something had gone wrong: Daddy, it turned out, was not perfect. Faced with the doubts of some of his own staff, he had waved them aside and submitted "Jimmy's World" for the big prize. As they used to say at the *Post,* "In for a dime, in for a dollar." Like the famous donors at Leonard Bernstein's fund-raiser for the Black Panthers, Bradlee had too much faith in his sense of the authentic even to question that fraud might appear in his midst. "To me, the story reeked of the sights and sounds and smells that editors love to give their readers," Bradlee writes. "The possibility that the story was not true never entered my head. After the fact, some reporters, particularly Courtland Milloy, a streetwise black reporter, told me that they had questioned the story. Milloy had taken Cooke in his car to look for Jimmy's house. When she couldn't find it, he shared his doubts with Milton Coleman. . . . Coleman told others he thought Milloy was jealous." Bradlee wanted to believe Cooke's résumé, and he wanted to believe her story; he had lost, if only for a moment, his instinct for skepticism, his bullshit meter.

That misbegotten summer, I arrived at the *Post*'s offices, on Fifteenth Street, and tried to pick out a route through the newsroom to my desk which would somehow afford me a view of Bradlee's office. He had designed the newsroom so that he could see his reporters and—what was at least as important—the reporters could see him; he faced out on his charges through a glass wall. Such was his sense of theater. For my part, I looked at him with the awe of a kid gazing at the blue whale at the American Museum of Natural History. He was, and still is, a magnificent sight, with slick silver hair, half glasses on a cord, an Audenesque spray of wrinkles, and those over-the-top broad-striped Turnbull & Asser shirts with white collars, which all the other editors began wearing to show their allegiance. With the newsroom still quiet, he plowed his way through the morning papers, then through the *Times* crossword puzzle (having first clipped out and discarded the grid, to make it harder). His feet were on the desk—the same jaunty pose that Robards had picked up for the movie—but he looked tired, close to beaten. Even an intern could see that.

The fact is, though, that Bradlee was not beaten, nor was the paper. Of all Bradlee's enduring contributions, perhaps the greatest was that he had finally made the *Post* strong enough to endure a crisis as painful as the Janet Cooke affair. He had built an institution— one of the strongest—in an anti-institutional age.

· · ·

It is typical of Bradlee's life that just when he begins to search for a title for his memoir a friend (in this case, David Halberstam) comes along and hands him the perfect one. *A Good Life.* None better. It must have been a gas to live it.

Bradlee is a lucky man; above all, he is lucky in his friendships. He has led such a charmed existence that even when he tries to enter the age of Oprah and Barbara and agonize a little in public about, say, one of his divorces, he can hardly contain his good cheer. Everything works out for the best. A former wife finds exactly "the right man" lickety-split, and the temporarily bitter son ends up just fine and working in the newspaper business. Bradlee does not pause to brood. In the newsroom, he was known to be a master of the minute-long conversation, coasting through the sea of desks like Nimitz on the poop, and woe to the numbskull who would detain him long. He was always moving, working the room. If he stopped to talk to you, you were golden; if not, you were meat. And then he was off. Even after great personal stress, he writes, "I put my nose down, and my ass up, and start driving toward the next goal." Bradlee is the picture of mental health. He admits to having paid for the services of five psychiatrists in his life, and one can only despair for the shrinks. (Bradlee declares one "an asshole" and pays scant homage to the rest.) The poor doctors had nothing to work with.

"Nothing profound; nothing radical," he writes. "I was neither."

As it happens, Bradlee is well aware of his luck, and has the good grace to spare us any mitigating details. His may be the least complaining memoir since *Yes I Can,* the story of Sammy Davis, Jr. Bradlee survived polio as a schoolboy, three years on a destroyer in the Pacific war as a young man, and a youthful stint on the shady side of Beacon Street. He grew up in the world of Robert Lowell— of *Mayflower* descendants and bankers and salt air—but without Lowell's self-consciousness. He prepped at St. Mark's and (more or less) studied at Harvard, which Bradlees had been attending since the eighteenth century. The only Jew Bradlee had ever met before college was a family friend, Walter Lippmann (who himself would not have known a sukkah if it had collapsed on his bean). Bradlee wound up as a cub reporter at *The Washington Post* after the war only after he blew off an interview at the *Baltimore Sun* because it was raining too hard that day. Just months after he moved to N Street in Georgetown, it chanced that John and Jacqueline Kennedy moved in a few houses away. The families met over the prams in the neighborhood; not long afterward, Bradlee had a pretty good source in the Oval Office (though not nearly as good as he believed).

In his foreword, Bradlee says that, as the son of a proper (if somewhat fallen) Boston family, he had been "trained from birth not to talk about family, money, or sex." The truth is that Bradlee appealed to and awed his contemporaries for precisely those reasons: family, money, and sex. In a newsroom filled with schleppers and strivers, he was an aristocrat of the old sort—that is, he betrayed no envy or embarrassment. There were a few people in the newsroom with money (one reporter's grandfather popularized the sugar cone, and another was heir to a newspaper chain), but only Bradlee carried himself with the ease of the moneyed. The fact is, he is not shy about money. He is the only newspaper editor I know of whose house (a two-and-a-half-million-dollar manse in Georgetown) and country retreats (the refurbished Grey Gardens in East Hampton and a spectacular manor house in rural Maryland) have all been featured in *Architectural Digest* or *House & Garden*. He is also the only editor who, even in his sixties, made women blush and men straighten their posture. Robards came close to matching the physical appeal: the chesty walk and muscled forearms, the schist-caught-in-the-cement-mixer voice. But he did not exceed it.

There really is something of the movie star in Bradlee—he is lit up from inside, like neon—and there are times in his book when he affects the style of the Hollywood memoir: breezy, whiz-bang, quick to be magnanimous. Bradlee, who will surely live to a hundred and fifty, seems oddly eager to pay homage even to those he could hardly stand, the better to get into heaven. Every name comes to him with its complimentary epithet: "the fabulous Sara Metin" (his sexy childhood governess); "the great Jack Barnaby" (his squash coach); "the great Paris doctor, Jean Dax" (his friend); "my secretary was the spectacular Marie-Thérèse Barreau"; "lunches, for me, often started at the Crillon Bar across the street from the embassy, where the great Sam White was more or less permanently installed at one corner"; "and then there was Bernard Valery, the joyous and resourceful correspondent of the New York *Daily News.*" In fact, there are moments when Bradlee's offhand good fortune is just mind-boggling: he takes jitterbug lessons from a Sulzberger; his engagement ring was "made for me by my pal René Tupin, managing partner of Cartier, and a fellow member of an eating club called Bistro Anonyme"; he meets "the legendary Vincent Astor, the tall, leonine, multimillionaire head of the famous Astor family, then in his late sixties, ailing and childless."

Of all Bradlee's friendships, none meant more to his career or added more to his glamour than that with John Kennedy. And *A Good Life,* unlike his first book, *Conversations with Kennedy* (1975), is better prepared to make sense of that relationship and that complicated man. Let me be the thousandth person to say that Bradlee and Kennedy were, as types, much the same. If Bradlee had been president, he would have been much like Kennedy: without ideology, mindful of style, reliant on expert elders, intelligent but hardly intellectual, long on vision and wit, short on temper and attention span. And Kennedy, who followed the press and its actors obsessively, would have been Bradlee-esque in a newsroom: excited by stories that broke news and balls, bored by "process stories"— what Bradlee calls "room emptiers." There were surely differences between the two men—for starters, their Boston status was different, Bradlee coming from the hive of WASPs, Kennedy from lace-curtain Irish Catholics—but they shared a sense of privilege and

fortune; they shared Harvard, the war, Georgetown, and an understanding of class; and they shared a penchant for gossip, detachment, irony, and courage.

Bradlee's friendship with and access to the president are something almost unthinkable today. Bradlee cannot quite bring himself
to say so in his book, but I doubt whether he would have let one of
his reporters cover a friend who had made it to the White House.
But at *Newsweek* he pretty much owned his friend and neighbor. "Little by little, it was accepted by the rest of the *Newsweek* Bureau [in
Washington] and by [the editors in] New York that Kennedy was
mine." On the night of the West Virginia primary, the Kennedys and
the Bradlees went to see a porno movie—"a nasty thing" called *Private Property* and "starring one Katie Manx as a horny housewife."
Imagine the uproar today.

Bradlee and Kennedy were not fools. They both knew that each
was capable of using the other, and yet they both enjoyed the duet.
They were young and were playing the headiest, most irresistible
game there is. In February of 1962, Kennedy pulled Bradlee off the
dance floor at the White House and gave him a scoop: "Francis Gary
Powers, the pilot of the CIA's U-2 spy plane, which had been shot
down by the Russians nine months before, had been swapped for
Rudolph Abel, a colonel in the Soviet intelligence agency." Bradlee
couldn't get the story in to *Newsweek* in time—it was too late in the
week to change a cover—but he did dictate it to his "sister" publication, the *Post*. "A moment from another world!" Bradlee writes.
"Imagine a reporter dictating an exclusive story, a lead story, sourced
from the President of the United States, from a telephone just off a
White House dance floor to the strains of Lester Lanin's dance band.
It was the kind of moment that made Kennedy nervous about me,
and me nervous about my relationship with him. It now seems also a
risky thing for the President to have done. But I was not nervous
enough to sacrifice the professional challenge and thrill." Distant
days, the days of access as a privilege of a journalist's luck or labor.

After the assassination, in 1963, Bradlee and his wife at the time, Tony Pinchot, spent a couple of "emotional weekends" with Jacqueline Kennedy at the Kennedy estate in Virginia. Already, the relationship seemed to be unraveling. "Too soon and too emotional for healing, we proved only that the three of us had very little in common without the essential fourth," Bradlee writes. A couple of weeks later, Bradlee received a note:

> Dear Tony and Ben:
> Something that you said in the country stunned me so—that you hoped I would marry again.
> You were close to us so many times. There is one thing that you must know. I consider that my life is over and I will spend the rest of it waiting for it really to be over.
>
> With my love,
> Jackie

Bradlee learned a devastating lesson in his relationship with the Kennedys. For all his seeming intimacy with Kennedy, Bradlee not only did not know the extent of Kennedy's womanizing but also had no idea that the list of mistresses included a mobster's moll and his own wife's sister, Mary Pinchot Meyer. When Meyer was found murdered in Georgetown, in 1964, Bradlee was deputized to go looking for her diaries. Once more, the journalist finds his personal life intersecting with Washington politics, and once more he reveals himself as a friend of establishment figures—a naïf, amazingly enough. When he goes to Meyer's house to look for the diaries—a document that would reveal the news of her love affair with JFK— he bumps into another searcher, one of the shadowiest figures in the history of the Central Intelligence Agency. "Now, James Jesus Angleton was a lot of things, including an extremely controversial, high-ranking CIA official specializing in counterintelligence, but he was also a friend of ours, and the husband of Mary Meyer's close friend, Cicely Angleton," Bradlee writes. "We asked him how he'd gotten into the house, and he shuffled his feet. . . . We felt his presence was odd, to say the least, but took him at his word, and with him we searched Mary's house thoroughly." Eventually, Tony Bradlee gave the diary to Angleton, Bradlee writes, "because he promised to destroy it in whatever facilities the Central Intelligence Agency had for the destruction of documents. It was naive of us, but we figured they were state of the art, and we got on with the business of mourning and memorializing."

Bradlee here is innately trusting of old-boy institutions and the men who ran them. He trusted Angleton to burn the diaries—and, of course, Angleton did not. Nor did Bradlee turn over the news of Meyer's liaison to *Newsweek.* "It is important to say that I never for a minute considered reporting that it had been learned that the slain president had in fact had a lover, who had herself been murdered while walking on the C&O Canal. . . . Mary Meyer's murder was news, not her past love affair, I thought then, and part of me would like to think so now." He helped the *Post* on the story of the love affair in 1976, and then only after the *National Enquirer* had published its own account.

Bradlee was in for another kind of shock after he published *Conversations with Kennedy.* While some reviewers found it treacly (even Bradlee's greatest admirers in the newsroom wondered why he was still so loyal to the mythologized Kennedy), Jacqueline pronounced it unworthy, saying that the salty language would offend her children and, besides, "it tells more about you than it does about the President." She never spoke to Bradlee again.

At *Newsweek,* Bradlee had been an average, if high-profile, reporter, an ordinary writer. ("Port Said is now an ugly, festering sore on the mouth of the Suez Canal.") But upon his arrival at the *Post,* Bradlee, having promised Katharine Graham no small part of his anatomy, became a genius of an editor. Nothing unprecedented here: Angelo Dundee couldn't much fight; Vince Lombardi was an unspectacular bruiser at Fordham. Generalship is not about fighting the battle; it's about inspiring the enlisted.

To understand the scale of Bradlee's achievement, it is important to know something about the mediocrity with which he began. *The Washington Post* in 1965 not only had no claim to rivalry with *The New York Times* but could not even claim to be the best paper in its city. Ever since the *Post* bought out the *Times-Herald,* in 1954, it had been profitable, but as an editorial enterprise it still was simply not competitive. It was, like most newspapers everywhere, pretty awful. In the capital, the *Star,* an afternoon broadsheet, was still supreme (though it was starting its slide). When Bradlee was hired as managing editor, the *Post*'s editorial budget was four million dollars, compared with twenty million at the *Times.* The *Post,* the saying went, did not cover stories outside the second taxi zone. The *Post* had one foreign correspondent—Murrey Marder. The *Times* had a few dozen. The *Post*'s Pentagon correspondent looked at other reporters' carbons to get stories; he was known as Black Sheet Jack. The one-man business department, S. Oliver Goodman, produced a column called "Business Notes," for which he rewrote the first paragraph of every press release he could get his hands on. In the afternoon, he and a part-time copyboy punched in the agate type for the stock page. Bradlee, in his first tours of the office, wondered aloud why the night managing editor went home at nine, and he was informed that the night managing editor was of the opinion that nothing much ever happened past nine. The *Post* did have Herblock, who is even now, in his eighties, the sharpest political cartoonist in newspapers, and it had one of the greatest sports columnists ever—Shirley Povich. And the editorial writers, especially Alan Barth, had a gift for decency, if you like that sort of thing. That was about it. The reputation of the paper was distinctly lightweight. Before Bradlee arrived, the *Post* itself had never won a Pulitzer.

To no one's surprise, Bradlee proved a ferocious office politician, and, since his newsroom competition was so weak and his relationship with Katharine Graham so strong (the Kay card, it was called), he wrested control of the paper in no time flat. At the stately *Times*, such maneuvering would have required decades. Bradlee found that the *Post* was filled with deadwood, and he set about reducing it to chips. When staff meetings ended, at least a few staffers usually left with an exit ticket. Ben Gilbert, the city editor and a Bradlee unfavorite, was suddenly appointed to a job with no description and even less importance. Exit Gilbert.

At the same time, Bradlee was trying to find ways to go bigtime—to compete with *The New York Times*, especially in Washington, where the *Times* comported itself more like an embassy than like a news bureau. Bradlee mastered the low art of budgets and the high art of getting the publisher to increase them. He hired young and not quite young reporters who loved his sense of adventure: Ward Just, who became the *Post*'s one real star in Vietnam; David Broder, who bolted the *Times* to lead political coverage at the *Post;* Hobart Rowen, who brought some sophistication to the *Post*'s coverage of economics; Don Oberdorfer, who became the city's leading diplomatic correspondent. Bradlee also helped make stars of Richard Harwood, Stanley Karnow, and Nicholas von Hoffman. And, besides covering official "white" Washington in greater depth, the *Post* discovered black Washington, jettisoned some older, racist editors, and hired talented black reporters, including Robert Maynard. Foreign bureaus opened in Paris, Moscow, Saigon, Bonn, and Tokyo. Moreover, with the help of a brilliant managing editor, Howard Simons, the *Post* discovered what they called SMERSH: science, medicine, education, religion, and all that shit.

It is to Bradlee's credit that he admits having come in very late to his first great story: Vietnam. While Ward Just's vivid battlefield reports went a long way toward saving the paper from mediocrity on the war, the coverage by the *Times* and the two wires, AP and

UPI, was far more distinguished. Bradlee was a kind of Roger Bald-win—ACLU liberal, but he had also been shaped by his years in the navy and was deeply suspicious of the antiwar movement. He recounts his own trip to Vietnam, in 1971, and says he ended up feeling "uncommitted politically as usual." His analysis is not exactly distinguished: "By instinct and habit, I was more interested in the whatness of the war than in the rightness or wrongness. I hated the idea that an authoritarian country like North Vietnam could wipe out a peaceful neighbor. But I didn't much like the idea that a cor-rupt country like South Vietnam in one hemisphere could be per-suaded to ask the United States of America and millions of its citizen soldiers to come to its rescue, with never even an attempt to enact a declaration of war."

Bradlee's achievement had nothing to do with his insight as a commentator. He had none, pretended to none. But that same year, when Neil Sheehan got a copy of the Pentagon Papers from Daniel Ellsberg, and the *Times* began to run excerpts, Bradlee knew what to do. His paper was ready, and so was he: his instincts finally kicked in. With the *Times* in trouble with the courts and forced to suspend publication of the Papers after three installments, Bradlee's national editor, Ben Bagdikian, got hold of another copy of the Papers. The *Post* had hours in which to assemble what had taken the *Times* many weeks, and while his top reporters tried to make sense of the Papers, Bradlee was on the phone to Katharine Graham, urging her once more to get into the game; against the advice of her lawyers, she did just that. ("God bless her ballsy soul.")

For the *Times*, the Pentagon Papers was a great beat; for the *Post*, it established for the first time an institution—a rival to the *Times*. Running the Pentagon Papers gave the *Post* the standing to begin its Watergate investigations the next year and the nerve to stay with them. Bradlee, a man of the establishment, had created a paper capable of playing in the biggest arena without bowing to the intim-idation of the attorney general or the Pentagon. He does not say so, but it seems that he had come a very long way since his cozy relationship with the Kennedy White House. Early in the Watergate story, Bradlee got a reward from one of the hoariest of the Washington Brahmins, Clark Clifford. He came on the phone "in that dramatic, triple-breasted basso profundo of his" saying, "Mr. Bradlee, I would like to tell you something. I woke up this morning, put on my bathrobe and my slippers, went downstairs slowly, opened the front door carefully, and there it was. The sun was already shining. It was going to be a beautiful day. And I looked up to the heavens, and said, 'Thank God for *The Washington Post.*' "

On the day of Bradlee's retirement party in the *Post* newsroom, in 1991, many stories were told about the latter-day Ben, the lovably crusty figure of journalism folklore. I especially liked a story about how one day Bradlee's secretary ("the fabulous Debbie Regan") approached the house grammarian, Tom Lippman, with a worried look on her face. It seems she had been typing letters from Bradlee's dictation and she was vexed. "Look, I have to ask you something," she said. "Is 'dickhead' one word or two?"

But of all the speeches made that day the one that was most memorable came from Meg Greenfield, the editorial-page editor. According to newsroom lore, Bradlee and Greenfield—the two top names on the masthead under the executives'—had a prickly relationship at times. (She is cerebral, given to reading history and Latin. He is not.) And yet Greenfield, nervous in front of the crowd and clearly filled with the sadness of the moment, paid precise tribute to Bradlee. What Ben had done, she said, was to make *The Washington Post* dangerous to the powerful, the dishonest, and the deceitful.

The champions of democracy, officeholders and voters alike, are not unanimous in their adoration of dangerous newspapers. Nor are newspaper owners. The Clintons long ago soured on an aggressive press. Clinton's rival, the Senate majority leader, Bob Dole, is also on record as being ambivalent toward the press. During Watergate, when he was the chairman of the Republican National Committee, Dole gave a speech in Baltimore that outlines some of his reservations:

> The *Post's* reputation for objectivity and credibility have sunk so low they have almost disappeared from the Big Board altogether. There is a cultural and social affinity between the McGovernites and the *Post* executives and editors. They belong to the same elite; they can be found living cheek by jowl in the same exclusive neighborhood, and hobnobbing at the same Georgetown parties. . . . It is only *The Washington Post* which deliberately mixes together illegal and unethical episodes, like the Watergate caper, with shenanigans which have been the stock in trade of political pranksters from the day I came into politics.

In his book Bradlee quotes Dole's speech at length. He is right to do so. It is a highlight of a good life. The shame is that so few value the presence of a dangerous paper.

As Hugh Grant walked down his Via Dolorosa last summer, a penitent stopping in at one video confessional after another, the film star made one remark that seemed close to true. On being asked by Larry King if the British press was giving him a tough time, Grant turned solemn critic, saying that in fact all British papers were now tabloids. Including the once venerable broadsheet of broadsheets, the London *Times*. It is not much of a stretch from Rupert Murdoch's *Times* to Rupert Murdoch's *Sun*.

American newspapers are suffering a less glamorous but no less homogenizing kind of doom. With one eye on Wall Street and the other shut tight, newspaper owners everywhere—except for a few, like the Sulzbergers of New York and the Grahams of Washington—are following the path to deadening mediocrity. Everything that cannot be made blandly profitable is killed outright. Spoiled by the wild profits of the eighties, the owners rarely have patience for a more modest yet distinguished future. The *Times* expands in recession; its inferiors brutalize themselves in the name of the Dow Jones averages. As Murray Kempton wrote after the Times Mirror Company's heedless execution of *New York Newsday* in July, "there cannot be much health left in a social order where corporations can clamorously proclaim a failure on Friday with entire assurance that therefore their stock will go up on Monday."

Few cities in the United States have a local newspaper that is preferable to *USA Today*. This is not to say that *USA Today* is a fine newspaper. It is not. It is a sprightly brand of fish wrap. And yet in a growing number of cities and regions newspaper owners have abused their franchise, slashing staff, cutting the "news hole," dropping aggressive reporting, and leaving little behind but wire-service copy, sports, and soft local stories designed to make readers feel all warm and fuzzy and inclined to place a classified ad. Despite its tinny bugle calls to a kind of national school spirit ("WE'RE ALL EATING BAGELS!") and color-keyed news crumbs, *USA Today* often provides a more tolerable reading experience than the local and declining sheet. It's simply depressing to read the *San Francisco Chronicle* or *Examiner,* the *Atlanta Constitution, The Denver Post.* Once great and near-great papers in major cities are in retreat. *The Miami Herald,* which used to be a vigorous daily even while constantly losing young talent to the *Times* and *The Washington Post,* has shut down bureaus and whacked away at its staff, and is now thin and anemic. The *Los Angeles Times,* the *Baltimore Sun,* and *The Philadelphia Inquirer,* all of which used to thrive on adventure and excess, show signs of decline. The *Chicago Tribune* is a shell in which the hollow carping of Mike Royko rings shrill. The blame for all this goes, in the main, not to the handcuffed journalists (there are still many terrific reporters at these papers) but to the owners, who pocket the key.

Along comes Bradlee's memoir to remind us of what was once so promising and is now endangered. Bradlee, who essentially created *The Washington Post* and guided it through Watergate, the biggest newspaper triumph of our times, probably intended his memoir as a breezy compilation of his greatest anecdotes. Many have already been played out in other books, by Woodward and Bernstein, and in Halberstam's *The Powers That Be.* It hardly matters. Bradlee's got a million of 'em.

But there is something sad about hearing Bradlee's joyous voice at this moment. I wonder whether, if a young Ben Bradlee came along today offering his left one, any willing plutocrat would take him up on the offer. The *Post* or the *Times,* each owned by a newspaper family, might, but who else? A Times Mirror paper? A Knight-Ridder paper? Newhouse? Gannett? Who is interested in a "dangerous" editor anymore?

At one point, Bradlee notes that in the ten years immediately following Nixon's fall, in 1974, the number of federal officials convicted of federal crimes rose from forty-three to 429. Shouldn't this be, both for the press and for democracy, cause for pride?

There has been much complaint in recent years about the aggression of the press, but the fact is that most aggression in the press is merely a pose. Sam Donaldson is not an aggressive reporter. He just plays one on TV. To do what the *Post* did during Watergate or to do what the *Times* did during Vietnam requires courage and incredibly hard work. The alternative to aggressive reporting is an unbearable coziness with power.

Among the pleasures of Bradlee's memoir are the moments of self-recognition and warning. Watergate established the *Post* as dangerous, but it also fixed the paper as a leading player in the capital—and therefore, paradoxically, as a member of the establishment. And with that membership "I began to feel subconsciously that what the world did *not* need right away was another investigation that might again threaten the foundations of democracy," Bradlee says. "What the newspaper did *not* need right away was another fight to the finish with another president—especially a Republican president, and especially a successful fight. Without the suggestion of a formal decision, I think the fires of investigative zeal were allowed to bank." The press, including *The Washington Post,* Bradlee concludes, was not fast or deep enough on the savings-and-loan scandals or other highlights of the Reagan-Bush years.

It is also true that Bradlee left some other things undone at the *Post.* His successor, Leonard Downie, Jr., found himself with plenty to do. The financial section has improved only lately. Downie loves "accountability" stories, pieces that show up betrayals of public trust, and there have been many more of those. Although Bradlee wisely trashed the "for and about Women" section and replaced it with a product of the New Journalism years, the Style section, he never managed to build a decent Sunday magazine. The last attempt, in 1986, ended in disaster when the first issue of a very expensive makeover featured a photograph of a black rap star and accused murderer on the cover, and a column sympathizing with store owners who refuse entry to young black men. The incident left the paper in a defensive crouch. In a city where the black population is intensely suspicious of all white institutions—including the *Post,* a monopoly paper—the magazine crisis only worsened relations.

It might have been predicted that the *Post* would face an identity crisis now that Bradlee is a vice president at large and Katharine Graham has given over nearly all the power at the paper to her oldest son, Donald Graham. The paper is less exciting to read, and its management is more bureaucratic. Although it has by no means set aside investigative reporting, it is sometimes more cautious about printing what it has.

Len Downie, a fair and intelligent man who has never pretended to compete with Bradlee as a figure of glamour, is both blessed and cursed. He is blessed because he inherited not the *Post* of 1965 but, rather, an institution created by Ben Bradlee—one capable of withstanding occasional catastrophe. The newsroom, which has become middle-aged, is still packed with reporters and editors who learned under Bradlee. Downie is cursed because, like so many modern editors, he must cope with modern problems which are no-win problems—money problems, information-superhighway problems, suburban-penetration problems.

Race is probably the most complicated and the most absorbing problem at the *Post*. Bradlee left the paper, to his immense relief, before having to deal fully with the complications of affirmative action and the era of sensitivity training. Downie, in a well-meaning attempt to diversify the newsroom and bring the paper closer to its city, has gone to great lengths to hire more minorities and generally make the paper more "sensitive."

The result is not always a pretty sight. At one gathering in Florida last year, *Post* editors were instructed by a "diversity consultant" to wear signs around their necks reading "I am stupid" or "I am ignorant," the better to understand the plight of the misunderstood and ignored reporter. At an earlier session, top editors were instructed to climb up on tall boxes that had been assembled in a circle, stand on one leg, and hold hands, the better to understand the concept of teamwork. As the sports editor, George Solomon, was trying to find his balance, he turned to the Style editor, Mary Hadar, and said, "Well, I guess the Bradlee era is really over."

16

※※

Good News Is No News

(October 1987)

On an upbeat morning in the U.S.A., Al Neuharth's jet lands at Boston's Logan Airport. Dressed in pearl-gray slacks, gray silk shirt, gray loafers, and a gray tie bordered with the color of dried blood, Neuharth seems a stumpy casino tout from Reno. His silver pompadour and chunky gold ring do little to cloud this impression. But he is one of the most influential men in journalism, and he is here to bring truth to the millions who read his creation, *USA Today.*

Neuharth heads for the capitol, where he is to interview the governor, Michael Dukakis. The limousine pulls up alongside one of the famous coin boxes, the handsome blue-and-white machines Neuharth designed to look like televisions. He worships television: a row of four Trinitrons plays soundlessly above his office desk all day long. "It keeps me in touch with the U.S.A.," he says.

Neuharth stands now on the statehouse steps, feet apart, hands on hips, surveying the noonday traffic on Beacon Street and the children playing ball on Boston Common. The tableau pleases him. He nods many times and permits a tight smile to crinkle his face. He can feel it wherever he goes, the great pulsebeat. Once more he is in the heart of the heart of the country. He has been in Boston no more than five minutes, and already he can sense its mood. And the mood is good.

On tour to celebrate the fifth anniversary of his paper, Neuharth is a press lord high and low, at home with the polished swell and the lumpen prole. And don't forget the "middlemost," for Neuharth does not. They are all his people, the great We and Us. Differences among citizens are never profound in Al Neuharth's U.S.A. THEY'RE LIKE US, EXCEPT THEY'RE RICH is one of his paper's recent headlines. He lowers his gaze to two little boys, one towheaded, one wearing a Boston Red Sox cap, and bends dramatically to their level. "Hello, fellas," he says—for his is the speech of the common man—"could we chat a minute? I'm from a newspaper. *USA Today.*" The lads trust this gray, imperial stranger, and they gaze up at him to answer all his questions. Neuharth listens, though he does not take notes. A staff photographer scrambles to the scene and shoots the boss at work. Neuharth is digging deep into the psyche of the U.S.A. And the psyche is good.

"Fine boys," he says, "fine boys."

Inside the statehouse at last, Neuharth and several of his reporters lob cotton-candy questions at the governor. When a politician is being interviewed, there is often an animal tension evident in his eyes. But We Are Not Critical of Governors, and Dukakis knows it. He can relax. This is the New New Journalism, or, better, the New Non Journalism.

Dukakis responds in kind, affirming his everlasting "belief in the rule of law" and his commonality with the people of the U.S.A. "I'm not a very complicated guy," he says. This is a brilliant stroke. Dukakis knows the program. The session reaches its climax when reporter Dan Greaney asks whether the governor grows his own food in a garden. Neuharth loves such populism, and he sends a smile Greaney's way. The governor jaws further. Later, Greaney confides, "I like questions like that. I asked the governor of Kentucky, Martha Layne Collins, if she knew what the name of her cow was. It was 'Sunshine.' I think that's kind of a nice thing to know."

A week or two later, Neuharth will write a column about his research in the state of Massachusetts: "Heavy history has unfolded here for more than 350 years. History is revered here."

It is a poetic lead, full of Neuharth's signature alliteration ("heavy history"), interior rhymes ("here," "years," "revered"), and his linguistic legerdemain ("revered," as in Paul). The rest is insight. "The Pilgrims landed at Plymouth Rock—by mistake." Lots of "presidents and poets" were born here. Digital Equipment employs 94,700 people. Neuharth makes little of these or any other facts. In his columns and in the paper's countless graphs, lists, and "brights," facts are popcorn, neither offensive nor nourishing. They just are.

There are a few major newspapers in the world that show such unyielding optimism, such an overwhelming desire to please and unite the citizenry, such an obdurate unwillingness to face the sorrows and complexities of the modern world. Most prominent among them are *Pravda* and *Izvestia*. But compared with *USA Today,* Soviet newspapers face an identity crisis. At least for now, a careful reader of *Pravda* will find stark descriptions of alcoholism, drug addiction, even sentiment against the war in Afghanistan to offset articles about heroic sugar-beet production in Murmansk.

USA Today is a more blithe, confident production. Not for nothing did Ronald Reagan toast the paper on the Washington Mall five years ago as "a testimony to the kind of dreams free men and women can dream and turn into reality here in America." Gannett executives may talk of the paper as a supplement, a "second read," but it was Neuharth himself who laid out his ambitions when he was drawing up his initial plans. He said, "It is impressive that *USA Today* could become the first read in the White House someday." Why not? From the beginning, *USA Today* was more than a new business. It was a new institution, in perfect sync with its times, a newspaper that would see the world the way Ronald Reagan does, as a television show that We Are All Enjoying Together.

The easy way to treat *USA Today* is as an amusement. It's always full of yucks. There are the daily quote boxes from sports stars in which, say, a Seattle Seahawk reveals his favorite pie filling and post-Cartesian philosopher. ("Mincemeat and Martin Heidegger, for sure!") There are the headlines—USA IS EATING ITS VEGETABLES, WE'RE IN A MOOD TO BUY—the reigning champion still being MEN, WOMEN: WE'RE STILL DIFFERENT. There's the world's worst "People" column, written by the indefatigable Larry King: ". . . **Thomas Wolfe** said you can't go home again and he was probably correct. . . . **Angie Dickinson** winds up filming *Big Bad Mama 2* the first of June. . . ."

There are the appeals for the people of the U.S.A. to express themselves: "Tell the USA what you'd do with 3,200 tons of garbage. 1-800-422-USAT."

And there's that Peter Pan view of the world. On a day last spring when the President took a beating in the Iran-contra hearings and Attorney General Edwin Meese was tied ever closer to the Wedtech contracting scandal and Senator Edward Kennedy proposed a $450 million comprehensive AIDS bill in Congress, *USA Today*'s banner story was ROYAL DUO, THIEF WORK CANNES. Seems Joanne Woodward lost her purse and Princess Diana was appearing at the film festival—"and this Côte d'Azur city couldn't be more alive with excitement."

There's always funny stuff, and favorites just keep appearing. A couple of days before visiting Neuharth at his office, I read this front-page story.

STYLE CUTS KNEES NO SLACK
By Kevin Anderson
USA TODAY

NEW YORK—Rising hemlines seem to have kicked off a mini-boom in fat-suction surgery to correct chubby knees.

Liposuction—removing pockets of fat with a suction wand through a ⅛-inch incision—has become routine only since 1980, used mostly for "saddle-bag" hips and "love handles" at the waist.

Dr. Lawrence Reed, a Manhattan plastic surgeon, was doing only three or four knee-area liposuctions a month—until hemlines rose at this spring's fashion shows. . . .

Never mind the telltale "seem" in the lead. Here the patina of absolute, nationwide truth is good enough, for it is obvious where such an item ends up. In conversation. Watercooler talk. The front page is not designed with an eye toward importance but rather for chat. In *USA Today* parlance, the top position on the front page is known as the "talker." Liposuction is something else. "That's a 'bright,' " Neuharth says.

A little T&A never hurt a front page either. According to *USA Today* editor and writer Peter Prichard's book *The Making of McPaper*, Neuharth once noticed a front-page picture of a leaping cheerleader. Her face was on the top half of the page, but it seems her breasts were too far south for Neuharth. "After all of the editors were seated, Neuharth strode over to the news rack. He opened the door and slammed it violently. He did that again and again, banging the door against the rack. The assembled editors stared, wide-eyed. He had their attention now. 'When you run a picture of a nice clean all-American girl like this,' Neuharth announced, '*get her tits above the fold.*' "

Because it is such a joke, *USA Today* is beyond parody. During the 1978 newspaper strike, Nora Ephron, Carl Bernstein, and other city lights produced a minor classic: *Not The New York Times.* The satire attacked everything about the *Times,* from its lapses into comma-tose writing to its steely promise of comprehensiveness. It stung.

The *Harvard Lampoon* published a parody of *USA Today* last year that ran headlines such as QADDAFI TO USA: I DIDN'T ORDER THESE PIZZAS and NATIONAL DEBT: BIGGER THAN A BREAD BOX? The Harvard boys did little more than celebrate their subject. *USA Today* knows how silly it is and doesn't much care. Neuharth was enchanted. So much so, he hired the *Lampoon* editor-in-chief, Dan Greaney, and they have been interviewing "garagemen and governors" together ever since. "*USA Today*'s a life-affirming kind of thing," Greaney says. "I was attracted to their vision of journalism. Of course, it's very hard to pin down what the definition is, but, anyway, I always wanted to be in show business."

Suddenly, the most popular newspaper in the country is edited on show-business terms. "The general editing approach is: What are they going to talk about tomorrow?" Neuharth says. He does not give a damn if he is vilified in universities or the *Columbia Journalism Review*. He finds the whole tradition of Lincoln Steffens and Woodward and Bernstein a bit puzzling: "Well, investigation, how do you define investigation? It's not our mission to prove that public officials are scoundrels, or that most are, or that you have to start with the assumption they are. Our investigative reporting—and you may chuckle at this—but our readers think it's investigative reporting when we present the only picture the vast audience out there gets of the salaries and contracts of all the big jocks in the country. Most investigative reporting is designed to define the scoundrels and paint them as scoundrels and run 'em out of town. That's not our mission."

Neuharth and his editors think they are changing the terms of journalism. "As I look back on it, it's not specific stories that I'm proudest of," says editor John Quinn, "it's the whole comprehensive approach. It's the style and drive of the newspaper. I'm looking more at the continuity of the package than for big hits in journalism. See, what our people do on Oscar night is as important as what we do on election night."

"Have you ever noticed that when you get together with your friends that this is the sort of thing you talk about?" says Susan Older, assistant features editor of the Life section. "You're probably talking about *Hill Street Blues,* not having some intellectual discussion of what's happening on Capitol Hill."

Newspapers have always recognized their tribunal function. In 1770 the *New York Gazette* wrote,

> *'Tis truth (with deference to the college)*
> *Newspapers are the spring of knowledge*
> *The general source throughout the nation*
> *Of every modern conversation.*

For centuries since, people have begun conversations, weighty or not, with "Did you read in the paper that . . ." But most serious newspaper editors do not view themselves as twittering party hosts who bring up "amusing" topics to get guests "going." If the liposuction story appeared, say, in the *Los Angeles Times,* it would be somewhere in the paper signaling it as an amusing footnote to the day. In *USA Today* everything is a footnote.

Neuharth indulges his readers. He caters to the common feeling that the world—the world of famines, wars, hatreds, and calamities—is too much with us. More than three paragraphs of Guatemala and your eggs go bad. Neuharth serves his paper sunny-side up.

The news decisions that Neuharth had to face on September 14, 1982, allowed him to set the tone for the five years ahead. That day, Lebanese president-elect Bashir Gemayel was assassinated and Princess Grace died from a car wreck in Monaco. At around deadline, Neuharth wanted a break, according to *The Making of McPaper.* He was driven by limo to his suite at the Capital Hilton and made a quick trip to the bar for a martini. He discovered that everyone was talking about Grace Kelly. Neuharth mentioned the assassination in Lebanon. No one cared.

"So I went back to the newsroom and told everyone, 'No question, the lead story has to be Princess Grace.' " The lead story was AMERICA'S PRINCESS GRACE DIES IN MONACO. The "major" papers played the Gemayel story as the lead. Certainly, no editor could possibly believe that people would be talking in offices and drugstores more about Lebanon than Grace, but the Gemayel death was a turning point in one of the most violent places in the world. Neuharth did not care. He stayed true to his vow to publish a paper edited "by the people." Gemayel was buried twice—first in Lebanon, and then in *USA Today*.

Neuharth still keeps that edition in a binder, and during an interview in his office he throws it onto his desk to survey the old handiwork. "It was the story our audience was interested in," he says.

The second most prominent story that day provided an opportunity to establish the paper's overtone of optimism. A plane crash in Spain was an obvious front-page story. The first headline read 55 DIE IN FIERY CRASH. Not upbeat enough. Neuharth changed it to MIRACLE: 327 SURVIVE, 55 DIE. "We plead guilty to the fact that we put a positive spin on things when we can," Neuharth says. "We don't start with the presumption that the country went to hell in a handbasket yesterday and therefore that must be projected this morning."

Ask staffers, from Neuharth down, what journalism they are proud of after five years, and many, Neuharth included, will talk only glancingly of certain stories, preferring to stick with "packages," "the philosophy of easy-to-find, easy-to-read," and how it is "harder to write five inches than fifty." Several stories and projects are mentioned repeatedly: coverage of the Los Angeles Olympics and, above all, coverage of the *Challenger* disaster, which included the headline PERFECT ISN'T POSSIBLE, FUTURE BELONGS TO THE BRAVE.

Tone controls the emphasis, even the content, of *USA Today*. An environmental reporter decided it was getting a bit absurd trying to write "happy news" about dioxin. Editors would say everything should have an "up," "today" angle.

"I got better play with good news, like when New York City made 'New York, New York' its official song," says John McGowan, who left reporting to work in public relations for Gannett. "I've spent years reporting, and I tried to do my job the right way. I covered the Sharon–*Time* magazine libel trial, and I sat there taking notes like everyone else, trying to think about what the defense would do next, what it meant, the usual things. Then they'd give me about one paragraph of space. But they've got a lot of younger people who are happy when they get five little paragraphs. It's a different kind of place. It's like a pep rally."

"When I worked there, people seemed like zombies or Stepford kids," says one former staff writer. "Everyone had kind of bought into the whole idea of 'We're not better than *The New York Times* or *The Washington Post,* we're just different.' "

USA Today isn't much for brains or character. It asks to be loved for its good looks and sunny personality. It is a bimbo.

Unlike the present generation of Sulzbergers, Grahams, and Chandlers, Al Neuharth is a small-town boy of ordinary legacy and education. When he became a big success, he would win an award named for Horatio Alger. He was born in Eureka, South Dakota (population 1,360), and worked in the composing room of the *Alpena Journal.* The family was poor and got poorer when Neuharth's father died after a farm accident.

Neuharth went to Northern State Teachers College for a few months before enlisting in the army. He served with distinction in the 86th Blackhawk Infantry Division during the war and came home to live with his bride in a trailer. He worked at a carnival darts stand and finished school. For a couple of years after graduating from the University of South Dakota, Neuharth was a reporter for the Associated Press.

In 1952, he and a friend raised fifty thousand dollars to start *SoDak Sports,* a statewide sports paper printed on peach-colored paper ("Reach for the Peach"). Neuharth saw his paper idealistically, as a bond among South Dakotans. The straight lines drawn by politicians and cartographers long ago were like a white picket fence to him, and all the folks inside the fence were kin. In the first issue, he announced that *SoDak Sports* would "bridge the gap between east and west, north and south, and make South Dakota one big 'sports' family."

The paper failed after a few years, but it could only be considered a financial death. For years thereafter Neuharth saw *SoDak Sports* as a valid idea for the future, a seed. "It's against that background that the philosophy of trying to help bring about the greater unity across the country began," he says. Neuharth was determined to set up a picket fence around the U.S.A. one day, and his tools would be sports and television. "Those are the areas you've got to play to," he says. "We have a love-hate relationship with sports. And we all watch television."

By the early sixties, Neuharth had worked his way up the ladder at what was then the Knight chain, where he was a reporter and city editor in Miami, and then jumped to Gannett, where he became a wunderkind executive. After only three years he was executive vice president of the company, occasionally improving a paper editorially but almost always developing new acquisitions into money-making machines. Unlike Knight-Ridder, the Gannett chain has never been known as an innovator in journalism. Gannett is foremost a company, and, in his way, Al Neuharth is foremost a company man. When he was asked how to pronounce Gannett, he once replied, "The accent is on the net."

Neuharth's boldest gesture as a young executive at Gannett was to begin *Today* in Brevard County, Florida. The dominant *Orlando*

Sentinel and *The Miami Herald* had always taken the county for granted, deeming it unworthy of the cultural and financial pretensions of nearby Orlando and Orange counties. Like an old-time populist, Neuharth introduced a theme of "One Brevard, one voice," and soon he was not so much a visiting newspaper executive as a Great Communicator. David Shaw, the *Los Angeles Times* media critic, called *Today* "perhaps the best paper of its size in the country."

The success in Brevard helped win Neuharth the presidency of Gannett by 1970. Neuharth had been talking with friends about setting up a national newspaper since 1954. It was time to put his dreams in place. By 1980 he had sufficient power, and his company had the money to do it. His first step was to gather his financial gurus around him at Pumpkin Center, his luxurious log cabin in Cocoa Beach, Florida (eleven television sets, fifteen telephones, wire tickers for AP and Gannett). There, they began to work on Project NN, known alternately as New Newspapers or Neuharth's Nonsense. As a technological enterprise, Gannett was in perfect position for a national paper. Not only had satellites become an extraordinary means of sending and receiving stories and layouts quickly and clearly, but Gannett already had in place what amounted to a nationwide staff. All its papers could be used, as both bureaus and farm teams. To the dismay of many in the chain, the project would tap millions of dollars and top talent from papers that could hardly afford tapping.

But the task involved far more than just money and hardware. They had to confront one of the principal problems of contemporary popular culture: how to attract attention in a crowded, noisy multimedia age. Neuharth understood well, perhaps too well, that he was no longer living in a world of print. Instead, he looked to the success of television—not the medium of Murrow and Moyers but of Musburger and Merv. The only principles were those of the market. "We plead guilty to wanting to make money," says Neuharth, who made $1.3 million last year. "Is that a crime?"

Neuharth felt "*USA Today* should be newsy. It should have lots of information—summaries, results, statistics, lists. It should have an upscale look. Red, white, and blue should be used subtly, as an identifier, but not in a way that would chase off nonpatriots."

Lenin is said to have limited the vocabulary at *Pravda* to around thirteen hundred words. Neuharth, ever the revolutionary, would have approved. In a memo to the staff, the editors wrote, "*Keep it tight:* Propel the story with punctuation. Colons, semicolons, bullets, and dashes can replace some words. . . . Condense background information. Don't prattle on for several grafs explaining what happened at Love Canal." Editors kept sentences simple. Reporters were warned against "falling in love with their own deathless prose."

As a journalist, Neuharth turned out to be an extraordinary adman. He instructed his editors to use "USA" instead of "American," ostensibly out of respect for "Brazilians and Canadians who are technically just as 'American' as people in the USA." But he also admits that the use of "USA" in headlines and the text of stories is a subliminal advertisement for the package itself.

And it has worked. In a period when scores of papers have gone out of business, *USA Today* is the only major newspaper to begin publishing in the past decade. What began as a phenomenon of mediocrity has become an institution, a market success. *USA Today* is now the most widely read paper in the country, having passed *The Wall Street Journal.* ("No. 1 in the USA . . . 5,541,000 Readers Every Day.") Gannett stock has soared in the five years since Neuharth founded the paper. Last June, the company announced that *USA Today* had moved into the black for the first time, showing operating profits of $1.1 million and surprising many Wall Street analysts who saw no opening for a new national paper.

•   •   •

Airplanes are laboratories of American elites. Somewhere a sociologist is working on "The Curse of the Flying Class." Because of the cost involved, people who fly regularly are likely to have an education and income well above the national average. They are consumers of hotels, rental cars, restaurants, best-selling books. And like all people who travel, they at times feel as if they are everywhere and nowhere, disconnected. How could they relate to any local paper? And who among them has time for two thousand words about any one thing? They skim above the earth and the earth's daily strangeness.

No one understood that new class better than Neuharth. His early market research told him that 850,000 people travel each day on the airlines, that 100 million people had changed residences in the past ten years, that 1,750,000 people stay in motels or hotels every night. These disembodied, well-to-do souls, he felt, cried out for attachment, for news of the old places they were nostalgic for. They would be his audience. It didn't matter to Neuharth that *The Wall Street Journal* and the national edition of *The New York Times* were dominating the very "top slice" of the audience. "We wanted the second to the seventh percentile," Neuharth says. "That's our slice."

Neuharth also understood the way the flying class reads. He saw his audience reading in line at the Eastern Shuttle, for three minutes between reading reports. They needed everything fast. Nearly every story would run about the length of a network news segment. Neuharth's charges learned to see virtue in the new approach. Older journalists who would not adapt could leave the room. "Look, I don't go beyond the jump on stories about contras," says reporter Peter Johnson. "A lot of people may say they do, but they don't. The paper revolves around the idea that people get their news from TV and their lives revolve around TV. We must be doing something right."

But length is only part of it. The tone of *USA Today* is also in touch with the life of the flying class. Air traffic and air safety often seem to be the paper's gravest concerns. And to a harried exec, with his coffee spilling down his sleeve because the guy behind him is jamming his knees into his lumbar zone, with his heart slamming against his ribs because his plane has been sitting on the runway for twenty-one minutes and the pilot hasn't the goddam courtesy to say when, *when* in God's name, this crate will leave St. Louis for the software conference in Jacksonville, where he has only the most important DOS presentation of the whole fucking computer *year*! . . . Well, who knows this man's needs better than Al Neuharth? Chad—do you think he wants to know about the intrigues of N'Djamena? In the long days of the flying class, airports exist, the Cardinals exist, Johnny Carson, Steven Jobs, the number of roses in the Rose Bowl Parade all exist. Lebanon, Iran, Iraq—problems that can be pushed to the margins of the mind—become marginal in *USA Today*. And, if only for that, the man on the plane, whose hips are fairly busting the armrests, is grateful.

This year Neuharth has sailed once more into the heartland, promising to visit and write about all fifty states on a journalistic tour of the country called BusCapade USA. Gannett spent $350,000 on a forty-foot Blue Bird Wanderlodge and staffed it with Buscateers who would help Neuharth write his column. Neuharth's prose style has always been Main Street surrealism, and he has been honing it for ages. Eight years ago, when a hurricane forced him and his second (now former) wife out of his home in Florida, Neuharth wrote the opening paragraphs about the storm for *Today:* "Hurricane David, the first major storm named after a male, acted very much like a loose woman all day Monday, dancing along Florida's East Coast and flirting dangerously with cities from Miami to Melbourne."

It was inevitable, then, that when *USA Today* began to show signs of turning a profit, Neuharth would reenter the temple of letters. His columns have embarrassed many of his colleagues. "BusCapade represents a lot of what we do badly," says one staff writer. "A lot of people around here are kind of humiliated by it." But Neuharth presses on. Not since Colonel McCormick of the *Chicago Tribune* flew around the world meeting statesmen and making an ass of himself in print has there been such a vainglorious tour.

> Potosi, Missouri—"People hereabouts are proud of being more middlemost than most of us. . . ."
>
> New Mexico—"They call it the 'Land of Enchantment.' It is. It is also the land of ambivalence. Curiously contrasting people and places."
>
> Louisiana—"Hot and heavy food. Hard drinking. Free living. But, churchgoing (mostly Roman Catholic)."

Happily, business tears him away from his reporting duties here and there. Although he has turned over the CEO spot at Gannett to John Curley, Neuharth is still very much in charge. After two marriages, he is single again but appears only rarely in the gossip columns. Business dominates his public life; he still travels about 250,000 miles a year in his restless Gannett jet. Even after he retires from Gannett in 1989, he will act as an "ambassador" for the company. Neuharth read the culture and saw the opening for *USA Today.* Gannett backed it, but *USA Today* is his paper, a singular vision of a corporate man. He will forever be its symbol.

His offices are suitably futuristic and a bit grotesque. There are walls papered with snakeskin, lots of the color peach, marble, and suede rugs. Outside Neuharth's office are two "neorealist" sheep. Staffers used to put chocolate kisses under the sheep's asses. With sinks of hammered brass and walls of brown marble, even the bathrooms look like imports from the Playboy mansion. Neuharth revels in the glory that is him. A huge bronze bust of Neuharth the size of an Easter Island statue stands in the lobby. It is known as "The Al-head."

Dressed once more in shades of gray, Neuharth leans back in his chair and shoots a quick glance at the silent TVs playing out soap operas and news above his desk. Though he is known throughout the building as a writer of sharp, even vicious memos, he long ago mastered the art of saying little in interviews. He begins to talk about the fulfillment of his dream, the success of *USA Today*. Evidently he has memorized his graduation speeches and press releases. He talks the way he writes, in alliterative, weird nuggets. Gravely, he concludes that *USA Today* tries to look at "the good and the bad, the glad and the sad."

Neuharth makes seriousness seem like an elitist, prissy sort of gesture. We Don't Take Ourselves Seriously, Why Should You?

The funny thing is that, in spite of itself, *USA Today* has proved that it's possible to be brief without sounding like an idiot. Lord knows why, but Neuharth lets an editor named Robert Wilson run a book-review page that carries intelligent, if fleeting, pieces that do not condescend to their readers. It is here, and perhaps here alone, that *USA Today* educates its audience. One page recently carried historian Ronald Steel on Gore Vidal's *Empire* and poet and novelist Jay Parini on James Dickey's *Alnilam*. In another forum, perhaps, the reviews would seem thin, but in *USA Today* they had a certain integrity. They did not stoop.

The sports coverage in *USA Today* is, in its way, unparalleled. If you are willing to leave the writing to Roger Angell and the sociology to Robert Lipsyte, *USA Sports* is a wondrous child's world. There is nothing quite like reading endless box scores and batting stats as a means of escape.

But the rest of the paper just doesn't try. It has no soul. The Life section is merely a press agent's dream, a littering field for hundreds of items daily. "Oh, I love it!" says PR prince Bobby Zarem. The Money section, too, can be entertaining, but there is no learning from it. As the world gets more difficult to understand, *USA Today* says it's all a lark.

Neuharth has contributed something to the culture that is at once cheery and cynical, a newspaper that imitates and celebrates the vacuity of television. Worse, he has identified a hurried, self-involved "slice"—the flying class—and has chosen to massage rather than nourish it. There is no sense of public mission in Neuharth's paper, only private enterprise.

USA Today is all about making money for itself. It is part of a near-revolution in the media: the traditional desire for profits has completely superseded its old partner, a sense of public responsibility. Publishing companies that used to finance serious fiction and poetry with best-sellers now jack up their profit margin by cutting the highbrow stuff out of the equation (prompting veteran editor Ted Solotaroff to refer to his business as "the literary-industrial complex"). Films have suffered as well. In the post–*Star Wars* age, the movie studios have shifted nearly all their attention and resources to the blockbuster. When they do make even the most mediocre bit of intelligent entertainment, we are told that such productions take tremendous "courage."

In recent times, the New Journalists, the underground press, the *New York Herald Tribune,* and dozens of other talents and publications have changed the language of American journalism. Neuharth, too, sees himself as an innovator. But *USA Today* is a product and nothing more. In the end, even its optimism has dangerous moments. Sometimes *USA Today* tries so hard to please that it distorts. AIDS CASES MAY BE ON THE DECLINE was the head for a recent story. A few paragraphs in, the story says, ". . . and the finding doesn't mean AIDS cases will decline." Doesn't that matter?

Neuharth is a new kind of Citizen Kane. But Kane's technique was to inflame, to outrage. His was an era of newspaper wars, and the paper that screamed most shrilly often won. Neuharth doesn't have to scream. Instead, he coos to his reader, "Everything is all right." His influence, his tone, can be felt in dozens of papers around the country, including some outside the Gannett family. Other papers have adopted his brevity, and even the Good Gray *Times* is studying the wonders of color. Nearly everyone has stolen the *USA Today* weather map. It is a fine weather map. Neuharth does not raise the old sort of Kane. He offers sugar. There is something terribly mean-spirited about it, as if he means to create a global village of village idiots.

The Xanadu of the era looms above the Potomac. Two rounded, silvery towers in Rosslyn, Virginia, house Gannett and *USA Today,* and as you fly over them, they seem ready to lift off at any moment. Inside, reporters are writing short, cheery paragraphs, and editors are making them shorter, cheerier. The generating intelligence is the great Al-head. "It's not exactly *The Front Page,* is it?" says assistant features editor Susan Older. "It's like, here we are on the starship *Enterprise,* sailing into the future."

—◊—

It is ten years later and somehow USA Today *no longer seems as shocking or ridiculous. It is true, the paper has gotten a little better, a little more attentive to the news, but what makes it seem almost stately is that so many big-city papers have declined so quickly. Papers from Miami to San Francisco have willfully eroded in a mad scramble to please the stockholder; in their attempts to be more "user friendly," they betrayed themselves and the readers. There are precious few cities now where* USA Today *is not the best paper in town. God help us.*

17

⟿⟁⟾

News in a Dying Language

(January 1994)

For one naive and splendid moment last spring, the newspaper romantics of New York believed they had a chance to claim the *Post* as their own. While lawyers piled up fortunes haggling over who would own the paper and who would owe what to whom, reporters in the riverfront newsroom paced nervously on a carpet the color of dried blood. "I hate this," one reporter, Colin Miner, said. "I just want to get back to dead bodies and chalk lines." Miner was young and had only recently been hired, but he had thoroughly inhaled the spirit of South Street. Meanwhile, Pete Hamill, the momentary editor of the paper and its would-be Lord Byron, sat near his office window and watched a loaded barge glide into the spidery shadows cast by the Brooklyn Bridge.

"You wanna know what I think would be God's paper?" Hamill said, rising from his chair. (He was then assuming that the *Post* might be his to reinvent.) "It would be a tabloid that's smart and hip, knowing. The tone of Rupert Murdoch's papers was always naive, like 'Holy Shit! They're Having Sex!' You can have classic tabloid sex and violence, but better, well written, and accurate. God's paper would have a coalition of audiences. We'd appeal to Koreans, Chinese, Japanese, Dominicans, Ecuadoreans, Haitians—the new immigrants. That's New York's future salvation. Anyone who still reads a newspaper is part of an aspiring class—the people who aren't zonked out yet on *Wheel of Fortune.* We'd try to get the kids of the immigrants, the first generation of English-speakers. Cover immigration. Have a green-card columnist. Make a feature section. Cover the streets. Even the foreign stuff would reflect the community. Cover the best murder trial in Tel Aviv. Get into the Caribbean. The paper's got to reflect the city more accurately than by just having drug dealers and guys in handcuffs plastered across the front page."

Hamill, who had made a career as a columnist by evoking a chiaroscuro New York of noble pugs and clubhouse hacks, was dreaming. And, what was more, he knew it. From the beginning, Rupert Murdoch had been the only participant in the negotiations with the will and the means to win the *Post,* and he would never hand the paper over to the likes of Hamill. It was depressing, then, to hear the cheer go up in the newsroom when it was finally announced that the owner of the *Post* would indeed be Rupert, Redux. Some jobs had been saved (though not Colin Miner's), but the *Post* would go on as a cynical paper—a right-wing feuilleton for the city's conservatives and an object of high camp for the rest. Still, it had been fine to hear a newspaperman dream, if only for a little while.

Just before Hamill gave way to the inevitable, he'd said he thought that one of the greatest models for any other newspaper was the *Forverts,* the *Jewish Daily Forward.* Like most Irish Catholics of his generation, Hamill was possessed of a fluency in Yiddish limited to words for sandwich meats and forms of human stupidity: it was the idea of the *Forward* he was responding to—the *Forward* as the king of New York's ethnic newspapers. For more than 150 years, publishers in New York have put out papers to capture the new arrivals at Ellis Island and Castle Garden and JFK as they stood blinking into the sun, starved for news and instruction. The best of those papers have been immigration primers, guides to the mysteries and manners of the New World. Signs of the old immigrations persist. *France-Amérique,* which began publication in 1828, is hanging on, and so is the *New Yorker Staats-Zeitung* (1834). *Il Progresso* (1880) folded in 1989, having been overtaken by a new Italian daily, *America Oggi.* (Ethnic papers have a way of breeding before they die. *Staats-Zeitung* was the Teutonic seedling from which the Ridder half of the Knight-Ridder chain bloomed, while the publishers of *Il Progresso,* at one time a pro-Mussolini paper, begat the old New York *Enquirer,* which begat the *National Enquirer.*) In all, there are more than a hundred ethnic papers in around thirty languages published in the city, and while it is sad that there are no longer, say, eight important Chinese papers, it is remarkable that there are still four. There are also papers published in Arabic, Armenian, Creole, Estonian, Hungarian, Korean, Latvian, Norwegian, Romansh, and Tagalog.

The *Forward,* which was founded in 1897, is not the oldest, but it is the model, the exemplar. At the peak of its influence, in the twenties, its circulation exceeded a quarter of a million, and in 1947 its fiftieth anniversary was celebrated at Madison Square Garden. It was once so powerful a paper that it helped engineer the election of a Socialist, Meyer London, to Congress. (That happened in 1914.) But no more. The *Forward* has been a weekly for a decade, and, having reached the age of ninety-six, it will count itself lucky if it can celebrate its centenary. It is written in a dying language for a geriatric population. Circulation is sclerotic, fourteen thousand being the official, and highly generous, assessment. Mordecai Strigler, a diminutive scholar with thick glasses and titanic energy, who is the present editor, has so much trouble finding writers able to communicate in Yiddish that he often writes half the paper himself. Over a period of forty years, he has used about thirty pseudonyms, A. Kore (A Reader), A. Ben-Ami (Son of the People), M. Ragil (A Simple Person), and Z. Kamai (An Old-Fashioned Man) among them. The most reliably generous section of the paper is the obituaries. Such is the state of Yiddish. In her story

"Envy, or Yiddish in America" Cynthia Ozick wrote, "Of what other language can it be said that it died a sudden and definite death, in a given decade, on a given piece of soil?"

The *Forward* these days is the product of four full-time staff members. Strigler is seventy-two, and the three others—the managing editor, Joseph Mlotek; the contributing editor, Abraham Wilk; and the news editor, Jacob Goldstein—are even older. "I come in, and *here* someone is sick, *there* someone is sick, so I have to finish things on my own," Strigler told me one afternoon. He slumped in his chair and raised his brows, Yiddishly, toward heaven. "What can I do?"

The *Forward*'s offices are in the Workmen's Circle building, on East Thirty-third Street, a flavorless site compared with the former headquarters, down on East Broadway. (The old *Forward* building, with some of its Yiddish pediments still in place, is now a Chinese cultural center.) By newspaper standards, the offices are quiet and trig. They reflect the prim neatness of the aged. But the modern era does intrude. Management has replaced the old Linotype machines with Apple computers and Yiddish software. And although the paper has a tradition of left-leaning secularism, the typesetters are Orthodox, since it is the Orthodox, and especially the Hasidim, who keep Yiddish alive as a language of daily conversation. (Hebrew, the sacred tongue, is usually reserved for prayer and religious scholarship.)

"The older people don't want to hear it when you say it's all dying," Strigler told me recently. "The Lubavitcher Hasidim speak Yiddish, but they don't want to read our writing. They have their own separate world—even their own paper, *Algemeiner Journal*. I don't know who I'm writing for anymore. Maybe two hundred younger people read us. But they are passive. They are not in the conversation. They are only observers of this old world. My daughter tries now to learn Yiddish. She is twenty-five. She's very interested. But if she and her generation will be readers of our newspaper I don't believe it. It's too late, because there are pockets of speakers but they don't have what to do. If they can be a rabbi or a lawyer, what have they to do with us?" Fortunately for Yiddish, Strigler's energy is legion. He edits the *Forward* in the morning and then walks to another office, in Chelsea, to put together a distinguished Yiddish-language magazine of politics and culture, the biweekly *Yiddisher Kemfer* ("The Fighter"). It is as if one man were running (and largely writing) both the *Times* and *The New York Review of Books*.

Like so many of his colleagues and his readers, Strigler has led the epic life of a survivor. Born near the Polish city of Lublin, he was ordained as a rabbi when he was sixteen. As a teacher in Warsaw, he was thrown into the crucible of the war with Germany. When the Nazis broke through the barricades with their tanks, the Poles pointed to him and said, "Jew." The Nazi soldiers hauled Strigler off to a concentration camp and carved swastikas into his cheeks and forehead with a razor blade. Over the next five years, he was sent from one concentration camp or slave-labor camp to another. He lost his parents and four of his sisters in the Holocaust. In 1945, an American journalist and writer named Meyer Levin went to the Buchenwald camp after it was liberated, and there he interviewed Strigler for what became the book *In Search*. Strigler described how he managed, mostly through sheer luck, to survive to the end of the war. He talked of how Nazi soldiers beat him and confiscated his manuscripts, how he saw them order people shot as unfit because of the slightest blemish. After a roundup of Jews in the Lublin area, "our camp was put on the march," Strigler said. "We had to go fifteen miles, in a column ten abreast. They told us to run, and they rode alongside the column and fired into it all the time, our comrades dropped around us, and we filled up to ten abreast and ran, and they shot, shot, shot." Once they had been herded into the Ishbitza ghetto, about thirty miles away from Lublin, a mass, orgiastic slaughter began. "I saw a German officer go up and look over a pretty little girl of thirteen who had just been taken off a train. Then he calmly took out his bayonet knife and ripped up her belly. I saw this."

Strigler has always been a remarkably prolific writer. Even now, he is capable of writing a dozen articles a week on topics as various as Israel, New York politics, biblical commentary, and the fate of Yiddish. But after he was released from Buchenwald he moved to Paris, and there he wrote as if truly possessed, spinning out a vast cycle of semifictional books on the Holocaust, which were among the first eyewitness accounts of horror: *Maydanek,* in 1947; *In Di Fabrikn Fun Toyt* ("In the Factories of Death"), in 1948; *Verk "Tse"* ("Plant C"), in 1950; and *Goyroles* ("Destinies"), in 1952. In 1953, he came to America, and he has worked here as a journalist in the Yiddish world ever since. Late in 1986, he became the editor of the *Forward,* succeeding the late Simon Weber. He does not wish to be its last editor, but that could turn out to be the case.

"A few years ago, I went out and tried to find an apprentice, but it was impossible," Strigler said. "To tell you the truth, I am sure in a year or two I will not be here. Maybe I'll go to Israel. My wife was a teacher at Hebrew University, and I don't know how long we'll stay here. They tell me that I can't move to Israel, that I'm the last one that can edit the paper. That's what they tell me." Harold Ostroff, the general manager of the Forward Association, which runs the paper, does all he can to cajole Strigler into staying. When I asked Ostroff if he would be able to find a replacement, he said, "There may be someone in this world. I don't see anyone in America." The decline of writers and of the circulation is so profound, Ostroff said, that he was already thinking about going monthly, if need be.

Even in its dotage, the *Forward* must evoke in the greatest newspaper dynasties (to say nothing of Murdoch, of the *Post,* or Mortimer Zuckerman, of the *News*) a sense of awe. The *Forward* grew out of an immigration of more than two and a half million Jews from Eastern

Europe between 1881 and 1925—an immigration that rivals the current influx of Dominicans and Chinese, and one that forever shaped the texture of New York life. The demand for Yiddish publications in New York was so great that by 1914 more than 150 daily, weekly, monthly, quarterly, and occasional journals were appearing.

Abraham Cahan, an editor of literary genius and imperious character, ruled the *Forward* in its golden decades—the first half of this century. Cahan had grown up in academic and revolutionary circles in Lithuania, and after he arrived in the United States, in 1882, he made a literary name for himself even before the *Forward* came into being. In 1895, he published a realistic novella of Jewish life on the Lower East Side. The headline over William Dean Howells's review of *Yekl, a Tale of the New York Ghetto,* in the *New York World,* read, THE GREAT NOVELIST HAILS ABRAHAM CAHAN, THE AUTHOR OF "YEKL," AS A NEW STAR OF REALISM, AND SAYS THAT HE AND STEPHEN CRANE HAVE DRAWN THE TRUEST PICTURES OF EAST SIDE LIFE. Cahan worked for four years at English-language newspapers, most notably with Lincoln Steffens at the *Commercial Advertiser,* covering murders, fires, Ellis Island, and the exploits of Buffalo Bill. By the time he settled at the *Forward,* in 1901, he had in mind a unique paper: one that would be a mix of *shund* and *literatur*—sensationalism and seriousness. He printed feature stories about the prostitutes on Allen Street and the peddlers on Delancey Street. He provided instructions in how to use a handkerchief, when to say "Pardon me," how to get along with the neighbors in a communal apartment. He advised parents to feed their children fresh fruits and vegetables. He ran a contest in which readers were asked for the best definition of the word *mazel* ("luck"), and printed a seminal front-page story headed THE FUNDAMENTALS OF BASEBALL EXPLAINED TO NON-SPORTS, which was accompanied by a helpful diagram of the Polo Grounds. At the same time, he printed fiction, essays, and poems by all the great names in Yiddish literature—an accomplishment that was celebrated when Isaac Bashevis Singer, who had first published almost all of his fiction in the *Forward,* won the Nobel Prize, in 1978.

The *Forward* under Cahan, Ronald Sanders wrote in his 1969 book *The Downtown Jews,* was "a kind of running Talmudic text for the secular cultural life of the Yiddish-speaking masses." Cahan was their secular rabbi, helping them ease their way into the New World. By far the paper's most popular feature was called "A Bintel Brief" ("A Bundle of Letters"), in which readers gave voice to their most personal concerns and posed plaintive questions. Cahan had pleaded with his readers to "send us *emmeser romanen"*—true-life novels—and the readers responded with remarkably vivid descriptions of tenement life and spiritual confusion. The column, readers said, was like a combination of "Dear Abby" and Talmudic argument. One worried young woman wrote, "Is it a sin to use face powder? Shouldn't a girl look beautiful? My father does not want me to use face powder. Is it a sin?" Elsewhere, mothers living in bleak poverty wondered if they should put their children up for adoption.

When the occasion demanded it, Cahan was also able to mobilize a skilled group of reporters to cover the news at least as well as the city's English-language papers. On March 25, 1911, a huge fire broke out at the Triangle Shirtwaist Company, a ten-story loft near Washington Square. The fire raged through the top three floors, where hundreds of girls and young women worked at their sewing machines. Fire engines arrived within ten minutes, but they could do little to stop the blaze. The water from their hoses reached only to the seventh floor and their ladders only to the sixth. Under the headline THE MORGUE IS FULL OF OUR DEAD, the poet and *Forward* reporter Morris Rosenfeld pieced together an astonishing account of the tragedy:

> Forlornly [the crowd on the street] stood and watched as one girl after another fell, like shot birds, from above, from the burning floors. The men held out a longer time, enveloped in flames. And

when they could hold out no longer, they jumped, too. Below, horrified and weeping, stood thousands of workers from the surrounding factories. They watched moving, terrible, unforgettable scenes. At one window on the eighth floor appeared a young man with a girl. He was holding her tightly by the hand. Behind them the red flames could be seen. The young man lovingly wrapped his arms around the girl and held her to him a moment, kissed her, and then let her go. . . . A moment later he leaped after her, and his body landed next to hers. Both were dead.

There were 146 dead, all told, and 100,000 people marched in a mass funeral ceremony.

Cahan was widely criticized among more religious and more intellectual Yiddish editors as a philistine bent on driving his audience into assimilation. And they were right: the *Forward* under Cahan was indeed a powerful instrument of assimilation. These days, Strigler and his colleagues like to say, with a sigh, that perhaps the paper did its job so well that it has put itself nearly out of business. The *Forward,* like the language itself, is in its preservationist stage. Aaron Lansky, a remarkable young man who in 1989 won a MacArthur "genius" award for rescuing hundreds of thousands of Yiddish books, told me, "My grandfather was a junkman in Fall River, Massachusetts, and he depended on the *Forward* for news. Who does that anymore? I'm afraid I can't think of anyone I know who reads it regularly, even in my circle of Yiddishists. Maybe this tells the whole story. The Hasidim speak Yiddish, but they will not read modern, secular Yiddish literature. To them, it is heretical. One night, I got a call from a Brooklyn collector who told me I had to come right away to Brooklyn, to Brighton Beach, to something called the Beth Am Center, an old Zionist labor center that was now being sublet to the Orthodox as a yeshiva. He had discovered that when the Orthodox moved in they found a library of fifteen thousand Yiddish books and threw them all down the cellar stairs. When we came to get the books, the Orthodox just glowered at us. For them, those books were heretical, because they discussed how Jews might live in a modern world. It is a great irony that the last Jews who speak Yiddish will not read these great books, let alone the *Forward*."

I doubt if there is any one paper in New York that is a worthy successor to the *Forward*. *Novoye Russoye Slovo* ("New Russian Word"), which is the leading paper in Brighton Beach, is distinctively Russian, with its passion for long opinion pieces, but it lacks the flair of the best Moscow papers. *El Diario–La Prensa* is the leading Spanish-language paper, with a circulation of fifty thousand, and features a broad range of opinion pieces, from conservative attacks on Fidel Castro to liberal pieces on Central and South America. But by trying to be an umbrella paper for all the Hispanic groups in the city it shows how radically different the interests of the city's Cubans and Puerto Ricans, Dominicans and Colombians are. The various groups are often better served by the imported papers available in Hispanic neighborhoods and at stores like Hotaling's, just off Times Square, that specialize in out-of-town publications. Caribbeans, too, have New York-based papers, but the imports, like the *Gleaner,* from Jamaica, are more popular.

Perhaps the most ambitious and among the wealthiest of the ethnic papers is the *World Journal,* which is a daily financed by a Taiwan conglomerate and is the leading Chinese-language paper in the country. Tih-Wu Wang, the Citizen Kane of the conglomerate, is a gigantic figure in Taipei. A former member of Chiang Kai-shek's military, he traded on his political and business connections to build a chain of papers in both Taiwan and North America. "The legend is he used to deliver his papers on a bicycle at the start, and now he might as well have a license to print money," Justin Yu, the *World Journal*'s immigration and crime reporter, told me over a long lunch one afternoon on Mott Street. "Mr. Wang comes on Chinese New

Year and holds a banquet at the Sheraton he owns, near La Guardia. Everyone gets an envelope with a bonus."

T. W. Wang is in his eighties and is sitting on a fortune. Taiwan sources say that years ago he bought a mountain on the island, and on that mountain he built a palace, and in that palace he built a glass floor with gold carp swimming underneath. It was a pretty effect, but this Xanadu made some squeamish local politicians very unhappy all the same, because it seemed to them an unnecessary flaunting of wealth. Soon it was announced that the estate would become a vacation center for employees. "Mr. Wang is a great story," Justin Yu said. "He even thought about buying the *Daily News.* But the American market is just a chicken leg compared to what he wants. It's peanuts compared to China."

For the *World Journal,* which was founded in 1976, the story that ranks in importance with the Triangle Shirtwaist fire was the tragedy of the *Golden Venture,* the freighter that ran aground on the beach at Far Rockaway in June 1993, loaded with hundreds of Chinese. Justin Yu and his partner, Alex Peng, covered the story with speed and grace, not least because they had been following the nuances and cruelties of illegal immigration from China to New York for years. Justin, who tends to do most of his phone work and writing while he is sitting at a small table at the back of his wife's toy store, in Chinatown, told me, "All the illegals come through the store. When someone comes into the toy store to buy a toothbrush, I know he's illegal and green, right off the boat. I get all my stories that way. One guy told me how he got to Houston via Mexico via Belize and how soldiers escorted him across the Rio Grande. They took a small airplane from Mexico to the desert and were met by a minivan and driven eight or nine hours to Los Angeles. Then they came here because there are no Fukienese in Los Angeles. The Fukienese own the bad carryout places. You know, the homeless live on that two-dollar fried rice they make."

Alex Peng makes his reporting rounds driving an old Lincoln and wearing two beepers on his belt. Husky and intense, he is sometimes described as the Chinese Jimmy Breslin. Peng doesn't resent the label, despite Breslin's outburst a couple of years ago when he called a Korean-American colleague at *Newsday* "slant-eyed" and a "yellow cur." Peng said, "I fully understand that Jimmy Breslin's reputation is no good among Asians, but he is an energetic, dynamic journalist. I learned a lot from him, just by reading. He is always there, and that's a rule: You gotta be there, you always go. If you sit in the office and work the phone, you get another kind of story."

New York's Chinatown is no longer limited to lower Manhattan, and one day recently Alex and I were in the Queens division, in Flushing, where many of the most prosperous Asians—from Taiwan, Hong Kong, and Korea—have settled. (Country folk from China itself are more likely to live in the overcrowded apartments in Manhattan.) Alex switched on a tape of one of his favorite singers, Engelbert Humperdinck, gunned the engine, and hummed lightly. I told him about the letters that used to appear in the *Forward*'s "Bintel Brief"—letters from parents who feared that their children were losing their Yiddish and their ties to Jewish culture.

"Yeah, sure. We get letters like that," he said. "Like 'My children won't go to weekend Chinese school and can't talk Chinese. What should I do?' Or 'My kids won't eat Chinese food. What should I do?' Nothing changes."

The *World Journal* publishes service information for immigrants, just as the *Forward* did—information on how to apply for a Social Security card, where to register to vote, where to collect your car if it has been towed, the schedule of the public libraries. But where the *World Journal* falls short is in its lack of independence. According to some members of the Chinese-speaking community, none of the Chinese papers in New York have shown that they are able to write in detail about, for example, the dominance of the tongs of organized crime. The *World Journal* and the three other Chinese papers—the Hong Kong–financed *Sing Tao,* the local *United Daily,* and the Beijing-sponsored *China Press*—all tend to skip lightly over areas considered too delicate to mention. When unionized waiters at the Silver Palace, a vast dim-sum emporium on the Bowery, picketed the restaurant last August because the owners wanted to cut their health insurance and take a percentage of the tips, the papers responded with minimal, euphemistic coverage. Because nearly all the other waiters in Chinatown are not even unionized, and because the tongs are so deeply involved in the restaurant business, the case had enormous importance for the community. It fell largely to the English-language press to cover the story.

Such limited coverage doesn't seem to bother even the best of the *World Journal*'s reporters—or not enough, at least. "News is business," Alex said. "Keep that in mind. Don't position yourself as a gatekeeper or a social conscience. Of course, we talk about all that, but news is business. If there is no profit, why you wanna do that? You are not the Salvation Army. C'mon, gimme a break!"

As we drove on through Flushing, Alex said that, like the editors of the *Forward,* he and his colleagues who grew up speaking and reading Chinese see their own children becoming Americanized. They can speak and understand Chinese but not read it. The *World Journal* will not be their paper. They, too, will drift toward the *News,* the *Post,* the *Times,* and, most of all, to television. "We're not counting on the younger generations to be our readers, but we have the confidence that we will always be a bridge for the newcomers," Alex said. "My kids seem to pick up their language from TV and the street: The other day, my four-year-old called me a schmuck. What language is that?"

In the end, one of the papers that seemed most promising on my search through the city's ethnic press was the English-language edition of the *Forward.* Started in 1990, it is a gigantic leap beyond much of the rest of the mainstream Jewish English-language press, which is generally so beholden to the Jewish charities for funding that it is no less cautious than the *World Journal* and *Sing Tao;* the slant is often so acute that one anticipates the millennium headline WORLD ENDS YESTERDAY; JEWS SUFFER MOST.

The idea for an English-language *Forward* had been drifting around the paper's offices ever since the other Yiddish papers in the city, like the *Tog* (the "Day"), began closing, in the early 1970s. But there was always resistance. What did English have to do with the *Forverts?* It was not until the early 1980s that someone came along who was ready to push the idea, and he was from outside the paper: Seth Lipsky, one of the leading writers and editors at *The Wall Street Journal.* Lipsky was an editor for the paper in Europe and Asia and also a member of its conservative editorial board. Like his mentor on the editorial page, Robert Bartley, he was, and still is, capable of writing in a mode just short of savagery. But, as happens with many editors easing into middle age—Lipsky is forty-seven—there came a time when he wanted his own show to run. The notion of an English *Forward* appealed to him more for reasons of the paper's history than out of any allegiance to *Yiddishkeit.* He is, of course, Jewish, but the extent of his attachment to religious custom was revealed to me one afternoon when we sent out for sandwiches. "Ham and cheese on rye, for me," he said. The *Forward,* Lipsky was quick to remind me, has always been a secular paper.

For years, Lipsky waged a campaign of noodging the *Forward* hierarchy—especially Simon Weber, who in 1970 had succeeded Abraham Cahan as editor, and who retained a great deal of influence at the paper even after Strigler became editor, at the end of 1986. Lipsky tried over and over again to convince the Forward Association that an English-language edition—not a mere translation but a separate entity—could one day turn a profit, and would almost certainly be a boon to Jewish journalism and learning. In advancing this cause, Lipsky visited Weber in the hospital, where the older man was recovering from a broken hip. "He was seventy-three, and in seventy-three years I don't think he'd ever heard an idea that he regarded as quite as insane as mine," Lipsky told me. "The *Forward*'s cause was secular Jewish language and literature, and along comes this kid from *The Wall Street Journal*."

The idea went nowhere until the spring of 1987, when Weber was in the hospital once more—this time with a general breakdown of his health. By then, Weber had taken a liking to Lipsky, a man of firm opinions ("I'm a hardheaded liberal, you might say") and tart good humor. There was an odd friendship between them, but the idea of an English *Forward* was still not moving ahead. This time, Lipsky was merciless.

"Si, look," he said. "You are on your deathbed, and in a matter of months you'll be gone. And if you don't do something, your newspaper is going to be gone with you. So if you are not willing to receive my emissary for me you should be willing to receive him for the sake of the *Forward*. And I expect you to do it."

Weber was silent a long time. And then he said, with his inimitable Old World gutturals, "And *khooo* is this emissary?"

"It's Sam Pisar," Lipsky said.

Weber was impressed. "Pisar," he said. "He can make things khappen."

Pisar, an international lawyer and a survivor of Auschwitz, met with Weber and the members of the Forward Association in Weber's hospital room, and could see that some of them were receptive to the idea of an English paper. They agreed to receive Lipsky.

"I came back from China to New York at my own expense," Lipsky said, recalling the meeting. "We met on a Saturday morning. I felt like Judge Bork going before the Senate Judiciary Committee. Everything was friendly, okay, and then Sam turns to me and says something that made me realize why he's so brilliant. He said, 'Seth, they don't want to know about the easy questions. They want to know about the difficult questions.'

" 'Like what, Sam?' I said.

"And he said, 'Like Jabotinsky. Where are you on Jabotinsky?'

"A chill fell over the room. It was like walking into a meat locker. I knew right away that this was the most important moment of my life."

It might well be appropriate at this juncture to explain the significance of the chill in the room. It was Theodor Herzl who founded modern Zionism, from a centrist, assimilated, slightly left-leaning bent. His opponent in tactics and temperament was Vladimir Jabotinsky, a Russian newspaperman who believed (some have said believed fanatically) in an armed struggle to create Israel. Jabotinsky advocated a "greater" Jewish state on both sides of the Jordan River. When the state was formed, Prime Minister David Ben-Gurion hung portraits on the wall of Herzl and Chaim Weizmann. But when Menachem Begin took office, in 1977, he added one more portrait—that of Jabotinsky.

Lipsky went on, "So, finally, I said, 'I know how you feel about Jabotinsky and how he appeared to your generation. But to my generation—or, at least, to me, looking back—the outstanding fact of Jabotinsky's life is that he called for the evacuation of the Jews from Europe in 1932.' What I was trying to say was that I don't want to fight about the past, but if you really want to I'll try to get down and mud-wrestle with you. After that, the conversation returned to an amicable plane."

Lipsky's dream was not realized until the Forward Association had a financial windfall. For many years, the association had owned the radio station WEVD-FM, named in honor of the socialist leader Eugene Victor Debs. Known some time ago as "the station that speaks your language," WEVD featured programming in Yiddish, Russian, Ukrainian, Spanish, Greek, and Turkish. But with time some of those languages died out in the city, and some became so prevalent that they had their own stations. WEVD was, as a business, losing ground. Then, in 1989, the Spanish Broadcasting Sys-

tem decided it needed a New York flagship, a fifty-thousand-watt
FM station. Not only did WEVD have the power, but it was one of
only thirteen stations with access to the transmission tower on the
Empire State Building. The SBS and the Forward Association cut a
deal. Harold Ostroff, who conducted the negotiations for the Forward Association, said that the total package should ultimately be
worth $65 million. Though much of the money will be a long time
coming in, even a fraction of it was enough to make viable the idea
of maintaining the Yiddish *Forward* while starting an English-
language edition. Lipsky published his first issue on May 25, 1990.

To all who ask, Lipsky spins out a ditzy theory of how the English
Forward could go from its current circulation, of 13,500, to something five times, even fifteen times, as big. His fantasy, like Pete
Hamill's dream of God's tabloid, is part mist, part ideology. "My theory about the newspaper market is that the billionaires circling the
city look only at the tabloid flank, but the weak flank in New York is
the *Times,*" he said. "The *Times* was built on a constituency of hardheaded liberals—largely Jews, though not exclusively. That constituency is shrinking in stunning numbers. The proprietors of the
Times have two choices: either shrink, which is not logical, or abandon
their traditional constituency and purpose, and pursue a much more
culturally diverse constituency—the African-Americans, the Hispanics. They are fine constituencies, but such a move will change the content of the *Times.* And that will leave only one broadsheet in New York
in a position to focus on that original constituency of *The New York
Times* and to grow, especially as a daily. And that will be the *Forward.*"

At the instant my eyebrow lifted, Lipsky smiled.

"I see you are dubious of the proposition."

Perhaps so. "Well, look at it this way," Lipsky went on. "You have
seventeen hundred dailies in America, and more than half of them
have circulations under fifty thousand. A daily that takes in a profit
can be sold for the price of a supertanker."

While Lipsky waits out that part of his dream, it is worth noting that the editorial contents of the English-language *Forward*—especially the aggressive news coverage and the sophisticated arts pages—are worthy of the Yiddish paper. From the start, Lipsky hired a range of quirky young talent, including one writer, Ilene Rosenzweig, whose previous employment had been with *Street News,* the paper of the homeless, and who is the author of *The I Hate Madonna Handbook.* Recently, he hired as executive editor Lucette Lagnado, late of the *Post* and *The Village Voice,* where she was the "Urban Guerrilla" columnist. Lipsky and Lagnado have published some excellent pieces from Moscow, Washington, and Jerusalem as well as irreverent coverage of the world of Jewish politics and culture. There has been a string of fine articles by Jeffrey Goldberg, late of *The Washington Post* and the Israeli Defense Forces, on the feuds within the Lubavitcher Hasidic community, and investigative reports on alleged fraud in Orthodox communities regarding medical insurance and state educational grants. "We don't have any sacred cows, kosher or otherwise," Goldberg told me. "We want to cover the Jewish community as rigorously as the *Times* or the *News* covers City Hall. We don't have that not-in-front-of-the-goyim sensibility." According to associate editor Jonathan Rosen, the virtue of the Yiddish *Forward* is "that it took the imagination as seriously as news." So, too, with the English edition. The paper has run excerpts from Philip Roth's *Operation Shylock,* David Rosenberg and Harold Bloom's biblical study, *The Book of J,* and, in serial form, the second volume of Art Spiegelman's *Maus,* the cartoon saga of the Holocaust and the relationship between the artist and his survivor-father that won a special Pulitzer Prize in 1992. Spiegelman, for his part, admires Lipsky's news columns—"Their anti-Semite watch is a good one, and they have a nice Diaspora beat." But he was astonished at the hawkish tone the editorial page took during the Gulf War. In despair, Spiegelman nearly pulled his strip, he said, "but the war ended too soon for me to act." No matter how conservative Lipsky may be on certain subjects, especially foreign affairs, his stewardship of the paper has been open and daring. Recently, he ran a column by writer and editor Philip Gourevitch resisting "the notion that American-Jewish culture can be understood as a matter of neurosis, cuisine, and television sitcoms":

> Sadly, a large portion—I'd venture that it's close to 50%—of the material that comes in to this office for review or publication conceives of Jewishness as something defined from without by persecution or hostility. Sitting in this chair on a bad day, you might think that Jews had finally succumbed to Sartre's insulting suggestion that if people stopped hating us we would cease to exist. . . . Sadder still is the fact that many Jews seem to cherish their self-perception as victims. This is a common idiocy of our age, hardly unique to Jews: to seek one's value in one's devaluation by others. We are hated, so we must be great enough to warrant hatred, the thinking goes, we are a cause, and easy righteousness is on our side.

Gourevitch's article, which goes on to urge secular Jews to find their identity in learning and the traditions of Jewish culture, is just not the sort of thing you would expect to find in *JewishWeek* or *Hadassah*.

Whenever Lipsky is asked why he threw away a big-time career at *The Wall Street Journal* to edit the English-language *Forward,* he says, "I did it for the prestige." He told me, "It's true. These are serious thinkers here. The *Forward* has a Nobel Prize. So they're not terribly impressed with Lipsky. It was just a question of trying to rise to their level."

Visitors to the *Forward* office, however, notice that while the Yiddish and the English staffs work on the same floor, they hardly mix. (The segregation is social *and* editorial. Neither paper runs translated articles from the other.) There is a bit of a cultural gulf in their interests. There are no Talmudic scholars on the English side, and, next to some of his staffers, Lipsky is a regular Maimonides. At one meeting, the English staff was talking about Hanukkah, and a reporter could not follow the drift.

"What's a dreidel?" he asked.

Jonathan Rosen, a Yale graduate who has also served as cultural editor and executive editor, told me that while the two sides come from different worlds, there is tremendous respect not only of the younger for the older but vice versa. The older generation is not the least bit deluded about the future of the Yiddish *Forward,* and hopes that the publication will go on, at least in English. "The *Forward* is a little like the State of Israel. It had a history, and now it has a history again," Rosen said. "I'll tell my parents' friends that I work for the *Forward* and their faces will beam, because they want so much to believe that Yiddish is being reborn. But Yiddish culture was disappearing even before the Holocaust. Shtetl life was changing. Lots of what we call Yiddish culture—films like *The Dybbuk,* which was made in Poland in the thirties—was already a self-conscious re-creation. Not authentic, already romanticized. What looks to us like authentic old Yiddish culture was already being made in a twilight era.

"The Yiddish *Forward* led a generation of American Jews into American life. Now they need to be led back to the sources of their culture. They have been born into ignorance—ignorance, not merely secularism. It's a little like the breakup of the Soviet Union. No one is Soviet anymore. You are Russian, Ukrainian. In the multicultural revolution, the notion of being American is not the same as it was. Jews have to discover that unless they embrace their identity they are not part of the equation. Jews are searching for an affiliation. Sometimes reading a newspaper can be an affiliation."

18

⁓⁓⁓

The Last Gentleman

(March 1993)

On a summer night in 1977, Murray Kempton left the news-room of the *New York Post* certain that he would never write his column for the paper again. He had threatened resignation many times before, but now he really meant it. The owner of the paper in those days, the Australian magnate Rupert Murdoch, had infuriated the staff with some outrage or other, and Kempton set off angrily for a night's marination that took him first to Greene Street, then to Great Jones, and finally to West Fourth, to Jimmy Day's.

There, as Kempton tells the story, he fell into conversation with a hooker, "drawn to me as I to her by the bond of there not being four teeth between our two heads." The two talked away the night—or, more likely, Kempton talked, and the hooker, enchanted by the sight of a bona-fide gentleman and the opportunity he pre-sented for a night of blessed unemployment, listened and laughed as she rarely had before.

Hours later, as if after a movie blackout, Kempton found himself on the floor in an unfamiliar apartment. He was still dressed in his customary three-piece suit and polished oxfords. Two small children were playing slapjack on his back. Kempton blinked the sleep from his eyes only to see standing in the doorframe the prostitute and a large and frowning fellow, "unmistakably her procurer and undisguisedly aggrieved."

The columnist, ever the well-bred guest, rose to his feet and extended a spindly hand to his host.

"How do you do?" he said. "I'm Murray Kempton, of the *Post*."

"Murray Kempton?" said the pimp, his expression brightening. "I've read you all my life. You made me what I am today."

"Thus inspired," Kempton recalls, "I made my way homeward as soon as ceremony permitted, with high confidence that my hostess could sleep the night in full possession of such teeth as she had left. I returned, of course, to the *Post* the next day, ready to carry on with a renewed sense of a mission that had not invariably been in vain."

Kempton's exasperation with the *Post*'s plunge into sleaze and right-wing politics finally overwhelmed him, and in 1981 he left for *Newsday*—a paper known, among those inclined to remark on its respectability in regard to that of the *Post* or the *News*, as "the tabloid in a tutu." Kempton has won all the important awards, including a Pulitzer Prize for commentary in 1985 and two George Polk awards, and even one-sixth of a Grammy (for his contribution to the liner notes of a multidisk Frank Sinatra album). His sense of mission, however, has not wavered. Now, with the *Post* and the *News* at war, and with the *Times* struggling to affect a youthful style without losing its stateliness, Kempton looms above it all—the one true original in the business. He is surely among the greatest of all living newspapermen, and yet he is for the most part a secret west of the Hudson River. His columns—there have been roughly 9,600 of them since 1949—have never been very popular in nationwide syndication. Most editors outside New York consider his material too local and his language too baroque for their pages. Moreover, Kempton does not live the life of a state-of-the-art pundit. He does not trade prophecy on the Sunday-morning talk shows, nor does he pad his accounts as the featured speaker for the annual convention of the American Meat Packers Association. He is not the president's debate coach or the First Lady's adviser. As he once put it, "I walk wide of the cosmic and settle most happily for the local, a precinct less modest than I make it sound, since my local happens to be the only city under the eye of God where the librettist for *Don Giovanni* could find his closest friend in the author of ' 'Twas the Night Before Christmas.' "

Kempton smokes a pipe, but he does not sit in his office chewing on the stem. He begins his day by reviewing the Associated Press daybook. He finds a story, pursues it, and rarely arrives at the *Newsday* offices, at 2 Park Avenue, to write until late afternoon. "I like to get around," he says. "I need a scene, something to look at. I'd rather die than try to write out of my head four days a week. I am a spectacularly bad interviewer. I usually make a twenty-minute speech and then the interviewee says, 'Well, you may be right.' "

In the course of business, Kempton has had breakfast with Frank Costello, lunch with Richard Nixon, tea with Huey Newton, and dinner with Nancy Reagan. He is the only journalist I know of who has seen Bessie Smith sing, Sal Maglie pitch, Westbrook Pegler type, Jean Harris weep, and Jimmy Hoffa fib. Kempton spent the evening before the first Cassius Clay–Sonny Liston fight, in 1964, in Miami with Malcolm X. As a youth, he was a member of the Young Communist League; as an adult, he has found a champion in the godfather of modern American conservatism, William F. Buckley, Jr. As a chronicler of political decline and individual struggle, he has influences ranging from the Earl of Clarendon, of the seventeenth century, to Grantland Rice and H. L. Mencken, of the twentieth. He does not write down to his audience of subway straphangers. He will compare Anthony (Fat Tony) Salerno to a Roman emperor, Richard Nixon to Sir William Yonge, and the former Bronx borough president Stanley Simon to Dreyfus and hope for the best. In addition to his columns, he has written hundreds of essays in a range of magazines. For *House & Garden,* he described his life and his apartment in a New York SRO; for *The Saturday Evening Post,* he recalled his arrest at the 1968 Democratic National Convention, in Chicago; and for *The New York Review of Books* he has written on the Newark federal prosecutor's collected wiretaps of Simone Rizzo DeCavalcante. His admirers make up an odd coalition. On his seventy-fifth birthday, in December, he received as gifts an American flag that had flown over the Capitol from Daniel Patrick Moynihan, the senior senator from New York, and an enormous bouquet of flowers from the wife of Carmine (the Snake) Persico.

If Kempton had been born in Japan, he would long ago have been declared a living treasure. "I grew up reading Murray, and the whole idea of him awed me," John Kifner, a foreign correspondent for the *Times,* says. "I had this romantic vision of this guy roaming the precincts and then going into a lonely newspaper office and then walking home on the empty streets having left behind this thing of beauty. I guess mine was the only room at Williams College to subscribe to the *Post,* and I got it so I could read Kempton." Jimmy Breslin, a fellow-columnist at *Newsday,* says of Kempton, "The man has brought more honor to newspapers than anyone in my lifetime."

Perhaps the only public man or woman in New York who has scant regard for Kempton is the city's former mayor, Edward Koch, who woke one morning in Gracie Mansion to find himself described as one who has "bullied the ill-fortuned and truckled to the fortuned," with the added note that "to walk in his wake has been to stumble through a rubble of vulgarities and meanness of spirit." The memory of such abuse still rankles Koch. "I thought my administration was one of the best in the history of New York City, and he didn't," he said not long ago, in a voice creaking with complaint. "I found him very unfair. But how can you have ill will toward a saint? He's Saint Murray."

The friction between Koch and Kempton was displayed one afternoon some years ago during a press conference at City Hall. Kempton arrived late, and as he sat down the chair beneath him collapsed.

"Here comes Murray Kempton breaking my furniture!" Koch cried out.

Climbing to his feet, Kempton said, "It's the *people's* furniture, Mr. Mayor."

If the greatest tributes come, in spite of themselves, from one's enemies, then surely the late chief of the Federal Bureau of Investigation gave Kempton's honesty as a journalist the ultimate accolade. In 1964, J. Edgar Hoover himself scrawled in the margin of one document, recently declassified, "When a newspaper hires a snake like Kempton they can expect the worst. . . . I am surprised that Scripps-Howard are taking on this rat."

Generations of journalists in New York have known a sense of awe when, after years of seeing the tiny photograph of Murray Kempton over his columns in the paper, they have finally run into him. Nicholas Pileggi, known for his book on the New York Mafia, *Wise Guy,* began his journalistic career in the city with the Associated Press, and he had the good fortune to meet Kempton on his first day on the job.

"I started work for the AP on January 6, 1956, and my first assignment was to cover a meeting of the joint council of the Teamsters at the Roosevelt Auditorium, on Union Square," Pileggi recalls. "Jimmy Hoffa had won control of the Midwest, and now he wanted to get his surrogate, a guy named John O'Rourke, elected in New York. Well, I was at a loss. This was really intricate, complicated stuff, full of political maneuvering. I had no idea what I was doing. And there was Murray Kempton, looking exactly like who he was—a great journalist taking notes, working. I'll never forget what he looked like. He was wearing a reversible tan-and-tweed raincoat with the tweed side out. I hadn't seen too many of those in Brooklyn. And he had this amazing red hair that just *launched* out of his head, like Elsa Lanchester's hair in *The Bride of Frankenstein.* It turned out he was unbelievably friendly and generous. I went up to him and introduced myself, and he started to fill me in on what was going on. Then he took aside a tall, bald guy, and the two of them were obviously talking about how I didn't know anything and how they had to help me out. So then the tall, bald guy comes up to me, takes a piece of paper out of his pocket, and says, 'Here, just read this over the phone to your editor.' And that's what I did. It turned out that he was Abe Raskin, the great labor reporter for the *Times.* The next day, I walked into the office and my editor said, 'You did okay. You had everything the *Times* had.' Murray Kempton had saved my life, with an assist from Abe Raskin."

Though Kempton's hair long ago turned white, he still has the sleek and elegant bearing that his friends remember from decades ago. He is not quite six feet tall, and if he eats at all he does not show it. He is the last gentleman, an amalgam of courtesy, formality, and kindness which is so rare that it strikes some as eccentricity. "He kind of reminds you of the wise Episcopal bishop," Russell Baker, of the *Times,* says.

In the service of his column, Kempton is everywhere. The novelist Nancy Lemann, who included a Kemptonian character in her book *Sportsman's Paradise,* says, "It seems that every time I get in from the airport the first thing I see is this wonderful white-haired gent pedaling his bicycle down Park Avenue." There he is on his rickety three-speed headed for a show of the Russian avant-garde at the Guggenheim. There he is walking up the steps of some courthouse in the Bronx rarely visited by the press. ("Real estate is New York's last available lodgement for the muse of classic tragedy," he will write for the next morning's paper. "Orestes and Electra are alive in Surrogate's Court and suing Clytemnestra for Agamemnon's office-building portfolio.")

I first saw Kempton at the Reagan-Gorbachev summit in Moscow, in 1988. In a pressroom built, it seemed, to satisfy the gargantuan demands of a five-year plan, he was at a distant table, hard at work. I was living in Moscow at the time and reading everything I could about Nikita Khrushchev, whose thaw in the 1950s was the antecedent to Gorbachev's perestroika. Unfortunately, the reading was dreary business—dreary until I read Kempton's columns in the *Post* on Khrushchev's trip across the United States in 1959. For Kempton's readers, that fantastic journey began on a runway in Washington:

> Nikita Khrushchev is an authentic, the real thing. He alighted on Andrews Field yesterday as a vice-president of the International Ladies Garment Workers' Union might descend upon Unity House. He even bore along in his wake his son-in-law, the editor of *Izvestia*. You could almost hear the echo: "Alexei is a bright boy, so I made him educational director of the local." . . .
>
> Poor Dwight Eisenhower stood waiting outside for Khrushchev's plane door to open yesterday as though he were waiting for some White House attendant to come in with a package that ticked.

In California, as a guest of Twentieth Century–Fox, Khrushchev watched a performance in which the chorus line from *Can-Can* revealed a row of buttocks to the guest of honor, and, Kempton reported, Khrushchev groused that the human face was more appealing to him than the rump. In Coon Rapids, Iowa, he was invited to the farm of Bob Garst. The farmer and his guest, along with the press herd, rollicked in the mud, all in the name of easing a crisis of diplomatic tension that would escalate, three years later, to the brink of nuclear confrontation. In Coon Rapids, Kempton was quite sure that he had witnessed the strangest apparition of his life:

> We shall not ever see again the scenes of a single yesterday; in a week, we shall have begun to doubt we ever saw them:

Nikita Khrushchev, heir of Lenin, Stalin and Peter the Great, standing, his ventilated shoes encased in silage, in a field of beheaded sorghum, watching his host, Bob Garst, go down to the earth to pick up handfuls of the infinite essence of the droppings of generations of prize cattle and throw them in the face of a banzai charge of cameramen. . . .

Henry Cabot Lodge, American Ambassador to the United Nations, Brahmin-born and schooled for command, bending over to ask the Chairman of the Council of Soviets if he hadn't seen enough. "See," said the Chairman, "the capitalist is trying to hide things from me." "This will be a jovial day," said Lodge. He spent it handling the microphone for the interpreters, a grand duke become overnight a Paris doorman. The air was filled with bursting smells of excess animal vitamin. "In all his life," said Khrushchev, "Mr. Lodge didn't take in as many smells as he did today."

There is not a journalist alive who would not cross an ocean (not to mention an oversized pressroom) to meet a man who can write like that (not to mention on a daily deadline). But Kempton was working hard that day in Moscow, and I figured the summit would be long and dull and there would be other chances to pester him. My hesitation turned out to be more courteous than wise. I never saw him in that pressroom again. He spent the rest of the summit wandering the streets of Moscow, ducking into the Museum of the Red Army and the Museum of the Revolution, and interviewing the children of revolutionaries and apparatchiks. Communist party officials were especially charmed to meet him. It was not often that they had a chance to talk to an American journalist who had built his early reputation on his defense of Communists and labor unions.

"How do you know so much about us?" they asked. "You must read a great deal of Sovietology."

"Actually," Kempton told them, "I have always thought the only Sovietologist worth reading is Anton Chekhov."

. . .

A few years after the Moscow summit, I met Kempton at a dinner given by Barbara Epstein, his closest friend and the co-editor of *The New York Review of Books*. He showed up late, apologizing for his deadlines. He explained that he had spent the morning at the John Gotti mob trial, listening to the testimony of Sammy Gravano, a bull practicing to be a canary. The remainder of the day was spent at a computer terminal waiting for the Muses to land. He was, of course, wearing his uniform—gray suit, white shirt, burgundy tie—but his pants cuffs were gathered with rubber bands, and there was a piece of heavy equipment strapped around his neck like a feed bag. It turned out to be a portable compact-disk player. He had ridden his bike from *Newsday* to dinner with the Valkyries storming in his head. "The arias smooth out the potholes on Central Park West," he explained.

I said that I was just beginning to get to know the New York papers again after a long absence, but that, on brief inspection, the Mafia dons I was reading about seemed to me like some of the vain Communist party chieftains I had met in such precincts as Baku, Alma-Ata, and Karaganda.

"You know, most of these guys, when you meet them, are just as bad as respectable people," Kempton said. "They take their beatings like men. Except in narcotics. I never met anyone who dealt in narcotics who had even the remotest decency. Do you remember that moment in Henry Adams's *Mont-Saint-Michel and Chartres* when Adams speaks of the Virgin and Child looking down on a dead faith? Well, John Gotti believed in all of it. He believed in a dead faith."

For years, Kempton has been writing that it is correct to say that mobsters are usually homicidal maniacs, but that it is folly to believe in an "invisible government" somehow "responsible for all the woes of our society not directly traceable to Soviet weather experiments." In American myth, the mafiosi are omnipotent lords, when in fact their palace is more often a row house in Bay Ridge or a split-level in Manhasset. "Slaves they certainly are of our credulous imagination; and we go on picking over them," he once wrote. "They are, after all, that precious asset to journalism, men who have crossed the shadow line beyond which they can no longer sue for libel and where they can thus be blamed, with impunity, for *everything*."

"Murray was the first writer I ever read to say that mobsters didn't control the world, that they were mostly just truck drivers without jobs," Nick Pileggi says. "He would hear about, say, Angelo Innuendo, of the great artichoke empire, who lived at such-and-such an address. Well, instead of swallowing the myth Murray would check out where the guy really lived, and, of course, it would turn out to be a ten-thousand-dollar house somewhere in Queens. The guy was a nobody. Not a prince—a nobody. And Murray got to know these guys because he'd see them in court. Someone would get arrested, and their brothers and cousins would all come to the trial. Murray would get to know them, and they would read what he wrote, maybe agree, maybe disagree, but they got to know him all the same. A few years later, inevitably, it was those guys who were on trial, and now Kempton had a personal relationship going. He knew who was who. He enjoyed a fluidity of movement in a world that had been closed to everyone else."

Kempton first met Gotti and his lawyer Bruce Cutler outside a courtroom in 1991. "Duke was playing Kansas for the NCAA basketball title, and John decided to bet Cutler on the game," he said recently. "Gotti took Duke. No points, no odds. He just took Duke, and Cutler agreed. I turned around and said, 'Mr. Gotti, perhaps you ought to give odds, considering Duke is a heavy favorite.' Gotti said, 'Why don't you mind your business, you son of a bitch?' That was our introduction."

But, as the trial dragged on, both Gotti and Cutler saw Kempton as somehow apart from the rest of the press. "John Gotti respects Murray, because he has always been fair about John Gotti," Cutler told me some time afterward. "The man has a sense of history."

Kempton had, it is true, dined with Frank Costello when Gotti was just a boy. And so when Gotti was found not guilty one of his friends invited Kempton to a secret sanctum of Little Italy, the Ravenite Social Club, on Mulberry Street.

"This place of such mythology looked like a rec room in Queens," Kempton told me. "John was there, looking very fine, drinking sambuca, very pleased with himself, feeling immortal, the poor son of a bitch."

I asked Kempton if he ever really liked any of the mobsters he had come to know.

"I have tremendous admiration for Carmine Persico," he said. "There's just a dignity about him. Of course, he is a killer, a real killer. But I love him because of his wiretaps. They are just wonderful. I remember one in which his cousin Freddie DeChristopher— a bit of a sleazebag, really—testified to one of Persico's conversations. They had been talking about Carmine Galante, a man universally hated by his colleagues. They had all been playing cards, and Galante had been riding someone at the table, an Irishman. Galante just kept it up with all manner of obscene anti-Irish comments. Finally, Persico said, 'Get out of the game!' and Galante did, slinking off for home. The next day, Galante came back to the card game, begging, 'Please! I'm sorry! I'll never do it again!' It was wonderful. Persico said about Galante, 'He's not such a bad guy. He was just brung up wrong.' "

Over the years, Kempton's arch affections for made men have confused his readers, causing them to believe that he was championing the cause of random murder when in fact he was trying to write about character against a comic background. The governor of New York, Mario Cuomo, once called Sydney Schanberg, a columnist at *Newsday,* and asked, in a voice truly distressed, "How do I get Murray Kempton to love me?"

"Governor," Schanberg said, "why don't you try getting indicted?"

. . .

Kempton's various publishers have done as badly by him and his talent as the editors who have left him off their op-ed pages. He has produced three books, and all of them are now out of print. *Part of Our Time: Some Monuments and Ruins of the Thirties* (1955) is a classic account of the odyssey of some of the country's radicals, well known and obscure; *America Comes of Middle Age* (1963) is a collection of columns published in the *Post;* and *The Briar Patch: The People of the State of New York vs. Lumumba Shakur, et al.* (1973), which won the National Book Award, is about the Black Panther movement and the court system.

With a nudge from William Buckley and Sam Vaughan, an editor at Random House, Kempton has sorted through his columns and essays of the last quarter century in the hope of publishing a new collection. Vaughan's assistant sent me a twelve-hundred-page stack of photocopied clippings, and I read them straight through in a couple of days—an astonishing experience. Reading Kempton, over time in newspapers or all at once in a book, is like watching an endless parade of the great characters of American life: Whittaker Chambers on the witness stand, Carmine DeSapio at Tammany Hall, Adlai Stevenson campaigning, Louis Armstrong backstage in his undershorts, exhausted between sets. Kempton's sense of the absurd and his ability to sketch a scene in a few sentences, to deflate the pompous in a phrase, make the parade as rich as any great novel. Here, describing Billy Graham's crusade come to New York, Kempton does as much in the space of a column to deflate unctuous piety as Sinclair Lewis did in all of *Elmer Gantry:* "Before I say another word about Billy Graham's opening, I should like to say that, if Jesus Christ crucified for our sins was good enough for Johann Sebastian Bach and Fyodor Dostoevski and Georges Rouault, He is much too good for the likes of me, and I shall make no sport of any honest prophet of His." In paragraphs to come, of course, Kempton brings the pastor to his knees, just as he said he would not: "The vengeful God is a stallion; in Graham's hands he is a gelding."

History is much the richer for Kempton's judgments. Those who avoid them do so at their peril. David Mamet, for one, would have done well to read just a few paragraphs of Kempton's visit to the trial of Jimmy Hoffa before he gave Danny DeVito and Jack Nicholson a script that would make a saint of a lout:

> They will, in our lifetime, run excursion trains to Washington so that young lawyers can watch Edward Bennett Williams postpone the frying of some damned soul. It is a good use for trains. To watch Williams and then to watch a Department of Justice lawyer contending with him is to understand the essential superiority of free enterprise to government ownership. The Justice Department used forty FBI agents to sew Jimmy Hoffa in a sack last March; yesterday Edward Bennett Williams almost had him out. . . .
>
> When Judge Matthews broke in to announce a recess, there was a low sigh of appreciation from the audience—Williams draws Washington audiences who understand each nuance of his work the way the Milanese do La Scala—and Ed Williams, saving himself, walked back. Jimmy Hoffa did not even look at him.
>
> "Is that all," he said querulously, "he's going to say about this fraud and deceit?" One of his retainers said: "Relax, Jimmy."
>
> To have no sense of sin is to have no taste, and to have no taste is to be a loser at the end; Edward Bennett Williams can save you only in the nonessentials.

Fans of Kempton know many of these set pieces well. But they constitute not merely a set of triumphant riffs, a scatter of portraits. They add up, over time, to a portrait of their author. Kempton's essay in *Part of Our Time* about the early years of Alger Hiss and his yearning to overcome the "shabby gentility" of his surroundings in Baltimore is partly an essay in autobiography, a glimpse of the sources of Kempton's motivations and sense of character and mercy. On his mother's side, Kempton comes from a grand lineage of Episcopal bishops and political potentates, a fallen Virginia family that moved north to Baltimore after the Civil War. His great-great-grandfather James Murray Mason was the author of the Fugitive Slave Act of 1850 and later became the Confederate ambassador to Britain. James Mason's grandfather George Mason was the author of the Virginia Bill of Rights.

"By the time it got down to us, my family was very uneven," Kempton said one evening. We were in his apartment, a tiny place in the West Eighties, drinking coffee and beer. The living room was filled with books, papers, and Kempton's one indulgence, compact disks. It was his day off. He was dressed in a three-piece suit.

"My maternal grandmother was a Randolph—pronounced 'Randoff'—and that made me feel totally inferior," he went on. "The Randolphs were like the Guermanteses in Proust. My grandfather was like Synge as Yeats describes him: 'He was a solitary, undemonstrative man, never asking pity, nor complaining, nor seeking sympathy.' On my father's side, we were extraordinarily dim. Come to think of it, I have never known why my father and my mother ever married. I was never able to ask."

Kempton's father, a stockbroker, died of influenza when Murray was three years old. The family, with the memory of grand Confederate circumstances still in them but with few resources to sustain the glory, began to fray at the collar. There is in Kempton a powerful sense of failure, of being on what he calls the "losing side" of things. "Baltimore had five private schools at the time," he said. "I went to Boys' Latin, which was secondary in all aspects. Not so very long ago, I got a letter inviting me to the fiftieth reunion of my class. But I wrote back declining the invitation. I just could not face my classmates. I couldn't face my awfulness as a child. I totally messed up. I made the class a total disgrace. I was supposed to edit the yearbook and never got it done. It's a shameful memory, and it returns to me, absolutely, in this strange, shameful way."

Kempton is known in New York for elaborate courtesies, for ending a phone conversation with "God bless you." He cannot countenance a cad. The worst villain in any of his recent pieces may have been the late diet doctor Herman Tarnower, who disappointed the headmistress Jean Harris in love and paid a price for it. Kempton pitied Harris, especially when she took the witness stand and said that the doctor's inattentions had made her feel like an empty suit. Jimmy Breslin tells the story of arriving late at Harris's trial for the murder of Tarnower and looking to his colleague for an update.

"What's going on?" Breslin asked Kempton.

"Well," Kempton said, "I was with her through the second bullet." But then, with infinite sadness in his eyes, he added, "There were four, you know."

Kempton writes, above all, about human character, about honor or the lack of it. Perhaps the letter he has received that he cherishes most is one from Fat Tony Salerno saying that Roy Cohn "always stated that you were an honorable man."

The yearning for honor, Kempton told me, comes as much from reading as from the gentility of his ancestors. "As a boy, I read the G. A. Henty books, and from that I gathered how to conduct oneself," he said. "They were historical novels about Edwardian Englishmen plunked down at Agincourt or wherever and then behaving with absolute aplomb. I've always taken honor very seriously, particularly since the possession of it has been a lifetime struggle. As a journalist, you must have honor. You have to go places where you are a stranger, so good manners are also essential. I suppose I carry them to the point of eccentricity sometimes, but they can be useful. You know, I often get the sense that *everyone* in this country truly wants to be a gentleman. I was once in Nashville in the mid-fifties. We were all standing in front of the steps of the state capitol, where some fascist was giving a speech to a demonstration. The evils of integration, and so on. I was drinking in those days, and so I was a little slow in leaving. Two guys came up and accosted me, and I said, 'Gentlemen, how is it you can come to the state capitol and give a speech on the steps without wearing a necktie!' They were absolutely shaken to the bone and slithered off with apologies."

At Johns Hopkins, Kempton was a star undergraduate. "Murray was eight years or so ahead of me at Hopkins, but by the time I got there he was still considered the great editor of the school paper, the *News-Letter,*" Russell Baker says. "Murray was the campus radical and was known for going after the Hopkins president, Isaiah Bowman, who had been Woodrow Wilson's geographer at Versailles. Bowman was a tyrannical old man, known as a hopeless conservative even though he was probably a Wilson Democrat. Kempton challenged the mossback and was loved for it."

Kempton got a summer job at the 1936 Democratic National Convention, in Philadelphia, as a page for H. L. Mencken. After Mencken finished typing a sheet of his column, he would lift it high above him and shout "Copy!" and then wait for young Kempton to snatch it away and carry it off to the telegraph room. "By then, I was also reading Mencken's things in the *Baltimore Evening Sun,*" Kempton told me. "I read a lot of things then. But the trouble was I didn't read anything closely in those days except Lenin and Trotsky. Ahhh, well. You read that shit for absolute truth. But I suppose my Marxism-Leninism was an affectation, like everything else."

As a way to escape the dreariness of Baltimore, Kempton joined the Communist faction of the sailors' union in August and spent the rest of the summer working on a mail boat that ran between Baltimore and Norfolk, Virginia. His membership in the union did not last long. Within a year, disillusioned by the Moscow trials and other horrific news from the East, he had quit the Communists and joined the Socialist party of Norman Thomas. After graduating from Johns Hopkins, in 1939, he worked for a while as a relief investigator in Baltimore and then moved to New York, to work as an organizer for the Campaign for Youth Needs, and then to Peekskill, to work for the International Ladies Garment Workers' Union. He also wrote pamphlets for the Young People's Socialist League and the Workers Defense League.

In 1942, Kempton was hired by the *Post* to write about labor issues, but three months later he was drafted into the army. "It was really in the army that I read an awful lot," Kempton says. "There wasn't much to do—that's the nature of military services—and, oddly, in the army, you are generally given full run of your eccentricities. People accepted you with a certain inevitability. It was like when I was covering the Black Panthers. There was a basic lack of resentment among them, even of the guys in their midst spying on them. They figured everyone had to do something to get by, whether it was selling reefer or spying for the cops. In the army, no one cared if you read. Books were not a subject of conversation, which, in a way, is a bloody relief."

In his columns over the years Kempton has been, by turns, shy and comic about his military service in New Guinea and in the Philippines during the latter part of the war. He has used it mainly as another example of his alleged haplessness. In a famous column written after Adlai Stevenson lost in the 1952 presidential race—a heartbreaking loss for Kempton—he wrote:

> Man and boy, I've been losing since birth, and the only time I've ever won has been with the Democrats. . . . During the war, I had a brief, tenuous relationship with an outfit called the 38th Division. Its nickname was the Cyclone Division. Do you think they called it the Cyclone Division because it had swept through the enemies of freedom? Of course not. They called it the Cyclone Division because all its tents got blown down on maneuvers. That's how it is with my team every time. I can't even persuade my kids to be Republicans and escape the family curse.

But Kempton's war was no comedy. He has begun writing a memoir, entitled *Once Ain't for Always*—a line from Bessie Smith's "Lost Your Head Blues"—and the one chapter he has finished is a brilliant piece about the war. It is filled with the battlefield confusion and moral embarrassment of *The Charterhouse of Parma,* in which Stendhal's hero, desperate for action, takes part in the Battle of Waterloo without quite knowing it. On patrol in the Philippines, Kempton and his fellows were ambushed by the Japanese at a time when the Japanese had all but given up the war. "The one thing about being ambushed is that you can never take yourself very seriously again," Kempton told me.

After returning from the army and rejoining the *Post,* a fairly left-wing paper in those days, Kempton worked for two years as an assistant to the paper's labor editor, Victor Riesel. The two men would climb out onto the roof of the *Post* building, on West Street, and mull over the day's story. "Well, fellow worker," Riesel would say, "whom do we hack today?" In 1949, Kempton succeeded Riesel and quickly expanded his beat from labor to whatever it was that struck him as a good story on a given day. Like Mencken before him, Kempton reveled in the follies of politics, and, like no other newspaper voice of his time, he wrote about politicians as buffoons, treating them to the same dish of irony he offered to any other suspect character. There have been exceptions. Adlai Stevenson was his hero, and all others were measured against that standard.

In the 1950s, Kempton established his passion for mercy and justice on two great issues of the time: the treatment of black men and women in the South, and the treatment of American Communists in the courts and in the press. These were constituencies which at the time had few supporters. Kempton was nearly alone in championing men and women who had fallen under the spell of ideology and the Communist party and never seemed to cease paying for their folly. He defended radicals whose names are now all but forgotten: Eva Bittelman, Steve Nelson, Lionel Stander.

In the mid-fifties, Kempton went south with his typewriter, his phonograph, and his stack of jazz records. In Sumner, Mississippi, he watched Mose Wright, a field hand in his sixties, stand up in a courtroom and finger the murderers—two white men—of a fourteen-year-old black boy named Emmett Louis Till. Wright's courage gave others the nerve to do the same. "They will be belted and flayed as he was yesterday, but they will walk out with the memory of having been human beings for just a little while," Kempton wrote. "Whatever the result, there is a kind of majesty in the spectacle of the State of Mississippi honestly trying to convict two white men on the word of four Negroes. And we owe that sight to Mose Wright, who was condemned to bow all his life, and had enough left to raise his head and look the enemy in those terrible eyes when he was sixty-four."

In Atlanta and Washington, Kempton came to know Martin Luther King as a young man. King was an intellectual who "would not look incongruous as a side-man in one of Dizzy Gillespie's big bands," he wrote. "He is hip in the word's deepest and finest sense; the night his house was bombed by the Citizens' Council, he came out and told his neighbors to remember that their one, great unconquerable shield was the whole armor of love."

Kempton's writing about race surprised some liberal readers by its refusal to subscribe to a political correctness. At a time when others were writing patronizing articles defending the fighter Sonny Liston for his thuggish behavior, Kempton took a more complicated path. "The Negro heavyweights, as Negroes tend to do, have usually given that sense of being men above their calling," he wrote. "Floyd Patterson sounded like a Freedom Rider. We return to reality with Liston. We have at last a heavyweight champion on the moral level of the men who own him. . . . He has already helped us grow up as a country because he is the first morally inferior Negro I can think of to be given an equal opportunity. He will help us grow up further if he destroys the illusion that a man whose trade it is to beat another man senseless for money represents an image which at all costs must be kept pure for American youth."

The texture of Kempton's thinking has changed little since his first wave of popularity, in the fifties and early sixties, but he still has the ability to surprise. It does not require a high ceremony of state or a moral crusade to excite his sense of mercy. Six years ago, a woman named Jessica Hahn was a supporting player in the fall of the preacher Jim Bakker. The preacher's circle mocked Hahn as a tramp. A gentleman rushed to her defense. "She was delivered like a package of prime beef and she is to be commended for the spirit to bite the diner back," Kempton wrote of Hahn. "Her sponsors had trusted her to be used and she has defied them and made herself the user. And now some of the Assemblies of God stand at the Armageddon they had promised for the rest of us and the sound of battle resounds with a discord of strumpets."

Jim Dwyer, another columnist at *Newsday,* says that through example and discussions on the newsroom floor Kempton has taught a couple of generations of journalists to avoid self-congratulation and the easy judgment. "Beneath all of Murray's gentility and manners is a very serious question, 'Who do you think you are?' " Dwyer said. "He sort of compels you to behave like a gentleman and remember that you are probably not all that much better than the person you are writing about."

Kempton's fascination with, and even affection for, Richard Nixon over the years has always been troubling to the arbiters of proper liberalism. I asked him one afternoon why he responded so strongly to the demon of his era.

"I first met Nixon the day that Lee Pressman testified to the House Un-American Activities Committee and confessed his sins," Kempton said. "I was staying at the old Congressional Hotel, and Nixon was there, too. I called him, and we sat up talking until five o'clock in the morning. At one point, he said he was getting ready to run for the Senate against Helen Gahagan Douglas. He said he just hated to run against her, because he admired her so much!

"Nixon liked me because he'd known me for a long while. Once I got my balance in about 1962 and stopped blaming everything on one guy, I just sort of got fond of him. We would have lunch when he was in exile and was the ambassador of Pepsi. He was so wonderful, so smart about everyone's affairs but his own. I remember, years later, the day Mrs. Marcos was being booked and I was visiting him in his office. I said, 'Mr. President, I wish you would do my profession a favor and go out there and greet Mrs. Marcos in front of all the cameras.' Nixon looked gloomily into his coffee cup. He said, 'I can't do that, but I will call over there later.' Then he said, 'You know, this is a very vindictive country.' It was on the tip of my tongue to say, 'If this is a vindictive country, then why am I here sitting at your feet calling you "Mr. President"?'

"Nixon was just amazing. I came to meet him for lunch once in 1966, and he asked me where I'd been. He's always collecting information on everyone else. I said that I had just seen John Lindsay, and I was bubbling with enthusiasm; I said I thought Lindsay had a limitless future. Over Nixon's face swept a look of limitless pain at the ignorance of mankind, and then he said, 'Lindsay will have a fight with Rockefeller and go off to the Democratic party.' "

Kempton's affection for Nixon is also connected to a personal gesture that came amid the great tragedy of his life. Kempton does not invite personal questions, but it is clear that he has borne more sadness than should be asked of anyone. He is divorced from his first wife, Mina Bluethenthal, and separated from his second, Beverly Gary Kempton. He has five children, of whom one son was born with a severe learning disability, though he works, and lives an independent life. Another son, Mike, was killed, with his bride, in a car accident two decades ago.

"When my son Mike died, in 1971, the *Times* ran an obituary that described his activities in some detail," Kempton said. "He'd been involved in antidraft things—resistance, and so on. The morning after the obit ran in the *Times,* the doorbell rang. I went to the door, and there was a man in plainclothes with an envelope from the White House, a handwritten letter. The writer described our long friendship and how when he read in the *Times* about Mike it reminded him of me in the fifties and our meeting. It was amazing. Here was this essentially fictive friendship and the expression of admiration for an idealism totally at variance with Nixon's own politics. Well, I can't tell you how touched I was. There was something beautiful and lonely in that note."

I never quite understood why Kempton had stayed with his column for forty years until I watched him put one together. We agreed to meet one morning this past December and go wherever the AP daybook took us. It was a few days before Christmas, and Kempton was distressed. "I am afraid the pickings are rather thin," he said. But then, brightening, he added, "Of course, there is this marvelous case of the subway shooting. Maybe that's it. Let's go to Bellevue Hospital."

A rookie transit policeman named Derwin Pannell had been critically injured when two of his colleagues shot him in a Brooklyn subway station. The two officers did not realize that Pannell was working undercover and had been arresting, not mugging, a woman who had beaten the fare. They claimed that his gun was drawn; he said he had holstered the revolver. To complicate matters infinitely, Pannell is black and the other officers are white. Pannell was scheduled to give his first press conference at Bellevue.

I met Kempton on a corner near Lincoln Center. He wore an expression of high optimism. We took a gypsy cab downtown to Bellevue, talking over the woes of the New York Giants as they completed a pitiful season.

"I might have had some pity for the coach, but finally he is too self-referring to demand real sympathy," Kempton said. "My guess is that management has noticed this." Once more, his judgment was prescient. The coach, Ray Handley, was dismissed in late December.

"Happy New Year," the driver said as we pulled up to the hospital. "God bless you, sir," Kempton said, and we headed for the story.

For reporters covering politics or public events of any kind, an amazing amount of the day is spent waiting around—waiting for the jury to come in or the press conference to begin. At these group waiting sessions, Kempton is the dean but not the lord. He is deferred to, yet he is too funny, and too kind to his younger colleagues, to be anything but charming about his position. As we stood around, hour after hour, in the Bellevue lobby waiting for the Brooklyn district attorney to finish his ministrations to the fallen officer, Kempton regaled staffers from the *Post,* the *Times,* and the local TV stations with stories about the trombone mechanics of Jack Teagarden, the vocal triumphs of Johnny Mercer, and the brutal oddities of Jimmy Hoffa. When it was discovered that Kempton's name was not on the short list of reporters who would be allowed to visit Pannell for an interview, there were apologies all around and the name was added. None of those left off the list complained. "These are the small gifts I get for being ancient," Kempton said, and set off for the interview.

While Kempton and half a dozen other privileged souls went to visit the newsmaker, the rest of us lingered in the Bellevue lobby. I spoke with Ron Bell, a veteran cameraman for ABC, who has been covering stories with Kempton for years. "I remember when the pope was in the States a while back and we were all at the Alamo waiting for him," Bell said. "It was something like a hundred and ten degrees out, and everyone was cranky and soaking wet. People were passing out and being taken off to the hospital with heat exhaustion. Then I turned around and I saw Murray Kempton—in a gray wool suit, listening to some opera on his portable CD player, absolutely dry and happy."

An hour later, the interviewers were back. Everyone seemed bored and jaded except Kempton. He was bursting with theories about the case, and he tried out some one-liners on his *Newsday* colleague Ellis Henican, a few of which made it into the column. He was a pleasure to see—a columnist who depends on his effort and sensibility rather than on propinquity to the powerful.

"The truth is that I have no sources," Kempton said. He does not believe in them. Kempton has written, "Persons privy to events either do not know what is important about them or, when they do, generally lie, as even Lincoln lied to Greeley for purposes of seduction."

There are those in New York journalism who mourn the idea that Kempton has never written for the *Times,* a paper that would undoubtedly give him a wider, more influential audience than *Newsday*. But Kempton does not crave the gravity of the *Times*. He has always enjoyed the rakishness of his papers, the sense of outsiderness that came with the *Post* or with the *World-Telegram & Sun,* where he worked briefly during the mid-sixties. Besides, he has written, "Not the *Times* or a dozen *Timeses* could ever attain a consequence justifying identification as a Fourth Estate of the Realm. Journalism might at best be called the Third-and-a-Quarter Estate, to signify its status as a quadruped with three feet mired in each of the other three estates and the fourth pawing the air above the ground."

Kempton goes to court, reads cartons of documents, and visits the battlefields of El Salvador, because real reporting is what he admires in his favorite colleagues. A real reporter is what he wants to be. Jim Dwyer, of *Newsday,* says, "I was once at a luncheon at Columbia University for the Meyer Berger Award. During the lunch, Murray Kempton said, 'You know, I never won the Berger Award.' And one of the winners on this occasion—Sara Rimer, of the *Times*—said, 'Murray, you just won the Pulitzer!' Murray said, 'The Pulitzer is named for a publisher. The Meyer Berger is named for a reporter.'"

Kempton's disdain for publishers has only heightened in recent weeks, as he has witnessed the noisy arrival of Mortimer Zuckerman at the *News*, and the even noisier controversy surrounding the *Post*'s would-be publisher Steven Hoffenberg. "Zuckerman is a perfectly awful person," Kempton says. As for Hoffenberg, "he's like a bank robber who's taken a hostage—or, at least, that's what one of my friends at the *Post* says. The Securities and Exchange Commission can't land on him, or, if it does, that will lead to the end of the *Post*.

"When I was at the *Post*, we thought of the *News* with great awe," Kempton goes on. "It was a wonderful paper, but it ruined itself. There were editors there—especially in Washington—who felt inferior because national politicians would take calls from the *Times* but not from the *News*. Mike O'Neill"—who was the editor of the *News* from 1975 to 1982—"decided that it was a slum paper. So he tried to make it appeal to the upper middle classes, to make it into an easy-to-fold *Herald Tribune*. They came up with a culture section almost as dreary as the *Times*'s. They spent a bucket of money, and it went nowhere. You see, a newspaper is like a bad habit—if you try to alter it, it rarely works out. Now, the *Post*, which is losing all its best people to the *News*, was doing a wonderful job as a guerrilla operation. They came up with a lot of stories—and some of them were true! In the end, my view of this so-called tabloid war is that I just don't consider the character of publishers. I'm rooting for my friends—the reporters."

Kempton has just finished one of his best years, despite his claim to having had "a dreary patch of failures and repetitions." In July, when the press corps flooded Madison Square Garden for the Democratic National Convention, he quietly went off to Dallas and, almost alone among the columnists, was there to hear Ross Perot quit the race. He rode the train with President Bush on "his Via Dolorosa," in the last days of a losing campaign. Kempton sounded the valedictory note for the president weeks before his colleagues. It is characteristic of Kempton that he was kindest to Bush when Bush was clearly on the way out. When Bush was ascendant, there was no one who wielded a sharper lance. In 1986, when Bush was vice president and was aiming higher, Kempton wrote:

> The vice president of the United States could stand as symbol of every soul in prison if he were not so much more degraded than his fellows by the requirement that he not only clank his chains but loudly bless them in the bargain.
>
> Bush does show promise of pushing the state of the art to new heights of self-abasement, but that may be because his endeavors come from the heart. I once watched Bush at an aerobics class during the 1980 primaries. His companions in this flirtation with cardiac arrest were all thirty years younger than he, and yet, the closer he approached *extremis,* the more earnestly he smiled. Doggedness at the price of dignity was plainly his life's commitment and, had I been endowed with a wisp of political acuity, I would have known then that George Bush was born to be a vice president.

In a year when much of the press fell in love with Bill Clinton, Kempton was almost alone among liberals in not going all gooey in his writing about the new president. I brought up the subject one day while we were having coffee in the *Newsday* cafeteria.

"Clinton? I hear the man's name and I break out in a rash. It's a completely irrational matter, I know, but there it is," Kempton said. "The business of the draft bothers me. I like the guys who either went and served or the ones who refused and paid for it. There's such an awful piety in Clinton's actions. And the lying. Well, of course, I lied all the time in my life, and the only reason I stopped is that I kept getting caught out. That Clinton still lies like that at his age just means he has no real experience of life. As Yeats once said of Wilfred Owen, 'There's every excuse for him, but no excuse for those who liked him.' "

Although Kempton is still working at the top of his form when most journalists his age are retired or are lecturing the young, he does not get quite the attention he once did.

"There was a time when I was writing one of the few local columns in New York," Kempton said. "There was Meyer Berger, but I had it mostly to myself. That meant if there was a story out there and I let it slide for a few days no one would notice. Now there are twenty local columns, at least, many of them in my own paper. Things really changed when Breslin came along. I always had great admiration for Breslin. I suppose I'm competitive, but I never worried about Breslin unless a story went on for four days. It's almost as if he would bracket himself: he would be wildly off on one side the first day, off to the other side on the next, but on the third and fourth days he would hit the target absolutely, he'd knock the spots off it. What I always had going for me was that I knew everyone. If something came up on, say, Adam Clayton Powell, I would not begin with the delusion that he was a great statesman and then learn my lesson. I already knew the gentleman."

These days, New York is a tabloid city. The morning talk in elevators and coffee shops is shaped not by the *Times,* which reaches just one city household in ten, but by the voices in the tabloids. Many of the younger columnists are clones of Breslin's tough-guy-with-a-heart-of-gold style. There are no clones of Murray Kempton. To imitate him, after all, would mean to read what he has read, to see and feel what he has seen and felt, and to be blessed with his sense of mercy and language. "There is no Sonny Stitt to his Charlie Parker," says Pete Hamill. "Murray is so specifically himself that he cannot be imitated."

The editors at *Newsday* have occasionally heard complaints from readers that Kempton's style is too difficult, and it is true that on the rare day when he is off, his sentences require more work than the bleary-eyed morning reader is willing to expend. But this is nothing new, and in at least one instance served as a shield. In

1955, Victor Lasky sued Kempton for libel. Lasky initially won the case but lost on appeal. The reasoning of the judges was, in fact, Kemptonian: "The Supreme Court, Appellate Division, held that where the accused article was frequently cryptic in meaning, sometimes contradictory, and only dubiously suggestive of matters defaming plaintiff, and in absence of allegation of falsity, it was not determinable which parts of ambiguous article plaintiff might be relying on as libelous, complaint which failed to make specific allegations of falsity or proper allegation of extrinsic facts or innuendo was insufficient." In other words, since the judges themselves could not quite understand the article in question the appeal was upheld.

"Most people regard me, stylistically, as a freak," Kempton told me one afternoon. "It's someone's idea of baroque or rococo. There is an arch quality in there that grates on me when I read it. I look at my pieces and despair.

"My work is probably more detached now than it used to be. The attitude, not the style, has changed. In the fifties, when I did all those Southern stories, I was drunk a lot of the time, and when you drink there are these great passions and flights. It seems to come easily, but you never know when you are bad. The fact is, I've always been discontented with the way I write. This is a serious remark. But I don't have the feeling that as I get older my style is falling apart. It's such a jerry-built style in the first place, and if the pillars shake no one will ever notice.

"Writing four times a week is a little much, except if you don't do it four times a week, you struggle. I'm happiest writing every day. I spent eight years of my life not working for a newspaper— when I was freelance and writing a book—and they were the low points of my life.

"The right word should come to you, and yet I feel I'm getting slack. The most important thing is to know when you are bad. When you lose that, you can never really be any good anymore.

The work of old men is usually a comedown, at least for me. I pre-fer Beethoven's middle quartets to the late ones. The late Henry James is marvelous, but the wit is gone, and when the wit goes, that's the beginning of decay. Proust was immune. He stayed funny to the end."

At his seventy-fifth-birthday party, in the *Newsday* offices, a happy, noisy affair with a string trio and lots of champagne, it came Kemp-ton's time to speak. Mayor David Dinkins had come by to pay trib-ute, Senator Moynihan had given him his flag, and his colleagues had paid their respects. Now Kempton glanced down at his birthday cake, an enormous confection that portrayed, in icing of various colors, an elegant gent bicycling from one courthouse to the next. The birthday boy smiled. "Splendid," he said.

Then Kempton gave a short speech praising the staff, those who had helped him on stories and had won prizes for reporting on New York City. Referring to somebody's statement that the city was filled with "Murray wannabes," he said, "That really is hyperbole. I think of myself as a never-be"—the man on the losing side of things. Finally, he said, "I hope there will still be a few more gaudy nights. I hope there will be something that will make me as proud of myself as I have been of you." Sometime toward the end of next year, Murray Kempton will write his ten thousandth column.

———

Kempton passed that milestone, but in 1995 the Times-Mirror Company closed the New York edition of Newsday, *robbing the city of a wonderful tabloid and its greatest voice. At least there is reason now to visit Long Island. Murray Kempton publishes there.*

ACKNOWLEDGMENTS

These essays were all published in *The New Yorker* except for the Alger Hiss profile, which ran in *The Washington Post Magazine,* and the pieces on Reggie Jackson and Al Neuharth, which appeared in *Esquire.* I am grateful to the editors of all these pieces, not least for the permission to reprint them.

I am especially indebted to Tina Brown, who took me in at *The New Yorker* and has provided unending support. She has given new life to Harold Ross and William Shawn's great invention.

Two editors at the magazine, Jeff Frank and Pat Crow, have made me look better than I had any reason to expect, and so, too, have Rick Hertzberg, Henry Finder, Dorothy Wickenden, Elizabeth Pearson-Griffiths, Ann Goldstein, and Eleanor Gould. The fact-checking department, led by Peter Canby and Martin Baron, has saved my bacon more often than I like to remember. Thanks as well to my agent, Kathy Robbins, my editor at Random House, the owl-wise Jason Epstein, and Jason's assistant, Joy de Menil. I am also grateful to my remarkable parents and to my brother, Richard, and sister-in-law, Lisa Fernandez.

My greatest debt is my greatest pleasure: my sons, Alex and Noah, and my wife, Esther, without whom, nothing, nothing at all.

ABOUT THE AUTHOR

DAVID REMNICK is a staff writer for *The New Yorker* and a frequent contributor to *The New York Review of Books* and other publications. He received the Pulitzer Prize in 1994 for his first book, *Lenin's Tomb,* which was selected by *The New York Times Book Review* as one of the nine Best Books of the Year. Mr. Remnick lives in New York with his wife and two sons.

ABOUT THE TYPE

This book was set in Perpetua, a typeface designed by the
English artist Eric Gill, and cut by the Monotype Corporation
between 1928 and 1930. Perpetua is a contemporary face of
original design, without any direct historical antecedents. The
shapes of the roman letters are derived from the techniques of
stonecutting. The larger display sizes are extremely elegant and
form a most distinguished series of inscriptional letters.